AN HISTORICAL SURVEY
OF THE
OLD TESTAMENT

Eugene H. Merrill

BAKER BOOK HOUSE
Grand Rapids, Michigan

THE AUTHOR

Dr. Eugene H. Merrill is professor of Old Testament at Berkshire Christian College, Lenox, Massachusetts, a position he has held since 1968. A graduate of Bob Jones University, he also received his M.A. and Ph.D. from that school. In addition, he holds the M.A. in Hebrew from New York University and is in pursuit of a doctorate in Semitic languages at Columbia University.

During the summers of 1963 and 1964 Dr. Merrill was a Visiting Scholar at Union Theological Seminary of New York City, and in 1965 he received a study and travel grant to Israel from the United States Department of State. A frequent contributor to numerous religious periodicals and journals, Dr. Merrill is a member of the American Oriental Society, the American Schools of Oriental Research, the Evangelical Theological Society, and the Society of Biblical Literature. He has recently been selected as an Outstanding Educator of America.

TABLE OF CONTENTS

PREFACE

Having taught beginning Old Testament courses for a number of years, the author has felt the need for some time for a text which would meet some needs which he believed were not being met by other books in the field. Being firmly committed to the conservative school of thought, he has had to eliminate works which, because of their critical historical and theological biases, were completely unacceptable for the conservative freshman or sophomore student who is in the rudimentary stages of his Old Testament study. And yet many of the conservative books either have not had the depth of scholarship necessary for a college approach or have gone beyond the ability of the beginning student in their details and presuppositions. Moreover, many of them are restricted to too narrow an approach, such as an emphasis on content, historical background, doctrine, or other specific areas.

Since this study approaches the Old Testament as an historical record of God's revelation to the world through Israel, the historical structure of the Book has been the skeleton. But to this we have added information from the ancient Near Eastern world in which Biblical history took place, including discussions of geographical, historical, and archaeological matters which illuminate the Biblical story. Because of the current criticisms of the reliability of the Old Testament in its scientific statements, special attention has been paid to this aspect of the record.

Every effort has been made to eliminate paraphrases of the narrative sections of the Old Testament, but naturally some retelling was necessary in order to maintain coherence and smoothness. It was in those areas of the Scripture where the account does not speak so clearly of itself that special attention was felt mandatory. It is to be hoped that the student will study this volume as an ancillary to the Word of God, making it a servant of the Old Testament, so that the message of the latter might be more readily comprehended.

The author hereby expresses much deserved recognition to those who have contributed long hours in seeing this most enjoyable project to completion. First, to his wife, Janet, who typed the entire final draft and offered unending encouragement and inspiration, a special thanks is due. And warm appreciation is gladly given to Miss Pené Cansler of the Bob Jones University English department who offered invaluable suggestions concerning mechanics and style. Finally, the generous help and support of many of his students, particularly Mr. William Alford, must not go unrecognized. It is with a sincere prayer that this effort may create a love for the Old Testament as the inspired Word of God that this book is made available.

Deep appreciation is expressed to the National Union of Christian Schools for permission to use the four outline maps.

CHAPTER ONE

INTRODUCTION

Before the reader can properly understand any book, he should be familiar with its author, purpose, and over-all theme; preferably before he reads it in its entirety. This is particularly true of the Old Testament, for the uniqueness of its authorship and contents renders it especially vulnerable to misunderstanding. Many of the literary criteria applied to other works are simply not sufficient to make plain the true nature of this most important composition. For example, how many books consist in turn of thirty-nine books, written over a period of 1000 years by perhaps forty writers? How many profess the incredibly dogmatic claim that they are special revelation from God? How many speak of a people whose entire complex history is so inextricably bound to so many tremendously vital truths? In short, any book which has survived for well over two thousand years and has, more than any other literature, revolutionized the course of human history, must be approached with more than usual care, and with full consideration of its importance as literature, to say nothing of its character as the Word of God. Our study of the Old Testament must, therefore, be preceded by an analysis of the introductory materials essential to an intelligent and thorough appreciation of its nature and content.

THE BOOK ITSELF

The Contents of the Old Testament. The Old Testament is that collection of sacred writings which virtually since their composition have been considered by the Jews to be their Scriptures. The Christian Church of the first century recognized the Old Testament Scriptures as their source of doctrine and ethics, and when their own literature, known to us as the New Testament, was composed, it was added to the Old Testament and both together became accepted as God's Word written. The two have from these earliest times been known as the Bible (Greek *Biblos* or "book"). Since the pre-Christian era the Jews have recognized a threefold division in the Old Testament: the Law (Torah), the Prophets (Nebi'im), and the Writings (Kethub'im).[1] In process of translation from the original Hebrew to the various vernaculars, the Jewish division of the Old Testament was basically followed, though the orders of the books varied, but it has become customary among Protestants in recent times to speak of a five rather than threefold division in the English versions. They designate the first section "Pentateuch" (Greek *Penta-teuchos* or "five books"), which corresponds to the Hebrew division, Torah. These are the five books ascribed to Moses. The second division is that of History; twelve books of generally anonymous authorship which were included in the Hebrew division known as the Prophets, or, more specifically, Former Prophets because they were thought to have been written by early men (pre-ninth century) who were prophets or who at least had the prophetic gift. The third section is Poetry and consists of five books characterized by literature of a poetic or philosophical nature. David and Solomon were their authors, for the most part, although some were composed by lesser known or anonymous individuals. The fourth division is the Major Prophets, so-called because they are lengthy and were the product of well-known prophets or men with the prophetic gift. These consist of five books, two written by the same man. Finally, there is the collection of twelve books known as the Minor Prophets, or, in the Hebrew Bible, simply "The Twelve." These are not designated "minor" because they are relatively less important than the "major" but because they are generally much shorter than the latter. For example, Isaiah contains sixty-six chapters as compared with the one chapter of Obadiah.

You may have observed that a numerical pattern has emerged in the total books of each of the sections: five Law, twelve History, five Poetry, five Major Prophets, and twelve Minor Prophets, or a total of thirty-nine in all. The Hebrew Old Testament contains only twenty-two books (or twenty-four, if Ruth and Lamentations are counted separately), but in many cases these books consist of two or more of the books in our English versions. For example, the twelve books of the Minor Prophets in English are included in only one book in the Hebrew, which reduces the Hebrew total by at least eleven. And the books of Samuel, Kings, and Chronicles are not broken up into I and II, a factor which reduces the Hebrew total by three more.

THE BOOKS OF THE OLD TESTAMENT

Hebrew Arrangement	King James Version
Torah	*Pentateuch*
Genesis	Genesis
Exodus	Exodus
Leviticus	Leviticus
Numbers	Numbers
Deuteronomy	Deuteronomy
Nebi'im	*History*
Joshua	Joshua
Judges (and Ruth)	Judges
Samuel	Ruth
Kings	I Samuel
Isaiah	II Samuel
Jeremiah	I Kings
(and Lamentations)	II Kings
Ezekiel	I Chronicles
The Twelve	II Chronicles
	Ezra
Kethub'im	Nehemiah
Psalms	Esther
Proverbs	
Song of Songs	*Poetry*
Ruth (if not with	Job
Judges)	Psalms
Lamentations (if not	Proverbs
with Jeremiah)	Song of Songs
Ecclesiastes	Ecclesiastes
Esther	
Daniel	*Major Prophets*
Ezra-Nehemiah	Isaiah
Chronicles	Jeremiah
	Lamentations
	Ezekiel
	Daniel

Minor Prophets
Hosea
Joel
Amos
Obadiah
Jonah
Micah
Nahum
Habakkuk
Zephaniah
Haggai
Zechariah
Malachi

The names of the various sections as outlined above should not give the impression that the sections include only materials suggested by the names. Just because the first part is called "The Law" does not mean that it contains nothing but laws or rules or ritual. Law *per se* makes up only a part of the Pentateuch; there is also history, poetry, and prophecy. Likewise, there are law, poetry, and prophecy in the historical books; law, history, and prophecy in the Poetic Books, and so on. The names assigned to the sections indicate that the *major* themes or emphases of the sections are of one kind or another.

The historical period embraced by the Pentateuch is from the Creation (date unknown) to the beginning of the Conquest of Canaan by the Israelites at the end of the fifteenth century B.C. The Historical Books continue the history from ca. 1400 to ca. 420 B.C., the time of Nehemiah's reform. The Poetic Books follow no particular historical order, but reflect practically every age of Israel's history from the beginning to the end. We are not incorrect in saying, however, that the florescence of Hebrew poetry and wisdom literature appeared at the time of the United Kingdom under David and Solomon, because well over half of the poetic writings were compiled by these two men alone. The Major Prophets lived and ministered in the period from ca. 740 to 540 B.C. and the Minor Prophets embraced the longer span, from ca. 800 to 400 B.C. It is clear, then, that many of the prophets were contemporaries and probably were close personal friends in some instances.

The Composition of the Old Testament. The question must inevitably arise as to the process of selection of the

various books which make up the content of the Old Testament. This is especially true in the light of the fact that
there were other documents written in the historical period of
the Old Testament, and possibly in some cases by some of the
Biblical writers.[2] How did the early Hebrews know which of
these should be included in their Scriptures and which should
not? How can we be sure that the books which we now have
in our Old Testament should be there? What would happen if
archaeologists should suddenly discover another book written
by Jeremiah, for example, and subsequently lost? Would we
place it in our Bibles or would we have the authority to reject
it though we have accepted others of Jeremiah's writings?
These and similar questions indicate some of the problems involved in the area of Biblical study known as the "canonicity"
of the Scriptures. Of the entire collection of ancient documents, which should be and are in truth the very Word of
God?

The word "canon" comes from the Hebrew *qaneh* which
means "reed" or "rod." The *qaneh* was the reedy plant which
grew beside marshy waters, the stock of which was often
used by the ancients as a measuring stick because of its length
and straightness. It was a criterion by which the short
could be distinguished from the long, or the crooked from the
straight. In time it signified any standard by which anything
could be measured; specifically, the standard by which the authenticity or spuriousness of a literary document could be
evaluated. When applied to the Scriptures, a book was canonical or not depending upon its adherence to certain well-
defined principles. Most of these were more or less arbitrary,
but are nevertheless valid when considered together.

Jewish scholars, some even before the time of Christ,
agreed that any document to be canonical must have been written before 400 B.C. or thereabouts.[3] This, of course, is one
of the reasons that Jews of the first century A.D. rejected the
New Testament as Scripture. Also, they held that a document, to be Scripture, must have been written by a prophet or
an individual who at least had the prophetic gift.[4] Moses, the
first writer, was a prophet and, it was maintained, no prophet
ever arose after Malachi, the writer of the latest book of the
Old Testament. Therefore, until God should see fit to raise
up a new prophet there could be no new additions to the Scriptures. Also, a writing to be canonical had to be extant. This

means that even if a prophet had written other documents than those included in the Old Testament, if those writings had been lost and never recovered *before* the "close" of the canon (ca. 400 B.C.), they could not have been Scripture. The reasoning was that it would be incredible that God should inspire a man to write Holy Writ and then not be able to or desirous of preserving it. Once a Scripture was written, it was for the benefit of every subsequent age, not just the age in which it was written. If it could meet only the immediate needs of the generation in which it was compiled, it must not be Scripture; it lacked the timelessness which is a characteristic of true Scripture.

Perhaps the most important canonical criterion, however, was that of inspiration.[5] Any literature not written under the supernatural influence of the Spirit of God was automatically excluded from consideration in the canon, even if it met all the other qualifications. This was much more nebulous than the other standards, but it was at the same time the most important. There came to be a very early and universal consensus among Jewish religious leadership in regard to this matter of inspiration, and though the ways and means by which they ascertained the existence or nonexistence of inspiration cannot be determined by us today, nobody who accepts the supernatural character of the Old Testament would seriously question their opinions and conclusions in the matter. Further attention will be paid to this crucial question in the next section.

Apparently, the books of the Old Testament were canonized as soon as they were written, or very shortly after.[6] For instance, Joshua, the immediate successor to Moses, recognized that his forebear not only wrote the Pentateuch, but that it was the authoritative Word of God (Joshua 1:7-8; 22:5, 9). In effect, Joshua and his generation canonized the books of Moses. Similarly, the other books of the Old Testament were accorded recognition as Scripture in following generations, though their recognition as such may not have been as immediately forthcoming as in the case of the Pentateuch. It seems reasonably clear, however, that by the time of the third century B.C. at the latest all of the books we now recognize as Jewish Scripture were in the Old Testament canon. There is no convincing basis to the commonly held argument that the development of the canon was a very slow and uncertain matter, not achieving its final form until the end of the first century A.D. or later.[7]

The Nature of the Old Testament. The most honest evaluation of the Old Testament which can be made, on the basis of both internal and external evidence, is that it is the inspired Word of God. Up to the present day critics have taken issue with this conclusion, but its truthfulness has never successfully been assailed. Since its inception, the Old Testament has been subjected to attacks of all kinds in this area and reams of apologetic materials have been written to defend the Book in the face of all this criticism. The essential and inescapable question which the critics and we ourselves must settle is simply this—Is the Old Testament the verbally inspired Word of God, or is it not?

Sincere and honest men of all generations have taken pen in hand to prove that the Bible teaches its own inspiration and their labors are commendable, but this seems to be nothing more than the erection of a straw man in the present day conflict. The basic issue today is not so much whether the Bible claims to be inspired, for even some of the most radical critics of the Bible admit this, but whether the Bible can be believed when it teaches such a doctrine concerning itself. If the Bible is inspired, then any statement which it makes even with regard to its own inspiration must be believed; if, on the other hand, the Bible is not inspired, then any statement which it makes, including those about its inspiration, is suspect. An uninspired Bible certainly cannot make authoritative statements about its own nature. Even if the words of Jesus and the Apostles teach us that the Old Testament is inspired[8] (which they certainly do), how can we be sure that Jesus and the Apostles actually said such things unless we first of all believe that the Old and New Testaments are inspired? In short, we must first *a priori* accept on the basis of faith the fact that the Bible is inspired, and only then can we with confidence believe what it says about its inspiration as well as matters other than its inspiration. Nor should all this be alarming to the Christian. In the final analysis, what of all we believe do we believe on any other basis than that of faith? It is no more irrational to accept the doctrine of inspiration by faith than it is to accept any of the other doctrines of the Christian faith, all of which must be taken on that basis alone.

In fact, what essential truth of any area of life is not couched in a framework of faith?

Argument must not be wasted then on whether the Bible teaches its own inspiration, for assuredly it does, but on what the concept of inspiration means to the believer who has accepted this basic premise by faith. The answers are found in two key passages in the New Testament: II Timothy 3:16 and II Peter 1:20-21. Here it is possible to see both the source of the Old Testament and the means by which it was transmitted to the ancient writers. In the former passage Paul argues that "every Scripture" (the Old Testament) is "God-breathed" (*theopneustos*) and is profitable. The qualifying adjective "all" or "every" (as it may be translated), combined with the passive participle, indicates that every part of the Old Testament originated with God apart from any human assistance or inventiveness.[9] In other words, God is the ultimate author of the entire Old Testament. This, however, does not explain how the revelation of the Old Testament came from God, through man, to the written parchment or papyrus. Peter does explain this process of revelation. He writes that the "prophecy" (or Scripture) in "old time" (Old Testament period) was not a product of human ingenuity, thus agreeing with Paul, but that "holy men of God spoke as they were carried along (*pheromenoi*) by the Holy Spirit." This means that they spoke, but that what they spoke was somehow not their message but that of God Himself.

These two passages are sufficient to indicate both the origin of Scripture and its mode of transmission and should satisfy the inquisitiveness of any "honest seeker" concerning the essential nature of the Word of God. However, there still remain unanswered questions, matters which can be solved only by a certain amount of reconstruction and evaluation based on the available data. There are problems such as the very great variety of styles and vocabularies employed by the Old Testament writers. If the writers were only recipients of revelation and were, in a sense, passive while being spoken through, how can one account for this variety? Is it likely that God Himself would write in such a number of ways to express the one basic revelation of the Old Testament? Were the human writers nothing but automata, robots impervious to human sensibility and will? Such questions are valid and deserve answers, even though many of these answers must be sought in a largely inductive consideration of all the evidence.

We suggest, first of all, that passivity as implied by Peter involves nothing more than the delimitation placed upon the "holy men of God" as regards the origin of their messages; it has nothing to do with their expression of that message except to render that expression inerrant. They were not permitted to invent their message, but they were permitted to express it within the bounds of their own intellectual and cultural resources, at the same time being divinely shielded from error of message content. An uneducated, roughhewn Amos was given a divine message, but he was not expected to express it in a style and with words which were beyond his experience. On the other hand a refined, cultured, poetic Isaiah was entrusted with revelation and permitted to express it in the inimical manner so much admired in his writings. All the time, both men were preserved from error of fact or judgment of any kind.

Paul suggests in II Timothy 3:16 that the Old Testament is verbally inspired; that is, that every word is the Word of God as God intended it to be. This is also a matter of concern, especially in the light of the preceding argument regarding individuality of style and vocabulary on the part of the several writers. How is it possible for men to express revealed truth in their own ways and yet for the result to be considered the Word of God to the very smallest particle? If the writers were permitted to express themselves in their own ways, how could the product be considered the words of God's choice? Perhaps the best explanation may be derived analogically.

When a business man wishes to communicate with an associate or potential customer, he usually leaves the actual composition and expression of the communication in the hands of his secretary. Perhaps on leaving the office in the middle of the morning he informs her that he wishes to send a letter to Mr. A and he wishes to express ideas 1, 2, 3, and 4. He further notifies her that he will return in the afternoon to check the letter before it is mailed. She goes to work on the letter, and employing her own mode of expression and vocabulary, she eventually produces a letter which she feels will be satisfactory. That afternoon the employer returns, examines the letter, and says reassuringly, "That is exactly what I wanted you to say, sentence by sentence, word by word, and even punctuation mark by punctuation mark. If I had written it with my own hand I would not have said anything different in any respect." The secretary has expressed the intentions of her employer to the point of exactness, but she has done so in her own manner.

Bearing in mind the deficiencies in any such parallel, we may still see from this the essential idea of inspiration. Through some inexplicable means God revealed His intentions to the Biblical writers, who in turn recorded them in writing while retaining their own individuality and God's purposes at the same time. One essential point, of course, is that the writers were not merely stenographers. In His omniscience God had prepared them from before their creation to write what He wanted and in the manner of His choice.

It might be well to point out the differences between inspiration and other concepts which are sometimes confused with it. First of all, inspiration is not tantamount to dictation, except in the sense described above. Perhaps it may be safe to say that inspiration is dictated revelation, if a "mechanical dictation" is not meant. If the term "dictation" can be stretched to include a qualifiedly controlled mediation of divine truth to man, the use of the term may be legitimate. If it is associated with the idea of Athenagoras that the Scripture writers were nothing but musical instruments upon whom God played and that they lost contact with reality,[10] then "dictation" must be rejected as a descriptive term.

Too, one should not interchange the ideas of inspiration and special (or Biblical) revelation. The latter is the corpus of truth or information which originates in God and can be made known to man only by divine self-disclosure. Inspiration is the process by which this impartation of revelation took place in inscripturated form. Revelation *is* the truth; inspiration is the means of God to bring that revelation into human experience via the written page.

Another term frequently misunderstood is "illumination." This has to do with enlightening of the mind of the believer by the Holy Spirit so that he might be able to understand the Word of God. Paul says that this may be the gift of every believer and not just an esoteric few (I Cor. 2:9-16). The complete relationship, then, is as follows: God's truth, or revelation, is made available to His servants, the writers of Scripture, by inspiration, and the understanding of that truth in written form is possible through the Spirit's ministry of illumination, a blessing possible to all in whom He dwells.

The Languages of the Old Testament. The greatest part of the Old Testament, by far, was written in the Hebrew language, a branch of that larger family of languages known as Semitic. This was a vowelless, alphabetic tongue which apparently was the official vernacular of the Israelites at least as early as the time of Moses (fifteenth century B.C.). A few sections, notably in Daniel (2:4-7:28), Ezra (4:8-6:18; 7:12-26), and Jeremiah (10:11), were written in a language known as Aramaic, also a Semitic language and closely related to Hebrew. By New Testament times Aramaic had replaced Hebrew completely as the *lingua franca* among the Jews and it is most likely that Jesus Himself spoke this language except in synagogue discourses when He may have used the Hebrew. Following the completion of the Hebrew canon the Old Testament became translated into various languages such as Greek (the Septuagint version of ca. 250 B.C.), Syriac, and Latin.

Texts of the Old Testament. As the years passed following the composition of the original manuscripts by the prophets and other Old Testament writers, scribes copied these originals many times and they eventually disappeared. It is likely that they were written on such perishable materials as papyrus and parchments, which because of the rigors of Palestine's climate could not long survive. However, before these originals were destroyed every precaution was taken to make absolutely certain that they were exactly preserved in copies. An excellent example of the meticulous care involved in the successful transmitting of the sacred Scriptures may be seen in Jeremiah 36 where the prophet commanded his scribe, Baruch, to duplicate exactly the copy of the book which he had written and which King Jehoiakim had destroyed in the fire. This reverence for the Word of God written did not diminish with the passing of years; if anything, it increased with every generation. Scribes hundreds of years later than the time of the writing of the books devised most ingenious means of guaranteeing the accurate copying of the scrolls. For example, they would count the number of words in a chapter or even a book and then would check it by the number of words in their copy. If there were a difference, they would check the entire copy until they located the error and would correct it without hesitation. There is even evidence that they would determine the middle word or letter of a book and then would check their copy to see that its middle word or letter corresponded with that of the original.[11]

As more and more copies were made and a multitude of translations were produced it is easy to understand that slight differences in the texts began to appear, especially if the copying and translating were done by individuals who did not carefully enough ensure against copying errors. As a result, the manuscripts which have survived down to the present day, representing many Hebrew text traditions as well as numerous ancient translations and versions, do not agree in every single point. Yet, it is remarkable to note that even those texts which vary most do so in matters of very little importance, and certainly it is safe to say that their differences are of no theological or doctrinal moment whatsoever. Furthermore, those texts which vary most from the Hebrew *textus receptus* (received text) are not regarded by the scholars as possessing much independent authority on the whole, so the differences are even more minimized.[12]

Until just a few years ago, the oldest Hebrew manuscript dated from the tenth century A.D., and there were several others which dated a little later. The present Hebrew Bible was based mostly on these Medieval texts, and although conservatives, at least, believed they were essentially the same as the Old Testament originals, there was no way to demonstrate this with absolute proof. Then, in 1947 a revolutionary discovery was made at Wadi Qumran, on the northwest coast of the Dead Sea. There in a cave a shepherd lad found the first of over 40,000 fragments representing hundreds of scrolls, including parts of every book of the Old Testament except Esther. With great anticipation these scrolls were unrolled and translated over a period of years. The excitement of the find was due to the soon established fact that they came in some cases from a period at least 150 years before Christ. Here was a chance to see how the modern Hebrew texts compared with some written over 1000 years earlier than the ones which had previously been considered most ancient. And to the delight of those who had all along maintained the integrity of the modern Hebrew text, those of Qumran were in the majority of the cases essentially the same. The major differences (mostly in Samuel and Kings) can be accounted for by recognizing that in some cases the scribes at Qumran had preferred the Septuagint, or Greek, version, over the Hebrew, but this by no means proves that the Septuagint was the more accurate reflection of the originals as written by the Bible writers.[13]

In short, it is safe to say without hesitation that we possess the originals insofar as they were faithfully preserved by godly and exacting scribes down through the ages. It is not overstating the case to say that we possess the Old Testament of the prophets. This is only as it must be, for it is theologically inconceivable to believe that God who inspired the original manuscripts would permit them to lose their value as inerrant revelation by failing to preserve them. The very inspiration of the Old Testament assures its faithful textual preservation.

Modern Critical Theories. Within the past 100 years especially, scholars have developed various theories purporting to explain the Biblical phenomena. These postulates reject the explanation of the origin and development of the Biblical truth as found in the Bible itself and insist that the Bible must be judged according to certain literary, historical, and philosophical criteria. This entire process of evaluating the Bible with the end in view of ascertaining its "real nature" is known most commonly as Higher Criticism (not to be confused with Lower or Textual Criticism, a perfectly legitimate science having to do with matters of text composition and collation).

Higher Criticism first began to command the widespread attention of Old Testament scholars in the middle of the nineteenth century, following the era of German rationalism and French naturalism. Without question, one specific impetus was the revolution in the biological world occasioned by the publication of Charles Darwin's *The Origin of Species* in 1862. As Julian Huxley states, it was not long until every part of the intellectual world was permeated by this philosophy of gradual development, and everything including religion became explicable only in relation to it.[14] Through the work of such men as Julius Wellhausen and Abraham Kuenen, the Old Testament became reinterpreted in line with the presuppositions of evolutionary theological and historical development. The Pentateuch could no longer be considered a work of Moses because it allegedly presupposes a much higher theological development than Moses, even if he actually lived (which came to be doubted by many), would be capable of expressing. In fact, the Pentateuch could no longer be considered a unity because some of its teachings seemed to express later theological and historical concepts than others.[15] The critics assigned the remaining books of the Old Testament to various dates and authorship, depending upon their internal adherence to the literary and historical canons which had been set up by these men themselves.

This modern reconstruction of the Old Testament was based upon an earlier and widely held view that the Old Testament, and especially the Pentateuch, was made up of a multitude of documents which eventually were woven together skillfully by editors or "redactors." In many cases, it is held, the names of well-known individuals in Israel's history, such as Moses, were attached by these editors to the documents or the finished compositions to lend them the authority which they could not possibly otherwise obtain. This "documentary hypothesis" originated with Jean Astruc, a French physician of the eighteenth century, who observed that the Pentateuch employs the name *Elohim* for God in some chapters and verses and the name *Yahweh* (Jehovah) in others. He concluded that Moses must have used documents written by two different men, one who preferred one name for God and one who preferred the other. Moses, Astruc maintained, blended these two ancient documents which he had at his disposal and produced an edited form which we today call the Pentateuch. It is interesting to observe, however, that Astruc did not deny Mosaic authorship — he merely felt that Moses used existing documentary sources in his composition.[16]

As time passed and men began to consider Astruc's thesis, more and more scholars not only began to teach that literally dozens of various documents were employed but that Moses, after all, had nothing to do with even the composition of the Pentateuch, to say nothing of its authorship. Eventually this piecing together of the Pentateuch from a multitude of alleged sources developed the whole idea into a *reductio ad absurdum,* for it became clear that every verse, and even parts of verses, could have come from different hands if the principles of the critics were to be rigorously applied.

By the time Wellhausen appeared on the scene (1877) the opinion prevailed in critical circles that there were at least four primary sources for the Pentateuch, and these were indicated by the abbreviations J, E, D and P. These men maintained that J represented the document composed by the school of writers who preferred the Divine name Jehovah, E the writers preferring Elohim, D the writer of the Book of Deuteronomy, and P the writer of those sections of the Pentateuch having to do especially with priestly liturgy, sacrifice, and genealogical and chronological sections. Some included the Book of Joshua in this reconstruction and labeled the whole production the Hexateuch.[17] Without attempting to break the Pentateuch down into its various "sources" (which is difficult because the critics by no means agree on the content of each), it might be helpful to illustrate at least one of the most common examples. In Genesis 1 through 2:4a, the Creation account, the name Elohim exclusively appears as the name for God. Beginning in 2:4b, which is also an account of creation, the name Yahweh appears, though usually in connection with Elohim. This led the critics to assume that there were two original stories of creation and that these were edited and placed side by side in the Pentateuch. In this case, however, the critics do not believe that E wrote the first chapter of Genesis, but rather P, because they feel that the cosmogony and history there are later than E on the whole, and that only P lived late enough in history to be aware of knowledge pre-supposed in this creation account. The second account is assigned to J, however, because it employs the name Jehovah so freely.

In general, liberal scholarship taught that the documents originated no earlier than the ninth century, B.C., though it was usually admitted that some of the basic ideas may have come in oral form from as early as the time of Moses. The consensus was (and still is) that J was composed first (850 B.C.), followed shortly by E (750 B.C.), then D (early seventh century B.C.), and finally by P (after 586 B.C.). There were also thought to be certain geographical frameworks discernible in the documents. For example, it seemed that J represented the viewpoint of the Southern Kingdom, and was, therefore, most likely written in Judah or at least by a pro-Judah circle. On the other hand, E, it is supposed, was biased to a Northern position, and probably had Israelite orientation. The geographical disposition of D is not quite so clear, though the weight of opinion was that it was Judahite, and, of course, P, being post-Exilic, was heavily in favor of Judah, though it pretended to be much more ancient than either Israel or Judah, and, therefore, more neutral.[18]

The present situation in Old Testament scholarship is basically the same as it has been for fifty years or more, though the evolutionary hypotheses of Wellhausen have been largely abandoned.[19] The tendency today is to hold to the essential concept of four documents, but to allow them a much more ancient substructure than was formerly admitted. It is now felt that many of the written sources of the documents are hundreds of years older than previously thought and that some may actually have originated with Moses himself. The Scandinavian school, in particular, advocates a Mosaic origin for the basic themes of the Pentateuch, though at the same time stressing that these themes were transmitted only orally until they were finally written by later scribes.[20] The most current opinion is that J, representing one tradition of law and history, was written about 850 B.C. in the Southern Kingdom. About 750 B.C. E was written in the Northern Kingdom, expressing a slightly different viewpoint. About 700 B.C. some unknown scribes wrote D (Deuteronomy) to combat certain religious tendencies in both kingdoms (though Israel had already fallen), and for some reason this document was lost, not to be found until 621 B.C. when King Josiah of Judah found it in the Temple and made of it the core for the great spiritual revival which took place under his reign. P was not written until after the Babylonian captivity and was incorporated by the priests into the JED document which had slowly taken place by previous editing by many hands.[21]

As far as the rest of the Old Testament is concerned, it is quite widely held, with Martin Noth, that the books of Joshua through Kings are a part of the corpus of the Deuteronomist, mainly because these books allegedly express the same religious and historical philosophy as Deuteronomy.[22] The Poetical Books are assigned mostly to anonymous authors and are dated anywhere from David's time to 150 B.C. The Books of Chronicles, Ezra, and Nehemiah were written by the "Chronicler" about 400 B.C. The Prophets for the most part are thought to have written the books which bear their names, though there are notable exceptions such as Daniel and Isaiah 40-66. These last, because of their remarkable predictive prophecies, are dated after the events they prophesy because otherwise their perfect fulfillment cannot be understood. The remainder of the books not included in this resumé are considered to be anonymous and are dated on purely internal literary evidence.

The mass of "evidence" accumulated by critical scholarship over the years might lead some to think that its reconstruction of the Old Testament is unassailable, but this is far from true. Without answering each point in detail, which is neither desirable nor necessary here, may we say simply that the entire process rests upon the most tenuous, subjective evidence, all of which is based upon the assumption that only evolution can account for the Old Testament phenomena. What the Bible says about itself in these areas, and what Christ, the Apostles, and every tradition have averred, is completely rejected in favor of supposed irrefutable internal evidence, no matter how subjective that evidence might be. In other words, the Old Testament has been made to fit a prearranged philosophical and historical framework, even though on every page it cries out against such an artificial and untenable reconstruction.[23]

The Credibility of the Old Testament. The foregoing presentation of the critical approach to the Old Testament leads to some vital questions which we should at least cursorily consider. It is mandatory to know whether the Old Testament is what it claims to be, the works of Moses and the prophets, or whether it is a collection of documents by anonymous individuals who tried to give their compositions sanction by appending the names of Moses and the prophets upon them.

There are two major lines of evidence to establish the credibility of the Old Testament — internal and external — and we shall consider them in that order. First, the Pentateuch claims to have been written by Moses (Ex. 17:14; Num. 33:1-2; Deut. 31:22), and other books of the Old Testament concur without dissent (Jud. 3:4; II Kings 21:8; Mal. 4:4). Moreover, the intertestamental Jewish literature such as the Apocrypha and Pseudepigrapha bear similar testimony

(Baruch 2:2; II Maccabees 7:30). Also of great weight is the fact that the New Testament writers and speakers, including Jesus and the Apostles, mention Mosaic authorship of the Pentateuch scores of times (Matt. 19:8; Rom. 10:5; Acts 3:22; John 7:19). It is impossible to overcome such testimony, especially in the case of our Lord, for it must be held that He either did not know that Moses did not write the Pentateuch, which is a reflection upon His Divine omniscience, or that He "accommodated Himself to the ignorance of the people of His time," which constitutes an assault upon His integrity. In all accuracy we can aver that the man who denies Mosaic authorship of the Pentateuch denies to Christ *ipso facto* the Divine attributes. And the evidence for the remainder of the Old Testament is equally clear and convincing. Jesus believed in the historicity of Daniel (Matt. 24:15) and Jonah (Matt. 12:39-40), for example, and also maintained by inference that Isaiah wrote the entire book which bears his name (Matt. 12:17-21). This knowledge was shared by the Jews themselves, the Apostles, and universal church tradition.

The external evidence is varied and interesting. For our purposes, we shall divide it into three areas: archaeological and historical correspondence, scientific accuracy, and fulfilled prophecy. It should be stressed again at the outset that we do not believe that the Old Testament is the Word of God merely because external proofs can be adduced to support that claim, but because it claims to be and we accept that claim by faith. On the other hand, external support is welcome whenever it is available and we certainly should expect the Old Testament, if it be the inspired Word of God, to be accurate in all historical and scientific matters with which it deals. Yet, and this is vitally important, we must always bear in mind the fact that the Old Testament does not always profess to speak in twentieth century scientific terms, but often employs the prescientific language of the day in which it was written. This has no bearing on the question of verbal inspiration *unless the passage in question indicates clearly that it is revealing timeless scientific truth,* and that is often difficult to tell. When that clearly is its purpose, it speaks with absolutely scientific precision. Moreover, in matters of history we must bear in mind that the Old Testament purpose was not to outline historical data chronologically, though it does this in a great many places, but to emphasize God's dealings in history. It was not written as a modern historian might write it, but rather as a progressive disclosure of theological truth. This does not mean that it is historically unreliable, but only that it may be chronologically incomplete in places where there was no particular reason for including historical information that might ordinarily have been included. In any event, where the Old Testament does speak historically, it has yet to be proven in error. In fact, it very often has shed light on extremely complicated historical problems which otherwise would have remained enigmatic to historians.

THE OLD TESTAMENT AND HISTORY

The conservative has always considered the Old Testament historical record to be completely reliable in all points. With the advent of modern rationalism and naturalism, the Old Testament was subjected to a massive attack in the area of its historicity. Higher criticism, it was felt, had completely demolished the integrity of the Scriptures in this respect, for all kinds of alleged unhistorical or nonhistorical Biblical references had been uncovered. Historians "demonstrated," for example, that because there was no record of a Hittite people in ancient extra-Biblical history, there must be a mistake in the Old Testament where references to the Hittites are made (Gen. 15:20; 25:9, etc.). Similarly, Isaiah mentions an Assyrian king Sargon who, according to the prophet, must have lived near the end of the eighth century B.C. (Isa. 20:1). Yet, there were no Assyrian records of such a king, so Isaiah must have had false historical information. Another favorite target was Belshazzar who, according to the Book of Daniel, was on the throne of the Neo-Babylonian Empire when Cyrus the Great overthrew that empire (Dan. 5:30). Because secular historical records failed to mention such a name, Daniel must have made a serious blunder. One can easily imagine the embarrassment of the critical scholars when they discovered eventually that there were not only Hittite peoples, but these peoples constituted one of the most powerful empires in the Near East in the eighteenth through twelfth centuries. Excavations at Khorsabad in Iraq also uncovered the ruins of one of the most magnificent palaces

of all time, ruins which dated from the eighth century B.C.
Amazing indeed was the fact that the walls of this palace
were covered with the name of Sargon the Great (Sargon II)
as well as extensive pictographs and murals relating the
magnificence of his kingdom and power. We know well today
that there were few kings of Assyria about whom more is
known than Sargon; certainly he was a far cry from some
figment of Isaiah's imagination. The Babylonian Chronicles,
also recently discovered, describe the history of the Mesopotamian world in the seventh and sixth centuries and interest-
ingly point out the fact that while king Nabonidus of Babylonia was out on campaigns or treasure seeking (for he was
a lover of antiquities), his son Belshazzar was left back in the
city of Babylon to administer affairs in the capital. During
his tenure in Babylon the Medo-Persians under Darius the
Mede entered Babylon without resistance and summarily put
Belshazzar to death. Just prior to this, Daniel, who was
captive in Babylon and had predicted the collapse of Babylon, had been appointed to a position as "third ruler of the
kingdom" (Dan. 5:29). This statement had always puzzled
Bible readers, for if Belshazzar was first ruler, who was
second? With astounding accuracy the book of Daniel had
implied that there were two kings in Babylonia at once, but
until recent times historical scholars did not realize that Nabonidus had a son named Belshazzar and that both were
reigning in the period in question. The Old Testament proved
itself not only reliable, but much more reliable and informa-
tive than had been imagined even by conservatives!

The results of modern archaeological and historical research have been even more amazing in pre-monarchial
Hebrew history (before ca. 1000 B.C.). The most skeptical
scholars had maintained that Old Testament history beginning
with David was, at least in its main points, quite reliable.
They declared that anything earlier than that, however, was
outside the realm of that which could be designated true history. The figures of the judges, Joshua, Moses, and especially
the patriarchs were nothing but shadowy and idealized representations conceived by Israel to give its history and covenantal claims some kind of romantic and meaningful origin.
Anyone or anything pre-Abrahamic was immediately con-
signed to the realm of the legendary, if not fictitious, domains
of prehistory.

Now, however, all this estimation is rapidly being re-examined and rejected, even by men who just recently held to these opinions most doggedly. Those who taught a couple generations ago that Moses could not have written the Pentateuch because writing was not developed as an art until after the time of Moses have now been completely repudiated. We are not suggesting that these critics have accepted Mosaic authorship, for that is far from accurate, but they now say that Moses *could* have written the Pentateuch so far as the ability to write itself is concerned. Furthermore, they generally concede that the entire historical situation in Canaan and Egypt in the time of Moses and Joshua was exactly that which the Bible describes it to have been. Though these critics still do not usually admit that the persons in Genesis named Abraham, Isaac, Jacob, and Joseph are historical, most scholars freely suggest that what the Old Testament says about these patriarchs fits in perfectly with what is now known about life in the Near East in the period from 2000-1660 B.C.[24] Cuneiform tablets from such places as Nuzi, Mari, and Alalakh provide fascinating accounts of civil, social, business, and political life from this period or a little later, and the accounts given in the Old Testament from the Patriarchal Age fit harmoniously into the entire historical and cultural context. In other words, according to modern historical criticism, though the persons and events of Patriarchal times probably are not truly historical, they could be from the standpoint of their adherence to what is now known about the historical milieu of these ancient times. This, we feel, constitutes something akin to admission that the Old Testament, at least from Patriarchal times, is essentially historical. Such an admission was made by no reputable critical scholar only a few years ago. Thus are the vicissitudes of those who refuse to take God's Word for what it professes to be — an historical unfolding of God's revelation to men.

The foregoing is not intended to suggest that all Biblical scholars are now completely convinced of the absolute historical accuracy and reliability of the Old Testament. Unfortunately, this is far from true. Yet, there is no question but that it has come to be appreciated as a record of revelation which fits marvelously into an actual historical background, one which can be demonstrably verified by all the skills of modern historical research. This, however, leads us to another approach to Old Testament study, an approach which sees in the Old Testament not so much a chronological history based upon historical data as a "sacred history," or, to use the popular German term, *Heilsgeschichte* ("history of salvation").[25]

This "salvation history" is not a history in terms in which we are accustomed to regard the discipline. It is an interpretative history which expresses Israel's faith in Yahweh and His mighty acts on their behalf. That is, the Old Testament is a witness to Israel's faith, and though it has an historical background, its special and individual events may not be history in the commonly conceived sense. For example, the Exodus is a Biblical event which fits in nicely with the historical milieu of Egypt and Canaan during this period, but because of its supernatural character obviously cannot be considered factual history. There was an act happening in time and space by which Israel was delivered from Egyptian bondage, and this act was interpreted by Israel's prophets to have been an act of God. In the retelling of the event over centuries of time "spiritual accretions" were added which, though not absolutely factually accurate, nonetheless became history as expressed in creedal recitations and, therefore, legitimate salvation history as defined by its own canons.

The reason for such a reinterpretation of Old Testament history should be obvious. When the critics realized that they could no longer scout the essential historical reliability of the Scriptures, they were faced with the difficult task of explaining the miracles and other supernatural content. The only feasible thing to do was to admit that the framework of Old Testament history was valid, but that the miraculous events were merely prophetic interpretations of what God did in history. Even prophets who recorded the events did not believe that they happened exactly as they recorded them, but they "read into" the events their own theological judgments as to the meaning of the events. This, in effect, strips the Old Testament of its miraculous content without denying it the essential historicity which it has been proven to possess.

The conservative response is that one cannot reasonably postulate a dichotomy between types of histories without robbing the term "history" of its accepted definitions. How can it be said, indeed, that there is more than one kind of history, that which describes the sum total of the past? Anything less than this is less than history and must be relegated to the realm of pure myth. Of course, and not surprisingly, modern Old Testament scholarship does speak of these supernatural occurrences as "myth," intending by this term to convey the idea of religious myth as opposed to that which is strictly fictitious.[26] Nonetheless, any attempt to philosophize or semanticize history into at least two compartments seems to destroy any recognizable standard of what constitutes history. How a matter can be myth and history at the same time remains a yet insoluble problem.

Conservative Old Testament students generally concede, then, that the Old Testament is a collection of absolutely reliable historical documents. Efforts mady by some critics to rationalize the miraculous elements by cloaking them in the guise of mythical history or by straining to interpret them as pious inventions calculated to express only spiritual truth become in themselves arguments for its historicity. Specific cases of the miraculous in history will be discussed in the outline of Israel's covenant and national history to be considered later.

The Old Testament and Science

With the advent of modern scientism, primarily in the nineteenth century, has come an assault upon the scientific accuracy or reliability of the Old Testament. The same rationalistic spirit which attempted to undermine the authority of the Word of God in matters historical is also the genius behind the "Bible-Science" conflict. This should come as no surprise, for if the Old Testament can be proven invalid in one of these areas, there is every likelihood that it will be proven so in the others as well.

Perhaps we should approach this discussion with a brief definition of terms. It is not strictly proper for one to speak of a conflict between *science* and the Bible; rather, one should speak in terms of a "Bible-scientism" antithesis. "Science," by definition, is "a branch of study concerned with observation and classification of facts," and, therefore, has to do with natural laws and processes.[27] If we assume that God is the author of the Old Testament as well as the author of all law, including natural law, it becomes axiomatic that there cannot be conflict — God cannot contradict Himself. On the other hand, "scientism," a term coined recently to denote the modern philosophy of science, can and, in fact, does clash with the Scriptures. The problem should be apparent; science truly known and correctly interpreted is Biblical; scientism as an expression of man's interpretation of his environment is usually unbiblical. It would not even be incorrect to say that it is anti-Biblical.[28]

As we pointed out earlier, we should not expect the Old Testament to speak scientifically when its intention is to speak poetically or in ordinary popular discourse, for this is placing restrictions upon it that we would not place upon any other book or speaker. For example, when the Scriptures speak of the "four corners of the earth" or the "rising of the sun" we should not condemn them for speaking unscientifically for this is obviously colloquialism. Who would telephone the television weatherman after the news broadcast to inform him that he is speaking unscientifically when he says the same things? Let us be fair to the Bible and permit it to use the speech of the workaday world.

Furthermore, let us not judge the Bible as being unscientific when it speaks of miraculous events which seem to contradict the "rules" of natural science. The basic question is what is really scientific — that which we have observed and declared to be in conformity with present scientific law, or that which reacts according to Divine law. This is a vital point, for it raises the issue of whether God Himself is subject to so-called natural law, or whether, as the Creator of all things, including these laws, He transcends them. It seems obvious that only the latter can be correct, so any miracles recorded in the Bible must be interpreted as temporary suspensions of natural law. We might even go so far as to say, at the risk of being misunderstood, that there is no such thing as real miracle, but only relative miracle, and that what appears to be natural law may be only a restriction placed upon the universe by God for some specific purpose or other. Paul suggests that the whole world is currently out of joint (Rom. 8:22). And practically all of·the eschatological passages of the Bible speak of a time when "miracles" will be the rule rather than the exception (Isa. 65:25; Amos 9:13; Joel 2:28-32). Science, when it rejects the miraculous, is only rejecting something which it cannot explain on the

basis of known causes and effects. Many of the phenomena
which we today take for granted would have seemed nothing
less than miraculous to even our immediate ancestors for
the laws which control or permit these things were unknown
or misunderstood in their time. Given a supra-natural set
of laws, what could possibly be "the natural order" is impossible to imagine, though the Bible bears eloquent testi-
monies to such marvelous occurrences both past and future.

In brief, the basic conflict between the Bible and science
is one of philosophies. The alternatives are to accept by
faith the record of the Bible regarding creation, the Flood,
and miraculous acts of God or to accept by faith the reconstruction of all these events by ungodly scientism. The
evidence is there for all to see, the responsibility of the individual is to properly evaluate and interpret the evidence. If
one proceeds from the concept of an ontological sovereign
Deity he has no difficulty accepting the Biblical account;
if he takes as his premise a no-God thesis, he must explain
the evidence the best way he can. Our only approach in
supporting the scientific claims of the Bible is not to defend
it point by point in its scientific pronouncements, though it
is defensible, but to accept it as the Word of God with the
implicit corollary of its scientific accuracy.

Two or three examples of the scientific accuracy of the
Old Testament in a "prescientific" age will suffice, though
they by no means exhaust the possibilities. One of the best
known statements is that of Isaiah who spoke of God as
"He who sitteth on the circle of the earth" (40:22). Though
the fact that the earth is round may always have been believed
by a few, there is no question that until comparatively modern
times the consensus was that it is flat. For Isaiah in the
eighth century B.C. to contradict the prevailing scientific
opinion presupposes either a "lucky guess" or a highly advanced scientific notion known to him only by revelation. The
same applies to the statement in Leviticus 17:11 with regard
to the "life of the flesh consisting of the blood." Only a little
over 300 years ago, William Harvey discovered the full meaning of the blood's relationship to life. When Job spoke of
God's "hanging the earth upon nothing" (Job 26:7) was he
only speaking poetically? It does not seem likely, for though
the Book of Job is numbered among the Poetic Books of the
Old Testament, this need not imply that every statement in

it is poetic. Indeed, the context in this case argues that Job is speaking earnestly and scientifically, utilizing information which could have come to him only from God.

It is true that the Bible was not written as a science textbook, but it is equally true that it cannot be disproven in its scientific claims and that it bespeaks a scientific knowledge far in advance of its own time.

THE OLD TESTAMENT AND PROPHECY

The subject of fulfilled prophecy is another which has given great concern to modern criticism. If the prophets could accurately predict the future, even in a broad sense, to say nothing of specific details, then we must automatically yield to the Old Testament a certain amount of supernatural character. If they actually could not, then either their prophecies must be dated after the events they prophesied, or the fulfillment must be regarded as a fortuitous accident and only one of several possible interpretations to the prophecy. Both of these "solutions" have been applied by many scholars with the result that some entire prophetic books (Daniel especially) and great parts of others (Isa. 40-66) have been completely redated to allow for the prediction to follow the fulfillment. This obviously nullifies the prediction and makes it, instead, history. As for fulfillments which materialized after Old Testament times and which could not, therefore, have occurred before the prediction in the Old Testament books, these are usually described as fulfillments only in the sense that they have been "shaped" or interpreted by later men as having some correspondence to an Old Testament prophecy. For example, when Matthew states (Matt. 1:23) that the virgin birth of Jesus Christ was in fulfillment of Isaiah's prophecy (Isa. 7:14), he merely intends to suggest that of all the passages of the Old Testament this one most closely approximates what was really involved in the birth of Christ. This was not to say that Jesus was really born of a virgin, but that Matthew, as a Christian apologete, was interested in validating the uniqueness of His birth, and, therefore, used the "virgin birth symbol" suggested to him by Isaiah.[29] By employing such tactics, the critics can remove every possible Old Testament fulfillment in the New, but not without impunging the integrity and intelligence of every New Testament speaker or writer including our Lord Himself.

The problem of Old Testament prophecies which are fulfilled later in the Old Testament is not nearly so difficult to the critic, but still fraught with all kinds of problems relative to the evaluation by Jesus and the Apostles of the books and prophecies involved. The usual procedure is to assign a date to the book late enough to prevent its having been written earlier than the fulfillment. The book of Daniel, for example, alleges to have been written by Daniel no later than 530 B.C. Yet, it contains most remarkably accurate descriptions of the affairs of individuals and nations which did not even exist until hundreds of years after Daniel's time. The solution is to date Daniel at ca. 165 B.C., thus reducing his prophecies to an outline of history and current events. The same thing is done to the book of Isaiah, though in this case only a part of the book is redated. The first thirty-nine chapters are admittedly ascribed to Isaiah of Jerusalem, but chapters 40 through 66 are attributed to an anonymous prophet (or prophets) who lived not until after the Babylonian captivity (ca. 560 B.C.)[30] This is done because these last twenty-seven chapters contain such notes of comfort and hope and because they furthermore speak with such amazing predictive accuracy regarding events and persons who do not appear until after the death of Isaiah of Jerusalem (ca. 685 B.C.). It has always remained a puzzle to the critics that this Second Isaiah who, they admit, wrote the most glorious prophetic work of all, should remain anonymous though other prophets with much less polished works and with much shorter books should be remembered. All efforts to account for this disparity have failed, because there is just no proof to support such a writer in history or the Bible. Jesus quotes from these last chapters of Isaiah on several occasions and the Gospel writers invariably assign them to the prophet (Matt. 3:3; 8:17; Jn. 12: 38f.; Luke 3:4-5), and, of course, He does the same with Daniel (Matt. 24:15) and other disputed books. Once again, the integrity of our Lord is in question if these books were not written by the men and in the times to which they bear internal witness. The effectiveness of fulfilled prophecy as an evidence of the supernatural character of the Old Testament is amply demonstrated by the machinations to which the critics must resort in order to try to disprove it.

THE PEOPLE OF THE OLD TESTAMENT

In a very real sense the history revealed in the Old Testament is the history of a special people. These people, from earliest times known as the Hebrews, and progressively as Israelites and Jews, constitute the human theme of the Book. Naturally, their origin in a general sense is to be traced back to the very beginning, the creation of mankind; their existence as a special people, however, commenced with Abraham, to whom the ethnic covenant was given, along with Jacob (or Israel) through whom it became nationalized, and Moses through whom it became fully realized. The reason for the need of a special people through whom God could reveal His redemptive purposes to all the world is fairly obvious; why Israel was selected to be that people, however, is not quite so plain. In the final analysis, all that can be said is that God loved them (Deut. 7:8) and made them a special object of His grace.

Throughout the Old Testament, we see the continually unfolding vicissitudes of this people or nation, both in history and prophecy. What they failed to accomplish in Old Testament times was apparently reserved for them to accomplish in the eschatological plan of God, both in conjunction with and independent of the Church of all the ages. Theirs is a spiritual and a temporal kingdom, one which existed in both space and time, but which ultimately is restricted to neither.

There are other peoples and nations mentioned throughout the Old Testament, but these are only ancillary to *the* nation Israel and to God's acts and messages of revelation through that one nation. Though Egypt, Assyria, and Babylonia do not act outside God's over-all purposes, for He is the God of all the world, their main function still is understood only in connection with Israel. To understand the Old Testament, then, is to understand Israel in all its historical and geographical contexts; any failure to properly appreciate these must inevitably result in an inability to correctly interpret Israel's faith and its role as the channel of God's redemptive grace. Because of the extreme complexity of these considerations and because they actually do constitute the substratum of the Old Testament story, further remarks will be deferred until they can be utilized in the unfolding of that story throughout this book.

THE HISTORY OF THE OLD TESTAMENT PERIOD

The complete story of God's people in the Old Testament covers a period of many thousands of years, but within this span various epochs or eras become quite plainly discernible; these epochs, in fact, constitute the main outline for our study. We need merely to outline these periods at this point, indicating their dates (approximately in some cases), and the sections of the Old Testament which discuss them. The terminologies employed will become clear to the student as he proceeds to study each of these periods in its own historical order. The following outline indicates briefly the ground to be covered:

Pre-patriarchal Period	(ca.10,000-2100B.C.)	Genesis 1:1-11:26
Patriarchal Period	(2100-1800)	Genesis 11:27-50:26
Egyptian and Exodus Period	(1800-1406)	Exodus 1:1-Deuteronomy 34:12
Conquest and Judges Period	(1406-1050)	Joshua 1:1-I Samuel 10:1
United Monarchy Period	(1010-931)	I Samuel 10:1-I Kings 12:15
Divided Monarchy Period to Jehu	(931-841)	I Kings 12:15-II Kings 9:27
Divided Monarchy Period to Fall of Israel	(841-722)	II Kings 9:27-16:6
Kingdom of Judah Period to Fall of Judah	(722-586)	II Kings 16:6-25:26
Babylonian Exile and Captivity Period	(586-420)	II Kings 25:26-30; Ezra; and Nehemiah

Other books such as Ruth, Esther, and Lamentations shed valuable light on historical conditions during some of these periods, and, of course, the prophetic books contain long historical sections. In addition, the Book of Chronicles consists of a parallel history of the entire period from Saul to Cyrus (1050-530 B.C.), written from a slightly different viewpoint, and also contains helpful genealogical and chronological data which have a direct bearing on the history. Even the poetic books share in an understanding of Israel's history, for they reflect the philosophical, cultural, and theological conditions of the times in which they were written.

THE LAND OF THE OLD TESTAMENT

Because the Old Testament is an historical book, there must be some attention paid to its geography, for the stage upon which the drama of Israel's life is portrayed is essential to its role as God's chosen people. People live and act within a geographical environment which shapes to a measureable degree the fortunes of the people who live within it. This was true of Israel; in fact, it could be said that the influence of Palestine's geography upon the nation Israel was all out of proportion to what might be ordinarily expected. The basic reasons for this may be found through a careful examination of the physical, geological, and climatic features which comprised Palestine.

The land itself is only a tiny fraction of the great land mass known as the Near East, but its location within that mass more than compensated for its small area. From the most ancient times the world's population was centered in an area from the Indus Valley on the east, the Caspian and Black Seas on the north, Anatolia and the Mediterranean Sea on the west, and Egypt and the Arabian Peninsula to the southwest and south respectively. The two major centers of civilization within the greater part of the Old Testament history were in Mesopotamia in the north and east and Egypt to the south and west, Palestine itself being located right in between. Ancient historical records from both Babylonia-Assyria and Egypt record the fact that thousands of years before the time of Christ extensive trade was conducted between these two population centers; and because Palestine was located between the Mediterranean Sea and the impassable deserts of the Arabian Peninsula, it became the highway for virtually all of this traffic. This entire land area, stretching from the Euphrates to the Nile Valley, was known as the Fertile Crescent. It soon became clear that Palestine was to be the "bridge of the Fertile Crescent."

Israel's location seemed to make it ideally situated to absorb the cultures and material benefits of all the nations which passed through its territory in the process of conducting merchandise; and in some respects this is exactly what Israel did, as did all the indigeneous populations of Palestine before Israel. On the other hand, the peculiarly fractured topography of the land was conducive to provincialism and

insularism. The various chains of hills and mountains, criss-
crossed by streams and precipitous valleys, made of Palestine
a heterogeneous collection of enclaves which tended to produce
within themselves independent cultures existent in a variety
of forms. Let us look now at these geographical structures in
order to illustrate the preceding remarks.

Palestine is basically divided into north-south regions,
though there are some east-west features. Stretching normally no more than 150-200 miles from north to south and at
approximately 31-30 degrees latitude north, the land consists,
first of all, of a coastal littoral varying in width from a few
hundred yards north of Carmel to over thirty miles in the
extreme south. This coastal plain was lined at the edge of the
sea by high sand dunes and ledges which prevented the streams
from flowing into the sea from the central hills, thus reducing
a great part of the plain to a swamp in the rainy season.
Besides this, the coast line is so straight and unbroken there
were little or no opportunities for any maritime industry.
These two factors combined to limit settlement of the plain
except in the south, where the Philistines managed to maintain a pentapolis of cities — Gaza, Ashkelon, Ashdod, Ekron,
and Gath. Historically, the Israelites never settled in this
area, both because of the agricultural difficulties and because
of the Philistines and other native peoples who were successful in maintaining their possessions there.

The coastal plain gradually rises in elevation until it
blends with the central hills of Palestine toward the east.
These hills, from north to south, were known as the Galilean
Hills, Mount Ephraim, and the Hills of Judaea. The first two
of these mountainous regions is bisected by the Valley of
Jezreel and the second two by the Valleys of Sorek and Ajalon.
Though none of these hills is very high, and scarcely deserves
to be called a mountain, they are quite rugged and steep,
forming natural frontiers throughout the whole length of
the country. The Israelites found these hills largely abandoned by any indigenous population at the time of the Conquest,
so most of the important cities they built or rebuilt were located in the hills and valleys of Palestine. These include such
places as Hazor, Shechem, Samaria, Bethel, Shiloh, Gezer,
Lachish, Gibeon, Jerusalem, Bethlehem, and Hebron.

East of the mountains is one of the most interesting and
unusual geographical phenomena on the face of the earth —

the Great Rift. Beginning in south-central Asia a long, continuous geological fault ranges over a distance of several thousand miles, eventually culminating in the great lakes of southeast Africa. This fault produced a deep cleft in the crust of the earth which reaches its greatest depth in Palestine. The Rift enters the Near Eastern world in northern Syria, passes between the Lebanon and Anti-Lebanon Mountains, and reaches sea level at a point between Lake Huleh and the Sea of Galilee. From there it drops below sea level, reaching a depth of -650 feet at the surface of the sea of Galilee. The Jordan River, which flows down the Rift from Galilee, winds and meanders over 200 miles until it reaches its end at the Dead Sea. Here the Rift dips to the astounding dept of 1292 feet below sea level at the surface of the Dead Sea, and about 2500 feet below at the deepest point of the Dead Sea. This makes the area at the Dead Sea the lowest point on earth, over one thousand feet lower than Death Valley in California. From the Dead Sea the rift rises to about 600 feet above sea level in the arid waste south of the Dead Sea known as the Arabah. From this elevation it drops once again until it reaches sea level at the Gulf of Aqaba.

The Rift, with the River Jordan, experienced the greatest differences in vegetation imaginable in so small an area because of the vast differences in elevation. In the north, plants of the Galilean region most frequently abound, but at Jericho, near the Dead Sea, a luxuriant tropical life usually found only in equatorial regions thrives. There is evidence that tropical animals frequented this area in Biblical times. This whole system also provided a great barrier to travel from east to west, so that peoples on either side of the river had very little contact with each other. The primary crossing places were at Jericho in the south, near the Jabbok River in the central region, and near Beth-shean, just south of the Sea of Galilee, and even these places could not be forded except at certain times of the year.

The easternmost section of Palestine was known as the Eastern Plateau or Transjordan. This region consists of a high plateau to the north, which gradually lowers in the middle, and then rises to several thousand feet to the south. At one time this plateau, like the central hills of Palestine, was covered with a dense forest growth, and the pastures became proverbial for their ability to sustain great herds and flocks. Now both of these regions have become denuded of their vegetation, and only in limited areas do we see much growth. In ancient times the Eastern Plateau was inhabited by quite highly advanced peoples including the Ammonites, Moabites, Edomites, and various groups of the Amorites. Eventually, this land was conquered and settled by Israel, particularly by the tribes of Reuben, Gad, and a part of Manasseh.

We should also mention two other major geographical features. First, the Valley of Jezreel is an essential part of the land for it provided the richest agricultural territory of all. Furthermore, through it passed over ninety percent of the commercial and military traffic of Palestine. The plain stretches from the Carmel Hills along the Mediterranean to the Jordan Valley, forming a triangle whose apex is to the West. One arm of the triangle runs to the east and enters the Jordan Valley at Beth-shean, and the other to the northeast, where it leads to the Sea of Galilee. The principal trade route, the Via Maris, led from Egypt along the Mediterranean Coastal Plain, and a few miles north of the Plain of Sharon went inland through a mountain pass and entered the Valley of Jezreel. It crossed the valley and passed near Mt. Tabor, heading toward the fords to the south or north of the Sea of Galilee, and ending up in Damascus and even beyond, in Mesopotamia. Another principal route, that from Asia Minor, also had to cross the Valley of Jezreel, and on its way to Egypt had to pass through the same cut in the mountains as did the Via Maris. From most ancient times it became apparent that he who controlled this mountain pass could become powerful and wealthy. The city of Megiddo was built there, and along with several other fortresses became the key to the possession of this strategic and productive valley.

The final geographic area is known as the *Shephelah* or Lowlands. This extends from the coastal plain, in its southern reaches, east to the central hills, and down into the South (the *Negev*) until it blends with the undulating hills of the Sinai Desert. This land was very dry, at least in the extreme south, and was used primarily for pasturage. In the more northern part of the Shephelah, the territory between Philistia and Judah, many wars between the Philistines and Israelites were waged, and, in a sense, the whole region was a kind of buffer zone or no man's land.

The climate of Palestine has had a profound effect upon the geographical, and even historical, affairs of Old Testament peoples. There are only two real seasons there, the rainy and the dry. True to the Mediterranean pattern, the rains begin to fall in the month of October, maintain themselves to varying degrees throughout the winter months, and then increase for one last time in April. In the Old Testament these rain periods are called, respectively, the "former rains" and the "latter rains." From April through September precipitation is rarely or never experienced in most of the country.

The rain pattern is from west to east and from north to south; that is, the coastal plain generally receives the greatest amounts, and the Galilee experiences more than the Shephelah and Negev. The amounts range anywhere from forty inches or more per annum in the extreme north coast to less than two inches in parts of the most southern deserts. The central hills catch most of the moisture which does not fall on the plain, and what manages to cross the mountains falls on the Transjordanian Plateau, leaving the Rift with virtually no rainfall except in the area just east of the Valley of Jezreel. All this means that Galilee receives abundant rain and is, therefore, a good farming area, as are the Valley of Jezreel, the western slopes of the central hills, and most of Transjordan. If the soil were not so rocky and were otherwise more conducive to agriculture, the productivity of Palestine would be much greater than it already is, with the exception of the south where lack of moisture is prohibitive of any kind of agriculture except that induced by the most ingenious use of irrigation.

The rainfall is the most important climatic factor, but temperature is also worth considering because of its variety in this small land. In the summer the entire country is quite hot with temperatures in the Rift and the Negev reaching as high as 125 degrees F. This, combined with the humidity, uncomfortable except in the higher hills and in the deserts, produces almost unbearable conditions at times. In the winter the temperatures are quite raw because of the rains and infrequent snows. The major exception is the lower areas of the Rift, commonly resorted to today as winter havens.

Finally, we should give some attention to the rivers and streams. Besides the Jordan, which is by far the most important, there are its tributaries which flow into it from the

Transjordanian Plateau — the Yarmuk and the Jabbok.
Farther south there are two principal streams flowing into the
Dead Sea, also from the East — the Arnon and the Zered.
There is one main tributary flowing from the west, the Jalud,
which empties the Valley of Jezreel. The only two rivers of
any importance at all which empty into the Mediterranean
Sea are the Kishon, north of Mt. Carmel, and the Yarkon,
near the modern city of Tel Aviv. These are normally nothing
more than mere creeks except in the rainy season when they
may extensively overflow their banks. One feature of Palestine is the presence of *wadis* or "dry streams." These are
brooks which flow only in the winter, and, perhaps, only for
a few days in the deserts. They are very treacherous, however, and have been known to fill their banks so rapidly after
a violent rain storm that everything in their path, including
men and vehicles, has been swept to destruction. Unless the
water of these wadis could be harnessed and controlled, as
sometimes it was, it merely flowed out into the sea or was
absorbed by the porous soil, serving little or no useful purpose
to agriculture. This very soil, largely of limestone, retained
ground water on a more or less permanent basis, and was
tapped by the ancients, as it still is, for wells and springs so
necessary in the long dry months of summer.

The Book, the history, the people, the land — a knowledge
of all these in their interrelationships is essential in order for
us to successfully grasp the intended meaning of the Old Testament. With all this background in mind, let us turn now to a
closer examination of the Old Testament story itself, by God's
grace learning from it the mysteries of His redemptive revelation which point us as a "schoolmaster" to Christ.

---

[1] *Prologue to Ecclesiasticus;* Luke 24:44; Flavius Josephus, *Contra Apionem* 1:8 in *Josephus' Complete Works,* trans. by William Whiston, London, Tallis, n.d.

[2] cf. Num. 21:44; Josh. 10:13; II Sam. 1:18; I Kings 11:41; 16:27; 22:45.

[3] IV Esdras 14:45-46; *Baba Bathra* 14b-15a. For all these argu-
ments see William Henry Green, *Old Testament Canon and Philology,* Princeton, The Princeton Press, 1889, pp. 3-37.

[4] Robert Laird Harris, *Inspiration and Canonicity of the Bible,* Grand Rapids, Zondervan Publishing House, 1957, pp. 170-179.

[5] *Ibid.,* p. 178.

[6] Herbert Edward Ryle, *The Canon of the Old Testament,* London, Macmillan and Company, Ltd., 1895, p. 183.

[7] Robert Henry Pfeiffer, *Introduction to the Old Testament*, New York, Harper and Brothers, 1941, pp. 50-70; Curt Kuhl, *The Old Testament: Its Origin and Composition*, trans. by C. T. M. Herriott, Richmond, John Knox Press, 1961, pp. 27-33.

[8] Jer. 10:35; Matt. 5:18; II Tim. 3:16-17; II Pet. 1:20-21.

[9] Benjamamin Breckinridge Warfield, *The Inspiration and Authority of the Bible*, Philadelphia, The Presbyterian and Reformed Publishing Company, 1948, p. 296.

[10] Gustave Oehler, *Theology of the Old Testament*, Grand Rapids, Zondervan Publishing House, 1883, p. 469.

[11] Ernst Würthwein, *The Text of the Old Testament*, trans. by Peter R. Ackroyd, New York, Macmillan and Company, 1957, p. 15.

[12] D. Winton Thomas, "The Textual Criticism of the Old Testament," *The Old Testament and Modern Study*, Ed. by H. H. Rowley, Oxford, Clarendon Press, 1951, pp. 244-245.

[13] F. F. Bruce, *Second Thoughts on the Dead Sea Scrolls*, Grand Rapids, Wm. B. Eerdmans Publishing Company, 1964, p. 96.

[14] Henry Morris, *The Twilight of Evolution*, Grand Rapids, Baker Book House, 1963, pp. 14-15.

[15] Pfeiffer, *op. cit.*, pp. 50-70.

[16] Edward J. Young, *An Introduction to the Old Testament*, Grand Rapids, Wm. B. Eerdmans Publishing Company, 1958, pp. 128-130.

[17] Walter J. Harrelson, *Interpreting the Old Testament*, New York, Holt, Rinehart and Winston, 1964, pp. 30 ff.

[18] Bernhard W. Anderson, *Understanding the Old Testament*, Englewood Cliffs, Prentice-Hall, 1957, pp. 382-383.

[19] John Bright, "Modern Study of Old Testament Literature," *The Bible and the Ancient Near East*, Ed. by G. Ernest Wright, Garden City, Doubleday and Company, Inc., 1961, pp. 16 ff.

[20] C. R. North, "Pentateuchal Criticism," Rowley, *op. cit.*, p. 70.

[21] Anderson, *op. cit.*, p. 383.

[22] H. H. Rowley, *The Growth of the Old Testament*, New York, Harper and Row, 1963, pp. 45-46.

[23] O. T. Allis, *The Five Books of Moses*, Philadelphia, The Presbyterian and Reformed Publishing Company, 1943, p. 261.

[24] W. F. Albright, *From the Stone Age to Christianity*, Garden City, Doubleday and Company, Inc., 1957, pp. 241-243.

[25] Gerhard von Rad, *Old Testament Theology*, Vol. 1, Edinburgh, Oliver and Boyd, 1962, pp. 50-51; For a good exposition of this concept, see James Barr, "Revelation Through History in the Old Testament and in Modern Theology," *Interpretation*, 17:193-205, April, 1963.

[26] Artur Weiser, *The Old Testament: Its Formation and Development*, trans. by Dorothea M. Barton, New York, Association Press, 1961, pp. 57-59.

[27] *Webster's New Collegiate Dictionary*, Second Edition, Springfield, Massachusetts, G. & C. Merriam Co., Publishers, 1953.

[28] Robert Lewis Reymond, *A Christian View of Modern Science*, Philadelphia, Presbyterian and Reformed Publishing Company, 1964, p. 17.

[29] Morton Scott Enslin, *The Literature of the Christian Movement,* New York, Harper and Brothers, 1938, pp. 397-398.

[30] Anderson, *op. cit.,* pp. 399-402.

CHAPTER TWO

IN THE BEGINNING

THE ANCIENT NEAR EASTERN WORLD

The pre-patriarchal period of Biblical history embraces more than the affairs of any single nation; indeed, it may properly be called the period of universal dealings, for at this pristine time God made Himself known indiscriminately to individuals and nations alike. A knowledge of the historical background in which this original revelation took place is almost indispensable to its complete understanding.

Aside from certain "palaeolithic" remains which are variously dated as early as 100,000 years B.C., the first geniune evidence of village occupation in the Near East is from the so-called Neolithic Age (ca. 8000-4500 B.C.). This civilization centered around the Tigris-Euphrates River system and in one or two other spots, notably Jericho and Abu Ghosh in Palestine.[1] There seems to be no doubt that Mesopotamia was the cradle of civilization, for the earliest remains in Egypt, long held to be the oldest, we know to be a great deal later, and those elsewhere are also from a later age. We know little about this earliest time except that rather primitive conditions are generally reflected, though there are some surprising exceptions. It appears that man was primarily a community dweller and that he practiced some forms of agriculture and herding.

Beginning with the Chalcolithic Age (4500-3000), man began to use copper extensively in the Fertile Crescent and made the first efforts discernible archaeologically to dwell in cities. Sometime during this period great city states developed and occasionally became rather powerful and widespread in their influence. The racial characteristics of these

Mesopotamians are uncertain, though it is clear that sometime during this era there was an incursion of peoples identified as the Sumerians. These people developed the first true
and independently observable culture and concentrated it on
the Persian Gulf at the mouths of the Tigris and Euphrates
Rivers. Their neighbors, and perhaps their predecessors,
appear to have been composed of various Semitic or proto-
Semitic mixtures, for it is likely that the Sumerian gods,
clothing, and certain other features which seem to be Semitic
in form and style were borrowed from peoples with whom
they came in contact in Mesopotamia. There is no doubt that
by 2500 B.C. there was a highly advanced Sumerian culture
which could name among its accomplishments great skill in
ceramics, art, and literature.[2]

In the meantime a civilization was slowly evolving in
the Nile Valley; certainly by 4000 B.C. there were city states
(nomes) maintaining themselves up and down the valley.
These remained independent of each other for at least a
millennium, but by 3000 B.C. had been united under a common
head, the founder of the First Dynasty. The culture of the
Nile seemed crude in comparison to that of Mesopotamia, at
least at first, but very quickly these populations made great
strides so that by the beginning of the third millennium the
level may have been about equal in both areas. The situation
was somewhat the same in the Jordan Valley, though advancement there was much inferior as a whole.

The history of Egypt from 3000-2000 consisted of organization and centralization of power in the first two dynasties
(3000-2800), a tremendous peak of building, including the
Age of the Pyramids, in the Third through Fifth Dynasties,
or Old Kingdom (2800-2600), and a decline featuring civil
wars and internal disintegration throughout most of the Sixth
through Eleventh Dynasties (2600-2000). Though there were
problems of various kinds, the civilization of Egypt through
this long period was remarkably stable and homogeneous with
considerable contact with the outside world.[3]

In Mesopotamia, on the other hand, the situation was
much more complex. There, city state after city state gained
the ascendancy only to be toppled and replaced. The Sumerians maintained only a very tenous grip on their lands though
their culture continued to dominate and even to spread widely.

Very little is know from the period following 3000 B.C. until near the end of that millennium, except that there was an utter lack of stability and centralization in the Land Between the Rivers. Eventually, however, a man with sufficient power and leadership rose at Accad, a city state on the Euphrates, and began to establish the first world empire, the Accadian. This figure, Sargon the Great (ca. 2360-2305),[4] pushed in all directions, even reaching to the northwest as far as Anatolia and the Mediterranean Sea. His dynasty occupied Mesopotamian control until about 2180, when a people known as the Gutians moved in from the mountains and dominated for about 100 years, only to be replaced themselves by a new city state dynasty, Sumerian in character, at the city of Ur. This so-called Third Dynasty of Ur remained in power until 1950 B.C., or well into the Patriarchal Period of the Old Testament.

Palestine during this thousand year period was passing through the epoch known as the Early Bronze Age (ca. 3000-2000 B.C.), a period from which there is a paucity of historical information, though material remains are quite impressive from this area. It appears that there were rather advancing cultures, especially in the Jordan Valley, throughout most of this age, but for some as yet undetermined reason the civilization came almost to a standstill under the influence of thousands of semi-nomads from the north and east. For most of the later part of the Early Bronze Age Palestinian culture passed through this "dark age" not to emerge from it until the turn of the Middle Bronze Age (ca. 2000 B.C.) when a cultural rise again becomes quite evident.[5]

The Ancient Near East prior to 2000 presents a picture which only in its last millennium becomes quite understandable; even then there are gaps which make any complete interpretation an impossibility. Several points of importance do emerge, however. Civilization throughout the entire region was much more complicated and refined than was thought true only a few years ago. Moreover, there were great movements of people everywhere except in Egypt, though even this was true in earliest times. Finally, the historical context suggested by Genesis 1-11 is in accordance with the knowledge of this age gained from extra-Biblical literature and archaeological excavation. These will be discussed in more detail as they bear upon the Biblical record.

VIEWS OF CREATION

At no point are the Bible and modern scientism more in conflict than in their cosmogonies. We have on the one hand the simple, unsophisticated, yet majestic account of Genesis; and on the other the complex evolutionary hypothesis of scientism. The Biblical account makes God the Creator; scientism explains creation as a fortuitous combination of original gases, whose origin, in turn, defies explanation up to the present time. Genesis allows for a period of only several thousand years from creation to the present; scientism maintains that billions of years are necessary to allow for the slowly developing evolutionary process. The Bible states categorically that creation was a once and for all event, a completed act; scientism holds that there is continuous creation and that this creation can lead only to higher and more complicated results.[6]

Following Whitcomb and Morris, we would suggest that scientism rests upon two main assumptions in its effort to explain the origin and maintenance of the universe.[7] First of all, the unproven and unprovable theory of evolution provides the key to the understanding of the present. Things are as they are because they have come through a long process. It is inconceivable to the evolutionist that the complex organisms of today were not originally only one-celled, and he asserts that even before that they somehow became alive though they originated in inorganic matter. The second premise is that of uniformitarianism, a term which suggests that the present is the key to the past. That is, the rates of change, whether positive or negative, which are observable today and which can be calculated, have always been the same in the past. If a mountain erodes today at the rate of one millimeter per century, and it appears to have eroded 100 meters, that mountain must, according to the uniformitarian, be at least 100,000 centuries or ten million years old. The whole argument is based upon the undemonstrable assumption that the rate of the erosion has always been constant. If some unknown factor in the past had either speeded up or retarded the rate of erosion, then there would be absolutely no way to determine the age of the mountain in question.

In support of the great age theory of the universe, many measuring tests have been developed. Besides the erosion technique described above, there are more scientific explanations such as the potassium-argon and uranium 235-lead tests. In addition, there is the carbon 14 test which is applied to organic materials. These all work on basically the same principle: that certain materials under certain conditions tend to decay and change into other materials.[8] For example, potassium deteriorates into argon at a consistent rate. If a given deposit of potassium and argon is found, the ratio of the two amounts found should indicate how long the process has taken place in that particular deposit. In most cases this will appear to be measured in the hundreds of millions of years, if not billions. The fallacy of the entire procedure becomes obvious when two or three factors are given special attention. First, it must be proved that the original deposit was pure potassium with no lead whatsover; or at least, the original ratio must be known. Obviously, neither of these is possible because no scientist was there to record this information. Second, we assume that there has been no "leakage" of the deposit; can we be sure that no lead has percolated into the deposit, or that no potassium has leaked out, etc.? Unless and until this can be firmly demonstrated, it cannot claim to be truly scientific. Finally, if there had been some means whereby the potassium-argon ratio could have been quickly formulated as it now exists, what appeared to be millions of years old might be only thousands. There has as yet been no scientific means of dating the age of inorganic materials without a great deal of assumption lying at its foundation.[9]

Similarly, there is no way to date organic remains conclusively, for even the carbon 14 test has been gradually discredited as a certain means of dating materials any earlier than a very few thousand years old. The variables are so great that as eminent an archaeologist as G. Ernest Wright says that he feels no confidence in using this means for very ancient materials.[10] Yet, as with the other tests just mentioned, the scientists continue to use carbon 14 and to base allegedly sound conclusions upon it, knowing full well that only assumed premises can make it justifiable at all.

Scientism teaches that the earth is the product of aeons of evolutionary development because, apart from the Scriptures, it has absolutely no alternatives. The universe *must* be old because it looks old and because nothing but great age can account for its development. The assumptions of evolution and uniformitarianism are made, and the phenomena must be made to conform to them; anything less, to scientism, is unscientific. In so reconstructing the origin and development of the universe, scientism acts on faith—faith in the infallibility of its postulates. What, then, makes the Christian position any less tenable? We too act on faith, but the object of our faith is the God of creation who has revealed Himself as Creator and Redeemer in the Old and New Testaments. If true scientific principle demands an observer and recorder of phenomena, the Genesis account only can be considered scientific, for only it dares make the claim that there was an Observer present—The Triune God.

THE ACT OF CREATION (Genesis 1-2)

The Cosmological Approach (Genesis 1:1-2:3). The Critics have long maintained that there are two separate strands of tradition regarding the creation, and that these appear in Genesis in parallel passages, Genesis 1:1-2:4a and 2:4b-7. This erroneous view rests upon the use of the Divine names in the passages, Elohim and Yahweh (Jehovah) respectively, and fails to take into account the fact that it might have been the writer's purpose to discuss creation from two different viewpoints. The name Elohim suggests the power and majesty of the transcendent God of creation, so it is only natural to expect that when the creation of the universe is in view that name should be employed. Yahweh is the personal name of God whereby He reveals Himself to man; it is the covenant name of Him who is immanent and who deigns to have intercourse with man (Ex. 3:13-15; 6:1-4).[11] In Genesis 2, where the creation of man is the key point, we would expect the very name which is used.

The first act mentioned in Genesis is the creation of the original mass of "heaven and earth" (vv. 1-2). This was "in the beginning," an expression which to the practical, nonspeculative Hebrew mind simply meant the absolute beginning: in this case the beginning of everything but God. The verb used to describe the creative act, *bara*, is that which means "creation from nothing" (*creatio ex nihilo*), and it is used, furthermore, only with Deity.[12] The scientific implication is clear. The mass, the totality of all which is, came purely and simply from nothing by Divine fiat. This is indeed a refreshing distinction from scientism which says in so many words that everything which exists must have, in some form, always existed. This is tantamount to dualism or at least to the concept of eternal matter, both of which are unscriptural and irrational.

Exactly what this primeval mass consisted of we have no way of knowing. All that is certain is that everything in the universe was reconstituted from this original material. And the process of that reconstitution is related in the immediately following verses.

Without a break the account goes on to describe the next event of the first day of creation: the appearance of light (1:3-5). Verse two had indicated that the earth was "without form and void" (*tohu wavohu*) and that darkness enveloped the face of the entire watery surface of the earth. Now that darkness was dispelled and light from some unnamed source began to break forth upon the unfinished scene. This light in turn was separated from the darkness, which apparently was on the opposite side of the globe, and day and night became distinguished. The entire process thus far completed was performed on "day one," an expression highly suggestive of a twenty-four hour period of time. Certain scholars attempt to interpret these days as geological ages; they feel this enables us to reconcile the Biblical statements with the scientific evidence of vast periods of time before man's appearance. Besides the literary objection of the expression "day one," however, there is the problem of the delicate balance of nature which depends upon the co-existence of animals and plants. Yet, according to verses 11-20, there was one day, or "era," between the appearance of plants and the creation of animals. The difficulty of answering these objections is greater than that of accepting these as literal days.[13]

On the second day the "firmament" was created (1:6-8). This Elizabethan term means quite the opposite of what one might ordinarily suppose, for there is no suggestion of solidity at all. The actual meaning is that of space, expanse, or even atmosphere. The idea is that God created an atmosphere which, among other things was to "divide the waters from the waters." This strange language can only suggest that in the earliest period of earth's history there was a body of water above the earth as well as the seas upon the earth.[14] Exactly what form this super-terrestrial water took is a mystery, but the most reasonable assumption is that it consisted of a kind of canopy of vapor, translucent enough to permit the light of the sun, but opaque enough to prevent many outer space agents from entering the atmosphere. The plausibility of this will be further considered later on. The atmosphere is called Heaven, meaning in this context not the dwelling place of God, but simply any height above the surface of the earth itself.

On the next day, the waters were gathered together into one place and the dry land appeared (1:9-10). Thus is described the formation of the continent or continents. As soon as this was accomplished, plants began to shoot up from the earth, each plant and tree so created that it would bring forth only according to its own kind (*min*). This is a very direct assault upon the evolutionary hypothesis which not only allows but necessitates a violation of this principle. Evolution cannot take place, according to its own canons, without development from one kind to another, an idea flatly contradicted here.

The fourth day witnessed the positioning of "lightholders" in the heavens to be the source of light from that day forth (1:14-19). The light which up to that point had emanated from some other undefined source now originated from the sun, moon, and stars. It is interesting to observe the accuracy of the Hebrew here, for the moon is not called a "light" in the original language, but only a "lightholder" or reflector.

The verb *bara* is used once again in verse 21 to describe the beginning of animal life (1:20-25). Obviously, the verb is used here in connection with every kind of animal but man, for it is repeated later on to speak of the creation of man as a separate act. The implication is that there are three distinct acts of creation, and, therefore, these three must be unrelated generically. The first was the original mass; the second is here with the animals; and the third is in verse 27 in relation to man. The evolutionist who suggests that man evolved from a lower form must face squarely this differentiation of Genesis. For just as *bara* means to make something from nothing in a material sense, it also, and here specifically, means to create something which had never existed before.[15]   Man is so different from the animals which preceded him that he must be a special object of God's creative power, just as those animals were different from the plants which had been created before them.   Animals, like plants, are to reproduce *after their kind*.   It will be the law of nature that they do so in distinction to the law of evolution which declares that one species must come from another.

Finally, on the sixth day, man himself was created (*bara*) (1:26-28).   The nature of man is implied—he was to be in the image (*tselem*) and likeness (*d'muth*) of God—and his function is clearly spelled out; he was to multiply, fill the earth, and dominate all things.   The abbreviated account given here is greatly expanded in chapter two, for all that is intended here is the mere mention of the fact and purpose of man's creation.   Chapter two enlarges upon both a great deal. Because of the great emphasis on man's having dominion over all nature, at least in the animal world, and its attestation in subsequent history until the Flood, it appears that this was a most essential point.   To what extent this domination was possible is uncertain, but it surely involved much more than is commonly thought.   It is very likely that the remarkable conditions described by the prophets with regard to millennial life were the common, ordinary features of man's life in his innocency (Isa. 11:6-9; 65:25; Hos. 2:18).   "The lion and the lamb shall lie down together, and a little child shall lead them" may not be poetic after all, for the evidence clearly supports the possibility that man at one time could do this very thing. All this fortifies the earlier contention that natural law, after all, may be nothing more or less than restrictive measures placed upon man as a result of sin.   What might man do apart from this curse?   The innocent Adam and the sinless Christ, with their domination of nature, answer that question eloquently (Mark 4:39-41; 6:48-50; Matt. 17:20; Luke 19:30-35).

Finally, God told man what he might eat, a diet consisting only of vegetables, both for him and for all beasts (1:29-31). Only after the Flood did men and animals become carnivorous, an indication of the deteriorating relationship between them, a deterioration which permeated the entire earth as a result of sin (Rom. 8:19-23).

The seventh day was set apart as a day of rest, for within six days God had created all things and now He rested (2:1-3). The thought is not that of God's weariness and need for respite, but merely His cessation from creative work. His was now a task of maintenance, not creating. This flies in the face of evolution which must hold to some form of eternal creationism, and it is really more scientific than scientism which claims that creation is an on-going process. For one of the cardinal principles of true science is that matter can be neither created nor destroyed; it can only be converted to non-reversible heat energy. The seventh day was set apart by God; from that time man was to commemorate the creation on the sabbath day as a monument to God's power and glory.

THE DAYS OF CREATION

First Day	The heaven, earth, and light	(1:1-5)
Second Day	The expanse	(6-8)
Third Day	The dry land and plants	(9-13)
Fourth Day	The sun, moon, and stars	(14-19)
Fifth Day	Water and air animals	(20-23)
Sixth Day	Land animals and man	(24-31)
Seventh Day	Cessation from creation	(2:1-3)

The Anthropological Approach (2:4-25). The parallel account of creation in chapter two deals almost exclusively with man. The passage begins by describing the purposelessness of a creation without a sub-regent acting on God's behalf in nature (2:4-7). The stage is set, the scene is drawn, but there is no prime actor to give it all life and meaning. Then the creation of this actor is described in most profoundly simple terms. The verbs employed here are of great interest, for they relate the steps involved in the creative act. In 1:27 man was created (*bara*), meaning that the concept of a man first came into existence. Now man is made (*asah*—1:26) and formed (*yatzar*). *Asah* refers to the assembling of anything, *yatzar* to the perfecting of that which is made. All together they suggest the tender and loving care which God lavished upon this His chief created object.

Of paramount importance is the expression "image and likeness" in 1:26 as it relates to the creation process of 2:7. The formation of the body itself poses no particularly difficult problems comparatively, but the concept of man as a living soul (*nephesh chayyim*) is a little more obscure. We read (Gen. 1:30) that even the animals possess a "soulishness" (*nephesh*), so man's uniqueness lies not in the mere soul itself. His difference from the animals must be explained in the light of "image and likeness" and in the process by which the *nephesh* is granted. The only realistic interpretation seems to be that man's body was inbreathed by God and that as a result of the relationship of this act to the body itself, man became a *nephesh* in God's image and likeness. The animals apparently were created, body and soul, by a spoken word of God; man was created through a process of inbreathing which transmitted to him in a peculiar and unique manner the characteristics constituting God's image and likeness. Such attributes as personality, sensibility, will, and reason separate man from the animal world and allow us to speak of him as a creature related in some wonderful way to God.[16]

"Theistic" or "threshold" evolution teaches that the spiritual nature of man was immediately created, but that his physical makeup was the result of a long process of evolution. When *homo sapiens* had sufficiently advanced beyond the higher primates, he was given a soul by God, and this is what is meant by the Divine inbreathing.[17] We can see that this is nothing more than ordinary evolution except that the uniqueness of man resulted from an instantaneous creative act. The position must rest upon the basic assumptions of atheistic evolution; the two stand or fall together. Surely the evidence for sub-human societies can be explained in some other way than saying that they represent a stage in human evolution, perhaps the stage before man finally evolved into the image of God. From the scanty bone fragments and material remains which exist, little can actually be proven about the periods from which they supposedly come. What is demonstrable may suggest only that some human beings advanced more quickly than others, or that certain hereditary or environmental factors contributed to aberration in physical and mental growth patterns. The existence of pygmies in Africa in the neighborhood of giants indicates that people can have vastly different skull sizes and bodily shapes and yet be from the same period and virtually the same place.[18]

The next matter of import in the account of man's creation is the location of his original home (2:8-17), a place called Eden ("delight") whose location is highly speculative.

It is true that four rivers are named in connection with it, two of which, the Tigris and Euphrates, are known from extra-Biblical sources. If the Flood were universal and as destructive as the account implies, there would be no means of locating pre-Flood geographical places, however, for the beds of rivers and other geographical features would certainly have been tremendously altered. The most outstanding fact about the garden of Eden concerns the two trees in its midst, the Tree of Life and the Tree of Knowledge of Good and Evil. That these trees had no inherent ability to produce either life or knowledge should be clear from even a superficial understanding of Old Testament theology which is markedly free of the superstition which such an assumption would require. Rather, the trees were symbolic or sacramental; that is, eating or refraining from eating of them would express faith and obedience in the God who issued the command. Whatever they imparted they imparted only as vehicles of God's gracious bestowal.[19]

The existence of the Tree of Life in the garden is indicative of the fact that man was not created with life in its fullest realization. He was created as an immortal candidate for eternal life, but the conferment of this life depended entirely upon his reaction to the Divine probation—the prohibition to eat of the Tree of Knowledge of Good and Evil. Chapter three shows that he did not overcome the satanic temptation to eat of this tree, so he was automatically barred from the Tree of Life (3:22-24). We can only assume that had he obeyed God fully, he would have eaten of the Tree of Life and immediately received the life of the highest order represented by the tree. God pointed out to man that if he did eat of the Tree of Knowledge of Good and Evil, he would thenceforth become a creature subject to death: a creature to whom physical death would be a necessity, though another way would be provided to guarantee him eternal life in response to faith.

In the last part of chapter two man was given a companion who was "meet" or "fit" for him (Gen. 2:18-25). Adam certainly had observed that all animals had their mates, but when he gathered them all before him and gave them their names he found not one among them which was suitable to his particular needs. God therefore extracted from Adam one of his ribs, from which He fashioned a woman. Adam said that she should be called Woman (*isha*) because she came from

Man (*ish*), stating that from that day it would be part of the Divine purpose for man and woman to be joined together as one flesh. The last statement, that they were naked and were not ashamed, proleptically speaks of the tragedy of sin which was to ensue so early in their experience together.

The Fall of Man (3)

The story of man's original sin hangs like a black shadow over the beauty of everything which had so far transpired. In some unexplained way sin was hatched in the heart of Satan who now, in the form of a serpent in the garden, tempted man successfully to follow him in his rebellion against the Almighty (Isa. 14; Ezek. 28). Because the serpent was naturally more subtle than any other creature, Satan took advantage of it to accomplish his end and became incarnate in it. Through a series of questions and doubtings he finally convinced the woman that the only reason God had prohibited the eating of the Tree of Knowledge was that God was jealous for His own superiority, and that His superiority would be jeopardized by man's acquisition of Knowledge. If the woman had only reasoned carefully, she would have realized how preposterous the whole Satanic proposition was, for if God were so terrified that man would be equal to Him in knowledge, why would God create the very means of man's acquiring that knowledge? But woman, who had already misconstrued the prohibition of God in her debate with Satan (3:2-3), was unable to let her reason rule over her emotions. When she realized the desirability of the Tree, she partook of it, sharing it with her husband, who ate with her. Immediately their spiritual eyes were opened and they recognized all too late the enormity of their transgression, for their nakedness for the first time became to them a source of embarrassment and an indication of their deeper and more serious spiritual nakedness.

The Knowledge of Good and Evil was not merely the ability to distinguish between the two, but the complete understanding of all that they involved. This knowledge could be gained in two ways. Presumably if the temptation had been resisted, man would have gained this knowledge by Divine revelation, without having experienced evil. Because he did not, however, he became aware of the nature of Good and Evil

by now experiencing the Evil, marking its infinite contrast
to the Good which had made up the totality of his experience
before he sinned. He now had the Knowledge he wanted, but
at the cost of his own physical and spiritual existence. All
that could now possibly avail was an act of Divine saving
grace.

When they recognized that they were physically and
spiritually naked, man and woman hid themselves from God
who nonetheless found them and extracted from them a confession of sin. God then proceeded to speak prophetic curses
to all three—Satan, woman, and man. To Satan He promised
immediate retaliation, as represented in the perpetual crawling of the serpent and ultimate destruction by the seed of the
woman. This reference to the seed (singular) of the woman
(not the man as would ordinarily be the case) is the first
Messianic promise in the Old Testament (3:15; cf. Isa. 7:14).
This seed, which can only be Christ, the virgin born Son of
God, would eventually destroy Satan and sin forever. God
predicted that the woman would experience pain in childbirth
and subservience to her husband, both of which were to remind her henceforth of her part in tempting her husband
(I Tim. 2:12-15). Finally, the man was told that the ground
would be cursed, and as he expended his energy and very life
in an effort to produce from it the food of life, he would weary
himself in agonizing toil even to the point of death, and would
eventually return as dust to that very soil. As though to
palliate the awfulness of the curse upon man and woman, God
slew an innocent animal and made from the victim garments
of skins to cover them. The fig leaves of their own invention
were insufficient, for what was actually involved here was
the need of spiritual covering, something which would be accomplished only by faith in shed blood (Heb. 9:22).

Man was then barred from the Tree of Life. The moral
anomaly of a sinful human being eating of the Tree reserved
for the innocent, and thereby achieving eternal life, was rep-
rehensible to God. Man might be saved, but having forfeited
the way of the Tree of Life by his disobedience, he must now
cast himself upon the mercy of God and through faith in the
divinely ordained system of sacrifice achieve what could have
been his without the shedding of blood.

THE GENEALOGY OF ADAM AND EVE (4-5)

The Family of Cain (4:1-24). Sometime after man's sin children were born to Adam and Eve. The first of these was named Cain ("gotten"), for it is likely that in him Eve saw the fulfillment of the promised seed of Genesis 3:15. She felt that this one whom she had gotten by God's grace might be the one who could crush Satan once and for all. Eventually a second son, Abel, was born. In course of time both sons took up their own occupations, Cain as a tiller of the ground and Abel a keeper of sheep.

On a certain occasion they appeared before God bearing their offerings. Abel and his offering were accepted while Cain and his offering were rejected by God apparently because of Cain's improper attitude and/or lack of true faith (Heb. 11:4; I Jn. 3:12). God gave Cain an opportunity to repent and warned him about what would happen if he did not. But the enraged Cain slew Abel one day in the open field. God called him to account, and finding Cain yet unrepentant, sentenced him to the life of a vagabond, perhaps to be understood as a nomadic life. Yet, He graciously shielded him with Divine protection, lest any human being should kill him in revenge.

The first murderer was then sent out into the land of Nod where he and his wife, who no doubt was his own sister, founded a civilization at a city named Enoch. It is probable that several generations had passed and that Cain had produced hundreds of descendants by this time, though a city by Old Testament standards was certainly not necessarily very large. This perhaps was no more than a cluster of beduin tents where a type of simple life was practiced. After seven generations from Cain, Lamech appeared in the genealogy with special recognition. This man, the first bigamist, produced three sons, Jubal, Jabal, and Tubal-cain, each of whom became proficient in an art or skill, presupposing rather high cultural development these many thousands of years before Christ. Lamech furthermore sang the first recorded poetry, a verse of boasting arrogance against God and society. The trend of the Cainite civilization had become unquestionably clear and the outlook for world history extremely pessimistic.

The Family of Seth (4:25-5:32). Following Abel's death, a son was born to take his place, appropriately named Seth ("appointed"). He in turn sired a son named Enos, meaning "weak man," a clue that illustrates the true condition of fallen man as recognized by the godly Seth. It was at that time, however, that men began to call upon the name of Yahweh. It has even been suggested that the proper translation is that men now "began to call themselves by the name of Yahweh."[20] It is surely possible that we have here the recognition by the Sethites that the God of heaven had revealed Himself through them as a witness against the unrighteous Cainites.

Chapter five is essentially a genealogy of Seth which traces his posterity through to Noah and his three sons. We are immediately struck by the references to the extremely long lives of these pre-Deluge patriarchs. Many scholars have tried unsuccessfully to discredit the literalism of these life-spans.[21] The years mentioned cannot be based on a lunar calendar rather than solar, as some suggest, making a year only one twelfth as long as these appear, for in the case of Enoch, for example, this breaks completely down. It is as great a miracle for Enoch to beget Methusaleh at the age of five as it is for Adam to live for 930 years. Whitcomb and Morris suggest that before the Flood, while the vapor canopy was still in the heavens, deadly age-causing rays from outer space were filtered out from the atmosphere and men simply were not subject to aging factors.[22] Certainly it is clear that for an immediate realization of God's command for man to be fruitful and multiply and fill the earth, man must be able to produce children much more prolifically than now. Extension of his productive years would greatly facilitate this. The Sumerian King List of Berossus, which purports to list all the ancient kings both before and after the Flood, is also of great importance in the argument. It is interesting to note that these kings allegedy lived not just hundreds but many thousands of years. A few, in fact, reigned as many as 40,000 years![23] These figures are greatly exaggerated but they testify to the fact that man's memory could recall a time when people lived much longer than they did in more modern times. The Old Testament and these traditions both refer to a common reality, the longevity of these persons, but the latter over the course of thousands of years of oral (though possibly written) transmission have completely corrupted the original facts. The Biblical figures, having come from either Divinely preserved historical documents directly to Moses, or from immediate revelation to the great Lawgiver, reflect the actual case as is made clear from all the evidence.

Two figures of this godly race stand out more vividly than the rest—Enoch for his godliness and Methusaleh for his great age, 969 years. The former "patterned his life after God" with the result that he was excepted from the principle that "it is appointed unto man once to die." In simple majesty the account states that "he was not for God took him" (Gen. 5:24).

THE FLOOD (6-9) [24]

The parallel races of men described in chapters 4 and 5, those of the Cainites and Sethites, continued to multiply through many generations. As long as there was separation between them, the knowledge of the true God could be maintained even in the face of increasing wickedness on earth. The time finally came, however, when that division was no longer preserved, for we learn in 6:1-2 that an intermarriage of the two took place, resulting in an absorption of the covenant race except for Noah and his family who alone retained their faith. Some would suggest that the "sons of God" in this passage were angels while the "daughters of men" were human beings, and that there was, therefore, connubium between angels and men.[25] Though this interpretation appears to have some support, especially from Job (1:6), Peter (II Pet. 2:4), and Jude (6, 7), the overall arguments against it seem to outweigh it. Jesus described the angels as sexless beings (Mark 12:25). Moreover, the purpose for carefully outlining the fortunes of the Cainites and Sethites in chapters four and five is meaningless apart from assuming that Cainites and Sethites are intended in chapter six, and that their intermarriage was the immediate cause for the Flood.

Regardless of the identification, we observe that the world was a place in which there were none who followed after God. God decided to alter His procedure (which is the meaning here of "repent") and to destroy man from off the earth within a period of 120 more years (6:3). One man alone found grace in His eyes. Noah, whose name means "comfort" or "rest" was chosen to be saved from the flood and to be the means of reestablishing the human race in a post-Deluge world. We are told that he, like Enoch, "patterned his life after God," but the reason for his selection by God must still rest ultimately in the fact that he became an object of God's special sovereign grace (6:8).

Because it was God's intention to destroy men alone, only those animals which could not survive flood waters needed to be saved along with Noah and his family. Following Divine specifications, Noah proceeded to build a vessel which would be large enough to accomplish the task of preserving at least two of every species, except, of course, the above-mentioned creatures which would survive even better apart from an ark. The dimensions, following the eighteen inch cubit, were 450 x 75 x 45 feet. The craft was divided into three decks, each of which had an area of about 33,750 square feet, so the entire capacity was roughly one and one half million cubic feet. This is an important fact, for one of the most prevalent arguments against the universality of the Flood is that the boat could not have accommodated all the animals and food necessary if two of every kind were preserved.

Modern taxonomy estimates that there are about one million different species, over ninety-five percent of which, however, could conceivably have existed outside the ark.[26] This means that there were no more than 50,000 animals in all—though Whitcomb and Morris believe the figure should be no higher than 35,000[27]—and the average size of these would be about equivalent to that of a sheep. Simple calculation leads to the conclusion that all of the animals could have been accommodated on one deck by itself, leaving the other two for food storage and other purposes. Of course, there was no water problem, for it is likely that rain fell throughout the greater part of the Flood time.

After the long period of preparation was completed, during which Noah served God as a "preacher of righteousness" warning and urging the people to repent (II Pet. 2:5; Heb. 11:7), God instructed him to enter the ark with two of every unclean animal and seven of every clean (6:19; 7:2). The seventh of each was no doubt for sacrifice following the deliverence, and more of them were taken also to ensure their continued existence. Having shut the door of the ark, God opened the "floodgates of the heavens" and for forty days the rains fell, apparently never having done so before. If the concept of the "canopy" be correct, we assume that it became the source of this deluge, and depending upon its thickness, could have deposited literally hundreds of feet of water upon the earth. In addition, the "fountains of the great deep" were broken open and water from subterranean reservoirs began to gush forth with unrestrained fury and rose perhaps thousands of feet, sweeping all before it and destroying all non-aquatic creatures. In addition, it is likely that the continents dropped considerably causing even more extensive flooding. The waters covered all land, even the highest mountains, by the 150th day. God's purpose was achieved.

After 150 days the water began to recede, most of it returning to its underground sources and filling the greatly deepened ocean beds. Probably the continents also rose, thrusting up great mountain peaks in the wake of phenomenal tectonic pressures (Ps. 104:6-9). Finally, after sending out birds to determine the state of the earth, Noah disembarked, setting foot on dry ground for the first time in over a year. All about him was chaos, for the civilization which had presumably reached such a peak of development before the Flood had been reduced to oblivion. Yet in the midst of all this, Noah set out to offer sacrifices of thanksgiving and praise to his Creator and Redeemer, sacrifices which God accepted, promising never again to destroy the earth with the waters of a Flood (9:8-17).

Arguments for a Universal Flood. One of the most critical and debated problems involved with the Flood story has to do with its extent. Was it local in scope, covering only the Mesopotamian area perhaps, or was it universal? If it was universal was it only anthropologically universal or was it also geographically universal? The Biblical narrative itself almost certainly implies a universal Flood, one which covered the face of the whole earth and which destroyed every creature on its surface. The only way that this can be circumvented is to believe that the writer, or Noah himself, was using the "language of appearance": the Flood appeared to be universal because it covered everything within man's immediate scope of observation.[28]

Whitcomb and Morris again have some telling arguments which the interested reader should consult, among which are the following:[29]

1. The depth of the Flood (Genesis 7:19-20). If the Flood were only in a restricted area, it is difficult to compre-

hend the fact that it covered the highest mountains, even in a small area, without overflowing to other areas. The fact that water seeks its own level seems to be decisively against a local Flood.

2. The duration of the Flood. It appears that the Flood lasted for over one year in all from the time Noah entered the ark until he left it; most of that time the water was upon the earth. No local Flood in history ever lasted that long. Any flood which endured for such a long period would, therefore, have to be universal.

3. The size of the ark. Why would Noah build a vessel large enough to accommodate all the land species on earth when all he needed was one large enough to save the species indigenous to Mesopotamia, of which there must have been very few?

4. The need for an ark at all. More fatal to the local Flood is the utter lack of any need for an ark in such an event, for Noah could easily have walked from the scene of the impending disaster, taking with him any animals which were in any danger of drowning. Why spend 120 years building a boat for which there was no real need?

5. The testimony of Peter. In his second Epistle (3:3-7), Peter argues that at the end of this age God will destroy the world with a fiery judgment. He bases his argument for the extensiveness of this judgment on the analogy of the destruction by water in Noah's time. If Peter is trying to teach a universal devastation by fire, which he assuredly is, why would he compare it to a merely local Flood of Noah's time?

Other Basic Questions. The extent of the Flood raises related problems, especially if the waters covered the whole earth. One of the most intriguing of these is the source of the Flood waters and their disposition following the deluge. We have suggested that the canopy of water above the earth, coupled with the "fountains of the great deep," could easily account for the water's source, particularly if the land masses were not as high as they are presently and therefore required less water to submerge them. As the waters rose to greater and greater heights, their tremendous weight began to cause the earth's crust to sink in some places and to be folded higher in others. The result was that during or right after the Flood the ocean beds were considerably deepened and the land masses reduced in size, through probably they increased in height. Psalm 104:6-9, which speaks of the Flood, expresses the idea quite well, especially in verse 8 which says literally, "the mountains ascend, the valleys descend." The continental shelves which ring the continents of the world at a distance of several hundreds of miles in some cases and which are several thousands of feet below the ocean's surface, indicate that at one time the oceans were very much smaller, or that the continents have sunk. The former, it seems, is just as easy to prove as the latter, and the Flood would provide the very factors needed.

Another interesting speculation has to do with fossils and rock strata. Scientists commonly use these as indications of age, but only at the risk of very circuitous reasoning. For example, they allege that the age of a rock can be determined by the nature of the imbedded fossils; also the age of those fossils is indicated by the level of rock in which they are found.[30] But the basic question here is, how can we account for rock stratification and for fossil indices? The scientist is hard put to explain both of these phenomena, usually resorting to uniformitarian hypotheses which are completely unsatisfying to the unprejudiced individual. What current process now at work in nature could ever, even in billions of years, produce the Grand Canyon? How can whole beds of millions of fossils be deposited by the ordinary processes of erosion and deposition presupposed by the evolutionary theory? Yet, a catastrophic occurrence such as the Flood could account for both. As billions of tons of materials were swept up and suspended by the Flood waters, they were eventually deposited and in a generally predictable order. Heavy and light materials or materials with varying viscosity would be laid down in discernible layers, exactly as we may observe them today. Fossils, too, would naturally follow a general pattern of deposition, both because of their shapes and sizes and because of their varying abilities to escape the Flood waters. The less complex the organism the less adaptibility to danger and the earlier the burial in water and mud. Obviously the simple marine creatures would be deposited first, and this is what the case really is in the fossil index. The more complex the organism, the higher it would climb away from the encroaching waters and the later it would be entombed. The highest orders of all, the more intelligent mammals, would drown last of all. We would expect to find them on the top strata, and that is precisely where they are usually found. Exceptions to the index are common, but some are explainable by later overthrusts and faulting.[31] However, in a sudden catastrophe, in some cases even large mammals would be trapped at the outset. Local circumstances and the reworking of deposits during the Flood would also affect the location of fossils.

The problem of the formation of canyons is also germane here. Under no uniformitarian set of principles can they be understood, for the conditions requisite for their original state and for their formation could not exist under these assumptions. The waters of a Flood several hundered feet deep returning to their beds in the oceans with the eroding force presupposed by as brief a period of return as that described in the Bible could cut their way through the freshly deposited materials of the Flood in a few years where the uniformitarian presumption would require millions of years. In other words, given soft soils and swiftly moving water, both of which are a tacit concomitant of a universal Flood, the problem of the canyons disappears.

Finally, let us consider briefly the great glaciers, tropical fossils in the polar regions, and woolly mammoths. Scientists generally agree today that at one time the earth enjoyed a tropical climate throughout and that tropical plants were to be found everywhere. As a matter of fact, fossils of these plants have been found as far north as the Arctic Circle. Moreover, hunters and other people have found the frozen carcasses of woolly mammoths in the Siberian tundra and these were so well preserved that their meat was still edible![32] When they were cut open tropical plants were found still undigested, but perfectly intact, in their stomachs. Scientism has a very difficult time accounting for all of this, but the universal Flood presents some solutions that are worthy of consideration. The canopy of water, previously discussed, no doubt provided a "greenhouse effect" which rendered the climate of the earth equally warm throughout. When this canopy disappeared as rain, normal climatic changes ensued, and the polar zones became frozen. Anything living there also froze becoming trapped in the mud and rock laid down by the Flood. If the process of drowning, entombment, and freezing were quick enough, thousands of animals could be preserved indefinitely. Uniformitarianism has no adequate solution to these problems, but the Flood, rightly understood, is quite satisfactory. By allowing for a proper "stretching" of the Biblical chronology, as we shall see later, the date of the Flood could be between 10,000 and 6000 B.C. The usual scientific dating for the last Ice Age is about 10,000 B.C., which ties in nicely with the above reconstruction. After the Flood, the polar areas froze, the climate made even more subsequent changes, and eventually the frozen area receded to the North and South polar regions. The Ice Age was over, leaving the scarred remains so evident in the northeastern part of the United States and other places.

We have said a great deal about creation and the Flood so far because the writer feels keenly that these matters are of paramount importance, for they form the foundations for all that ensues in Old Testament history. The reliability of that history depends largely upon the reliability of these accounts properly interpreted. It is not mere naiveté to say that they stand or fall together.

The Noahic Covenant (9). The first act of God following the Flood was the acceptance of the sacrificial offering made to Him by Noah, and the subsequent promise by God that He would never again destroy the earth by a Flood. Catastrophism was not to be the rule from that time forward, except at the end of the world (9:9-11). Nature was to continue an orderly course, or was to be "uniform," manifesting its stability in the regularity of the seasonal cycles and by unending alternation of day and night.

God continued His promise to mankind by outlining the basic features of the covenant which He was about to make with Noah, the covenant which formed the real basis for God's having spared man from extinction in the first place. In virtually the same words of those of the Adamic covenant, God informed this second father of the human race that he was to be fruitful, and multiply, and replenish the earth (9:1-7). However, we note a very decisive difference. Man was to continue to have dominion over all things, but this domination was to take the form of forced subservience rather than the docile, voluntary acquiescence demonstrated by nature before the Flood. Evidently man's environment was now hostile to him in a way that was not apparent before.

The whole universe was "out of joint" as Paul was later to imply. The best that man could expect was control of his environment by sheer strength and ingenuity. This control by force was to issue in the slaughter of animals for food, an occurrence not noted before. In fact, it seems almost certain that such a thing was actually prohibited before the Flood. At the same time, man was to be very careful concerning the shedding and eating of blood, for in some peculiar sense the blood was sacrosanct. It was to be poured out upon the ground and not consumed, for it represented life. Feeding upon that which was so sacred would be inconsistent with the high premium which God placed upon life, even that of an animal. This explains the later Mosaic stipulations concerning the meticulous use or nonuse of blood (Lev. 17).

In line with this Divine equivalence of life with blood, God states that the shedding of human blood to the point of death was punishable by the death of the one who had shed the blood, whether man or beast (9:5-6). This by no means implies merely human, individual revenge, but rather the prerogative of organized man, or government, to assume this function of reprisal. The basic reason for such a harsh punishment is that life is sacred; especially, because man is in the image of God. To slay one in the image of God is to assault the very God whom the image represents, just as the desecration of the national flag constitutes an attack upon the nation for which it stands.

The covenant is further outlined beginning in verse 8 where God again enunciated the promise that never again would He destroy the earth by a flood, though this by no means ruled out the possibility of destruction by God through some other agency (II Peter 3:1-7). Then, as though to visibly guarantee to man the inviolability of the covenant, and also to be consistent with such covenant arrangements, God set in the heavens a rainbow as a sign of the promise. Whenever man viewed the bow from that day hence, he was to take heart in the realization that God who had made the covenant would be faithful to its contracts.

Following the declaration of the Noahic Covenant, we are introduced to the immediately following course of human history (9:18-28), a tragically sordid beginning to the new human civilization. Noah had no sooner received the promises of God as contained in the covenant when he showed dramati-

cally the utter inability of mankind to measure up to his covenant responsibility. He planted a vineyard, drank from the
wine which it produced and lay in a drunken, naked stupor
within his tent. His son Ham found him there and with
none of the common filial regard expected of a son, refused
to cover his father and keep from his brethren the awful
details of his father's shame; in fact, there is every likelihood that he acted in the situation with a positive assertion
of the latent immorality which seemed to characterize him, or
certainly his son Canaan. Upon awakening, Noah issued a
prophetic statement of cursing and blessing upon the three
sons, expressing in capsule form the affairs of the three
great branches of mankind as they would develop in history.
These were not racial divisions as is apparent from chapters
10 and 11. They seem rather to be constituted along spiritual
lines. Canaan, the son of Ham, was cursed in his father's
place, the curse manifesting itself primarily in Canaan's servitude to his brethren (Josh. 9:22-27). Shem, the meaning of
whose name is "name," was to be Canaan's master. Japheth
was to be enlarged and was to dwell in the tents of Shem and
also be dominant over Canaan.

We should be careful to note that there is no basis here
for assigning the Negro race to bondage because of any
Divine curse. The Hamites, from whom the negroid races
undoubtedly sprang, were not objects of the curse. Only
Canaan, a tiny part of that great group of humanity, was involved. Moreover, Canaan by no stretch of the imagination
can be considered negroid, for they settled primarily on the
eastern Mediterranean and any mention of them in the Old
Testament seems to suggest that they were not racially distinct from the Hebrews or any other peoples with whom they
came in contact. The subjugation of Canaan was fulfilled in
its defeat at the hands of the Hebrews under Joshua and, later,
of the Phoenicians who were related to the Canaanites under
Babylonia and Persia, and of the Carthaginians (Phoenician
colonists) under Rome in the Punic Wars.

The exaltation of Shem was bound up in the fact that God
would reveal His saving Name to the world through Shem.
Shem was to be the vehicle of Divine revelation and salva-
tion, a concept amply illustrated in Abraham, Isaac, Jacob,
David, and the whole Messianic line down to and including
Christ, all of whom were Shemites (Semites). The idea of

Japheth's dwelling in the tents of Shem may include both the occupation of the Near East by Gentile nations throughout history and the extension of the Gospel message to the non-Jewish world, the latter being far more likely.

THE DISPERSION OF THE NATIONS (10-11)

One of the stated objectives of the Noahic Covenant was for man to scatter abroad upon the face of the whole earth so that he could exercise rule over every part of the creation. The events described immediately after the Flood indicate, however, that the descendants of Noah were slow to carry out this obligation. This is especially noticeable when we arrange the events of chapters 10 and 11 in their proper chronological order and perspective. We find the first description of post-Deluge humanity in Genesis 11:1-2 where we learn that everyone on earth spoke a common language, presupposing a common civilization and culture, and, therefore, certain geographic cohesion. This is in antithesis to the covenant which stipulated that man was to overspread the whole earth; indeed, the expression of that antithesis is found in 11:4 in the remark by the builders of Babel to the effect that they wished to countermand God's will by remaining where they were, a gregarious community.

The listing of the nations in chapter 10, then, must be anticipatory of the dispersion of man by God as disclosed in chapter 11, verses 8 and 9. The latter passage explains *how* and *why* the nations were divided; the former *where* they settled.

The genealogy of Noah in chapter 10 is an account of the origin of the nations and their earliest ethnical characteristics, for verse 32 states that of Noah and his sons "were the nations divided in the earth after the Flood." We learn that the descendants of Japheth settled basically in the South Central Asia and European areas (11:2-5). The Hamites were early located primarily in Africa, with the notable exception of Canaan (11:21-32). The Shemites lived in the Mesopotamian and Persian region of the Near East (11:21-32). These are not hard and fast distinctions, for there are too many exceptions and overlappings and too much subsequent migration from place to place to make the division constant. Furthermore, there is absolutely no hint that we have here any reference to races or colors. Such differences must have developed later, probably after the Tower of Babel incident.

One or two points of special interest in chapter 10 must suffice. First, we observe that Nimrod, the Cushite, moved eastward to found the kingdoms of the Plain of Shinar (10:8-10). This is a good example of a Hamite who moved into Semitic territory to establish a culture, a situation described also in extra-Biblical literature.[33] Also, we learn in verse 25 that a certain Semite by the name of Peleg ("division") lived on the earth at the time of its division. There is only one account of such a division in the Bible and that is in connection with the dispersion of man after Babel. The mention of Peleg in the Semitic genealogy, therefore, gives us valuable information in approximating the date of Babel.

Chapter 11 begins with the story of Nimrod (at least he best fits the situation) and his migration to Mesopotamia (not "from the east" as in the KJV). When he and his colleagues settled they decided to build a city and a tower, the purpose of the latter being to provide a visible monument to the desire of mankind for homogeneity in the face of God's clear commands to disperse. We have no suggestion here that the tower had any religious connotations whatsoever— rather, there is obviously a very definite anti-religious or at least anti-God spirit—though such towers in later Babylonian history did serve as temple towers or shrines in some sense.[34] Man was not attempting to reach Heaven; on the contrary, the struggle was one of man against God in the interests of human independence.

The result of this flagrant disobedience of the covenant conditions was the dispersion of mankind by God, a scattering which seems to follow naturally the confusion of human speech. Because man would not spread throughout the earth voluntarily, God confounded his language so that he was unable to conduct the most ordinary affairs of life, with the result that he lost his sense of fellowship with every other man. Men began to gather into small enclaves, each possessing its own speech. They became widespread from the necessity of being distinguished from others with whom they now had so very little in common. This, then, explains the origins of the various worldwide civilizations, each with different languages and customs, and yet all possessing certain common traditions such as those of Creation and the Flood, traditions based upon a common experience in their dim pre-Babel world.[35] Perhaps the beginnings of the races may also be found here, for if it was God's purpose to render man incapable of cohesion, the separation of men into races would compound the difficulties inherent in the confounding of languages. As a result of both, mankind would be up against physical and sociological obstacles the like of which he had never before experienced and which he would never be able to completely overcome no matter how hard he might try. Indeed, the very efforts of modern man to minimize and even erase linguistic and racial differences is indicative of the nature of the problem created at Babel. God's continuing plan is that man should overspread the earth, and modern man reacts as his ancestors did at Babel—he wants to unite as One Man against God's will. The name of the place, Babel, indicates "confusion" (though etymologically it means "gate of god"), and this term exactly describes man's timeless condition in rebellion against his Creator.

Because the Shemites were selected to be the bearers of the covenant promises according to Noah's prophecy, our interest from this point on centers on them. The last part of chapter 11 records the Semitic genealogy from Shem to Abram, the man who was to become the father of a chosen people through whom God would manifest Himself to the rest of the world in saving grace. This genealogy is interesting in many respects. It is noteworthy that the ages of the individuals listed are much shorter than those of the pre-Deluge patriarchs. This may suggest a change in the environment in which man lived, a change detrimental to his health. Or it may simply have reflected the increasingly deadly toll of man's cursed existence. In addition, by totaling up the years of the various generations we may arrive at approximate dates for the period between Abraham and the Flood, though the probability of gaps in the genealogy and careful interpretation of the data contained therein may well extend the period considerably longer than that reached by a simple addition of the figures. Biblical historians now agree that Abraham was born about 2166 B.C.[36] According to a strictly literal exposition of genealogy, the Flood must be dated no earlier than 2600 B.C., a figure which is obviously too late. Evidence of thriving and uninterrupted civilizations both in Egypt and Mesopotamia as far back as 4500 B.C. supports this contention. The solution is to attach to the genealogical information certain interpretative criteria which allow the pre-Abrahamic period to be expanded,[37] though such expansion cannot stretch to the tens of thousands of years required by uniformitarian anthropological hypotheses. We may be safe in saying, on the basis of both the scientific and Biblical evidence, that the Flood occurred about 8000-7000 B.C. and the Tower of Babel dispersion about 7000-6000 B.C.[38]

The way the genealogy of chapter 11 proceeds leaves no doubt in the mind that the family of Terah of Ur, especially as traced through his son Abram, was to occupy a very special place in redemptive history. The whole course of the Genesis historical account swings from national and international considerations to the biographical story of Abraham and his family, particularly those of his descendants who were chosen by God to mediate the covenant blessings. To these individuals, known initially as the Patriarchs, we now direct our attention.

---

[1] G. Ernest Wright, "The Archaeology of Palestine," *The Bible and the Ancient Near East*, Ed. by G. Ernest Wright, Garden City, Doubleday and Company, Inc. 1965, pp. 92-93.

[2] Samuel Noah Kramer, "Sumerian Literature; A General Survey," *The Bible and the Ancient Near East*, Ed. by G. Ernest Wright, Garden City, Doubleday and Company, Inc., 1965, pp. 332-333.

[3] John Bright, *A History of Israel*, Philadelphia, Westminster Press, 1959, p. 32.

[4] The dates here are those of the "low chronology" of W. F. Albright; cf. Edward F. Campbell, "The Ancient Near East: Chronological Bibliography and Charts," *The Bible and the Ancient Near East*, Ed. by Wright, pp. 288-293.

[5] Wright, *op. cit.*, pp. 96-110.

[6] Colin Ronan, *Changing Views of the Universe*, New York, The Macmillan Company, 1961, pp. 180-181.

[7] John C. Whitcomb and Henry M. Morris, *The Genesis Flood*, Philadelphia, The Presbyterian and Reformed Publishing Company, 1963, pp. 130-132.

[8] Donald Collier, "New Radiocarbon Method for Dating the Past," *The Biblical Archeologist Reader*, Vol. 1, Ed. by Doubleday and Company, Inc., 1961, pp. 330-337.

[9] Frank Hole and Robert Heizer, *An Introduction to Prehistoric Archaeology*, New York, Holt, Rinehart, and Winston, 1965, p. 151.

[10] Lecture at Hebrew Union College, Jerusalem, July 21, 1965.

[11] Geerhardus Vos, *Biblical Theology*, Grand Rapids, Wm. B. Eerdmans Publishing Co., 1954, pp. 77, 129.

[12] Francis Brown, S. R. Driver, and Charles Briggs, *A Hebrew and English Lexicon of the Old Testament*, London, Oxford University Press, 1962, p. 135.

[13] For good arguments for the twenty-four hour day see Edward J. Young, *Studies in Genesis One* (1964), pp. 103-105. Young himself does not reach any conclusion as to the length of the days. Also, Henry M. Morris, *Studies in Science and the Bible*, pp. 33-38 (1966). Both, Presbyterian and Reformed Publishing Co.

[14] Whitcomb and Morris, *op. cit.*, p. 77.

[15] C. F. Keil and Franz Delitzsch, *Biblical Commentary on the Old Testament; The Pentateuch*, Vol. 1, Grand Rapids, Wm. B. Eerdmans Publishing Company, 1948, p. 47.

[16] *Ibid.*, p. 63.

[17] Ernest Charles Messenger, *Evolution and Theology*, New York, The Macmillan Company, 1932, p. 144.

[18] W. E. LeGros Clark, *The Antecedents of Man*, New York, Harper and Row, 1963, p. 23.

[19] Vos, *op. cit.*, pp. 37-43.

[20] W. H. Griffith Thomas, Genesis: *A Devotional Commentary*, Grand Rapids, Wm. B. Eerdmans Publishing Company, 1946, p. 64.

[21] John Skinner, *A Critical and Exegetical Commentary on Genesis*, New York, Charles Scribner's Sons, 1910, p. 129.

[22] Whitcomb and Morris, *op. cit.*, pp. 399-405.

[23] Merrill F. Unger, *Archaeology and the Old Testament*, Grand Rapids, Zondervan Publishing House, 1954, p. 46.

[24] For the following discussion of the Flood, I am heavily indebted to John C. Whitcomb and Henry M. Morris, *The Genesis Flood.*

[25] Frank Delitzsch, cited in Gustave Oehler, *Theology of the Old Testament*, Grand Rapids, Zondervan Publishing House, 1883, p. 135.

[26] Whitcomb and Morris, *op. cit.*, p. 68.

[27] *Ibid.*, p. 69.

[28] Bernard Ramm, *The Christian View of Science and Scripture*, Grand Rapids, Wm. B. Eerdmans Publishing Company, 1954, p. 240.

[29] Whitcomb and Morris, *op. cit.*, pp. 1-35.

[30] William Charles Putnam, *Geology*, New York, Oxford University Press, 1964, pp. 440-441.

[31] Whitcomb and Morris, *op. cit.*, pp. 271-275.

[32] Charles Schuchert, *Outlines of Historical Geology*, New York, John Wiley and Sons, Inc., 1947, p. 37.

[33] Skinner, *op. cit.*, p. 208.

[34] G. Ernest Wright, *Biblical Archaeology*, Philadelphia, Westminster Press, 1957, p. 26.

[35] John Bright, "Has Archaeology Found Evidence of the Flood?", *The Biblical Archaeologist Reader*, Vol. 1, Ed. by G. Ernest Wright and David Noel Freedman, Garden City, Doubleday and Company, Inc., 1961, p. 33.

[36] See p. 98.

[37] O. T. Allis, *The Five Books of Moses*, Philadelphia, The Presbyterian and Reformed Publishing Company, 1943, pp. 295-298.

[38] Whitcomb and Morris, *op. cit.*, p. 489.

CHAPTER THREE

THE FOUNDING FATHERS

THE HISTORICAL BACKGROUND[1]

In Mesopotamia. At the end of the Third Millennium
Mesopotamia was quite generally under the domination of the
Third Dynasty of Ur, a political entity flavored with Sumerian influences but Semitic in character. In about the middle
of the twentieth century B. C. this dynasty was overthrown
and supplanted by rival states at Isin and Larsa, both of
which maintained at least a tenuous existence until the close
of the eighteenth century. In the meantime the center of
power gradually shifted up the Euphrates to the city of Babylon where, about 1830 B. C., Shumu-Abum founded the
First Dynasty of Babylon. The might of this state increased
with the passing of the years; by the time of its famous
sixth king, Hammurabi (ca. 1728-1686), it had extended in
all directions at least as far as any preceding empire. This
level was maintained until ca. 1600 when a violent incursion
into the Mesopotamian world by a savage people known as
the Kassites ushered in the Babylonian "Dark Ages," a period
which was to last for all practical purposes until the rise of
the Neo-Babylonian Empire in 626 B. C.

There were other nations making their impact on this
part of the ancient world at this time, notably the Assyrians.
Their history before 2000 B. C. is very obscure, but by the
turn of the millennium they were making their presence felt
in a way that indicated the future role they were to play in
international affairs. The first monarch of great repute,
Shamshi-Adad I (ca. 1748-1716), began to reign in the time of
the Hebrew Patriarchs and was for a time a contemporary
of the great Hammurabi. For some time there was intense

rivalry between Assyria and Babylonia, both vying for control of Mesopotamia, until the Kassite invasion of 1600 put Babylonia out of contention and opened the way for a gradual building up of Assyrian strength and influence. It was not until well after the Patriarchal Period, however, that Assyria was to be reckoned as a first rate power in Near Eastern diplomacy.

In Egypt. The Eleventh Dynasty of Egypt, which marked the beginning of revival of power in that kingdom, commenced its authority about the time of the beginning of the Patriarchal Period (ca. 2133 B. C.). It was shortly followed by the Twelfth Dynasty under Amenemhet I (1991-1962), a dynasty which was to become one of the most important in Egyptian history, but which in turn was followed by a period of disruption hardly paralleled in the life of any other nation ancient or modern. For about 200 years the Middle Kingdom (Twelfth Dynasty) made Egypt equal in prestige and power to Mesopotamia in the Near East, and it is now well known that the two cradles of civilization carried on extensive contacts of all kinds.[2] Just as Babylonia had pushed out in many directions in extending its sway over other peoples, Egypt now began to do the same, reaching as far south as the land of Nubia and as far east and north as the Arabian peninsula and southern Syria, including, therefore, Palestine. This imperialism was shortlived, however, for in about the year 1730 Egypt succumbed to a people known in history only as the Hyksos, an apparently semi-nomadic Semitic race which gradually began to settle near and just within the borders of northeast Egypt, and then occupied the whole northern part of the country by military force. The identification of these people has been one of the thorniest of historical problems, for they left little of material remains, especially of literature, whereby they might be studied. There is no question, however, that they made some major contributions to Egypt, including the use of the chariot and a new type of fortification known as a revetment wall.[3] What is most important is that they completely disrupted Egyptian civilization, creating a lacuna in that nation's history which is difficult to fill. And for at least 150 years (ca. 1730-1580) they maintained their grip, until finally under Ahmose I of the Eighteenth Dynasty they were expelled.

In Palestine. The period from 2000 to 1600 B.C. in Palestine was characterized by an almost complete break with the civilization which had existed in the third millennium. Before 2000 there had been many important city states, the archaeological remains of which suggest that they were strongly fortified and rather remarkably advanced culturally.[4] Then, almost without intermission, and certainly without explanation as yet, these city states were overwhelmed in a series of devastations which rendered them completely incapable of continuing their existence. Because the remains from the period following this conquest indicate nomadic and semi-nomadic life, it is assumed that Palestine met the same fate that Egypt did later, and possibly through the Hyksos or people very similar to them. Historians now know that there was a tremendous movement of peoples everywhere in the Near East at this chaotic period in history, and the overrunning of Palestine may reflect the results of such mass migration in the Fertile Crescent. Throughout the Patriarchal Period Palestine seems to have been the home of semi-nomadic people; not until the middle of the Middle Bronze Age (ca. 1700 B.C.) is there much evidence of sedentary population.

THE OLD TESTAMENT AND THE PATRIARCHAL PERIOD

Until recent times the Old Testament account of the Hebrew patriarchs and their historical background was discounted and considered nothing more than legend or "sacred myth." The tremendous wealth of information available today, thanks to the systematic excavation of nearly every part of the Near East, has overthrown much of the argument against the historicity of the period.[5] Now scholars generally concede that the history depicted in Genesis 12-50 is reliable, though, in their opinion, the figures of Abraham, Isaac, Jacob, and their families are only retrojections from much later Hebrew history. They are "aetiological"; that is, they are figures invented by Israelite historians to account for the origin and development of the nation from prehistorical times.[6] Naturally, one cannot prove the existence of the patriarchs for as yet no archaeological evidence mentioning them has been found, but if we now can establish that

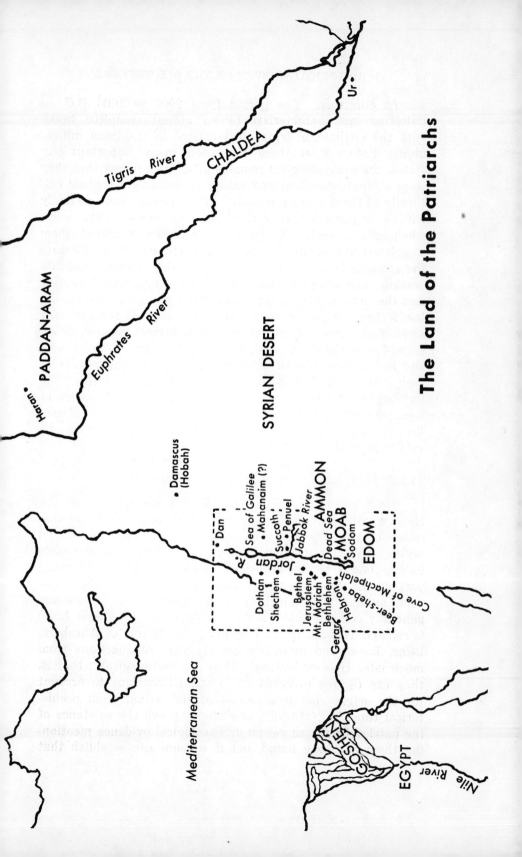

The Land of the Patriarchs

PADDAN-ARAM

Haran

CHALDEA

Tigris River

Euphrates River

Ur

SYRIAN DESERT

Damascus (Hobah)

Dan

Sea of Galilee

Mahanaim (?)

Succoth

Penuel

Jabbok River

AMMON

MOAB

Dead Sea

Sodom

EDOM

Jordan R.

Dothan

Shechem

Bethel

Jerusalem

Mt. Moriah

Bethlehem

Hebron

Beer-sheba

Cave of Machpelah

Gerar

Mediterranean Sea

GOSHEN

EGYPT

Nile River

the period in which they lived is the same as that which Genesis accurately describes, there is no valid reason for dismissing their historicity.

As examples of the reliability of the Old Testament in the light of what is now known extra-Biblically about the Near East history and culture, let us examine the Biblical narrative. The move of Abram from Ur to Haran is consistent with the now recognized fact that both cities were centers of moon god worship; it is only logical that Abram, still untaught in his new faith, would seek out a place of residence whose religious practices were familiar to him (Gen. 11:31).[7] Or, the picture in Genesis of Palestine as a land of few or no cities, largely settled by semi-nomads such as Abram came to be, is consonant with what we now know for certain about Palestine at this time in history. The story of Abram's migration from the Negev to Egypt at a time of famine (seen again later in the story of Jacob) also is consistent with much Egyptian literature describing the immigration of thousands of Semites into Egypt at this same period and for the same reasons.[8] The selling of Joseph into Egypt with a Midianite caravan and his subsequent elevation to a place of prominence in the Twelfth Dynasty is amply attested in Egyptian sources which, though they do not mention Joseph, do describe similar advancements of Semites in Egyptian government.[9] The familiarity of Joseph with the Egyptian customs of his day and the recording of those customs by Moses in Genesis is strengthened by secular literary material from Egypt which speak of these same customs.

In addition to the specific instances listed above there is the overall feeling that the patriarchal historical milieu rings authentic. There is nothing whatsoever in the Old Testament, whether in individual statements or occurrences or in general background, which fails to square with the knowledge of the Near East gained in the past one hundred years; as the archaeologist's diligent toil yields more and more information, the historicity of this Patriarchal Period becomes more and more firmly supported.

ABRAHAM (11:26-25:8)

After the dispersion of mankind at the Tower of Babel, the knowledge of the true God seems to have become even more limited. There is absolutely no Biblical evidence of any believers at all in the time of Abram, a fact which may account for his having been called by God from idolatrous circumstances in Ur of the Chaldees (the same Ur of the previously discussed Third Dynasty). Still, God maintained His faithfulness to man by singling out an individual in this apostate world condition through whom the covenant promises might be promulgated and realized. This is in line with the principle already discernible that though God's blessings fell upon all mankind they were mediated through individuals such as Adam, Noah, and now Abram.

We know little of Abram's background except that he was a Semite of Mesopotamia whose immediate ancestors were pagan worshipers of the moon god, Sin. We are told that his father migrated from Ur to Haran on the northern curve of the Fertile Crescent and that he (Terah) died there when Abram was seventy-five years old. The New Testament informs us that Abram had been called by God to leave Ur (Acts 7:2-4), so we may assume that Terah's move may have been encouraged or even motivated by this call to his son. The circumstances of that initial revelation to Abram are clouded in mystery, but in some way unmistakable to him God called him to set forth in faith to a land which He would show him (Heb. 1:8-12). No doubt these directions were preceded by a Divine self-disclosure so plain and forcefully impressed upon Abram that he immediately forsook his old religious and even geographical environment to embrace the faith of Yahweh, the true and only God. In any event, God made a covenant with Abram, an agreement in which He promised to bless the patriarch immeasurably and to make him and his descendants a blessing to all the world (12:1-3).[10]

After leaving Haran, Abram with his wife Sarai and nephew Lot traveled south into Palestine, settling first at Shechem (a name given only later to this place), at a place near Bethel, and finally in the Negev. At each of these places he built an altar, a symbol of his new faith and of the awareness of the presence of his God wherever he went

(12:4-9). After a time, he moved on down into Egypt to escape a famine in Palestine, for though the Near East might suffer from lack of rain, Egypt, "the gift of the Nile," could always rely upon the unceasing faithfulness of the great river to overflow its banks annually and provide the necessary topsoil and irrigation. As he traveled toward Egypt he revealed his human nature by instructing his wife to explain to the Egyptians that she was his sister and not his wife, for he feared that according to the custom the Egyptians might be attracted to her beauty and kill him in order to make her available to them legitimately. This half-truth (for she was, indeed, his half-sister) by so saintly a man is understandable when we remember that only recently had God revealed Himself to the patriarch, and then surely in a very limited way. We cannot expect Abram to measure up to Mosaic truth when he antedated the giving of that truth by over half a millennium; yet, he cannot be excused, for even the law codes and culture of his day advocated standards of truth. The Egyptians did take Sarai as Abram feared, but when God began to afflict them for it, they recognized Abram's deception, and graciously restoring Sarai to him bade them leave the country (12:10-20).

Abram and Lot next moved northward to Bethel where they soon found that their greatly enlarged herds and flocks were too numerous to be sustained in the same pastures. To avoid the risk of serious hostility between them, Abram wisely suggested to Lot that he (Lot) select the land which he wished to have and he (Abram) would take what was left over. Lot, after assessing the situation carefully, chose the well-watered plain of the Jordan, probably south of the Dead Sea, and "pitched his tent toward Sodom," one of the cities of the area. God then appeared to Abram and attached geographical promises to the covenant by assuring him that all the land that he could see would be his and his descendants' (13).

Chapter fourteen is one of the most difficult in the Old Testament from the standpoint of historical perspective, for though it describes actual historical persons and events these cannot be identified with anything known as yet from other than Biblical sources. It seems that a coalition of four Near Eastern kings invaded the plain of Jordan and subjugated the

five city states there including Sodom. The kings all bear
names which are in no way anachronistic to the nineteenth
century and which may even be tentatively identified with
monarchs from this period, but no way has been found as
yet to equate them with kings which were contemporaries. It
was long maintained that Amraphel, the king of Shinar, was
Hammurabi. Two basic objections to this are (1) that no
other kings with the other names mentioned were contemporary with Hammurabi, and (2) Abraham, if the Biblical
chronology is to be accepted at face value, antedated Hammurabi by over three hundred years.[11] It is best at present to say
that the identifications of these kings are uncertain and to
trust that in time the archaeologist's spade will clear up the
whole matter.

For twelve years these eastern kings maintained suzerainty over various parts of Palestine, but then a rebellion
took place on a wide scale, the cities of the plain being among
the participants. This coup was quashed, the cities sacked,
and various captives, including Lot of Sodom, carried off to
the north. Here another historical difficulty creeps in, for
Abram, with 318 servants, set out after these kings and
overtook them near Damascus where he soundly defeated
them and rescued Lot and the other prisoners. It is impossible to comprehend that Abram with such limited forces
could rout four kings and their armies; but, upon closer
scrutiny, such does not appear to be the case. For one thing
the four eastern kings were not necessarily there in person,
and there is no evidence that their armies were very substantial. If these were great imperial monarchs we may surmise that they had sent only token forces to campaign in Palestine. Furthermore, what troops they did have were spread
over a much larger area than the plain of Jordan alone, so
that it is only reasonable to conclude that a relative handful
were directly involved with the cities of the plain. This being
the case, Abram could well have pursued and defeated the
contingent necessary to defeat Sodom and carry off some of
its inhabitants. Besides this, we read that Abram had con-
federates who, we suppose, went with him, and these may
have amounted to several hundreds of men (14:13).

Following his victory Abram returned to Mamre, but on
the way was intercepted by Melchizedek, king of Salem, who

appeared bearing bread and wine. As priest of the most high God (*El Elyon*), he blessed Abram and received from him tithes of all which he possessed. Buber maintains that Melchizedek was a Canaanite priest of a tribal deity named El Elyon and that Abram ignorantly confused him with the Hebrew God, or even identified El Elyon with Yahweh.[12] This is totally without support of any kind, especially when the New Testament is considered. The seventh chapter of Hebrews deals with Melchizedek, pointing out that he was a mysterious figure who had neither beginning nor end, neither father nor mother, and that he was the prototype of Jesus Christ, the High Priest of the New Testament. It would indeed be strange for the writer of Hebrews to associate Christ with a Canaanite priest. Besides, the strange description of Melchizedek, both in Genesis and Hebrews, leads to the conclusion that he must have been more than a mortal being; indeed, the only possibility is to ascribe Deity to him. Because God did appear many times in the Old Testament in bodily form (a *theophany*), it is not incredible that He so appeared here. The only possible objection to this being a *theophany* is that Melchizedek is called the "king of Salem"; it is difficult to imagine God as the king of this earthly place (Jerusalem). However, the word *salem (shalom)* in Hebrew means "peace," so we may assume that He is not being called the king of a place, Jerusalem, but the King of Peace, a term reminiscent of Isaiah's description of Messiah (Isa. 9:6). Moreover, the name Melchizedek itself literally means "king of righteousness," another appellation attributed to God. In summation, it seems that God had appeared to Abram once again to graciously remind him of His presence, and in respect of God's saving power in victory over the kings, Abram offered a tithe of his possessions.

The promise of an Abrahamic seed is continued and elaborated in chapter 15 through 18:15 in the following way. God appeared in a vision to Abram and disclosed that though Abram was old he would sire a child. Abram proceeded to argue that the only heir he possessed at present was Eliezer, his servant, whom, in line with the prevailing Near Eastern custom, he had no doubt adopted as his inheritor.[13] God corrected the false impression that Eliezer was to be heir by revealing explicitly that Abram and Sarai would have a covenant son. The promise was strengthened by a continuation of the vision in which Abram witnessed a slaughter of animals and their division into two rows.[14] Between them passed God and Abram symbolically, the total effect suggesting the binding of God and Abram together in a blood relationship the nature of which would lend to the covenant promise a certain unconditional indissolubility. Added to the ceremony was the prophetic declaration of a future 400 year bondage in a strange land (Egypt), followed by a reoccupation of Palestine, the land of the Amorites.

In their desire to realize God's covenant promise, Abram and Sarai, who was barren, decided to have children by Hagar, their Egyptian handmaid (16:1-3). According to the Nuzi tablets, ancient Hurrian cuneiform documents dealing with custom and law of this period, the action of Abram and his wife in this respect was perfectly legitimate.[15] Any children born of this proxy arrangement would be considered legal heirs of the husband unless and until children should be born of the wife herself. Hagar conceived, but because of the jealously of Sarai was banished into the wilderness. There God met her and promised her that she too would be the mother of a great people (16:10), a people known historically as the Arabs. Ishmael, the son whom she bore, was to be the head of this mighty nation.

Finally, thirteen years after this, God appeared once more to Abram, revealing Himself this time as the Almighty God (El Shaddai) and promising that though Abram was now ninety-nine years old he would be the father of a nation of kings. As an evidence of God's faithfulness, Abram's name was changed to Abraham. Whereas he had been "great father" (abram), he from now on would be known as the "father of a great people" (abraham). The fulfillment was so imminent and certain that God proceeded to declare to Abraham the sign of the covenant—circumcision. As the rainbow had been the token of the Noahic Covenant, the rite of circumcision was to be the sign of the Abrahamic Covenant, a sign which Abraham immediately put into effect in his own household, including Ishmael who had meanwhile returned home. In conjunction with all this, Sarai's name was changed to Sarah ("princess") by virtue of her impending role as mother of the promised race. In spite of this apparent demonstra-

tion of faith, both Abraham and Sarah found the promise of
a child still too much to accept. They both laughed, with the
result that God told them the child would be named Isaac
("laughter").

Soon thereafter Abraham was outside his tent at Mamre
one day when he was approached by three strange visitors
whom he, according to custom, began to entertain lavishly.
In the course of their conversation one of the three announced once more to Abraham that he would have a son in the
near future, an idea which was so preposterous to the aged
Sarah, who was eavesdropping within the tent, that she again
laughed to herself. At this the chief visitor, the Angel of
Yahweh, rebuked her, and despite her denial reminded her
that the child of a surety would be named "laughter," a name
to remind the patriarch and his wife perpetually of their
little faith.

Following the conversation, two of the angelic strangers
departed to Sodom to warn the city of its imminent destruction occasioned by its great wickedness before God. The
third, the Angel of Yahweh, remained with Abraham, who began to "bargain" with Him concerning Sodom for Lot's sake.
After much entreaty, Abraham elicited from the Angel the
promise not to destroy the city if even ten righteous inhabitants might be found therein. At the conclusion of the discussion, we are told that "Yahweh" left Abraham. This
striking identification of the Angel of Yahweh with Yahweh
Himself is indicative of the Deity of the Angel, and of the
fact that God could and did reveal Himself in bodily form in
the Old Testament.[16]

The angels finally reached their destination at Sodom
and were greeted at the city gate by none other than Lot, who
urged them to spend the night with him, though he, like Abraham, did not at least initially discover their angelic nature.
In the night certain perverted men surrounded the house
and demanded to "know" Lot's visitors with a carnal knowledge, for the men involved were homosexuals. The very term
"sodomy" derives from this situation of debauchery which
seemed so characteristic of the city. Lot refused to release
his visitors to them, but offered to send out his unmarried
daughters whom these perverted men could abuse in whatsoever way they desired. Only by the intercession of the

angels was this prevented, and after the wicked Sodomites became blinded by God the heavenly messengers warned Lot of the destruction of the city which would immediately ensue. Fruitlessly Lot went to the homes of his daughters and sons-in-law, desperately trying to warn them to flee the wrath of God, but they were little inclined to hearken to the voice of one who had reared them in such an atmosphere. Resignedly, Lot took only his wife and two single daughters from the city, but his wife, deaf to the warning of the angels not to turn back, did so and became a pillar of salt. With a deafening roar, the entire earth erupted, and perhaps by means of volcanic explosion fire and brimstone were rained from the skies until all that was left of the city was a charred ruin which defies location to this very day. Lot and his daughters fled to near-by Zoar and from thence to the mountain caves overlooking the horrible scene. But the sin of Sodom was carried out with them, for in their utter frustration at having been de-nied husbands and children, both of which were considered essential to blessing, the daughters of Lot made him drunk, committed incest with him, and bore him two children: Moab, the ancestor of the Moabites, and Ben-Ammi, the father of the Ammonites (19:37-38).

In Genesis 20 is an account which reminds us of Abra-ham's deception of Pharoah in chapter 12, but this time, though the situation is similar, the circumstances are not the same throughout. This time Abraham migrated to Gerar, a small kingdom between Canaan and Egypt, and on the way advised his wife to keep her true relationship to him secret. Abimelech, the king of Gerar, convinced that Sarah was Abra-ham's sister, took her into his household. In a dream God appeared to Abimelech, however, and disclosed Sarah's true identity, whereupon Abimelech, whose own family had begun to suffer Divine retribution for the king's mistake, released Sarah and entreated Abraham, designated here a prophet, to pray for his family's healing. This was done, and without further ado Abraham left for Mamre once again.

Shortly after this escapade, Sarah became with child and bore Isaac, the realization of all their fondest hopes and dreams and the fulfillment of the Divine promise of a cove-nant son. The birth of Isaac provoked Hagar and Ishmael to mockery, however, for they now stood to lose the claims of inheritance. For this they were sent once again into the desert, where for a second time they were sustained by God's mercy and reminded that they too would produce a great nation. At about the same time Abraham and Abimelech made a covenant with each other to respect each other's territorial rights, for their lands were contiguous. They sealed this agreement at a place called Beer-Sheba (well of the oath) in the Negev.

Only a few years after the birth of Isaac, God demanded that Abraham take this only begotten son and offer him up as an offering to God. Though Abraham could not reconcile the idea that Isaac had been given as the son of promise with God's request now that this son be sacrificed, the patriarch had realized by now the wisdom of acting in obedient faith. Apparently without hesitation he took Isaac with him to Moriah to a certain mountain where the act might be performed. While ascending the mountain, Isaac noted that his father had everything necessary but the sacrificial victim itself. When Abraham gave the assurance that God would so provide, Isaac went obediently forward, and even when told the shocking truth that he was to be the sacrifice, acquiesced and voluntarily submitted himself to the knife. In this moment, expressive of the highest measure of faith, God spoke and provided a substitute. Having passed this most severe test of faith, Abraham was comforted by God with the promise that all the blessings of the Covenant, so frequently reiterated in the past, would most assuredly be his (22:15-18).

The day finally came when Sarah died, an event which prompted Abraham to acquire a burial place which forever after would be made holy by the bodies of the saint and his family. After negotiations with a certain Ephron, a Hittite, the burial cave and the field in which it was contained were purchased; there the mother of kings was buried. Abraham now saw plainly that his own life must soon end, so he called his faithful servant to him and commissioned him to go to Mesopotamia to seek a wife for his son, Isaac, who, as yet, has not produced a covenant son of his own. After much seeking of Divine guidance, the servant arrived in the city of Nahor where he met Abraham's kinfolk, and especially the beautiful maiden, Rebekah (24:15). Convinced that this was the proper selection for his master, the servant presented Abraham's request to Laban, the girl's brother and guardian. He agreed that in view of all the circumstances this must be the will of God. After a parting blessing from her family, Rebekah departed for Canaan where she married Isaac, bringing to him the comfort he needed following his mother's recent death.

The final years of Abraham are recorded in Genesis 25 where we read that he took a second wife, Keturah, who also bore him a family including Midian, the father of the Midianite tribes. He eventually bestowed his patriarchal blessings, which consisted of both material and spiritual provisions, upon his many sons. Isaac, as covenant son, naturally was most richly favored. Finally, after 175 years of pilgrimage, Abraham died and was buried at Machpelah by his sons Ishmael and Isaac.

Isaac (25:9-27:46)

In the chain of patriarchal history, the link of Isaac is the weakest. It is almost possible to pass directly from the life of Abraham to that of Jacob without interruption, and one tends to get the impression that Isaac's only importance at all is that he was the son of Abraham and the father of Jacob. This surely is not a fair interpretation of Isaac, however. The reason for the brevity of the narrative concerning him may not be so much his lack of importance as his conformity to the will of God. His was not a life of bizarre escapades which made him the subject of much discussion. In silent, obedient faith he pursued the will of God, carefully ordering his life as His servant.

The first event of importance in the life of Isaac following his marriage was the birth of his twin sons, Esau and Jacob (25:21-26). These two, who struggled together even in their mother's womb, bore testimony in this fashion that their lives together would be fraught with competition, a competition which would result in the subordination of the elder to the younger. Esau, born first, became a hunter and the favorite of his father, whereas Jacob, who pursued the more domesticated life of a nomadic herdsman, was especially favored by Rebekah. This unfortunate family division became the source of grievous trouble in days to come.

The course which the lives of the two men was to take in their relationship with each other first became clear when Esau, returning hungry from the hunt, begged his brother to give him a bowl of soup in return for which he would surrender his birthright. It is unlikely that Esau expected Jacob to take him literally and seriously in this lopsided bargain, though such transactions have been recorded elsewhere in Mesopotamian sources,[17] but Jacob was not one whom Esau could treat so lightly in such a serious matter. Evidently all was done according to due process of law, for Esau never challenged the validity of the transaction later on, though he regretted it bitterly.

After another famine had come and gone, one in which Isaac had moved to Gerar where he deceived the king (perhaps Abimelech II or III) about his wife as his father Abraham had done, Isaac returned to the place called Beer-Sheba. There, as also his father had done, he made a covenant with the Philistine king with regard to property rights and trespassing. The brazenness of Isaac in palming off his wife as his sister in this instance is matched only by the extreme naiveté of the king of Gerar in believing him, for their fathers had similarly become involved in only the previous generation. It seems that whereas history repeats itself, human nature remains basically the same.

The main thread of the narrative is taken up once more in Genesis 27. Isaac, an old man by now and blinded by the years, called in Esau, his elder son, and informed him that he was about to bestow upon him the patriarchal, covenant blessing—pending Esau's preparing for him once more a meal of the venison stew for which he was renowned. While Esau was gone about his father's bidding, Rebekah, who had overheard the whole thing, suggested to Jacob the means whereby he might disguise himself and extort from Isaac the promised blessing. Jacob, in compliance, dressed himself in his brother's clothing, placed upon his hands and neck animal skins to resemble the hairy body of Esau, and brought to Isaac a dish of "savory meat." Finally convinced, though with reservation, that Jacob was Esau, Isaac blessed him with the irrevocable patriarchal blessing.[18] This promise, of a spiritual nature as opposed to the purely material provisions of the birthright which Jacob had already obtained from Esau, was nothing more nor less than the covenant of Abraham of which Isaac had become the custodian.

Upon Esau's return, he persuaded Isaac of his identity, but Isaac, who had just pronounced the blessing, was unable to retract it though he had been deceived into giving it to Jacob. Esau recognized the validity of even this transaction and without appealing for a reversal of any kind merely begged for an additional blessing for himself. One was given, but compared to that of Jacob it was emasculated of any real significance. Esau did envision revenge, however, and planned to slay Jacob after his father's death. Again Rebekah, coming to Jacob's assistance, engineered his escape from Esau by convincing Isaac that Jacob should go to Haran, the homeland of their kinfolk, under the pretext that there he might find a wife.

JACOB (28:1-38:30)

Jacob ventured to Haran where he soon located the home and family of his mother. On his way the Lord had appeared to him in a dream at Bethel, certifying to him that the covenant promises given to his fathers would be his as well (28:-101-15). His arrival at Haran, then, was filled with a realization that the future was bright before him. After staying there for a few weeks, he was invited by his uncle Laban to remain indefinitely and to work for him for wages. Jacob agreed to this proposition with the understanding that his wages for seven years' work should be the hand of Laban's younger daughter, Rachel. We may surmise, in accordance with what has been learned from the Nuzi tablets and other sources, that Laban actually adopted Jacob since he at this time was without sons of his own as far as we know.[19] This meant that he stood to inherit Laban's estate, provided, of course, that no sons were born to Laban later.

When the seven years had passed, the wedding date was set and the seven day feast begun. At its conclusion, the veiled bride and Jacob were united in marriage and ushered into the darkness of their tent home. In the morning, however, Jacob was infuriated to discover that he had married not Rachel, but her sister Leah. Laban hastily explained that the custom of the land was that the elder daughter must be married first, but apparently not convinced that Jacob's

wrath was ameliorated by this information, agreed to offer
Rachel also, with the proviso that Jacob would labor seven
years more. In addition, Laban added to the dowry two hand-
maidens, one for each of the wives.

The motif of the barren wife [20] is noticed again in this
context, for Rachel, because she was more favored by Jacob
than was Leah, was unable to conceive. Leah, by way of Divine compensation, was fruitful and soon bore to Jacob four
sons: Reuben, Simeon, Levi, and Judah. Rachel then attempted to make up for this lack in her own productivity by offering to Jacob her maiden, Bilhah, who bore two sons, Dan and
Naphtali (cf. Gen. 16:1-3). Leah, who had ceased bearing in
the meantime, retaliated now by presenting Zilpah, her
servant, to her husband; as a result of this union, two more
sons were born to Leah by proxy, Gad and Asher. In an
effort to renew the fertility of his mother Leah, Reuben
brought her some mandrake plants superstitiously believed
to be aphrodisiac. Leah refused to offer some of these to her
rival, Rachel, and upon partaking of them herself was able
to produce yet two more sons, Issachar and Zebulon. The
plants obviously had no inherent beneficent effects, for the
Scripture says plainly that the children were born because
"God heard Leah" (30:17). Finally, after much prayer and
agony of soul, Rachel was blessed of God and gave birth to
Joseph, the first of the two sons she was to have.

At least fourteen years had passed by this time, and
Jacob decided to return to Canaan. Laban, however, persuaded that the secret of his success lay in Jacob, urged him to
remain for any wages he would name. Jacob generously
agreed to remain on, provided that he would become owner of
all the cattle and sheep of Laban which were not purebred.
Immediately upon the consummation of this agreement, and
unknown to Jacob, Laban instructed his sons to remove all the
inferior animals from the flocks and herds and to pasture
them at a distance of three days' journey from the homestead. When Jacob went to claim his property the next day
he found that it had become nonexistent, but because the
contract specified only that he should have all except the
purebred he was in no legal position to do anything but accept the fact that he had been at least temporarily outsmarted.
With a mixture of superstition and ingenuity Jacob devised
a means whereby he might not only regain his rightful prop-

erty, but might also punish Laban for his craftiness. He peeled
the bark from certain rods which he placed in the watering
troughs near where the cattle customarily bred. When they
drank from the water, viewing all the time the striped, spotted, and speckled rods, the offspring which they produced
later bore the markings of the sticks. By thus ensuring such
"marked births" Jacob was soon able to acquire quite a herd,
for even the purebred cattle of Laban gave birth to impure
progeny. Furthermore, Jacob would not put the rods in the
troughs except when the better cattle came to drink, with the
result that whatever cattle Laban did retain were of the weaker and less valuable variety. The whole matter smacks of
gross superstition, but that the above results actually did accrue is clear from the following passage which states that not
Jacob's shrewdness, but God's grace, was responsible for the
miraculous result (31:9).

During all this Laban had frequently attempted to counter Jacob by changing the conditions of his wages, but all to
no avail, for God continued to overrule in Jacob's favor until
the patriarch became very wealthy. Finally relations had become so strained that Jacob, in line with Divine guidance, decided to leave Haran and return to Canaan. His wives supported this decision, for they had seen their father's guile,
and, besides, were angry because Laban's own sons, born
since Jacob had come to Haran, were now holding the rights
of primo-geniture, leaving Jacob with no inheritance at all
and in possession of only that which he had managed to gain
despite Laban's connivance. One day when Laban had gone
to a sheepshearing, Jacob seized the opportunity to make his
abrupt departure taking with him his entire family and all
his goods. When Laban became aware of the move, he pursued the travelers, finally catching them at Gilead near the
border of Palestine and Syria. With hypocritical indignation
he scolded Jacob for not having notified him of his plans, assuring him that had he done so he would have been sent off
with a blessing. Besides, Laban had not been permitted to bid
farewell to his daughters and grandchildren. Finally, and this
is most important, Jacob had had the gall to steal the household images (teraphim), the possession of which entitled the
owner to the inheritance rights of the firstborn, rights which
had originally belonged to Jacob as Laban's adopted son.[21]
Jacob, of course, was unaware that Rachel had, indeed, stolen

these images, and he stoutly protested that the person with whom the images were found should be put to death. Rachel had taken the images to her tent and placed them under the camel saddles and blankets upon which she was seated when her father came into the tent to search there. Laban, out of respect for his daughter's physical condition, did not insist that she rise, so the hiding place remained secret.

After Laban had demonstrated that apart from Divine prohibition to the contrary he would have slain Jacob, the two agreed that further argumentation was fruitless. Thereupon they contracted together to leave one another in peace with the specific understanding that neither would ever encroach upon the property of the other and that Laban's daughters would always be treated with the care and respect consonant with their position. A ceremony of attestation followed consisting of the erection of stones of witness whose presence there on the border of the two countries was to be a perpetual reminder of the inviolability of their covenant (31:49). At last, Laban returned to his own home.

Jacob was next threatened with the realization that he must now prepare to meet the brother from whom he had fled twenty years before. Somehow Esau had learned of his return, and in a series of maneuvers Jacob plotted how to make their encounter as safe for himself as possible. First, he sent messenger to spy out Esau's strength; they returned with the disheartening news that he was accompanied by at least 400 men. Next he resorted to earnest prayer in which he both pled for God's help and reminded Him of the covenant which He now must not break. Then he sent gifts of animals on ahead to palliate his brother's ruffled feelings. Having done all that he could think of, Jacob separated himself from his family near the Jabbok brook where, in a most unusual encounter, he began to wrestle a strange nocturnal visitor. Whether this was in a vision or in the flesh is unimportant. The main thought is that Jacob persistently refused to release the man from his grip until he had blessed him, an indication that Jacob recognized the heavenly nature of the assailant. As a result he was blessed, indeed, in a most singular fashion. In this hour of great need Jacob was told by the angel that God was with him, a fact that was expressed in the change of Jacob's name to Israel (32:28). He had been "supplanter," but because he had prevailed with God he was to be a "prince of God." Surely no greater word of comfort could have been given Jacob, for as prince he would live to continue the promised line of covenant blessing.

The next day the dreaded meeting took place, but with inexplicable kindness Esau welcomed his brother warmly, even refusing to accept the proffered gifts. Still, Jacob was wary of accepting his brother's invitation to visit him in Edom, so with typical persuasiveness convinced Esau that he would follow him there at a slower pace, a promise which he had no intention of keeping. As soon as Esau was out of sight, Jacob turned due west and with great haste crossed the Jordan into Canaan.

With little lapse of time Jacob and his family settled at Shalem (Shechem) in the central highlands adjacent to a Canaanite community headed by a certain Hamor and his son Shechem. The latter became infatuated with Dinah, Jacob's daughter, and assaulted her, an occurrence which prompted Hamor to negotiate with Jacob over the marriage of the two. Jacob readily agreed to this, but Dinah's two brothers Simeon and Levi were greatly incensed over the whole affair and stipulated that such a marriage could be consummated only if the men of Shalem would agree to join Israel in covenant and express that unity by becoming circumcised. To this all were agreed, but just after the rite had been effected, and the Shalemites were all, therefore, physically incapacitated, Simeon and Levi, with sword in hand, proceeded to decimate the entire male population (34:25-29). Fearing now that other Canaanite communities would seek to avenge this massacre, Jacob fled from Shalem to Bethel, having first carefully buried the teraphim and other Syrian cultic objects under an oak tree.

At Bethel, the scene of his dream of the ladder twenty years earlier, Jacob once again was reminded of the presence of God and His continued blessing despite the enormous inconsistencies in the patriarch's life. From there he proceeded to Ephrath near Bethlehem where in childbirth Rachel died and was buried. Finally he reached his destination of Mamre where he found his father still alive though extremely feeble. Shortly thereafter the old saint died; in an act of joint respect his two sons buried him at Machpelah (35:29).

For several years Jacob lived an uneventful life in the Negev. The narrative then continues with the introduction of Joseph at the age of seventeen. Because he was the son of Rachel, the favorite wife, he was accorded special privileges, among them the right to be clothed in a long, flowing robe of many colors (or pieces), a garment which indicated his genteel position in life. Not only was he the family pet, however; he was also the recipient of dream revelation, a fact which only increased the animosity of his brethren toward him for they invariably were depicted in the dreams in roles subordinate to Joseph (37:5-11).

One day Jacob sent his sons to Shechem, his original Palestinian homestead, where they were to feed their flocks on the comparatively richer pastures to be found there. The patriarch deployed Joseph to Shechem to learn of their activities, but he failed to find them there. A stranger who had seen the brethren go to Dothan, a town to the northwest which lay on the Coastal Highway, directed him to go there. As Joseph approached, the brethren observed him and determined to take this opportunity to do away with him. Reuben, no doubt sensing the special responsibility which he bore as the eldest son, advocated that they not shed their own brother's blood, but cast him into a pit where he might starve to death. All the time it was Reuben's intention to rescue Joseph later on and send him back to Mamre. Meanwhile, and in Reuben's absence, a Midianite caravan bound for Egypt with a rich cargo of spices from Gilead appeared upon the horizon. Judah, eager to "kill two birds with one stone," suggested that they rid themselves of Joseph by selling him as a slave to the merchant for twenty pieces of silver, accomplishing thereby both the removal of their hated brother and a profit at the same time. By the time Reuben returned the transaction had been completed, and the brothers, now at a loss as to how to account to Jacob for Joseph's disappearance, soaked the boy's cloak in animal blood. When Jacob later examined this telltale evidence he could only conclude that Joseph was dead, not knowing that, indeed, his favorite son was even then in the employ of an Egyptian nobleman (37:-35-36).

The lengthy account of the selling of Joseph into Egypt can be understood only when we recognize the hazardous predicament of Israel at this time in history. His descent into Egypt paved the way for the later migration of the entire family of over seventy souls, a migration which eventually would result in the settlement of Israel in Egypt for more than 400 years. We have noticed that God's purpose in the Old Testament was to reveal Himself through men and nations in His mighty saving power. In order for this revelation to be clear and unimpaired, it was necessary that the vehicles through whom He spoke be preserved from anything which would render them incapable of fulfulling their divine commission. That message of promise had been entrusted to Israel and his sons and families; if they should fail to hold it in trust the witness to the true and only God would be jeopardized.

We have already seen that the effectiveness of Jacob and his family as the bearers of the covenant to the world had been imperilled. This was apparent in the attempted union between Israel and the Shalemites, a union prevented only by the timely action of Simeon and Levi. The influence of the Canaanite immorality is also seen in the incest committed by Reuben against his father's concubine, Bilhah (36:22). But it is in chapter 38 that the need for the removal of Israel from Canaanitish ethical and religious contexts is best discovered. We learn that Judah, son of Jacob, had married a Canaanite woman and that over the course of the years they had three sons. The eldest of these also married a Canaanite, Tamar by name. This son was thereafter struck dead by God for some unnamed sin, and, after the so-called Levirate custom (Deut. 25:5-10), his brother was supposed to marry her to raise up children in his brother's name. The younger brother refused to do so, however, perhaps because of pride or envy of his brother, so Yahweh slew him also. This left only Shelah, the youngest brother, who was yet a child. Judah promised Tamar that if she would wait she might marry Shelah when he was grown. Evidently the desire to have a son in this covenant line, or at least the pure desire to be a mother at all, encouraged Tamar to wait these years. When the boy was grown, though, Judah reneged, which meant that Tamar who no doubt was very unlikely by this time to find another husband, was destined to remain childless. To preclude this possibility, she disguised herself as a prostitute and meeting Judah on the road to Timnath, seduced him. Because Judah had no money with which to pay for her favors, he left his staff, bracelets, and personal signet as pledges.

When Tamar became pregnant she was haled by Judah into the presence of witnesses and was questioned by the indignant Judah who demanded to know the identity of the man involved in this sordid business. When Judah's personal effects were then summarily brought forth and exhibited for all to see, the mortified accuser could do nothing but admit his guilt. Though one of the children born of this relationship, Pharez, was destined to become an ancestor of David the king and of Christ Jesus Himself, an amazing example of God's overruling providence, the whole sorry picture, nevertheless, bespeaks the urgent need for God's people to be removed from Canaan to a place where they could be socially and spiritually insulated from any such reoccurrences. In all the ancient world, no place better satisfied this need than Egypt; hence, the placing of Joseph there in God's prescience.

JOSEPH (39-50)

The geographical background of the patriarchal narrative now switches to Egypt; for that reason Joseph must be considered the focal point of our discussion. His life there and the life of the Israelites in general against the backdrop of Egyptian culture will be discussed in the following chapter.

Joseph fortuitously was sold into the hands of an Egyptian nobleman, Potiphar, who was also the captain of Pharaoh's guard. Quickly Joseph gained the favor of his master and was appointed overseer of all that he had. Unfortunately, he also incurred the attentions of Potiphar's wife who became enamored of his handsome features, his intelligence, and overall demeanor. Frequently she attempted to entice him to sin with her, but stoutly he maintained his fidelity to his master as well as to his God. One day she seized him in desperation. In his frantic effort to escape her designs he left his cloak behind, circumstantial evidence which was sufficient to have him incarcerated in the federal prison. The fact that Joseph did not suffer capital punishment may suggest that Potiphar's wife had become rather notorious at this sort of thing. We may even conclude that the only reason he was imprisoned at all was because the presence of the cloak implied that Joseph had at least cooperated in the affair.

Immediately upon Joseph's imprisonment he began to be promoted until he finally became a trusty over all the prison (39:21-23). While in this capacity he later encountered two men, the butler and baker of Pharaoh, who, for some reason, had been thrown into the same prison. They related to him dreams which they had had, for he had testified to them that his God was the giver and interpreter of dreams and that as God's servant he could give them the meaning they sought. As it turned out, the butler was restored to his position in Pharaoh's court, exactly as Joseph had interpreted; whereas the baker was removed and hanged, again in line with the dream he had dreamed. Joseph had requested the butler to make known to Pharaoh his innocence, but it was not until two years later that the ungrateful man remembered Joseph, and then only because another dream, this time by Pharaoh, brought his own dream and its consequences back to the butler's mind.

It seems that Pharaoh saw in his dreams seven fat cattle followed by seven lean ones which devoured them, and after that seven healthy ears of corn which were consumed by seven withered ears (41:1-8). When all the sorcerers and magicians of the realm were unable to offer any sensible interpretations, Joseph, summoned at the advice of the butler, without delay made known all the ramifications of the dreams, acknowledging that God had enabled him to see that seven years of bounty were approaching in Egypt to be followed by seven years of famine. Amazed and convinced by this exhibition of wisdom, Pharaoh, following the counsel of Joseph that a wise administrator be found who could regulate the collection and distribution of food during this time, appointed Joseph himself to a position of minister of agriculture or some such office, proclaiming that the Semitic wise man was to be second only to him throughout the kingdom.

Commensurate with this position and with Joseph's reputation as a man in "whom the Spirit of God is" (41:38), Pharaoh gave him the daughter of the chief priest of On (Heliopolis), to be his wife. Asenath bore him two sons, Ephraim ("fruitful") and Manasseh ("forgetting"), whose names suggested that Joseph had become prosperous and had forgotten all his miseries. When the years of famine eventually came, Joseph proved the wisdom of Pharaoh's choice, for God used him to save both Egypt and Israel from disaster.

The widespread famine was beginning to take its deadly toll in Canaan, and Jacob was forced to send his sons to

Egypt for grain (42:1-2). Upon their arrival they were presented to Joseph who recognized them at once. They, however, could not even guess his true identity for the passing of some thirteen years coupled with the Egyptian language and dress of their brother effaced any possibility of recognition. When they had stated their request, they were curtly rebuffed by Joseph who accused them of being spies and cast them into the prison. This and the following treatment of the brothers by Joseph may be explained as an attempt to teach them a badly needed lesson, an irresistible opportunity to play a practical joke, or a combination of both. Whatever the purpose, Joseph succeeded in frightening them to the point that they could not but rue the fact that they were in Egypt before this austere figure.

Finally, Joseph permitted them to return home. He retained Simeon as a hostage, however, and warned them not to come back to Egypt without their youngest brother, Benjamin, who had not accompanied them this first time. On their way home they discovered, to their utter consternation and amazement, that the money they had taken to pay for the grain was still in their possession. They told their father about the whole series of events, but despite Simeon's arrest in Egypt he refused to let them return to Egypt if they had to take Benjamin as well. When the grain was exhausted, however, Jacob finally relented and all ten brothers returned once again for supplies. This time Joseph amazed them by inviting them to a feast at his home and uncannily he seated them around the table in the order of their ages. When they prepared to return to Canaan once more, Joseph told his servants to put their money in their grain sacks and his silver divining cup in the sack of Benjamin. After the brothers had gone a short distance, they were overtaken by Pharaoh's troops who in searching them found the money and cup. Fearing now the death of Benjamin and the death of their own father which would inevitably result, they fell upon their faces before Joseph, begging his mercy, a gesture which Joseph could no longer endure. At once he revealed his identity to them with tears and embraces; finally convinced that this lord was indeed their long-lost brother, they rejoiced with him, though in absolute bewilderment at this turn of events. Joseph proceeded to outline to them the providence of God, who had sent him to Egypt with the brothers as unwitting accomplices. And he declared that God had done so to remove from them this temporary threat of extinction by the famine and from the less clearly discernible but more dangerous threat of Canaanite assimilation. He followed this disclosure by entreating the brethren to return to Canaan for their father and families and to live with him in Goshen, the choicest part of Egypt (45:1-15).

Even Jacob was convinced when he saw the gifts sent by Joseph with his sons, so he with all his posterity emigrated from Canaan, the land of promise to which his family would not return for over 400 years. Upon arriving in Egypt he was presented to Pharaoh, whom he blessed, and was assigned by him a dwelling place in the northeast delta region of the land. For seventeen more years, all during the famine and afterward, Jacob lived in Goshen, his last years of peace contrasting sharply with those tumultuous years which had preceded the entrance into Egypt.

When the day of Jacob's death appeared imminent, he requested that his remains be carried to Machpelah for burial; he blessed the two sons of Joseph, Ephraim and Manasseh, deliberately giving the inheritance promise to the younger, Ephraim, rather than to Manasseh; and he blessed all twelve of his sons with the beautifully poetic and prophetic patriarchal blessing of Genesis 49. We note the tenth verse with special interest, for in the words "The sceptre shall not depart from Judah, nor a lawgiver from between his feet, until Shiloh come; and unto him shall the gathering of the people be," we see in clear focus the covenantal Messianic promise. Later it became abundantly clear that the tribe of Judah, ancestor of David and the Christ, was the object of God's special concern in history.

In accordance with his wishes Jacob was buried in Hebron with his fathers. After the interment Joseph and his brothers returned to Egypt to live out their days. Now that Jacob was dead the brothers expressed a fear of retribution, but Joseph assured them that they had nothing to fear from him, for he had forgotten all in recognition of the fact that God had used all the past historical events to preserve for Himself this remnant of witness to the truth. Then Joseph, at the age of 110 years, lay at death's door with the prophecy on his lips that God would lead His people out of Egypt one day; moreover, he demanded of his brethren and descendants the promise that when that day should come they would carry his body with them (Josh. 24:32). Though he had lived all but seventeen years in Egypt, he knew in his heart that his real home was the Land of Promise, the inheritance of Abraham, Isaac, and Jacob.

EGYPTIAN CULTURE AND LIFE IN THE PATRIARCHAL PERIOD

The beginning of the Patriarchal Period was centered in Mesopotamia, very briefly, and then in Palestine. We saw that there were extensive references in Genesis to Near Eastern customs and traditions, most of which have been rather remarkably illustrated by such finds as the Nuzi tablets and the documents from such places as Mari and Alalakh.[22] Many of the contemporary Egyptian cultures may also now be studied as a result of archaeology and more advanced historiography, and they shed a great deal of light on the Biblical accounts of Jacob and Joseph during the course of this Middle Kingdom period. The following cannot hope to be exhaustive, but can at least point out the fact of the incredible accuracy of the Genesis account of life in Egypt at this time. This, besides substantiating the Biblical historicity itself, supports strongly the Mosaic authorship of the book.

Besides the incursions of Abram and Jacob into Egypt for food, which has been illustrated from Egyptian literature which speaks of such movements by Semites on a very major scale, we have other matters of importance by way of illustration. For example, the abundance of dreams, the despotism of Pharaoh, famines of seven years duration, and the elevation of Semites and other foreigners to prominent places in Egypt—all these are Biblical concepts which appear in non-Biblical Egyptian documents.[23] In addition, there are matters of custom which are of great interest. For example, when Joseph was summoned out of prison to appear before Pharaoh, he shaved himself and dressed in Egyptian clothing in order that he might not offend the king by appearing in his Semitic beard and clothing.[24] Also, Joseph advised Pharaoh to retain twenty percent of the food in the seven years of plenty, a custom attested by secular documents. The segregation of the Egyptians and Semites at the meal table is in line with the Egyptian feeling of superiority and religious separation. The "divining cup" of Joseph was a common instrument of wise men of the Middle Kingdom who sought occult wisdom. Joseph's advice to his father and brethren not to reveal their occupation as shepherds accords perfectly with the knowledge that the Egyptians could not countenance sheep and shepherds for they themselves were cattlemen.[25] One of the most striking examples of all is that entire section of chapter 50 which deals with embalming and burial practices of the Egyptians. We are told that the embalming of Jacob lasted for forty days and was followed by a thirty day period of public mourning. The Egyptian Book of the Dead, an extensive collection of miscellaneous data pertaining to death and burial, comes from this period of history and specifies that the process must be that as outlined in Genesis (50:2-3).[26]

Besides these specific references, there is nothing whatsoever in the very tenor of the Bible to suggest that the account is amiss at all. Surely, unless one extremely familiar with Egyptian life and customs had written this book, there would be some kind of inconsistency somewhere along the way with what is known from ancient Egyptian sources; but this just is not the case. And, conversely, the evidence available from these extra-Biblical materials has considerably illuminated the Genesis story of the patriarchs in Egypt. Further consideration as to the relationship of the Biblical narratives to the historical situation as we know it from other sources must be reserved for later discussion.

---

[1] For the best discussion from the standpoint of the "low chronology" see John Bright, *A History of Israel*, Philadelphia, Westminster Press, 1959, pp. 41-59.

[2] W. F. Albright, *The Biblical Period From Abraham to Ezra*, New York, Harper and Row, 1963, p. 3.

[3] W. F. Albright, *The Archaeology of Palestine*, London, Penguin Books, 1956, p. 86.

[4] G. Ernest Wright, "The Archaeology of Palestine," *The Bible and the Ancient Near East*, G. Ernest Wright, ed., Garden City, Doubleday and Company, Inc., 1965, p. 101.

[5] Albright, *The Biblical Period From Abraham to Ezra*, p. 2.

[6] Theophile J. Meek, *Hebrew Origins*, New York, Harper and Row, 1960, p. 2.

[7] Gen. 11:31;   Merrill F. Unger, *Archaeology and the Old Testament*, Grand Rapids, Zondervan Publishing House, 1954, p. 112.

[8] G. Ernest Wright, *Biblical Archaeology*, Philadelphia, Westminster Press, 1957, p. 28.

[9] *Ibid.*, p. 36.

[10] On covenants in the ancient Near East see G. E. Mendenhall, *Law and Covenant in Israel and the Ancient Near East*, Pittsburgh, The Biblical Colloquium. Reprinted from *Biblical Archaeologist*, Vol. 17, May, September, 1954.

[11] H. H. Rowley, *From Joseph to Joshua*, London, Oxford University Press, 1950, pp. 57-58.

[12] Martin Buber, *Moses*, New York, Harper and Row, 1958, pp. 96-97

[13] Henry J. Cadbury, ed., *Annual of the American Schools of Oriental Research*, Vol. 10, New Haven, Yale University Press, 1930, Tablet H60.

[14] W. F. Albright, "The Hebrew Expression for 'Making a Covenant' in Pre-Israelite Documents," *Bulletin of the American Schools of Oriental Research*, No. 121, pp. 21-22, February, 1951.

[15] Cadbury, ed., *op. cit.*, Tablet H80.

[16] Gen. 16:17;   22:11;   Num. 22:23;   Jud. 5:23;   6:11;   13:3; II Sam. 24:16.

[17] Cyrus Gordon, "Biblical Customs and the Nuzu Tablets," *The Biblical Archaeologist Reader*, Vol. 2, Ed. by David Noel Freedman and Edward F. Campbell, Jr., Garden City, Doubleday and Company, Inc., 1964, p. 23.

[18] *Ibid.*, p. 27.

[19] *Ibid.*, p. 25.

[20] Gen. 16:1, 25:21;   Jud. 13:2;   I Sam. 1:2.

[21] Gordon, *op. cit.*, p. 25.

[22] G. E. Mendenhall, "Mari," *The Biblical Archaeologist Reader*, Vol. 2, Ed. by David Noel Freedman and Edward F. Campbell, Jr., Garden City, Doubleday and Company, Inc., 1964, pp. 3 ff.

[23] J. A. Thompson, *The Bible and Archaeology*, Grand Rapids, Wm. B. Eerdmans Publishing Co., 1962, pp. 43-49.

[24] Ira M. Price, *The Monuments and the Old Testament*, Philadelphia, American Baptist Publication Society, 1907, p. 104.

[25] Unger, *op. cit.*, p. 133.

[26] Samuel A. B. Mercer, *The Religion of Ancient Egypt*, London, Luzac, 1949, pp. 313-317.

CHAPTER FOUR

CREATION OF A NATION

OLD TESTAMENT CHRONOLOGY

The date of the Exodus, the most important historical event in Israel's past, is so crucial to the rest of the story that it is mandatory that we give some consideration to the problem of ascertaining that date and as many other important dates as possible. Obviously, there is no reckoning of time in the Old Testament with reference to B.C. or A.D., nor, indeed, with reference to any fixed and known point, so the matter is more complicated than it might ordinarily seem. For years the dates of Archbishop Ussher, a British prelate of the seventeenth century, were accepted almost universally. This scholar had added up all the years between the time of Christ and the close of the Old Testament historical record, thus determining the final date of that record. Then he added backward the genealogies and other chronological data in the Old Testament, making allowance for such matters as co-regencies or inter-regna of the kings, parallel or synchronistic evidences, and passages which tied various parts of the Old Testament together. On the whole, he succeeded very well, at least as far back as Abraham, though he probably misdated the patriarch by some one hundred years too early.[1]

With the advent of the modern age of archaeological and historical scholarship, Ussher's chronology has become somewhat discredited though even now his dates are not corrected as much as one might think. Certain persons and events known in the Bible became datable because they were mentioned in literary and other material remains which have been discovered in the past century or so. These extra-Biblical data provide points of reference which can be dated with absolute certainty. One major breakthrough came with the uncovering of the Assyrian Eponym Lists which listed all the years from 893 to 666, each being named for the *limmu* or prime minister of Assyria elected for that year. In addition to the names of these officials the tablets contained accounts of the most important events of each year. Thus, we have an unbroken series of events embracing more than two centuries of Assyrian history and touching upon the histories of other nations as well.

In the year of a *limmu* named Bur-Sagale the Assyrians noted a complete eclipse of the sun, which, for various religious and scientific reasons, must have impressed them deeply. Modern astronomy has calculated that this eclipse could have occurred only on June 15, 763 B.C., for the mathematical precision of such phenomena permit them to be calculated hundreds of years later with no appreciable margin of error. Ninety years earlier than this eclipse in the year 853 the most noteworthy event was the Battle of Qarqar, a battle which Shalmaneser III of Assyria claims to have won over a Palestinian-Syrian coalition including Israel and her king Ahab.[2] From the internal Biblical evidence this battle must have occurred near the end of the reign of Ahab for only then was he on friendly enough terms with Syria to ally himself with them in battle (I Kings 22:1). This point of contact was most important but it alone was hardly conclusive. More information was forthcoming, however, in the form of the Black Obelisk, a stele erected by Shalmaneser III in honor of his subjugation of his enemies, including King Jehu of Israel. This unhappy king of Israel is depicted kneeling in submission to his Assyrian overlord in the eighteenth year of Shalmaneser, an occurrence which, then, can be dated, for the dates of Shalmaneser are known from the Eponym Lists. The Black Obelisk date is 841 B.C., apparently in Jehu's first year.[3] The Book of Kings says that there were twelve years between Ahab and Jehu, so the dates 853 and 841 are thereby established in their Biblical relationship to Ahab and Jehu.

From this information it is relatively easy to reconstruct the rest of the Old Testament chronology. The lengths of the reigns of each of the kings of Israel and Judah are given, both before and after the time of Ahab and Jehu, and by simply adding them up we may arrive at the accession years of each and learn the dates of many of the events mentioned in connection with them. We must not oversimplify the matter, for there are such factors as coregencies and inter-regna to consider; because the two kingdoms of Israel and Judah used different systems of reckoning time at different periods in their histories, diligent study must be made of all the data in order to work out a self-consistent, harmonious reconstruction.[4]

Ahab, who must have died ca. 853/52, reigned for twenty-two years, so ascended the throne of Israel in 874 (I Kings 16:19). His father, Omri, reigned twelve years, having been crowned in 886 (I Kings 16:23). Elah, his predecessor, reigned two years or from 887-886 (I Kings 16:8). His father Baasha maintained a rule of twenty-four years from 910 to 887 (I Kings 15:33). Nadab, son of Jeroboam, reigned two years from 912 to 910 (I Kings 15:25) while Jeroboam took the kingdom in 931 B.C. and ruled for twenty-two years (I Kings 14:20). Because Jeroboam seized the throne of the Northern Kingdom upon the death of Solomon and Solomon reigned for forty years, his dates must be 971-931 (I Kings 11:42), the dates of his father, David, 1011-971 (I Kings 2:11) and so on. Working from a different angle, we have a very important statement in I Kings 6:1 which informs us that Solomon began to build his temple in his fourth year (967/66) which was also the 480th year after the Exodus. This places the date of the Exodus at 1446 B.C. In Exodus 12:40 we learn that Israel was in Egypt for 430 years; therefore, Jacob's migration there must have been in 1876 B.C. When Jacob had his audience with Pharaoh, he had stated that he was then 130 years of age (Gen. 47:9), indicating that he was born in 2006 B.C. His father had been sixty when Jacob was born, so Isaac's birthdate is placed at 2066 B.C. (Gen. 25:26), while Abraham, 100 years old when Isaac was born, must have been born in 2166 (Gen. 21:5).

The chronology earlier than that is most uncertain, for, as we have already pointed out, strong evidence exists to convince us that there were gaps in the earlier genealogies, perhaps as many as thousands of years being unaccounted for chronologically. From Jehu on to the time of Christ, however, the dating is almost certain, for the Biblical figures, combined with materials such as the Babylonian Chronicles and the various King Lists,[5] spell out in detail the passing of the years. The entire chronological system, especially in later times, is controlled by other factors such as the Canon of Ptolemy from Egypt, the sources available to historians such as Josephus, Herodotus, Tacitus, Berossus, and others, and certain other independent witnesses which provide valuable checkpoints and criteria with which to support or correct the Assyrian Eponym data and the Old Testament figures themselves. That our present understanding of the Old Testament chronology, especially from the time of David and later, rests on a scientific and accurate basis is not disputed. Dates earlier than that are subject to "reinterpretation" by the critics in many instances, but to the objective student the over-all framework is consistent and valid.

THE HISTORICAL BACKGROUND AND DATE OF THE EXODUS

The historical milieu of the Exodus period can be comprehended only in the context of the several centuries which preceded it, especially in Egypt. We have already lightly touched upon the role of Egypt in the Near Eastern scene, but only in very general terms. Now it will be useful to go back and gather up the strands which when woven together will provide the setting for the Egyptian-Israelite relationship lying at the very foundation of the Exodus movement.

The rise of the Twelfth Dynasty at about 2000 B.C. inaugurated an era of Egyptian power and influence hitherto unmatched. Yet Egypt even in this period was not concerned so much with the outside world as with her own peculiar internal interests. There was, however, an interest in Egypt on the part of outsiders; history records the movement of thousands of people to and from Egypt all throughout this time. These peoples seemed to be Semitic primarily; though most of them were merchants who went to Egypt only temporarily for trading purposes, some remained there to occupy various parts of the country. Sesostris III (1878-1843) was one Pharaoh of the dynasty who was interested in expansion. We have evidence that he pushed as far north as Shechem in Canaan. From the period of a predecessor, Amenemhet I (1991-1962), comes the story of Sinuhe, an Egyptian physician, who describes his travels throughout the Mediterranean in an epic known as the *Tales of Sinuhe*.[6]

Near the beginning of the eighteenth century the Egyptian government collapsed under the influence of the Hyksos whose domination gradually was achieved, though it consisted first of all of a mere coexistence with the Egyptians. As these "shepherd kings"[7] moved into the land in great numbers, the Egyptians feared a takeover, but their efforts to remove them or prevent further immigration proved too late. By 1730 B.C. at least all of Lower Egypt was firmly in Hyksos hands. Unfortunately the Hyksos were not active in producing a material culture so comparatively few remains from the period have survived. They were not totally unproductive in these areas, however, as we now know from their military equipment, indicating the use of the horse and chariot for the first time in Egypt. And we also possess abundant literary remains consisting primarily of scarabs containing Hyksos personal names.[8] They moved the capital of Egypt from near Memphis to a site known as Avaris in the northeast delta region. There they maintained rule until they were finally expelled (ca. 1580).

Some Egyptian control was sustained through this Hyksos period; namely, the Thirteenth through Seventeenth Dynasties in southern Egypt, but their influence was nil because they themselves were embroiled in internal problems. Out of the last of these dynasties, however, came a figure, Ahmose (ca. 1580-1548), who became the founder of the powerful Eighteenth Dynasty. It was he who united Egypt against the Hyksos oppressors and finally drove these Asiatics from the borders of Egypt up into Palestine and even farther.

At this point we must consider the Biblical record concerning Jacob and Joseph. We have already suggested that Abraham visited Egypt during the Eleventh or Twelfth Dynasty, a fact quite consistent with our knowledge of those periods, and that the date of that migration may be around 2090 B.C. The next contact with Egypt concerns Joseph's enslavement there, the date of which must be about 1900. This would be in the reign of Amenemhet II, so it was probably the dream of the next Pharaoh, Sesostris II (1894-1878), which he interpreted. This king elevated Joseph to his position of governor, a promotion which certainly cannot be disproven. The argument is sometimes advanced that the migration of Jacob into Egypt at about this time was the same as the Hyksos invasion and takeover, and that this accounts for Joseph, a Semite, reaching such heights in Egyptian government.[9] This theory seems to be overthrown by the insistence of Joseph in observing Egyptian customs both before and after

his father's arrival.   This would be wholly inexplicable if
the king of Joseph's time were an anti-Egyptian Hyksos.
Moreover, it is not necessary for us to assume a Hyksos king
in order to account for Joseph's elevation, for as we have
already shown there are other examples of Semitic advancement in the Middle Kingdom.

Jacob must have entered Egypt in the reign of Sesostris
III (1878-1841) who not only was an expansionist abroad, but
who was successful in breaking the power of the local nobility
(nomarchs) and confiscating their land for the crown.
This would be the time of Joseph's administration in which
he had advocated to the king the acquisition of lands in the
time of famine in order to be able to dole out foodstuffs as
the need arose.   Joseph died during the reign of the next
king, Amenemhet III, in about 1806 B.C.   The Twelfth
Dynasty itself came to an end not less than twenty-five years
after that date.   For the next 200 years the Israelites lived
in comparative peace and prosperity in Egypt, the rule of
the Hyksos no doubt contributing to this state of affairs in that
they too were largely Semites.   It is interesting to note that
the Israelites lived in Goshen (or Raamses) all this time, and
that this was the location of the Hyksos capital, Avaris.
Evidently, though the Hyksos and Hebrews were not one and
the same, there were very definite similarities and closeness
of relationship.

We read in Exodus 1:8 that "there arose up a new king
over Egypt, which knew not Joseph" and that this monarch
proceeded to deal harshly with the Israelites lest they defect and join in with Egypt's enemies (possibly the recently
evicted Hyksos).   This king, it seems, must have been Ahmose,
first king of the Eighteenth Dynasty and enemy of the hated
Hyksos, with whom he prejudiciously related the Israelites.
In this sense he "knew not" Joseph or had no sympathy with
the Hebrew cause.   He placed the Israelites in bondage and
required them to build public works, including the cities of
Pithom and Raamses (Ex. 1:11).   The difficulty involved
with this assertion will be considered under the arguments
concerning the date of the Exodus.

Ahmose managed to unite Egypt and drive the Hyksos
not only out of the country but even out of Palestine and into
oblivion.   His successors followed up his brilliant victories
by occupying Palestine and other nearby lands and building

strong fortifications against the possibility of ever being invaded again by northern hordes. It is very likely that there were still thousands of Semites in Egypt following this defeat of the Hyksos, among whom surely the Hebrews would constitute a large element. Amenhotep I (1548-1528) very likely carried out the oppressive measures of Ahmose against the Hebrews, and it is entirely possible that he was the Pharaoh who made the decree that all the male infants of the Hebrews should be slain (Ex. 1:22). We learned earlier that the Bible date of the Exodus is 1446 B.C. and Moses was eighty years of age when he led the people from Egypt (Ex. 7:7). This means that he was born in 1526, a date which fits in nicely with the reign of Amenhotep I if he were indeed the Pharaoh who had made the infamous decree.

Thutmose I (1528-1508) led many campaigns into Palestine, even as far as the Euphrates, but he is best known in history, perhaps, as the father of Hatshepsut (1504-1483). This ambitious woman married her own half-brother, Thutmose II (1508-1504), in order that she might have a legitimate claim to the throne. When he died under rather inexplicable circumstances, she married her daughter to her stepson, Thutmose III (1504-1448).[10] Only after her death was Thutmose III able to take the throne by himself. It is very tempting to identify Hatshepsut with the daughter of Pharaoh mentioned in Exodus 2:5, for her age at the time would fit the situation perfectly as would her boldness in rescuing a Hebrew baby and rearing him within the very palace of the king.

Thutmose III occupied himself with at least sixteen campaigns into Palestine and beyond to the north, and he also apparently pushed into the south for some considerable distance. The chief opposition which he faced was from the newly emerging kingdom of the Mitanni which was located on the upper reaches of the Tigris-Euphrates River system. After Thutmose had reached terms of peace with these new neighbors the Pharaohs frequently married Mitannian princesses from then on to solidify their friendly relationship.[11]

Thutmose III was followed by Amenhotep II (1448-1423), who may have been the Pharaoh of the Exodus, and he in turn was succeeded by Thutmose IV (1423-1410). Throughout this whole period Egypt maintained its strength and continued to be active in conquest and trade in all directions. But then a noticeable decline began to appear. Amenhotep

III (1410-1377) had his hands full with a rising discontent within Egypt, a turmoil related to the ascendancy of one god or the other. His son Amenhotep IV (1377-1358) settled the matter by originating or refining a monotheistic religion[12] which revolutionized Egyptian theology and also made an indelible political impact. To symbolize his reverence for his new god, Aton, whom he worshiped in the form of the sun disk, Amenhotep changed his name to Akhnaton and moved the capital of Egypt to a new city which he named Akhetaton. Its later name, Tell el Amarna, is found in connection with the Tell el Amarna letters which were discovered there.

These letters consisted of communications from the various kings of city states, particularly in Palestine, who were under the Egyptian hegemony. Because Akhnaton was so consumed with the internal religious problems of his land he had little time to protect his provinces from outside interference. As a result these provinces were laid open to attack by all kind of marauding peoples including some known as the Habiru (or 'Apiru). The king of Jerusalem, for example, wrote an urgent appeal to the Pharaoh to send even a few troops if at all possible, for the Habiru were overrunning the land. As we shall see there is every probability that these invaders were none other than the Hebrews who had escaped from Egypt some fifty years or more earlier.

Before Egypt collapsed entirely, the eccentric Akhnaton died (perhaps violently) and was followed by his young son-in-law, Tutankhamon (1358-1349), who attempted to restore the worship of Amon. Then, with two more rulers, Ay (1349-1345) and Haremhab (1345-1318), the Eighteenth Dynasty came to a close.

The Nineteenth Dynasty was founded by Rameses I who reigned for a very brief time (1318-1317), but who was to give his name to one of the most illustrious families in history, the Ramessides. He was followed by Seti I (1317-1301), who resumed the imperialistic policies of the early kings of the preceding dynasty, and passed on to his successor the beginnings of a renewed empire. This successor was the famous Rameses II (1301-1234), the length of whose reign suggests his stability and endurance. Though he no doubt appropriated to himself many glorious feats which he never accomplished at all, he nevertheless was the single means of restoring a great measure of Egypt's prestige in the world.

Were it not for the Hittites, who were beginning to assume tremendous proportions in the north and northwest, Egypt under Rameses II might well have achieved its greatest extent and power. The Hittites, though, were his constant problem, and it is likely that following the disastrous Battle of Kadesh in 1286, he was never able to subdue them.[13] The Nineteenth Dynasty ended with his son, Merneptah (1234-1222), who was also his general in Rameses' later years. This king managed to occupy as far north as Beth-shean in Canaan and, as a matter of fact, left a monument which bears the earliest reference to Israel outside the Bible.[14] After his death, however, the empire collapsed; never again was Egypt to exercise any extensive control outside its own borders.

The preceding rather lengthy discussion of Egyptian history from the end of the Hyksos Period through the Nineteenth Dynasty has been deemed necessary because of its bearing on the date, route, and interpretation of the Exodus and conquest. Now, specific arguments for the Biblical dates must be brought to bear with a consideration of the most pertinent historical and archaeological materials available. We have already seen that I Kings 6:1 teaches that the Exodus must be dated at 1446, but this date is denied by the majority of scholars, especially the liberal critics who date it in the middle of the thirteenth century.[15] The consensus is that either the text of I Kings 6:1 is corrupt, the historian who wrote the words was not in possession of the facts, or the figure "480" must be interpreted. It is urged, for example, that there were twelve generations from Moses to Solomon; if each generation is about twenty-five years in length, there would be only a period of 300 years from the Exodus to the building of the Temple.[16] This would permit the date of the Exodus to be no earlier than ca. 1260 B.C., a date generally maintained by the critics.

We see, then, that the validity of the chronological information in I Kings 6:1 is at stake; this in turn has a bearing upon the whole problem of Old Testament historicity. There is other information within the Bible, however, which may be cited to strengthen the 1446 date. In Judges 11:26 Jephthah reminds the king of Ammon that the Israelites had been in Ammon for 300 years. Jephthah can be dated no later than 1100 B.C., so the arrival of Israel in Transjordan could be no later than 1400 B.C., a remarkable agreement with I

Kings 6:1. We believe that all that is necessary is for statements such as I Kings 6:1 and Judges 11:26 to be accepted
at face value, particularly when there is no textual or other
internal reason for rejecting them. When other factors are
considered and correctly interpreted, we feel that the Biblical
date as indicated by these passages will be absolutely corrob-
orated.

Besides this inherent Biblical witness to the Exodus date,
there are supporting arguments from Egyptian and Near
Eastern history and archaeology. For example, the Moses
stories fit into the historical milieu of the early Eighteenth
Dynasty more easily than in any other period of Egyptian history. The command to purge all Hebrew infants well accords with the period immediately following the Hyksos expulsion under Ahmose and Amenhotep I. The daughter of
Pharaoh could hardly be any other than Hatshepsut, daughter
of Thutmose I, for only she of all known Egyptian princesses
would have the audacity to rear a Hebrew male child in the
very palace of Egypt despite her father's orders otherwise.
Also, Moses was in Midian for a total of forty years before
he could return to Egypt, a stay necessary until the death of
the Pharaoh from whom he had fled (Acts 7:23; cf. Ex. 7:7).
There was only one king of Egypt before Rameses II who
reigned over forty years and that was Thutmose III, a contemporary of Moses. The Pharaoh of the Exodus, Amenhotep
II, had a son who became Pharaoh, but it was not his eldest
son. The question is, What became of the eldest son? Could
he have been the son slain by the God of Israel? Moreover,
the son who did succeed him was Thutmose IV, the Pharaoh
who left the famous "Dream Stele" which was found between
the feet of the Great Sphinx. On this inscription Thutmose
IV records the fact that he had been told by the Sphinx in a
dream that though he was not the eldest son of his father, he
would nonetheless be the next monarch, a very strange turn
of events to say the least.[17]

The Tell el Amarna Letters, written in the first quarter
of the fourteenth century, recite the appeals for help by the
chieftains and princes of the various small city states and
provinces of the Egyptian Empire, especially in Palestine and
Syria. These kings were desperate because their cities were
being overrun by people call 'Apiru, a term now considered
by some to be equivalent to Habiru in Babylonian and Hebrew

in the Old Testament.[18]   The only ways possible to deny that
these 'Apiru are the same as the Hebrews under Moses are to
conclude that Israelite is not synonymous with Hebrew and
that there were other Hebrews besides Israelites, a valid assumption in the light of the present evidence,[19] or that some
of the tribes never were in Egypt at all and that these 'Apiru
represent tribes indigenous to Canaan.   In other words, there
were not twelve tribes in Egypt, possibly as few as one, and
the final establishment of the twelve tribe confederacy was
the result of hundreds of years of development in which
scattered tribes slowly came together.[20]   These arguments
appear to be without historical confirmation and certainly
have no Biblical support.   There is no way to disprove that the
'Apiru of the Tell el Amarna Letters are identical with the
Hebrews and that they represent the invasion of Canaan by
Israel under Joshua as early as 1400 B.C.

The destruction of Jericho was dated until very recent
years at ca. 1400, thanks largely to the work there by John
Garstang.   When Garstang's work was completed some thirty
years ago, there was almost universal agreement that his
dates were correct and that the destruction of City D, the
stratum in which the walls had fallen outward, was by the
Israelites in 1400.[21]   Albright, who agreed with this date initially, has now modified his opinion, and in the light of
further evidence, including Kathleen Kenyon's recent work
at Jericho, has come to accept a date of 1325 or later for
Jericho's fall under Israel.[22]   Yet, Garstang has not been
completely discredited, if at all, in the opinion of many scholars.[23]

Very interesting also are inscriptions found in Egypt
which mention the name of the tribe Asher.   These must be
dated in the fourteenth century and would agree most favorably with the Biblical date for the Exodus and Conquest.[24]
The critic, by assuming that the tribe of Asher did not participate in the Exodus, is able thereby to overcome this evidence,
but this again seems to be merely a way to explain away the
original unity of Israel and their composite departure from
Egypt under Moses.   It is difficult to explain how Asher
could be in Canaan a hundred years before the critics date the
Exodus except by maintaining that Asher was not part of
the movement.   There is also the Stele of Merneptah, previously mentioned,[25] which mentions "Israel" as a power in

Canaan about 1219 B.C. If the Exodus did not take place
until 1300 at the earliest, and the period of wandering was
another forty years, we wonder how Israel could be represented as a mighty power as early as 1219; especially if,
as the critical view alleges, the formation of Israel into any
kind of a confederacy did not take place until hundreds of
years after the Conquest. This is indeed a difficulty in the
late date, and though it does not prove the early date, it
certainly favors it.

Now, we must consider the evidence against the early
date, for there are certainly arguments in that direction.
Exodus 1:11 states that the Israelite slaves in Egypt built the
treasure cities Pithom and Rameses. These cities have been
excavated and the evidence indicates that they were built
by the Hyksos originally, perhaps in the eighteenth century.
Later they were rebuilt by Rameses II, but this was not until
the thirteenth century.[26] In addition, there is evidence of
Semitic slave labor having been used in the construction of
the cities in Rameses' time.[27] The problem is this: How
could the Israelites have built these cities in 1290 B.C. when
the Exodus, according to the Biblical dating, occurred 150
years earlier? In response, it is by no means certain that the
city of Rameses was named after the Pharaoh of that name. In
fact, Genesis 47:11 states that Jacob and his family settled in
the land of Rameses when they entered Egypt in the nineteenth century; unless we postulate an anchronism, for which
there is not the slightest proof, we must conclude that there
was an area by that name before there was ever a Pharaoh
Rameses. It could well be that there had been an ancient
Rameside dynasty long ages before and the Ramessides of
the Nineteenth Dynasty were named for them, the city also
having taken this name.[28] In any case, there is no need to
assume that the mention of the city of Rameses proves that
the Exodus must have taken place during the reign of Rameses II. The reconstruction of the cities in the thirteenth century could very well have been done under Rameses II, but
the presence of Semitic slaves is not sufficient evidence to
prove that the Hebrews of the Exodus were the Semites in
question.

Nelson Glueck has shown that there were no sedentary
populations in Edom and Moab between the twentieth and
thirteenth centuries B.C. When Moses requested permission

for Israel to pass through Edom (Num. 20:14), and when he
by-passed Moab to avoid warfare with the Moabites, how
could he have expected any interference if there were no
people in these countries during the late fifteenth century?[29]
The answer is quite obvious from a careful study of the Old
Testament record and even a superficial knowledge of Biblical geography. We are told that Moses wanted to take the
Kings' Highway, a road which passed through an extremely
narrow mountain pass into and out from the city of Petra
(Sela). This pass could easily be defended by only a very few
hundred well-trained troops, and they need not be sedentary
peoples.[30]   Nomads or semi-nomads could well have occupied
the area in such sufficient numbers that they precluded
Israel's passing through their difficult land; yet the nature
of their existence would explain the lack of any material
remains such as permanent structures.[31]   Likewise, Moab
could have been settled by tribes people who, though not so
advantageously situated, were spared by the Israelites because
they were akin to them ethnically (Gen. 19:37). The absence
of remains of a settled people need not militate against the
early date of the Exodus if the people simply did not leave
remains. *Argumentum ad silentum* is not sufficient to overthrow the Biblical position.

Archaeological research has shown rather conclusively,
if the evidence has been correctly interpreted (a moot point
oftentimes), that there was no large scale destruction in
Canaan in the fourteenth century, but that there was such
devastation in the thirteenth.[32] If Joshua conquered Canaan,
where is the evidence if this did not happen until only after
1250 or so?   Again, we feel that the problem results from an
incorrect interpretation of the Biblical record.   The Books
of Joshua and Judges leave the impression that Joshua's campaign was not wholly successful.[33] In many instances places
had to be taken more than once, which suggests that they were
not demolished the first time, and perhaps not at all until the
time of the Judges in the thirteenth century.   In fact, it seems
to have been Joshua's policy not to destroy the cities of the
enemy, but to only defeat them in the field of battle (Josh.
10:28-42). [34] A good example of this policy is seen in Joshua
11 which describes the Northern Campaign.   The battle
against the coalition of northern kings centered around Hazor,
and only Hazor of all the towns mentioned was destroyed by

the Israelites. The others were left "standing on their mounds."[35] There is little evidence of violent destruction of Canaanite city states in the fourteenth century simply because it was not Joshua's intention to destroy them.

Extra-Biblical arguments are far from conclusive in support of either position, but there is no question that the Old Testament leans to the early date of 1446 for the Exodus and 1406 for the beginning of the Conquest. Only by assuming a series of movements by Israelites into Canaan can this evidence be overthrown, and such an assumption must rest on the most tenuous support.

ISRAEL IN EGYPT (EXODUS 1-14)

Let us now return to the Biblical narrative. After the expulsion of the Hyksos about 1580 B.C., a native Egyptian monarch, Ahmose I, became Pharaoh. It is possible that he is the Pharaoh "which knew not Joseph" (1:8), in the sense that he was now prejudiced against all Semites because of the Hyksos domination through which Egypt had so recently passed. To prevent Israel from becoming a threat to Egypt's security, he placed them under bondage. Exodus 1:11 relates that they built for Pharaoh store cities including Pithom (Zoan) and Rameses (Avaris), but this oppression did not deter whatsoever the enlargement and strengthening of Israel. Finally, the Pharaoh (probably Amenhotep I or Thutmose I) deemed it necessary to slaughter all the Hebrew male infants in an effort to curb the population. It is in this period of genocide that Moses was born of Levite ancestry.

When the child had reached the age of three months, his mother found it impossible to conceal him in the house so she fashioned a reed basket which she waterproofed and placed among the rushes in the Nile. The infant Moses was laid in this floating cradle while his sister Miriam watched nearby to see what would become of him. It just so happened that Pharaoh's daughter, possibly Hatshepsut, coming to bathe near where the basket floated, noticed the ark with its pitiful cargo. Her heart was so touched by the sight that she, forgetting her prejudice and her father's edict, rescued the child, whom she named Moses (Hebrew—"drawn forth"; Egyptian—"son"). She decided to adopt the child, and following the farsighted advice of Miriam, who witnessed all this, sought out a Hebrew nurse to attend him. This nurse, of course, was Moses' mother who was able, therefore, to train him in the traditions and customs of her Hebrew heritage at the same time that he was nurtured in all the arts and sciences of Egypt (Heb. 11:23-27).

Little is known of Moses' life in his first forty years except that he became highly favored in the royal household. One day, however, he witnessed the beating of a Hebrew slave by an Egyptian foreman and in a fit of anger slew the Egyptian. Fearing reprisal because of his Hebrew background, he fled to a distant land, 200 miles to the east of Egypt, Midian. There he met Jethro (or Reuel), a priest of Midian, and after marrying his daughter Zipporah settled down to live with him. For forty long years, all through the reign of Thutmose III from whom he had fled, Moses remained in the Arabian desert tending the flocks—a far cry from his days of luxury in the courts of Heliopolis.

The purpose for his having been driven to the desert was dramatically explained one day when Moses was in the south Sinai peninsula at Horeb tending his father-in-law's sheep. There God appeared to him in a theophany consisting of a bush which burned but was not consumed; for the first time in 400 years, as far as we know, God revealed Himself in an audible way by identifying Himself to Moses as the God of Abraham, Isaac, and Jacob. He followed this declaration with the call to Moses to lead Israel, whose prayer and groaning He had heard, from Egypt back to the land of promise, the covenant land. When Moses protested that he was incapable and was unsure of the response he would receive from his people, God reiterated His promise by revealing Himself in a new name. Moses had asked what name of God he should use when describing to Israel their call from Egypt, and God replied that he should mention to them that I AM had sent him (3:14; 6:3). This name, simply the first person singular of the Hebrew verb, *hayah* ("to be"), would indicate to Israel that God was the one who eternally exists and that He would be more than sufficient to protect, accompany, and bless them every step of the way. The expression of that name in the third person singular gave rise to the name *Yahweh,* "He is." This name of God is usually rendered "LORD" in the King James Version, "Jehovah'" in the American Standard Version, and "Yahweh" in the Anchor Bible and certain others. To be sure, this name had been known to the saints of old, but not in its full meaning. They knew the name, but not its significance for this hour of deliverance. They were about to be redeemed, rescued, and reconstituted as a covenant nation, and *Yahweh* meant all of this. The name, in other words, was to be the name of God in His redemptive, covenant capacity.[36] It was in the power of this Name that Moses was to return and lead his people forth; such power he would need, for Pharaoh would by no means permit them to leave.

After further argument by Moses as to his capabilities as a leader, God silenced his objections once and for all by a series of signs: the changing of his shepherd's rod to a serpent, his affliction and deliverence from leprosy, and the promise that his elder brother Aaron would serve as his spokesman. Furthermore, as a token of God's promise, He revealed to Moses that Israel would worship Him at this mountain (Sinai), and then they would realize God's covenant faithfulness. Finally Moses agreed to go; after having bidden his father-in-law adieu, he took his wife and two sons toward Egypt. On the way his wife and he parted over a dispute concerning the circumcision of their elder son; she returned to Midian, not to rejoin him until he later returned to Horeb. Aaron in the meantime had been led by God out of Egypt to meet his brother in the wilderness and together they returned to Egypt to assume their ponderous responsibilities.

Upon the initial encounter with Pharaoh, no doubt Amenhotep II, they suffered a setback, for he refused to permit Israel to go and worship Yahweh in the Wilderness of Sinai as Moses requested (Ex. 5:1-2). In fact, he interpreted Moses' request to be a result of too much leisure and punished his insolence by increasing the severity of Israelite slavery. In great discouragement Moses and Aaron turned to Yahweh who proceeded to reaffirm His promise, the same promise made to their fathers many centuries earlier. He told them, moreover, to return to Pharaoh again and this time they would perform mighty works in His name before him. If he still refused to permit them to worship in the desert, God would bring upon Egypt a series of plagues so severe that Pharaoh would be compelled to grant their request. The second audience was no more successful, and though Aaron's rod became a serpent and swallowed up the serpents which the Egyptian magicians, by Satanic power, were able to create, the king was adamant. Thereupon God unleashed upon the land the plagues, ten in all, which, in spite of temporary indications to the contrary, left Pharaoh unmoved in his determination to resist Israel's demands.

THE TEN PLAGUES

1.	The turning of water to blood	(Ex.	7:19-25)
2.	The frogs	(Ex.	8:1 -15)
3.	The lice	(Ex.	8:16-19)
4.	The flies	(Ex.	8:20-32)
5.	The cattle disease	(Ex.	9:1 - 7)
6.	The boils	(Ex.	9:8 -12)
7.	The hail	(Ex.	9:13-35)
8.	The locusts	(Ex.	10:1 -20)
9.	The darkness	(Ex.	10:21-29)
10.	Death of the firstborn	(Ex.	12:29-30)

The miracles of the rods, plagues, and so on have always been a source of consternation to the critics who dismiss them as exaggerated accounts of natural phenomena of nature at best. For example, they maintain that the turning of water into blood was simply a darkening of the Nile by some muddy materials which had been carried down the river from Ethiopia and central Africa. The lice were merely sand fleas, which are common today, and they were caused by the stirring up of the dust in which they breed. The total darkness was caused by a tremendous dust storm which blotted out the sun.[37] The objections to such circumventions of the miraculous should be obvious, for they completely fail to explain all of the plagues, and the incredible results which followed are not explicable on the basis of purely natural occurrences. How could it be that only in Goshen, where Israel lived, there were no flies or darkness? Granted even that forces of nature were at work in some cases, how is it that these forces excluded Israel from their devastating effects? No answer apart from God is sufficient to account for these facts; to say that these stories are only legendary or spiritually interpreted memories of God's mighty acts in nature is begging the question and relegating history to nonsense.[38]

The tenth and final plague, the slaughter of the firstborn of Egypt, was the most horrible and momentous of all.

To the Egyptians it indicated the superiority of Yahweh over their gods of life and death, but to Israel it spoke of His gracious deliverance and salvation. It occasioned the institution of one of the meaningful services of the Hebrew religious year, the Passover, a rite which forever after would commemorate God's selection of the slave band Israel to be His special people, the proof of that selection being their marvelous deliverance from the Tenth Plague and Exodus from the land of their bondage.

The description of the Passover in chapter 12 is filled with meaning for both Israel and the Church. Every Israelite household must select a lamb on the tenth day of the month Abib (Nisan), the month which from henceforth was to be the first in the religious year. This lamb was to be tethered in the dooryard of the home until the fourteenth day when it was to be slaughtered "between the evenings" or between the going down of the sun and absolute darkness. The blood from the victim must be applied to the two sideposts and the lentil of each house with a sprig of hyssop. The entire roasted flesh of the lamb was then to be eaten with unleavened bread and bitter herbs. During this hurried meal the family must be in a state of preparation, dressed for a journey. The lamb typified the lamb of God mentioned by John the Baptist at the baptism of Jesus (John 1:29) and prophesied by Isaiah, particularly in Isaiah 53. The blood spoke of atonement, which in the Hebrew literally means "covering." The application of the blood indicated the faith of the one making the application in the ability of the blood to protect him from the wrath of God, or, as later theology was to express it, to save him from his sin (Lev. 17:11; Heb. 9:22). The roasting by fire conveyed the idea of judgment, which Christ vicariously suffered; the wholeness of the victim's body revealed that "not a bone of his body should be broken" (Ps. 34:20; Jn. 19:36). There were other typical elements as well, but these are sufficient to indicate the spiritual nature of the Passover feast as well as its meaning in the historical context of the Exodus.[39]

That fateful night of the fourteenth of Abib finally came; when God's judgment passed over the land of Egypt, only those homes sheltered by the sprinkled blood escaped the awful toll which was exacted upon the firstborn. In sorrow and rage Pharaoh, who also had lost his firstborn son, commanded the Israelites to leave his land. With the clothing and valuables which they had "borrowed"[40] from the Egyptians, they left in haste from Rameses in Goshen, fleeing to Succoth near the edge of the Sinai wilderness. The magnitude of the migration staggers the imagination, for over 600,000 adults plus the children and animals entered the sojourn (Ex. 12:37). In fact the multitude was so great that the critics account for it by suggesting that the term "thousand" in Hebrew (aleph) should be transliterated into a military term meaning a certain contingent of troops.[41] If an aleph contained on the average no more than fifty men, it might mean that only 50 x 600 adults left, or 30,000. Together with children the total under this reckoning would amount to no more than 120,000 persons, a much more understandable figure. The line of reasoning just presented is inconsistent, however, with the totals given by tribes later on, where there is no question whatsover as to the meaning. As difficult as we know it must have been to manage and sustain such a crowd in a desert for forty years, we are obliged to accept the Biblical account, for the entire Exodus account is in the spirit of the miraculous, the miracle of this great host being but one of many examples.

Following the Passover feast, and apparently while in Succoth, Moses was further instructed concerning its significance. For seven days following the feast itself there was to be a secondary, though related, observance known as the feast of Unleavened Bread. Leaven, generally a symbol of sin in the Scriptures, was to be removed from the home as a sign of the separation of its inhabitant from the sinful elements of his past life. Moreover, because God had graciously spared the firstborn of Israel at the Passover, all firstborn sons were to be dedicated to His service (11:11-13). All firstborn animals, on the other hand, were to be offered in sacrifice if they were sacrificial animals; otherwise they were to be substituted for by a sacrificial animal. For example, the ass, because it was a valuable work animal, could be "redeemed" by a lamb which would die in its place. The male children of Israel could likewise be redeemed by a lamb in lieu of service to God.

The journey was resumed from Succoth; contrary to expectation God forbade Moses to take the coastal highway from Egypt directly to Canaan because that way crossed Philistine territory, and God knew that when Israel met the warlike Philistines they would desire to turn back to Egypt. A more southerly route was selected, though its details are irrecoverable because of the present lack of Biblical and archaeological information. In any event they camped near Etham, thought to be at the northern end of the Bitter Lakes, from whence they turned again and encamped before Pi-hahiroth, "between Migdol and the sea" and near Baal-zephon. These places have never been identified, so the route at this point is highly speculative.[42] We are told that they were shut in by the desert and the sea, no way being available to them but the sea itself. Pharaoh, by this time regretting the fact that he had permitted all these slaves to escape, pursued the Israelites with a picked unit of charioteers, finally overtaking them at their encampment near the sea. At this time, however, God intervened and in a most incredible miracle parted the waters of the sea to permit the entire Israelite host to cross on dry ground. The pursuing Egyptians, essaying to cross in the same path, were overwhelmed by the returning waters which God permitted to flood to their original bed.

This entire miracle, including the place of crossing, demands further investigation in the light of the criticisms which have assailed it on nearly every hand. It is generally pointed out, and correctly, that the word describing the sea in the Hebrew, *Yam suph,* means Reed Sea and not Red Sea,[43] and this is taken to mean that the crossing place was very shallow.[44] However, this same term applies to the entire Gulfs of Suez and Aqaba as far as we can determine (Ex. 10:19; Josh. 2:10; Dt. 11:4; Num. 21:4). The argument that the Reed Sea must imply a shallow body of water is thus overthrown for the Gulf of Suez is hardly so. In fact, even the Bitter Lakes, Lake Timsah, and Lake Ballah, are deep enough, or certainly were in ancient times, to demand a miraculous act of God for Israel to pass through and for the Egyptian charioteers and horses to be drowned. We may allow that Israel crossed one of these lakes, the writer's opinion being that it was the southernmost, the Bitter Lakes, and still believe in the full need for a miracle. Such explanations as a blowing back of shallow waters by a strong wind or the crossing point being merely through a swamp in which the Egyptians became lost and ensnared are only feeble attempts to skirt the miraculous nature of the Exodus.[45] It is not enough to say that a small renegade band fled through shallow water, lost its pursuers in the darkness, and later reinterpreted these events as miraculous mighty acts of God on their behalf. The massive structure of the Judaeo-Christian faith can hardly be supported by such a shaky foundation. Only a genuine miracle, as recorded here, can account for Israel's memory of this forever after as the greatest historical event in their national experience (Amos 3:1-2; Hos. 11:1; Ezek. 20:5-6; Ps. 66:6; Ps. 136:10-11).

ISRAEL IN SINAI (EXODUS 15-NUMBERS 21)

After singing the praises of God in one of the most stirring poems of the Old Testament, Moses continued to lead the way to Marah, three days' journey south of the crossing point. If the average day's journey was fifteen miles, a figure comparable to such a journey under such circumstances today, the Bitter Lakes crossing point is somewhat substantiated, anything farther north being too far for three days and any place farther south not necessitating three days. At Marah the water was too bitter to drink; hence the name *marah* ("bitter"). The water became palatable, however, when Moses cast a certain medicinal plant into it; the water remains pure to this day.[46] From Marah they journeyed on to Elim ("palms"); a month or more after their departure they moved into the Wilderness of Sin in the southern part of the peninsula. There, possibly in view of Egypt which lay across the Suez Gulf, they began to long for the old life which they had left only recently. They tired of the lack of meat and bread. One familiar with the desert can sympathize with their plight, for the heat and aridity, coupled with the difficulty of traveling, must have been extremely taxing.

To alleviate their appetite God promised to shower upon them quail and bread in such supply that they would never again lack these necessities in all their journey. At the first appearance of manna they were dumbfounded because of its source and nature; all they could exclaim was *"ma na?"* ("what is it?"). To memorialize this wonderful event a supply of the manna was conserved in a pot and later placed in the ark of the covenant.

The next stop was at Rephidim where Moses struck a rock to secure water; it was there also that Israel encountered its first enemy. Swooping down upon the Hebrews' rear flank and attacking the elderly and infirm, the Amalekites, a nomadic and fierce tribe of the Sinai interior, struck Israel hard, but not without retaliation. Untrained militarily as Israel presumably was, she was not lacking in leadership or resources; as Moses raised his hands in benediction over the Israelite hosts with their captain, Joshua, they prevailed in the power of God over their enemies. At the conclusion of the fracas, Jethro, Moses' father-in-law, arrived at Rephidim with Moses' wife Zipporah and their two sons, Gershom and Eliezer (18:1-6). He had heard rumors to the effect that Yahweh had delivered Israel from Egypt and wanted to verify these accounts. Having been assured of the truth of all these matters, Jethro, as priest of Midian, offered up a burnt offering in praise to Yahweh. The question of Jethro's relationship to the faith of Israel is too involved to be considered fully here, but the evidence available would surely indicate that he was intimately familiar with Israel's God.[47] The fact that he says that now he knows that Yahweh is superior to the gods of Egypt does not mean that he questioned that up until now; he is simply saying that now he has seen it proved beyond any reasonable doubt. Noticing that Moses was continually troubled by the hordes of people who came to him for advice and judgment in thousands of petty matters, Jethro warned him that he would overtax himself and advised him to set up a court system of minor judges who could settle at least the more insignificant cases. To this advice Moses gave heed, though apparently the system had only very temporary use.

Jethro left Rephidim, and shortly thereafter Moses did also. Israel's next stop, and their most important, was in the Plain of Sinai before the mountain where Moses had first seen the manifestation of God in the burning bush. Here were to take place some of the most important events in Israel's history, for this place was, in many respects, the cradle of the Theocracy ("rule by God"). A covenant had been made with Abraham, inherited by Isaac and Jacob, expressed ethnically in Israel. A remarkable deliverance had been effected by God when this people had fled from 400 years of bondage in Egypt. And now this rather heterogeneous band, Israel, was at the threshold of a new and vital experience, the giving of the covenant law that would lend their loose federation cohesion enabling them to know the will of God in government, society, and worship.

Moses, as the mediator between Yahweh and Israel, was summoned by God to the summit of the holy mountain where God told him that the time for the creation of a nation of believers had come. In unmistakable language He informed Moses that he was to remind Israel that He, God, had delivered them from Egypt by His mighty power, that He would confirm and enlarge the terms of the ancient covenant with them, that He expected faithful obedience from them, and that on the condition of their obedience would make of them a kingdom of priests and a holy nation (Ex. 19:4-6). Agreeing to this condition and in solemn oaths, the representatives of Israel prepared themselves for the reception of the details of this covenant. Three days later in a great demonstration of power, God appeared before Moses in fire and thunderings and earthquakes and set the stage for the giving of the Book of the Covenant, the very heart of the Theocratic economy (Ex. 20-23).

After the law was announced and spelled out, it was accepted in a ceremony of covenant agreement by a council of elders representing the twelve tribes. The seventy elders gathered about an altar and a circle of twelve pillars especially erected for the occasion; sacrificial offerings were made and the blood of the sacrifices was sprinkled in turn on the altar and the participants. As in the case of the Abrahamic Covenant, the slaughter of animals and the use of the blood as an intermediary agent bound the parties of the contract into an indissoluble relationship. God and Israel had become "blood brothers" in a very real sense. Following this, God summoned Moses up to Sinai once again in order that He might give him the Decalogue (Ten Commandments) on the tables of stone as well as instructions concerning a place of worship where He might meet Israel (24:12-18).

The tabernacle and priesthood are discussed in the remainder of the Book of Exodus (25-40). Now that Israel was a nation with a king (God) and a body of laws (Torah), there must be a provision made for Israel to have communion with God. This involved both a place of communion and a means whereby communion might be a possibility since sin barred any possibility of direct access to God. The parts of the tabernacle and the acts of the priests have highly symbolical value, so it will be necessary that we discuss them in some detail in the next chapter.

The historical narrative is resumed in Exodus 31 where we learn of the selection of men who were to oversee the construction of the Tabernacle with all its accoutrements. Because of the extreme complexity of all the work involved, it was necessary that men be endowed with the Holy Spirit in order to have the requisite skill and wisdom. The two chief foremen, Bezaleel and Aholiab, were especially singled out as chosen instruments of God under whose direction the work was carried out successfully.

While Moses was on the summit of Sinai receiving all these aforementioned laws and instructions, the people down in the plains concluded that he was gone never to return. In their opinion, Yahweh had forsaken them and nothing real was ever to come of the covenant. Bereft of their human leader also, they resorted to the manufacture of an image of gold which would become to them a tangible object of worship. This image of a bull (not calf) was not that of a foreign god but was supposed to represent the pedestal upon which Yahweh stood.[48] The fact that the feast which followed was dedicated to Yahweh is sufficient to prove that the sin was not a departure from God, but an attempt to hypostatize God, at least in a secondary way. This was clearly prohibited in the second commandment.

In the midst of the orgy of feasting and dancing, in which Aaron apparently took a prominent role, God related to Moses what was transpiring below and threatened to destroy Israel for its sin. Upon hearing this Moses urged God to remember His eternal covenant; then he went down from the mountain with the tablets of stone upon which God had inscribed the commandments. Almost symbolically, he cast the stones upon the ground when he saw the awful picture before his eyes; the breaking of the stones seemed to suggest the terrible breaking of the Law which had so recently been given. In his rage Moses took the image, smashed it into pieces, ground it to dust which he threw into the nearby brook, and caused the ringleaders to drink of the water. He then proceeded to excoriate Aaron for his part, though Aaron tried vainly to excuse the act as a miracle beyond his ken, for he stated that when certain gold objects were cast into a fire, the golden bull appeared as though by magic. The conclusion of the matter was reached when Moses commanded the Levites, who by now seemed to exercise a certain religious authority, to slaughter the guilty parties, whereupon at least three thousand men perished. Moses now turned to God and in some of the most moving and selfless words ever penned requested God to forgive Israel, offering to give himself for his people if God might see fit (32:30-32). God instead forgave the people and reassured Moses of His continued presence with them.

God then revealed Himself to Moses in a most magnificent way. Having called him to the temporary tent of meeting outside the camp,[49] He manifested Himself to Moses and all the people in a pillar of cloud which rested over the tent. Then He informed Moses that He would permit him to see His "back parts," though not His face, as a testimony to Moses that He would continue to be with him in the days ahead. What he saw was no doubt the reflected glory of God, the effulgent radiance of His presence, and nothing physical; for the Father, as a spirit, would not manifest Himself otherwise (John 4:24). Moses then was summoned once more to the top of Sinai where he was given a set of tablets to replace those which had been broken. When he reappeared the brilliance of God's presence as reflected on his face was so intense that Israel could not bear to look upon him unless he covered his countenance with a veil (34:29-35; II Cor. 3:13).

The construction of the tabernacle, manufacture of the vessels, garments, and other objects, and anointing of the priests are described in Exodus 35-40. The mass of details in these chapters indicates clearly the preciseness of the work and the fact that each and every item had great importance in the eyes of God and is instructive to those who will study it carefully.[50] When the Tabernacle was finally reared and the furniture placed therein, God filled it with His presence glory.[51] When the cloud appeared by day and the fire by night over this holy shrine, Israel was to know that God was there and that when they moved He was leading them on to new experiences.

Next, the priests were anointed and consecrated in accordance to the Divine instruction (Lev. 8), following which they offered their first sacrificial offerings (Lev. 9). Two of Aaron's sons, Nadab and Abihu, presumed to make an offering with "strange fire" and were slain by the Lord as a result

(Lev. 10:1-7). The harshness of the punishment would serve as a warning to others that the very technique of offering to God was a sacred procedure laden with meaning which could not be abridged. At about the same time Moses was commanded to number the people and arrange them in order that they might continue the long journey to Canaan (Num. 1-2). They were to march according to camps, three tribes on each side of the tabernacle and the Levites surrounding it on all sides. Each camp had its own standard and whether marching or settled was to position itself in the same order.

The selection of the tribe of Levi for special service followed next (Num. 3), though it was implied even earlier. Formerly, the firstborn of every house of Israel was to be dedicated to God for perpetual service, but now God selected a whole tribe, Levi, to render this service. Every firstborn could be represented by a Levite according to the Law; in the event that there were not enough Levites for each firstborn (as the case actually was), the remaining firstborn were to be redeemed from their service by the sacrifice of five shekels apiece (3:44-51). The Levites themselves were divided according to families into the Gershonites, Kohathites, and the sons of Merari, these three having been the sons of Levi the patriarch. To each of these groups was given a special responsibility in regard to the services, care, and transportation of the Tabernacle and all that pertained to it. The further instructions concerning the selection and consecration of the Levites are given in Numbers 8.

Finally the day came for resuming the journey to the Land of Promise (Num. 10:11). For over a year Israel had rested at Sinai while the nation was being formed; now, with a blowing of trumpets, they proceeded to the Wilderness of Paran. Hardly out of sight of Sinai, however, they began to complain again about their condition, the chief grievance being the lack of meat and spicy Egyptian foods. Moses, about at the breaking point from the burden of the people, was given seventy elders who were filled with the Spirit and delegated to help him in his overwhelming tasks of ministering to so great a host (11:24-30). Then God sent an abundance of quail, but the people in their greed began to devour them without an offering of thanks. At this God slew a great many; in memorial of their lust the place of their death was called Kibroth-hattaavah ("graves of sinning").

From here they moved to Hazeroth, the place where Miriam and Aaron rose in rebellion against Moses, ostensibly because he had married an Ethiopian woman.[52] The real reason for their attitude was a feeling of envy because they apparently did not entertain the intimate relationship with God which Moses enjoyed, though they, too, could lay claim to the title "prophet." In retaliation, God summoned Miriam and Aaron before Him; possibly because Miriam as a woman and as the prime instigator had sought to undermine the Divinely appointed authority of her younger brother, she was struck by leprosy. Only after earnest intercession by Moses was she healed and permitted back into the camp.

Upon reaching the Wilderness of Paran, Moses sent spies into Canaan (Num. 13:1-25). Israel nearly had come now to Canaan's southern boundaries; it seems that Moses' purpose was to enter Canaan from the south. Twelve men were appointed to take a trek throughout the land and to report on their findings. Forty days later they returned to Kadesh-barnea where Israel now camped. Ten of them brought back a pessimistic report of great giants and high walled cities in Canaan which Israel could in no wise overcome. Only two, Caleb and Joshua, tried to convince Israel to trust God and to move in and occupy the land by His grace. Their arguments were not convincing, however, and in a near rebellion the nation decided to hearken to the majority report, overthrow the leadership of Moses and Aaron, and return to Egypt. God threatened once again to disinherit Israel and to make of Moses a mightier nation yet, but true to his prophetic calling, Moses interceded for them as he had so often done before with the result that God spared them from death, but sentenced them to wander for thirty-eight more years, or a total of forty, never to reach Canaan except as represented by their children twenty years of age and under (14:22-24). Only Joshua and Caleb, because of their obedience, were going to see that land.

Upon hearing this, Israel attempted to make an immediate entry into Canaan from the south but was soundly defeated at Hormah by a Canaanite force. This was only the first of many events in that next thirty-eight year period, but very few of those are recorded in the account of Moses. Perhaps the most outstanding is the rebellion of Korah, Dathan, and Abiram (Num. 16). These men, with their families and friends, decided that Moses and Aaron were arrogating too

much authority to themselves and challenged them to prove
the uniqueness of their Divine calling as mediators between
Israel and God. The challenge was accepted, but when these
pretenders attempted to offer sacrifice, the earth opened up
beneath them and they were swallowed up together with their
unbelieving families and their tents and possessions. Rather
than accepting this as a sign of God's blessing upon Moses and
Aaron, however, the nation protested; were it not for the
intercession of these two faithful men of God, once more God
would have destroyed the nation "as in a moment" (16:45).
In a final and convincing act each tribe was to supply a rod
which, with Aaron's rod, was to be placed in the Tabernacle
overnight. The rod which would shoot forth buds would be
the symbol of its owner's call from God. On the next day, the
rods were examined and, of course, Aaron's budded and even
brought forth flowers. All arguments being now silenced
forever, the rod was placed beside the ark of the covenant, a
worthy retirement for an instrument which had been so
singularly used of God.

At long last the period of wandering about the oasis of
Kadesh-barnea and vicinity was over and Israel moved into
the Wilderness of Zin. There Miriam died at a very advanced
age. And in the vast desert there was no water; the people
so complained that Moses, in a burst of anger, struck a rock in
violation of God's command in an effort to procure water
(20:7-11). This was to cost him the privilege of entering the
Land of Promise, though God assured him that he could see
it from a distance. This denial to Moses, who for so many
years had unfailingly followed the will of God until this moment of anger, can be understood only in the light of the
principle that of those to whom God has granted great blessing
and responsibility does He at the same time expect unswerving
obedience. A lesser man would no doubt have gone virtually
unscathed, but a "little" sin in such a spiritual giant loomed
larger than the aggregate sin of a whole generation.

When Moses realized the impossibility of penetrating
Canaan from the south, he decided to do so from the Plains of
Moab just across Jordan from Jericho. To reach this area he
must pass through the Kings Highway if at all possible. This
route wended its way north from the Gulf of Aqaba through
the Kingdom of Edom, particularly its capital city, Sela (Petra
in Greek). The route traversed terrain impassable except

where there were narrow mountain passes. The result was that caravans or armies were compelled to go almost single file; if the Edomites so wished they could withstand many thousands of invaders with a few hundred well-trained troops. Moses, therefore, sought permission from the king of Edom to pass through his land, but the permission was denied (20:17-21). While he decided what to do next, his brother Aaron died and was buried at Mt. Hor. And Israel was attacked near there by the Canaanite king of Arad, a battle which Israel won (21:1-3).

Moses next turned south, apparently deciding to go east of Edom through the Syro-Arabian Desert, but when the way became too difficult, he had to retrace his steps north and make the effort to venture up through the Arabah and bypass Edom on the west. Somewhere along the way, the people began to murmur once again, and this time fell victim to serpents which God set upon them. Only when they looked in faith upon a bronze serpent which Moses had made and placed upon a pole did they recover from the plague (21:9); even then many people died.[53] They finally reached the mouth of the Wadi Zered, just to the north of Edom at the southeast corner of the Dead Sea, and proceeding up the Zered Valley, which formed the border between Edom and Moab, they arrived at the Plains of Moab which lay just south of the Amorite kingdom. There they remained for the most part until they crossed the Jordan under the leadership of Joshua.

ISRAEL IN TRANSJORDAN (NUMBERS 22-DEUTERONOMY 34)

In the course of entering the Plains of Moab and while they were settled there, Israel encountered many obstacles. The first of these was the battle with the Amorite settlers who occupied the territory north of Moab (21:21-25). Sihon, their king, in response to a request by Moses to permit the passage of Israel through their land, refused to comply, whereupon Israel attacked, defeated them, and occupied their holdings. This first of the Israelite possessions was later settled for the most part by the tribe of Gad. As a follow-up Israel's armies went north of Sihon's realm to the land of Bashan; after a short skirmish they defeated Og, the king of Bashan, and occupied this area which later was the home of half of the tribe of Manasseh (21:33-35). Thus, in two quick assaults, Israel occupied virtually everything east of the Jordan and north of Moab.

The most serious test of all, though not in the form of military action, came in Israel's contacts with the Moabites (22-25). Moses had refused to force his way through Moab, despite the ease with which this no doubt could have been done, because he recognized the ancient relationship between Israel and Moab. Nevertheless, the king of Moab, Balak, when he saw how Sihon and Og had both been defeated by Israel, feared that his kingdom was next in line to be assimilated by these powerful Hebrew nomads. At the same time he felt that military strength would be incapable of defeating them, so he resorted to the realm of supernatural power. He called a certain soothsayer, Balaam by name,[54] to come from Mesopotamia and curse Israel for him, believing that in this way Israel would become immobilized. At first Balaam refused to come, for God had forbidden him. After much persuasion, aided by an offer of substantial financial remuneration, he decided that he could go, but he still insisted that he could speak only what God permitted him to speak. On his way to Moab Balaam encountered an angel of God in his way, but when he failed at first to notice the angelic visitor, his beast of burden upon which he rode spoke to him.[55] This, naturally, shocked Balaam, bringing him to the awareness that God was trying to reveal something further to him: that he must speak only the word of God.

As soon as Balaam arrived in Moab, Balak took him to the high places of worship and sacrifice where, after a series of cultic acts, he proceeded to curse Israel which he could see spread out in the plains below him. To Balaam's amazement and Balak's chagrin, only a blessing issued forth (23:9-10); Balaam admitted the impossibility of cursing that which God has blessed. Twice more Balak urged Balaam to curse Israel, but both times only marvelous prophetic blessings were proclaimed (23:18-24; 24:4-9). Finally, in utter frustration, Balak dismissed his hireling soothsayer who, nevertheless, was still not finished with his blessing. In an act entirely beyond his control he spoke one final word, one of the most glorious prophecies in the Old Testament. In somber tones he said, "I shall see him, but not now: I shall behold him, but not nigh; there shall come a Star out of Jacob, and a Sceptre shall rise out of Israel, and shall smite the corners of Moab, and destroy all the children of Sheth" (24:17). A representation of this same star centuries later would lead wise men from Mesopotamia to seek Him who was the object of this majestic prophecy (Jer. 23:5; Luke 1:32-33).

But Balaam's work was not yet finished. He apparently dwelled among the Moabites and somehow became instrumental in causing Israel to go after the Baal of Peor, a Moabite god. What he could not accomplish in a curse he did manage to achieve subtly, for thousands of Israelites, especially from the tribe of Simeon, began to "commit whoredom" with the daughters of Moab. This apostasy from Yahweh was not only a spiritual fornication, though it was that to be sure, but it was also very physical. This was the first contact with the immoral fertility cults of Canaan, the very essence of which was sexual aberration of all kinds. The result was death to 24,000 Israelites, for God had plainly declared that all such things were abominations and could not be tolerated if Israel was to survive at all.

At last the days of Moses' ministry came to an end, but before he died he was privileged to have a final glimpse of the land to the borders of which he had led his people. Also, there must be one who could take his place after his departure; God's choice for such a leader was Joshua (Dt. 31:14-23). Another matter which came to his attention was the request by the tribes of Reuben, Gad, and half the tribe of Manasseh to settle the lands east of the Jordan which they had already subjugated and which was ideal for pastures and farms. Moses granted the petition on the condition that the fighting men of these tribes cross the Jordan with the other tribes and help them occupy the western portions of Palestine. Then, and only then, could they return to their families and lands (Num. 32:20-33). Gad took the area formerly known as the Amorite kingdom, Manasseh settled in Bashan, and Reuben eventually occupied Moab. At the same time, Moses outlined the borders of Canaan where the other tribes were soon to settle (Num. 34). In addition he selected forty-eight cities in which the Levites would live and minister, because Levi as a religious tribe had no inheritance; six of these he designated as cities of refuge, three on each side of the Jordan (Num. 35; Dt. 14:1-10).

After reviewing all the law and making certain necessary additions and modifications thereto, Moses gathered all the people together for preparations for a final assembly (Dt. 27:1) He first commanded them to build an altar at Shechem, between mounts Ebal and Gerizim, when they entered Canaan (27:2-8). There they were to write the words of the law, presumably the Decalogue, upon stones and reaffirm their obedience to the terms of the Covenant. Following this, the Levites were to utter a series of curses which would become applicable upon the breach of certain points of the covenant, and the people were to accept the justice of these curses by giving their assent at the Shechem assembly (27:11-26). Then Moses pointed out another series of blessings and curses which would follow Israel's obedience or disobedience in the days ahead, and he concluded the list by summoning Israel into covenant once again with God then and there (28-30).

After this great gathering in which Moses spelled out God's requirements for His people, Moses wrote down all the law (31:9), gave Joshua a final charge (31:23), and recited a song in which he extolled God for His faithfulness to Israel (31:28-32:43). Then he gave his final blessing to the tribes (33), went to the top of mount Pisgah where he had his last view of the land of promise, and finally, at the age of 120 years, died in Moab where God buried him in an unknown grave (34:1-7). No more fitting epitaph could be given than that at the end of Deuteronomy: "And there arose not a prophet since in Israel like unto Moses, whom the Lord knew face to face...." (Dt. 34:10).

---

[1] See p. 98. Ussher dated Abraham's birth at 2247 B.C.

[2] D. Winton Thomas, *Documents from Old Testament Times*, London, Thomas Nelson and Sons, Ltd., 1958, p. 47.

[3] *Ibid*, p. 48.

[4] Edwin R. Thiele, *The Mysterious Numbers of the Hebrew Kings*, Chicago, University of Chicago Press, 1951.

[5] David Noel Freedman, "Old Testament Chronology," *The Bible and the Ancient Near East*, Ed. by G. Ernest Wright, Garden City, Doubleday and Company, Inc., 1965, pp. 265-281.

[6] John A. Wilson, *The Culture of Ancient Egypt*, Chicago, The University of Chicago Press, 1963, pp. 134-136.

[7] or "foreign chiefs;" cf. W. F. Albright, *From the Stone Age to Christianity*, Garden City, Doubleday and Company, Inc., 1957, pp. 202-203.

[8] Millar Burrows, *What Mean These Stones?*, New York, Meridian Books, 1957, pp. 193-194.

[9] So argued Josephus in *Contra Apionem* 1, 73; but see John Gray, *Archaeology and the Old Testament World*, New York, Harper and Row, 1962, p. 73.

[10] Merrill F. Unger, *Archaeology and the Old Testament*, Grand Rapids, Zondervan Publishing House, 1954, p. 144.

[11] John Bright, *A History of Israel*, Philadelphia, Westminster Press, 1959, pp. 98-99.

[12] There is no basis to the claim that Moses was influenced in his monotheism by Akhnaton. In fact, if the Biblical date for the Exodus be correct, and we believe it is, Moses preceded Akhnaton by nearly one hundred years. It is far more likely that Akhnaton was familiar with Moses' teaching.

[13] O. R. Gurney, *The Hittites*, Baltimore, Penguin Books, 1964, p. 35.

[14] Thomas, *op. cit.*, p. 139.

[15] H. H. Rowley, *From Joseph to Joshua*, London, Oxford University Press, 1950, pp. 132-138.

[16] G. Ernest Wright, *Biblical Archaeology*, Philadelphia, Westminster Press, 1957, pp. 50-51.

[17] G. Frederick Owen, *Archaeology and the Bible*, Westwood, New Jersey, Revell, 1961, pp. 202-203.

[18] Wright, *op. cit.*, p. 24; W. F. Albright, *The Biblical Period From Abraham to Ezra*, New York, Harper and Row, 1963, p. 26; see, however, Emil G. Kraeling, "Light From Ugarit on the Khabiru," *Bulletin of the American Schools of Oriental Research*, No. 77, p. 32, February, 1940.

[19] Rowley, *From Joseph to Joshua*, p. 55.

[20] Theophile J. Meek, *Hebrew Origins*, New York, Harper and Row, 1960, pp. 27-33.

[21] John Garstang, *Foundations of Bible History*, London, Constable and Company, 1937, pp. 61 ff.

[22] Burrows, *op. cit.*, p. 78.

[23] Unger, *op. cit.*, p. 148.

[24] Rowley, *From Joseph to Joshua*, pp. 33-35.

[25] See p. 104.

[26] Bright, *op. cit.*, p. 111.

[27] Burrows, *op. cit.*, p. 74.

[28] See Albright's interesting speculation along this line in *From the Stone Age to Christianity*, p. 223.

[29] Nelson Glueck, *The Other Side of the Jordan*, New Haven, The American Schools of Oriental Research, 1940, p. 146 ff.

[30] Denis Baly, *The Geography of the Bible*, New York, Harper and Brothers, 1957, pp. 245-251.

[31] Glueck seems to admit that there could have been nomads in Edom and Moab during this period; cf. "The Civilization of the Edomites," *The Biblical Archaeologist Reader*, Vol. 2, Ed. by David Noel Freedman and Edward F. Campbell, Jr., Garden City, Doubleday and Company, Inc., 1964, pp. 51-52.

[32] Albright, *The Biblical Period From Abraham to Ezra*, p. 27.

[33] Josh. 13:1-6; Jud. 1.

[34] Unger, *op. cit.*, pp. 163-164.

[35] The better translation of 11:13.

[36] Geerhardus Vos, *Biblical Theology*, Grand Rapids, Wm. B. Eerdmans Publishing Co., 1954, pp. 129-134.

[37] J. Coert Rylaarsdam, "Exodus," *The Interpreter's Bible,* Vol. 1, Ed. by George Buttrick *et al,* New York, Abingdon-Cokesbury Press, 1951, p. 839.

[38] Bernhard W. Anderson, *Understanding the Old Testament,* Englewood Cliffs, Prentice-Hall, 1957, pp. 40-41.

[39] Robert Jamieson, A. R. Fausset, and David Brown, *Commentary on the Whole Bible,* Grand Rapids, Zondervan Publishing House, n.d., p. 55.

[40] The better translation here is "asked." There was no intention of paying back, nor did the Egyptians expect it.

[41] A. H. McNeile, *The Book of Exodus,* London, Methuen, 1908, p. 75.

[42] Charles F. Pfeiffer, ed., *Baker's Bible Atlas,* Grand Rapids, Baker Book House, 1961, pp. 73-74.

[43] Francis Brown, S. R. Driver, and Charles Briggs, *A Hebrew and English Lexicon of the Old Testament,* London, Oxford University Press, 1962, p. 693

[44] Anderson, *op. cit.,* p. 49.

[45] Lewis Hay, "What Really Happened at the Sea of Reeds?," *Journal of Biblical Literature,* 83:397-403, December, 1964.

[46] According to Manasseh Harel, who was engaged in the Sinai Campaign of 1956, the waters at Marah are quite palatable. From lecture in Jerusalem, Israel, July 17, 1965. Harel is professor of geography at Hebrew University.

[47] Bright, *op. cit.,* p. 116.

[48] Martin Buber, *Moses,* New York, Harper and Row, p. 214.

[49] H. H. Rowley, *The Growth of the Old Testament,* New York, Harper and Row, 1963, p. 19.

[50] For a good study of the historical basis for the Tabernacle, see Frank M. Cross, "The Priestly Tabernacle," *The Biblical Archaeologist Reader,* Vol. 2, Ed. by David Noel Freedman and Edward F. Campbell, Jr., Garden City, Doubleday and Company, Inc., 1964, pp. 201-228.

[51] Shekinah glory; from Heb. *shakan-* "to dwell."

[52] It could be that this was an inter-racial marriage, though the Hebrew term "Cushite" could refer to natives of the Arabian peninsula; cf. Buber, *op. cit.,* p. 217. Of course, we assume that Zipporah had died by now.

[53] This may have been at Timnah or Punon, both places being rich sources of copper to this day. See Baly, *op. cit.,* p. 212.

[54] See my discussion of Balaam as a false prophet in "An Investigation of the Person and Work of the Old Testament Prophet of God," Ph.D. Dissertation, Greenville, South Carolina, Bob Jones University, 1963, pp. 139-155.

[55] See C. F. Keil and Franz Delitzsch, *Biblical Commentary on the Old Testament: The Pentateuch,* Vol. 3, Grand Rapids, Wm. B. Eerdmans Publishing Company, 1948, p. 173, for an explanation of this strange phenomenon.

CHAPTER FIVE

THE THEOCRATIC FOUNDATION

ANCIENT NEAR EASTERN LAW

There had been law codes in the Near East much more ancient than that of Moses. Hammurabi's Code of Laws, most famous of all, came from the seventeenth century, but even it was only the collection and refinement of Sumerian and ancient Semitic law from many centuries earlier.[1] All of the other nations of the Mediterranean world had their laws, some rather crude, to be sure, but all reflecting a great common tradition of jurisprudence. As Alt and others have pointed out, Mosaic law was quite similar to many of these, though there were notable exceptions.[2] For example, in Hebrew law there were two types, apodictic and casuistic law. The former are best illustrated in the Ten Commandments which were unique in ancient law in that they contained the simple injunction or prohibition without reference to specific cases. They set forth principles which are always binding and which must always be strictly observed simply because they are right. Casuistic law, as the term suggests, had to do with specific laws dealing with individual cases which might come up. This was not peculiarly Hebrew, for in Hammurabi's Code, to cite the best known example, there were nearly three hundred statutes dealing with that many possible infractions of various kinds. The formula in the casuistic law was usually phrased, "If a man do thus and so . . . then the punishment shall be such and such." There were no specific principles as such, no statements of universal legal obligation.

Beyond the mere form of the laws, that of Moses is definitely superior in moral and spiritual tone and is leavened with a spirit of mercy noticeably absent from other codes.

For example, Babylonian law stated that if a physician were performing an operation and the patient died, the physician's right hand was to be amputated.[3] No such harshness exists in Mosaic law at all, nor is there anything remotely similar. The closest would be the principle of *lex talionis,* or "an eye for an eye and a tooth for a tooth," and even this was closely and justly regulated by society. Many scholars argue that Hebrew law like others was based largely upon other more ancient law codes.[4] This is true only in the sense that all law codes had a common basis in ordinary human ethics and in established norms of what constituted right and wrong. No doubt Moses incorporated much such natural law into his code under Divine inspiration, but the distinctive features such as the apodictic law and those having to do with Israel's peculiar relationship to Yahweh can be accounted for only as revelation from God. The Theocracy was a unique institution and the legal framework, both civil and religious, in which it operated was on that account also unique even though elements within it resembled those found elsewhere. These will be discussed in greater detail when the individual law codes are considered.

ENLARGEMENT OF THE COVENANT AND MEANING OF THE THEOCRACY

The Old Testament clearly teaches that Israel had its origins in a family, that of Abraham, Isaac, and Jacob (Gen. 12:1-3). But it is equally clear that all through its patriarchal history it had no real national existence. It was merely a family or clan in Canaan before the movement to Egypt and all through its Egyptian sojourn was nothing more than a very loose association of people with a common racial and historical background, an association nonetheless recognizable because of the covenant which had brought it into being in the first place. Then at Sinai a very decisive event took place; the formation of these people into a nation of tribes which would be the custodian of the ancient faith of Abraham. This formation was not a simple matter, for these semi-nomadic wanderers now had to be welded together politically, socially, and religiously into a covenant people who could not only agree among themselves to stay together and keep the terms of the covenant, but who must resist all efforts on the part of others to destroy this solidarity. Added to all this was the fact that they had no land, only the promise of one to come, and no central government or law. Moreover, they had no formal statement of their faith or ritual in which to express it. All this had to be created at Sinai in order for the metamorphosis of a people into a nation to be realized.

The first part of the legal aspect of the Covenant at Sinai, that which was given to Moses in his first encounter with Yahweh on the mountaintop, is called the Book of the Covenant (Ex. 20-23). It in turn consists of the Decalogue ("Ten Words") or Ten Commandments (20:2-17), which in a sense formed the constitution of the new nation just as the Exodus events had proclaimed a declaration of independence; and also a series of religious, civil, and moral statutes calculated to guide Israel in these areas of life. The Code here in Exodus was the earliest expression of the Mosaic covenant, but not by any means its only expression. Also at Sinai were promulgated regulations concerning the place of worship, the priesthood, and liturgy. These constitute almost all of the book of Leviticus, the last seventeen chapters of Exodus, and the first ten chapters of Numbers. In addition, there are scattered places throughout the remainder of Numbers where certain ideas were expanded or repeated in the course of the wilderness journey. Finally, the Book of Deuteronomy, as the name implies ("second law"), consists largely of slight modifications of the Sinaitic Law or additions thereto which were given nearly forty years later in the Plains of Moab just prior to Moses' death and the Conquest. This repetition of the Law is sometimes known as the Deuteronomic Covenant, a designation which may be justified because of the ways in which this covenant differs from the one delivered at Sinai. Following Moses, however, there were no additional laws as such, though there were confirmations of the covenant from time to time all through Israel's history, usually at certain annual festal occasions or in times of spiritual revival (Josh. 24; II Chron. 15:12; II Kings 23:3; Neh. 9:38).

The name applied to these books of Moses, the Torah ("instruction"), is a singularly appropriate term, for it expresses the real essence of the Sinaitic and Deuteronomic revelation. The people had been called together, joined in a Theocratic society, and given a Divine commission as partners with God in an eternal covenant. The instruction of

Torah, in its social, political, and religious aspects, was to be the means of assuring both an understanding of and adherence to the terms of the covenant.

THE MOSAIC LAW

In one respect Mosaic Law was divided into three parts —civil, moral, and ceremonial or liturgical. Yet, because the Theocratic Community was essentially a religious society with no distinction between "church and state" such divisions are rather superficial. Every part of every law was religious as well as secular and impinged upon every part of the nation. It was a matter of religion to plant one's crops according to the Law, and it was a matter of state to offer the sacrifices in the prescribed manner. Yet, for practical purposes some arbitrary outline of the Mosaic legislation must be attempted so that its nature and purpose can be more fully understood.

Civil Law. Let us first consider the laws having to do with man and his relationship to his fellow. These are expressed first of all in the Ten Commandments, the last six (Ex. 20:12-17) containing the basic elements of society: honoring the parents, esteeming human life, regarding the sanctity of the neighbor's wife, the rights of his property, the value of his reputation, and not desiring anything belonging to him. The remainder of the laws interpret these basic commandments or indicate special applications of them.

There are many laws having to do with one's parents and family (Ex. 21:17; Lev. 19:3; 20:9; Dt. 21:18-21). It was taken for granted that the mother and father were the heads of the families, and unquestioning obedience was expected from the children. Akin to these were laws regarding marriage and sexual relationships. Of special interest in the former case is the marriage of an Israelite to a woman taken as a war prisoner (Dt. 21:10-17) and the permitting of divorce in the case of adultery alone (Dt. 24:1-5). There were certain marriages considered illicit, such as those within families (Lev. 18; 20:10-21), and, of course, any acts of sexual perversion were severely condemned (Ex. 22:16-17, 19; Lev. 19:20-22; Num. 5:11-31; Dt. 22:22-30). In addition, there were special prohibitions against prostitution, which was an especially dangerous temptation because it formed such an important part of Canaanite religion (Lev. 19:29; Dt. 22:13-21; 23:17-18).

There was a special reverence for old age (Lev. 19:32) and consideration for widows and orphans (Ex. 22:22-24; Dt. 24:17-18), the poor (Ex. 23:3; Lev. 19:9-10; 23:22; Dt. 24:19-22), and the handicapped (Lev. 19:14). For example, the farmer was not to reap the corners of his fields nor rake up the scatterings, so that the poor might come into his fields and take the leftovers. Furthermore, because Israel had been a stranger in Egypt they were to have particular regard for the strangers among them (Ex. 22:21; 23:9; Lev. 19:33-34). In this connection also there were laws regulating slavery and voluntary servitude. In times of dire need a Hebrew could sell himself to his neighbor for a certain price, and the money he thus obtained could be used to pay his debts. In turn he must serve his neighbor for a six year period, but was to be permitted his freedom on the seventh year. If he chose to remain with his master longer, he could indicate this choice by having his ear bored through with an awl in the presence of witnesses. In this way he expressed his voluntary indenturehood, a condition not altogether undesirable in many cases, for these servants had every need of life provided without the responsibility which accompanies independence (Ex. 21:1-11; Lev. 25:39-55; Dt. 15:12-18; 24:14-15). Involuntary slavery of aliens was permitted, though clearly not sanctioned by God. In any case the slave must be treated with mercy and the whole institution was subject to stringent regulations (Ex. 21:16; Dt. 23:15-16; 24-7). If a slave's eye or tooth were knocked out by the master, for example, the slave was to be freed for compensation. This naturally ameliorated the harshness of his bondage, for the loss of a slave would be a financial blow to his owner.

The Israelite's relationship to his peers was also covered by the law. Thieves were strictly dealt with (Ex. 22:1-5), as were arsonists (Ex. 22:6), tale-bearers (Ex. 23:1; Lev. 19:16), and rioters (Ex. 23:2). In the case of assault and battery, the principle was that of *lex talionis* or "an eye for an eye" (Ex. 21:18-36; Lev. 24:18-22; Dt. 25:11-12). Manslaughter or unpremeditated murder was punished but not capitally (Num. 35:6-29; Dt. 19:4-10). The slayer under the law must flee to a designated city of refuge where he was protected from revenge until he had a fair trial. If proven innocent he must remain in the city until the death of the high priest; if proven guilty of murder, he would be put to death. In cases of known and proven murder immediate vengeance was taken and the murderer was punished by death at the hands of the elders or avengers[5] (Ex. 21:12-15; Lev. 24:17; Num. 35:30-34; Dt. 19:11-13; 21:1-9).

The business dealings of the Israelites were included within the compass of the law. Such matters as the lending of money (Ex. 22:25-27), charging of interest on loans (Lev. 19:35-37; 25:35-38; Dt. 23:19-20), and using fair weights and measures (Dt. 25:13-16) were strictly regulated. They were also to beware of taking gifts (bribes) because such gifts tended to blind their eyes to right and wrong whether in business or otherwise (Ex. 23:8). If they had been entrusted with the care of their neighbor's goods, they were to make recompense for any loss of those goods incurred (Ex. 22:7-15) unless, of course, it was not the fault of the custodian in the case.

Because the land and soil were so important to the nation's economy, there had to be carefully defined regulations relative to their use. For example, every seventh year the land was to lie fallow both to commemorate the creation of the universe in six days and to give the land a chance to be replenished with nutrients (Ex. 23:9-13). In addition, every fiftieth year was to be a year of jubilee in which nothing was to be planted; therefore, both the forty-ninth and fiftieth years would be years of rest (Lev. 25:1-24). One interesting law in regard to the crops in the fields states that one had the privilege of plucking grapes or grain from his neighbor's fields if he were only passing through. He could not, however, expect to do so with a sickle in his hand (Dt. 23:24-25).

Other stipulations have to do with the inheritance of property and the redemption of persons and goods. To prevent the development of a poor element in society if at all possible, a family's possessions, including land or real property, were to be retained by the family forever. This land was to be properly marked by boundary markers which were never to be removed by anyone (Dt. 19:14). In the event the property had to be sold for some reason, it must in any event be returned to the original owner on the year of jubilee, with the exception of property within city walls (Lev. 25:25-34).

Any Hebrew who had had to become indebted to another was automatically released of his debt on the seventh year, the year of release (Dt. 15:1-11). In case of either selling the family property or of personal indebtedness we may presume that there was the possibility of redemption; this was true of Hebrews who had sold themselves into indenturehood as well. If a man had sold his property, it could be repurchased for him by his next of kin who would pay what it was worth less the amount for the remaining years until jubilee (Ruth 4:1-8). In other words, if the property had remained in the hands of the purchaser for twenty-five years, the next of kin would have to pay only half as much as the original price because the purchaser had had the use of it for half the jubilee period. If no one was able to redeem it or did not care to, the land would return to the original owner in the year of jubilee without cost to him. The use the purchaser had had of it for the preceding years was considered equal to the amount he had paid for it in the beginning. The year of jubilee was in effect throughout the entire land, so whenever and wherever property was sold the price was in proportion to the number of years left until the next jubilee (Lev. 25:25-34). The same principle of redemption applied to the release of Hebrews who were servants of foreigners living in the land. But they did not go out in the year of release though they could in the year of jubilee. If at any time in the course of servitude a next of kin desired to purchase the freedom of a servant, he paid a price commensurate with the number of years of servitude left until the year of jubilee and also in line with the original sale price (Lev. 25:47-55). As a whole, every effort was made to maintain personal independence and to guarantee possession of family property from generation to generation. Special consideration was given even the women who were able to inherit their father's goods if they had no brother who could do so (Num. 27:1-11; 36:1-10).

If a man died and left no children, his widow must marry one of his brothers and any children produced from such a marriage would be considered heirs of the deceased brother (Deut. 25:5-10; cf. Luke 20:27-40). We may assume, of course, that the second brother did not already have a wife of his own and that not all of the children born of the second marriage would be considered the posterity of the deceased.

Otherwise it seems that the law would be sanctioning bigamy on the one hand and a callous disregard for the desire of a man to have his own family on the other. The example of Judah and Tamar, which we have already discussed (Gen. 38), is most helpful in demonstrating the application of this "Levirate" law. Also, there are many allusions to the practice in New Testament literature. The case of Ruth and Boaz suggests that it was permissible for the widow (Ruth) to marry the next of kin outside the immediate family (Boaz) if there were no other male within the family proper.

Even kings must be guided by the Law, for in the Theocracy no one was exempt from its authority (Deut. 17:14-20). This meant that there must be justice in the courts (Deut. 16:18-20; 19:15-21; 24:16; 25:1-3), and that due respect must be had for authority of all kinds (Ex. 22:28; Dt. 17:8-13). One point of special interest in the administering of justice is that anyone hanged must be removed from the gallows before sunset of the execution day (Dt. 21:22-23). This reminds us of the removal of the body of Christ from the cross on the same day in which He was crucified (Jn. 19:31). The sense of justice extended even into the realm of warfare, where there were clearly spelled out principles of behavior toward the enemy (Dt. 20; 23:9). There were further regulations regarding the treatment of friendly aliens (Dt. 23:3-8).

In every society there are certain undesirable elements, and ancient Israel was no exception. These individuals were subject to the law in a very drastic manner, however, and persons such as witches (Ex. 22:18; Lev. 19:31; 20:27; Dt. 18:9-14), false prophets (Dt. 13:1-5; 18:20-22), and leaders in heresy (Dt. 13:7-18; 17:2-7) were dealt with very harshly. Such matters as transvestitism were especially singled out for condemnation (Dt. 22:5, 12).

Finally, there were numerous miscellaneous laws, some partially covered elsewhere, which had to do with the treatment of one's fellow man (Lev. 19:11, 13, 15, 17-18; Dt. 22:1-4, 8; 24:6, 10-13) and even with the kind treatment of animals (Dt. 22:6-7; 25:4). There were very few areas of life, indeed, which were not at least touched upon by Mosaic civil law. Had they been followed faithfully Israel would have had a most well-managed society, but the ideals herein embraced were usually badly neglected, especially in Israel's later history.

Ceremonial Law. The remainder of Mosaic law had to do with the more religious or ceremonial aspects of life, including the ritual of the cultus, though this last will be discussed separately because it is so important and also detached from the everyday life of the common people. Chief among such laws would be those dealing with the worship of God only and the rejection of idols and false gods (Ex. 20:2-11, 22-23; 22:20; 23:24, 32-33; 34:12-17; Lev. 9:4; 20: 1-6; 26:1; Dt. 4:14-24; 7:25-26; 11:16; 16:21-22). Also important was the stipulation that the proper place of worship was at the tabernacle (Dt. 12:1-14), though there was also the permission to worship wherever God had "placed His name" (Ex. 20:24-26); presumably that meant that the tabernacle was the central shrine to which all Israel must come for special occasions, but that in Canaan there would be the possibility of worshiping God in other places for ordinary occasions.[6]

Besides the Sabbath, which must be meticulously observed (Ex. 31:12-17); 34:21; 35:2-3; Lev. 19:30; 26:2), there were certain days of special religious importance. One day of every month was honored by a Feast of the New Moon, this probably being the first day (Num. 28:11-15). There were also seven stated feasts of the year, three of these necessitating a convocation of at least all the adult males of the land to the tabernacle. These three were the Feast of Unleavened Bread (Ex. 12; 23:15; 34:18-20; Lev. 23:5-8; Num. 9:1-14; Dt. 16: 1-8), the Feast of Harvest or Pentecost (Ex. 23:16; 34:22; Lev. 23:15-21; Dt. 16:9-12) which came fifty days later, and the Feast of Tabernacles or Booths, which came on the fifteenth day of the seventh month (Ex. 23:16; 34:22; Lev. 23:34-44; Dt. 16:13-15). In conjunction with the Feast of Unleavened Bread was the Passover, which actually inaugurated it (Ex. 12); at the time of the Feast of Tabernacles was the Feast of Trumpets on the first day of the seventh month, the Day of Atonement on the tenth day, and the week-long Feast of Ingathering which began right after the Feast of the Tabernacles on the fifteenth day. There were seven festal observances in all, then, grouped for the most part around the spring Feast of Unleavened

Bread and the autumn Feast of Tabernacles. The only exception was the Feast of Weeks which came in the third month or summertime.

The purpose of the spring feasts has already been discussed, and the Day of Atonement will be at a later point. The Feast of Weeks celebrated the harvesting of the early crops, usually barley. The Feast of Trumpets announced the commencement of the autumnal festal season; the Feast of Tabernacles, the week following which the people dwelled in rude huts in the fields, reminded Israel of the deprivations of their forebears who had lived in such dwelling in the wilderness; the Feast of Ingathering was for the purpose of celebrating the final harvest of the year. The critics have tried unsuccessfully from time to time to attach pagan Canaanite ideas to the origin of these various feasts. There is no evidence to prove, for example, that the Feast of Tabernacles was derived from a nature cult which met at that time of year to induce the forces of fertility to fructify the soil for the coming year. Nor can it be established that the Feast was only a modified New Year's celebration taken over from the Canaanites and other Near Eastern peoples who usually began their year in the fall.[7] We have no reason to doubt that the feast served the very purposes outlined in the Old Testament.

The personal lives and habits of the people, though in a sense incorporated within civil law, also had very perceptible religious overtones. There were principles of separation which were to remind Israel that it was a chosen people, a nation that was to separate from all others. Even in such matters as plowing with two different animals or wearing garments of mixed fabric there were strict requirements (Lev. 10:9-11; 11; 19:19; 20:25; Num. 19:1-10; Dt. 14:3-21; 22:9-11). There were also regulations of a hygienic nature which dealt with the purification of women (Lev. 12), detecting and curing of disease (Lev. 13-15; Num. 5: 1-4; Dt. 24:8), and uncleanness in general (Num. 19:11-22; Dt. 23:1-2, 10-14). The eating of certain foods besides those considered unclean for sacrifice was subject to legal definition as well (Ex. 22:31; Dt. 12:15).

Many Israelites, particularly the priests and Levites, dedicated themselves to God as lifetime servants, and others such as the Nazarites would enter into limited periods of service or devotion. For each case there must be definite procedural policies in the undertaking, maintenance, and cessation of such relationships. The priests, all of whom must be of the family of Aaron, were consecrated to their holy office by a very significant ceremony and in accordance with well-defined regulations which we have already discussed (Ex. 29:1-37; Lev. 8). There was one high priest and eventually, we assume, several thousand regular priests in Canaan. They had to observe ceremonial washings (Ex. 30:17-21), careful instructions in the making of ritual ointments and incenses (Ex. 30:22-38; Lev. 24:1-9) and exacting standards within their family and social lives (Lev. 21:1-22:13; Num. 18:8-19; Dt. 18:3-5).

The Levites were a quasi-clergy whose main function was to assist the priests, maintain the place or places of worship, and look out for the general well-being of the nation's spiritual life. It will be remembered that God had demanded that the first born of each family in Israel was to be given to Him as a token of gratitude for His having saved the nation from Egypt and from the death of the firstborn there. Later this was modified to permit the tribe of Levi to substitute for the firstborn of the remaining tribes, one Levite for one firstborn (Num. 3:5-36, 40-51; 4:1-33; 8:5-26; 18:20-32; Dt. 18:1-2, 6-8). In the event there were not enough Levites to match the number of firstborn, the remaining firstborn could be redeemed from service to God through payment of money.

One could become a Nazarite ("separated one") by making a vow to God that he would not shave his hair, touch a dead body, or drink any fruit of the vine or any intoxicating drink of any kind (Num. 6:1-21). There was no requirement that one make such a vow, but if a man or woman felt a special sense of gratitude or love to God for one reason or another, he could voluntarily assume the deprivation associated with being a Nazarite and for any length of time he wished. If he violated the terms of the vow in any way, however, he was required to begin the period of the vow all over again after he had made suitable offerings for cleansing. Samson and Samuel were two of the better known Nazarites, but their cases are unique in that they were made such through dedication by their mothers.

There were other vows besides the vow of the Nazarite in which objects, lands, and persons could be dedicated to Yahweh for varying lengths of time. When these objects of the vow were released from their obligation it was only at the price of a redemption payment which varied depending upon the object, the age of the individuals, and certain other factors (Lev. 27; Num. 30; Deut. 23:21-23). The first-born, the tithe on the crops and goods, and any other posses-sions which belonged to God automatically could not be devoted in a vow, for they were His without such a vow at all. Again, all such vows were purely voluntary and were made only as expressions of love and gratitude to God. Once under-taken, however, they must be carried through; any failure to do so would constitute an act of sin (Dt. 23:21).

Finally, there were miscellaneous instructions concerning the use of the land and crops at the arrival of the people in Canaan (Lev. 19:23-25), the payment of a religious tax or "ransom" annually (Ex. 30:11-16), special reverence for the Name and Person of God (Lev. 19:12), the disfigurement of their bodies in imitation of the heathen (Lev. 19:27-28; Dt. 14:1-2), and the eating of holy things (Lev. 22:15-16; Dt. 12:17-18, 20-28; 15:19-22). This last law had to do with the eating of materials offered in sacrifice either deliberate-ly or inadvertently. The only place where such food could be eaten was the place of offering, usually the Tabernacle. Later, when they settled in the land and the Tabernacle was too far away to make this practicable, they could eat their portion of the offering at home, provided they did not eat the blood which was sacred and belonged only to God.

Offerings and Sacrifices. There was a whole set of laws regarding the procedure of worship in Israel. God and Israel had entered into covenant; a place of worship, the Tabernacle, had been built; a priesthood and Levitical order had been established to represent the people before God. Now there had to be a means whereby Israel could express its religious devotion to God in an orderly, ritualistic fashion. This means was by offering to God something which one owned, the surrender of which would constitute a very real sacrifice. The need of man's heart has always been to express his devo-tion, thanksgiving, and love to God, and to find a means whereby his sins might be forgiven so that he might have unbroken fellowship with Him. All of this could be accomplished in the Old Testament via the offerings made from a heart full of faith. There was no salvation by the keeping of the Law, and no merit in the mere offering of one's goods to God; but when both were done in dependence upon God's grace and in a spirit of faith the worshiper could know the reality of the presence of God in his life.

Gustave Oehler has outlined quite well the content and purpose of Mosaic sacrificial ritual in his *Biblical Theology;* the following represents for the most part his study of the matter.[8] That offering was integral to Mosaic worship is easily seen when we consider all the passages devoted to it (Ex. 22:29-30; 23:18-19; 29:38-42; 30:7-10; 34:25-26; Lev. 1-7; 19:5-8; 22:17-33; Num. 15:1-31; 28-29; Dt. 14:22-29; 17:1; 26:1-15). We need now to consider briefly what could or could not be offered, how these materials were offered, and for what purposes.

There were bloody and bloodless offerings, the former, of course, being animal sacrifices and the latter vegetable or drink. Sometimes the vegetable offerings were made independently, but usually they accompanied the bloody offerings in one way or other. There were very strict rules in the selection of materials, both bloody and bloodless, and actually very few were qualified to be offered. Animals must be clean to be acceptable for sacrifice (Lev. 27:9, 11). This meant that of the large animals, only those which chewed the cud and had cloven hooves could be used (Lev. 11). Of water animals only those with both fins and scales were acceptable. Some twenty-two different birds were considered unclean, and so could not be offered or eaten (Lev. 11). Only the grasshopper of the small "animals" was suitable, and none of the so-called crawling animals such as the reptiles or amphibians were permitted. In addition, an animal, to be suitable for offering, must be domesticated.[9] It would hardly be a sacrifice in the true sense of the term for a man to hunt down wild game, which was not his anyway, and present it to God. This meant that a deer, for example, though it had cloven hooves and chewed the cud, could not be an offering. Also, an animal offering must be at least eight days old (Lev. 22:27), for only after eight days would an animal's chances for survival be guaranteed. It would hardly be a sacrifice, again, if one offered a new-born animal which might die shortly

anyway.   Finally, an offering animal must not be past its
prime of life (Lev. 9:3;   12:6;   Num. 28:3).   Usually this
amounted to about one year of age for a lamb and three for
a bull.   Besides representing the animal's greatest time of
value to the owner, the prime of life would preclude one's
sacrificing an animal so old that it would soon die a natural
death.

The vegetable offerings could consist of roasted corn,
flour, or unleavened cakes or loaves (Lev. 2).   These were
accompanied without fail by salt and usually also by oil and
incense (Lev. 2:13, 15).   It was prohibited to offer any kind
of leaven or honey, for these materials spoke of corruption.
The drink offering, which could be only wine, was also offered
in conjunction with other offerings.

The ritual of sacrifice was quite generally consistent, in
its main outlines, at least, no matter which kind of offering
was being performed.   The vegetable offerings were quite
simple, merely consisting of a presentation of the material at
the altar where it was burned (Lev. 2).   Drink offerings were
simply poured out upon and about the altar.   The animal offerings were more complex, however, and took the following
form.[10]   First the animal was led to the altar by the offerer.
Then the offerer laid his hands upon the victim's head, trans-
ferring himself thereby to the animal in a symbolical way.
Next the slaughter itself was accomplished, by the offerer in
a private service and by the priest in a public ceremony.   This
was usually performed by the slitting of the victim's throat.
When the blood had begun to flow, it was caught in a basin
and then sprinkled in various places, depending upon the
kind of offering.   Usually some was sprinkled on the altar
or its horns, toward the veil, upon various pieces of furniture
in the tabernacle, or, on the Day of Atonement, upon the
mercy seat in the Holy of Holies.   The reason for the use of
blood was that it might serve as an atonement (covering),
representatively covering the soul of the one making the offering.   Because in the Hebrew mentality blood was essentially equivalent to life, it was the life of the animal that was
covering the life of the offerer.   That guiltless life substituted
for the life of the sinful man who placed his faith in its
efficacy for hiding his sin.   The removal of sin is seen only
in the chasing off of the scapegoat on the Day of Atonement,
an event we shall discuss below.   After the proper applica-

tion of blood, the animal was burnt. The rising of the smoke suggested, perhaps, that the real essence of the victim was ascending to the presence of God who smelled its savour and was made satisfied in the act of sacrifice.

The various kinds of offerings should now be considered. The first of these was the simple burnt offering which was made twice a day at the tabernacle on behalf of all the people (Lev. 1). It was a sacrifice of devotion to God and consisted of a male lamb without blemish. On special occasions such as Sabbath, holy days, and feasts, the number would be increased to several lambs in both the morning and evening. The second type of offering was the Peace or Thank Offering which spoke of a peaceful relationship between God and the offerer (Lev. 3). It was not made to achieve a harmonious relationship between the two, but to denote the fact that all was well. In times of particular gratitude or special need one could offer a peace offering to God as an expression of love or as a supplicatory gesture. There was always a sacrificial meal with the peace offering with a strong possibility that the Hebrew thought of himself feasting at a common table with God. The fat, certain internal organs, and other choice parts of the sacrifice were burnt on the altar as God's portion. The breast and right shoulder were taken by the officiating priest who waved them horizontally and "heaved" them verticallly, in both motions indicating the presentation of them to both God and himself. The offerer, his family, the Levites who were present, and any poor who wished then sat down and consumed the remainder of the sacrifice. The priests and God already had been served their portions, that of God consisting of the burning of the choice parts.

The Trespass Offering was made by one who had been guilty of the infraction of a specific and clearly defined statute, whether this was concerned with only his neighbor or with God (Lev. 5). Only a ram could be used; no matter how rich or poor the offender might be, each had to make the same offering. This suggested that in point of law all were equal and all must make equal restitution. The choice parts of the ram were burnt and the priests consumed the rest. Naturally, one could not partake of the very offering which was atoning for his trespass, so the offerer received none at all.

The last of the offerings, the Sin Offering, was made for the establishment of a proper moral relationship with God (Lev. 4). There were three grades of offerings possible; one for the High Priest on the Day of Atonement and for the consecration of priest, one for the nation on the Day of Atonement and at festivals, and one for the ordinary Israelite whenever he felt the need. In the first class offering only a young bullock could be sacrificed. In the second class the victim was a kid of the goats. A goat or female lamb sufficed for the third class. The poor who could not afford a goat or lamb could offer a turtledove or pigeon, and those still poorer could offer only fine flour. If the offering were low grade, it was consumed by the priests; if first class, it was burned outside the camp except for the fat, which was burned on the altar.

One of the most important occasions of the year in Israel, and certainly a greatly significant religious event, was the Day of Atonement on which the entire nation was collectively atoned for (Lev. 16).[11] This ceremony, which formed a part of the autumnal convocation, followed a rather elaborate ritual the essential features of which are as follows. Early in the morning of the tenth of Tishri the high priest bathed himself completely and dressed in a garment all of white. He then slew a bullock at the great altar of burnt offerings. Next he carried into the Holy of Holies a censer filled with burning coals the smoke from which spoke of the prayer of the people. He then returned to the outer court to get the blood of the bullock which he carried into the Holy of Holies and sprinkled before the mercy seat. Following this, he returned once again to the outer court to slay the first of two goats which had been standing near by the altar. The blood of this animal was carried into the Holy of Holies and sprinkled on the mercy seat, thus atoning for the nation as the blood of the bullock had atoned for the priest himself. After this the blood of the two animals was mixed and sprinkled on the two altars and the interior of the Tabernacle, an act signifying the consecration of these sacred precincts for another year. The same blood was applied to the head of the other goat which, as the "scapegoat," was sent off into the wilderness without the camp bearing on his head the collective sin of the nation. In this manner the sin was not only covered, but also removed completely, at least for another year. Finally, the high priest bathed himself completely once again and changed back into his regular vestments.

Mosaic Law, then, with all its aspects and categories still was nothing more than the framework in which Israel expressed the fact that it was a covenant people and that it desired to worship the God who had called them and made of them a nation. The regulations, the statutes, the ritual—all were purposeful expressions of the covenant faith; though completely meaningless in and of themselves, they were absolutely indispensable for that people and at that time. They were not inventions of an ancient Semitic mind, but Divine revelation from their God.

THE TABERNACLE[12]

Though the Hebrews at a very early time realized fully that God could not and did not dwell in only one place at a time, they nevertheless came to see that He had chosen certain places above others as places where He might be found in a special way by His worshiping people. At first these places had been at altars and other simple shrines, later at Sinai itself, and now that the covenant had been given, in a portable tabernacle which could be carried on their journeys through the wilderness to Canaan. Once there, other arrangements would be made; by the time of Solomon, as we shall see, Yahweh's earthly dwelling place was in a massive Temple in Jerusalem. Eventually, even that was done away and, as Jesus said to the Samaritan woman, there would be no special place that would be considered as the proper place of worship (John 4:21-24). All dwellings then would be His as men worshiped Him in spirit and in truth. But until then, He would reside in a building made with hands, the Sinaitic expression of it being a tent made according to exact specifications.

The materials necessary for the construction of the meeting place are listed first (Ex. 25-30); then follows a description of the various pieces of furniture to be housed therein, beginning with the Ark of the Covenant. This latter was merely a chest-like box measuring some 45 x 27 x 27 inches and made of shittim wood (acacia) covered with a layer of gold. Its cover, known as the *kapporeth* ("mercy seat"), consisted of a slab of gold upon which rested two cherubim ("covering ones") who faced each other and whose wings touched over the Ark. In the corners of the Ark were rings through which gold plated staves could be passed enabling the Levites to carry it on their shoulders. The area directly above the Ark and between the cherubim was the immediate place of God's dwelling, the holy spot where settled the *shekinah* ("presence") glory of God. Within the Ark were the pot of manna and the tables of the Decalogue.

The table of showbread, also covered with gold, was 36 x 18 x 27 inches and contained rings in its corners so that it too, could be carried by staves. The main purpose of the table was to hold the bread, twelve loaves of which were to be baked every day as a symbol of God's abundant provision for Israel's material needs. There were, in addition, certain vessels of gold useful in the worship which were also set upon the table. Another object was the golden candlestick (actually a seven branched lampstand) which held seven oil lamps, one directly in the center and three on either side in a branch-like formation. There were joints in the branches made in the shape of flowers, the whole affair being most ingenious and artistic. The purpose for the candlestick was naturally to give light, but also to remind Israel that God was the source of the light of revelation.

The manufacture of the tabernacle itself is next described. It was to be 45 x 15 x 15 feet and divided into two rooms, the Holy Place and the Holy of Holies. The former was to contain the table of showbread, on the north side, and the candlestick, on the south side, while the latter housed the Ark of the Covenant. The dimensions of the Holy of Holies was 15 x 15 x 15 feet, constituting a perfect cube, while the Holy Place was 15 x 15 x 30 feet. The sides and rear of the tabernacle were made of thick planks stood on end and bound together by horizontal bars which connected them. They were secured at the bottom by being driven firmly into sockets of some kind. The top of the structure was covered by layers of various kinds of cloths and animal skins which draped down over the sides and back nearly to the ground. These coverings were interwoven in some cases into beautiful designs, whereas the purpose of others was merely utilitarian; to keep the elements out. The two rooms in the tent, for so it basically was, were separated by a curtain or veil suspended on a row of pillars. This veil was woven from four kinds of cloth—blue, purple, scarlet, and white (fine twined linen)—and contained embroidered images of cherubim. No one at all could go behind this veil except the High Priest, and he only on the Day of Atonement. The other priests could serve in the Holy Place. The ordinary Israelite was absolutely forbidden entrance to any part of the Tabernacle.

Other pieces of furniture were the altar of burnt offering, the altar of incense, and the laver. The altar of burnt offering was 7½ x 7½ x 4½ feet and was made of wood covered with a bronze grate to prevent it from being set a-fire. Conspicuous features of this altar were the horns which extended from every corner, horns like those of a bull and signifying strength and security. There were also rings in the corners of the altar so that it could be carried with staves. It was placed in front of the Tabernacle and was the center of all animal and vegetable sacrifice. The smaller altar of incense was located just in front of the veil in the Holy Place. It was sheeted over with gold and served the purpose of symbolizing prayer. As the smoke of the incense would ascend above the veil Israel would be reminded that God was accepting their prayer and would meet their needs. The laver was a wash basin placed directly in front of the altar of burnt offering. Its function was to contain the waters of purification with which the priests must wash their hands and feet before they could officiate at any of the Tabernacle services.

Surrounding the Tabernacle was the court, an open area one hundred fifty feet long and seventy-five feet wide. This court was encircled by a fence consisting of cloth hangings and standing seven and one-half feet high. There was one entrance to the court, an opening which was covered by a curtain of the same kind of cloth as the veil within the Tabernacle. Apparently the ordinary people were permitted in the court, but only in very small numbers because of its limited area.

There is no doubt that the Tabernacle and its furniture have great typical meaning, though this meaning can sometimes be more than what is justifiable.[13] For example, the showbread does remind us that Jesus was the Bread of Life and the candlestick typifies the fact that He is the Light of the world. The altar of burnt offering reminds us of Calvary where the Lamb of God died for the sins of the world, and the altar of incense is a type of prayer, even for the Christian. The veil, especially, is a type of the body of our Saviour, and it is striking that when His body was impaled upon the cross, the veil of the Temple at Jerusalem was torn in two, from top to bottom. The writer of Hebrews verifies this type when he declares that the veil, indeed, was representative of the body of our Lord (Heb. 10:20). To make every aspect typical of something in New Testament faith may be going too far, however, for the very nature of typology demands that it not be considered a type in the Old Testament if there is no clearly stated New Testament counterpart.

THE PRIESTHOOD

Of the three great institutions of the Theocracy—the Prophets, the Monarchy, and the Priesthood—the Priesthood was first in point of time. This is understandable because before Israel had ever settled in Canaan and had become a sedentary people requiring a king, its religion had already become well formulated. The prophets for the most part did not become numerous and prominent until the rise of the Monarchy, for they seemed to serve the function very often of keeping the kings "in line." Underlying the whole successive history of Israel was the religious or "cultic" substratum, an integral part of which was the order of priests.

We have already discussed the ceremony whereby Aaron and his sons were anointed to the priesthood after the giving of the instruction regarding the Tabernacle. From that day onward, only those of Aaronic descent could lay claim to the office of priest (legally), and the whole institution became hedged about with a great deal of regulation and meaning. The anointing, the dress, the function of the priest—all of these must be strictly according to the Law. For example, as far as the dress was concerned (Ex. 28) the principal piece of clothing was an *ephod,* an apron-like garment which hung down both the front and the back and which was joined at the shoulders only by shoulder pieces. Upon these shoulder pieces were placed two precious stones, one upon each shoulder, on which were engraved the names of the twelve tribes, six to each stone. This no doubt represented the fact that the priest bore upon his shoulders before God the responsibility for his people. On the front of the ephod was a breastplate which consisted of a square piece about nine by nine inches. To this were attached twelve precious stones arranged three to a row; they were engraved with the names of the tribes, one upon each stone. This may have suggested that the priest bore over his heart the concern for his people. In addition to these twelve stones in the breastplate, there were also two more, the stones of judgment. These were called Urim ("light") and Thummim ("uprightness") and were probably used by the priest as a kind of sacred lots or dice in determining the will of God in any particular matter (I Sam. 28:6; Ezra 2:63; Neh. 7:65). It seems that with the coming of seers and prophets the use of these stones diminished.

After the listing of various other pieces of clothing, Exodus 29 goes on to describe the process of consecrating a priest to his holy office. First, a bullock must be slain as a sin offering on behalf of the candidates who have placed their hands upon its head as a symbol of the transference of their sin to the victim. Next, a ram must be sacrificed as an act of consecration. Again the hands of the priests were placed upon the head of the animal which vicariously was dedicated to God on their behalf. The blood of the ram was taken and applied in order to the right ear, right thumb, and right toe of the candidates as an indication that they were consecrating their ears to hear the word of God, their hands to perform the will of God, and their feet to walk in the paths of righteousness.

Originally, only Aaron and his four sons were priests; under wilderness conditions this was sufficient, for they had, in addition, the assistance of the Levites who were, in a sense, lay ministers. Later, however, when Israel became more widely spread in Canaan and the exclusive use of one central sanctuary became impracticable, the number of the priests was increased eventually, perhaps to hundreds. Only the major services were then conducted at the Tabernacle or Temple, the lesser observances being regulated by the priests at the local shrines. The command that only the Tabernacle was to be the legitimate place of worship was obviously intended for the semi-nomadic life in Sinai and also for the three chief convocations of the year. Under later conditions a multiplicity of altars was not only permitted but authorized, though the precedence of a central place must always be understood.[14]

[1] D. Winton Thomas, *Documents From Old Testament Times*, London, Thomas Nelson and Sons, Ltd., 1958, pp. 27-28.

[2] Theophile J. Meek, *Hebrew Origins*, New York, Harper and Row, 1960, pp. 72-73. For the contrary view, see Erhard Gerstenberger, "Covenant and Commandmant," *Journal of Biblical Literature*, 53:50, March, 1965. For a discussion of the Law as a basis for the Covenant, see Meredith Kline, "Law Covenant," *Westminster Theological Journal*, 27:19 ff, November, 1964.

[3] George Barton, *Archaeology and the Bible*, Philadelphia, American Sunday School Union, 1937, p. 400.

[4] W. F. Albright, *From the Stone Age to Christianity*, Garden City, Doubleday and Company, Inc., 1957, pp. 268 ff.

[5] The avenger would be a member of the family of the deceased who was charged with the responsibility of taking the life of the murderer, though, of course, under the aegis of law and government. See Gustave Oehler, *Theology of the Old Testament*, Grand Rapids, Zondervan Publishing House, 1883, pp. 236-238.

[6] O T. Allis, *The Five Books of Moses*, Philadelphia, The Presbyterian and Reformed Publishing Company, 1943, pp. 178-184. For the view that the central sanctuary was a late development, see H. H. Rowley, *The Growth of the Old Testament*, New York, Harper and Row, 1963, p. 28.

[7] John Gray, *Archaeology and the Old Testament World*, New York, Harper and Row, 1962, pp. 107-108.

[8] Oehler, *op. cit.*, pp. 261-319.

[9] *Ibid.*, p. 269.

[10] *Ibid.*, pp. 274-283.

[11] *Ibid.*, pp. 309-319.

[12] For the critical view of the Tabernacle, see Frank M. Cross, "The Priestly Tabernacle," *The Biblical Archaeologist Reader*, Vol. 1, Ed. by G. Ernest Wright and David Noel Freedman, Garden City, Doubleday and Company, Inc., 1961, pp. 201-228. Cf. with this William C. Moorehead, *Studies in the Mosaic Institutions*, Dayton, W. J. Shuey, 1896, pp. 31 ff.

[13] See Gleason Archer, *A Survey of Old Testament Introduction*, Chicago, Moody Press, 1964, pp. 224-226.

[14] John Bright, *A History of Israel*, Philadelphia, Westminster Press, 1959, p. 147.

Chapter Six

CONQUEST AND CHARISMA

The Historical Background of the Period

Next to the story of Israel itself, which we will discuss in the course of this chapter, the nation whose affairs most interest us now is Canaan.[1] In the same breath we must hasten to say that this is not the account of just one nation, but many, for Canaan especially at this time was extremely fragmented and occupied by people with widely divergent backgrounds and interests. Most of these are listed in passages such as Joshua 9:1 where we read of Hittites, Amorites, Canaanites, Perizzites, Hivites (Hurrians), and Jebusites, all living in the same land and in some cases quite intermingled. Yet, they did not form one single nation at any time, though under the threat of the Israelite invasion they coalesced from time to time.

Following the Hyksos domination of Egypt, these Semitic warriors had retreated up from Egypt into Canaan, especially the northern reaches, where at least some of them were assimilated into the native Canaanite populations. The rest we suppose moved even farther north and were gradually lost to history as any kind of entity. With the impetus given them by this Hyksos accretion, the Canaanites (to use the general term for all the native population from as early as 3000 B.C.) became a greatly strengthened people who would no doubt have exercised larger influence than they did if Egypt had not so rapidly recouped after 1580 B.C. Especially under Ahmose I the Egyptians began to penetrate into the Fertile Crescent until they had annexed Palestine as early as 1550 B.C.[2] The Canaanites, therefore, became Egyptian vassals and remained so, at least theoretically, until the time of the Hebrew Mon-

archy 450 years later. Yet the hegemony of Egypt was ex-
ceedingly loose throughout much of this time; it is with no
surprise that we read little or nothing of Egypt in the Books
of Joshua and Judges.

The primary factor contributing to this state of affairs
was the reign of Amenhotep III and especially that of his successor, Amenhotep IV. These two kings, who lived near the
end of the illustrious Eighteenth Dynasty, witnessed the beginning of its demise, largely caused by their own inefficiency.
The government of Palestine was in the hands of scores of
petty "kings" who were answerable to Egypt, but who, it
seems, received very little help from Egypt. This is seen
especially in the Tell el Amarna Letters, to which reference
has already been made. When the 'Apiru (Hebrews) invaded
Canaan at the beginning of the fourteenth century under
Joshua's leadership, the various vassal kings under attack
wrote to both Amenhotep III and IV requesting their aid, but
because of other matters which occupied their attention these
two kings paid little heed.[3] The former was apparently concerned with his relationships with the Mitanni, a recently
friendly and powerful force at the headwaters of the Euphrates, while the latter was experimenting with a monotheistic philosophical concept which he had helped to develop.

Another reason that Egypt figures so slightly in the Biblical account of the period is that the Canaanite populace
under its jurisdiction lived primarily in the plains of Palestine,
whereas the Israelites occupied the hills. There was actually
very little contact between the Canaanites and Hebrews, except for that initial confrontation recorded in both the Book
of Joshua and the Tell el Amarna Letters, and that was un-
affected by Egyptian interference. By the time the Israelites
had encountered the Canaanites again on a large scale, in the
time of Deborah, Egypt was safely out of the way because of
the Hittite threat from the north. The one time that Egypt
did regain effective control over Palestine was in the beginning of the reign of Rameses II (1290-1224), but during this
long reign the Hittites drove the Egyptians south or at least
contained them in Palestine where the latter maintained only
a shaky rule.

The Mitanni, whom we mentioned above, came to prominence in the early fifteenth century B.C., for some time exercising primary control of Upper Mesopotamia. In fact they

were such a threat to Egypt that the two nations warred almost continually throughout the fifteenth century. About 1400 B.C. the Hittites began to push eastward and engaged the Mitanni in conflict with the result that the latter nation was forced to turn to Egypt for help. Relations between the two peoples became so good that Amenhotep III even married a Mitannian princess, but the Hittite menace ended this period of peace. By 1370 the Hittites had occupied Mitanni and became neighbors with Egypt in Syria.[4] Both countries were concerned with internal matters for a few years, during which time Israel accomplished much of its conquest of Canaan, but finally hostilities broke out again between them. Rameses II, as we have seen, tried to restore Egyptian suzerainty over the whole area, but the Hittites proved too much for him. Nevertheless, the Hittites could not occupy or even be concerned much with Palestine either because of their problems with the newly aroused Assyrians and other powers to the north and west. Thus, Palestine lay wide open for Hebrew conquest throughout the fourteenth and thirteenth centuries, a situation accounted for only by God's gracious ordering of the times.

The Hittite Empire collapsed ca. 1200 B.C., in the time of Gideon, and the Assyrians who gained the ascendancy[5] had been increasing in influence from ca. 1300 B.C. With the overthrow of the Hittites they encountered very little resistance from any source. The end of the Nineteenth and all of the Twentieth Dynasties in Egypt were powerless to resist Assyria and, in fact, could not even interfere in Palestine. Yet, in its infancy Assyria was unable to press any farther south than northern Syria, so once again, as in the preceding century, Palestine remained aloof from the great powers all through the period from 1200-1100. But another force must be reckoned with, and that is one which is emphatically described in the Bible. At about 1200 B.C. the Palestinian coast, especially in the south, was settled by the Philistines who had recently come from Asia Minor and Egypt, but originally from the Aegean.[6] There had been Philistines there from much earlier days (Ex. 13:17), but their numbers were now greatly augmented. It was they who threatened Israel in the days of Samson, especially (ca. 1075 B.C.), and who almost extinguished God's people later on in Samuel's day (ca. 1050).

Not until David's Jerusalem reign was Israel able to overcome them and reduce them to tributaries.

The Babylonians during all this time were slumbering in their Dark Ages under the domination of various peoples from the north and east; only sporadically did they show any strength, and then not in any way that affected the settlement of Israel in the Land of Promise.

With this historical sketch, as limited as it must be, we can see more readily that the stage of the Near Eastern world was set for the momentous event of Israelite conquest and settlement. The great powers, beset with conflicts between themselves and with problems within, had little time to be concerned with the migration of a band of desert peoples into so insignificant a place as was Palestine at that time. The many small city states within its borders, disunited as they were and confined largely to the plains, could offer little concerted opposition to Joshua's invaders. Only the Philistines, and occasionally the surrounding little nations such as the Ammonites, Moabites, and Midianites whom God raised up for the purpose, could and did provide a means of chastening His people in their hours of unbelief. At no other time before or since could the Hebrew tribes accomplish the Divine objective in Canaan.

THE CONQUEST (Joshua 1:1-Judges 3:7)

Preparations (Joshua 1:1-5:15). Moses died about 1406 B.C. and the conquest of the promised land of Canaan commenced immediately thereafter. Joshua, the newly appointed leader of Israel, must have reflected very carefully on the weighty responsibility that was now his, and perhaps with great trepidation he viewed the prospects of what lay ahead. Moses, his mentor and example, was no more; that fact in itself was sufficient to create in Joshua a feeling of inadequacy. Yet, this moment for which the nation had hoped for nearly forty years was here, the moment when they would finally occupy in reality the land which had been guaranteed to their forefathers hundreds of years earlier, the promise of which had only recently been reaffirmed to them. Joshua knew what he must do, but would he have the courage and resourcefulness to do it?

In the midst of his dilemma God spoke to Joshua and instructed him to set out for the inheritance, reassuring him that He was with him every step of the way even as He had been with Moses. To guarantee the continuance of the Divine presence, Joshua and Israel must saturate themselves in the Law of Moses so recently given to the nation. They knew that God must work in a very special way at this time, for the command to cross the Jordan and enter the Plains of Jericho would otherwise be precluded by the flooding Jordan, for this was the spring of the year, the time of barley harvest, when the melting snows of the Lebanons came plunging down the Rift Valley sweeping all before it (Josh. 3:15). Ordinarily the river at this place could be crossed only in the late summer, but the immediacy of the command of God meant that the impossible must be accomplished now as it had been at the Red Sea exactly forty years earlier to the very month.

Apparently Joshua's strategy was quite well in mind for some time before the attempted crossing, for he sent out some spies to Jericho, the city which guarded the pass from the Jordan Valley to the Central Highlands to the west. He recognized the absolute necessity of first subduing this fortress, both to allow his forces to proceed past it and to prevent any Canaanite threat from the rear after he had moved to the interior of the land. These two spies stealthily mapped out the strengths and weaknesses of the ancient city, but nearly at the cost of their lives for their presence was soon detected. Only through the bravery of a certain harlot of the city, Rahab by name, were they able to escape and carry their intelligence back to Joshua at Shittim. This courageous act on her part elicited from the spies a promise that she would be spared the wrath of Israel when the city was sacked (Josh. 2:8-22). Far more rewarding than this was the fact that this infamous woman was brought into the covenant family, by God's grace, becoming the ancestress of King David and of Messiah Himself (Ruth 4:18-22; Matt. 1:5).

Once the spies' report was digested and tactical decisions had been formulated, Joshua commanded the people to form a line of march and make their preparations to cross the river. The priests, bearing the Ark of the Covenant, were to proceed first, and the nation would follow at a distance. The faith involved in such an action is difficult to visualize, but perhaps with the memory of the Exodus still in their minds, the people

stepped forward in ready obedience. When the priests' feet
barely touched the edge of the raging flood, it ceased its flow
and stood "in a heap" several miles up the river at Zaretan,
in repetition of the Exodus miracle. Some would suggest that
an earthquake caused the high limestone cliffs of the Ghor to
slide into the Jordan where it narrows at Zaretan, thus
causing the waters to be dammed up. Other occurrences of
this nature are cited from history.[7] This, of course, is a
distinct possibility, but it must be kept in mind that appearance of an earthquake at precisely the moment when it
was needed is no less a miracle than any other way of stopping
the river. Furthermore, the Scripture states, as though deliberately, that the priests and people passed over the Jordan
on *dry* ground, not through puddles or mud as one would ordinarily expect following a natural event such as an earthquake.

Once the passing had been successfully completed, Joshua
commanded that twelve stones be taken from the river bottom
and piled in a heap on the western side of the river as a memorial of the miraculous passing. Likewise, a heap of stones
was placed in the middle of the river as a testimony of God's
miraculous power on behalf of His people (Josh. 4:1-9). This
crossing, like that of the Exodus, was to be a reminder to all
generations to come that Israel was a redeemed people, a people with a special redemptive mission. This done, the Israelites were circumcised, the rite having been neglected in the
wilderness, and they celebrated the Passover. How fitting
that the tokens of both the Abrahamic and Mosaic Covenants
should be enacted here and now, just as Israel reached its
promised destination! And how singularly appropriate that
these were followed almost immediately by the appearance of
the Captain of the Lord's Host, who reminded Joshua that this
new land was holy ground (Josh. 5:15). The nation then encamped at Gilgal, a site which remained their base of operations for several years.

The Central Campaign (6:1-10-10:14). There is no question that the city of Jericho was strongly fortified and that
under ordinary circumstances could easily withstand a siege
of several years. The walls were high and thick, the access
to the city was most difficult because of the steepness of the
slopes of the ancient mound, and there was a plentiful supply
of water within the enclosure. Special means must be under-

taken, then, if Joshua was to take the city with a minimum of time and effort. For the second time in a very few days, Joshua ordered the people to form a strange line of march and to prepare to walk around the mound of Jericho once each day for six days and seven times on the sabbath. He commanded the priests to blow their trumpets all this time, and especially instructed the people to shout with a loud cry once the thirteenth circumvention had been made. Following this, they were to annihilate the population of the city, retaining nothing of the material goods, for both population and spoil were "accursed." This means that everything and everyone in the city were objects of God's special wrath because of their idolatrous propensities which would occasion Israel's downfall if they were permitted to remain alive. In technical language, Jericho was under the *cherem* ("ban") of God, and must be devoted to Him in extermination. Israel was waging "holy war."[8]

The results which Joshua anticipated resulted, for at the shout of the people, the walls fell down "under it"; that is, down the slopes of the mound (Josh. 6:20). There is no point in explaining this miracle as another perfectly timed earthquake, or a result of the shock produced by thousands of people marching in precise cadence, or by assuming a wall-shattering note from the trumpets of the priests.[9] These are hardly possible from a scientific standpoint unless, as in the case of the crossing of the river, one wants to understand any one of these as the means which God used at the necessary moment to carry out His purposes. In this case, the miracle is not diminished one iota. Though the remains of the wall from this period are disputed at the present, Garstang, at least, feels that he has located them; he offers fairly convincing proof that these walls, dating from the end of the fifteenth century B.C., did indeed fall outward.[10] This is remarkable when we consider that in ordinary warfare we would expect the walls to fall inward beneath the blows of the battering rams and other instruments of war extant in that period. Only one part of the wall was spared, that on which rested the house of Rahab, unless we maintain that Rahab and her family had been brought out of the city before the walls collapsed, a possibility allowed by the text. Finally, the entire city was burned and everything destroyed according to the commandment of the Lord (6:24).

Tragically, there was one man who presumed to disobey the clear will of God in this matter of the *cherem*. Achan ben Carmi, in the midst of the tremendous conflagration, saw certain items of value in Jericho which he could not resist. Greedily he took them to his tent, buried them beneath its floor, and kept the whole matter a secret. When Israel attempted to take the city of Ai, however, their sound defeat revealed to them that someone had incurred Divine displeasure. This small city, possibly a military garrison attached to the city of Bethel,[11] was able to repel 3,000 Israelite troops and kill about thirty-six. In the wake of the overwhelming victory over Jericho so recently, this reversal was particularly bitter. Joshua fell upon his face before God in supplication asking the reason for the defeat by such inferior forces. God responded by revealing to Joshua the means whereby the guilty party might be exposed. Achan, realizing that all was lost, confessed before Joshua that he had broken the terms of the *cherem* and taken that which was rightfully devoted to God alone. The whole affair resulted in the death of Achan and his family, who no doubt were aware of what he had done but who had collaborated by maintaining silence (7:22-26).

Once the matter was cleared up, a second siege against Ai proved successful thanks largely to a clever system of ambuscades. The city was reduced to a ruin and the king hanged. Apparently the elimination of Ai paved the way for an effortless conquest of the central hill country of Canaan, for we next learn that Israel assembled together at the ancient and sacred site of Shechem.[12] There between Mt. Ebal and Mt. Gerizim Joshua built an altar at the place where Abraham had built one many centuries earlier. In obedience to the dying instructions of Moses the nation listened to the law and the blessings and curses associated with their destiny as the chosen people (8:32-35). The fact that Israel met no opposition in the central hills is not to be explained by the fact that there were already tribes related to them who had lived there for many generations and who now gladly welcomed their invasion. Rather, it seems more likely that there were very few people living in this area at all, a point established by the archaeological evidence.[13] The Canaanites, we must remember, concentrated along the coastal areas and the plains; in the central hills especially we would expect Israel to have very little contact with them.

This was not so true for the hills south of Ai, however, for there were concentrations of peoples known in the Old Testament as Amorites. These peoples, when they heard of the success of Israel, banded together to resist the encroachments of these savage nomads (9:1-2). One enclave, however, that at Gibeon, decided that the odds were on the side of Israel and that the only wise course was to join the enemy (9:3-15). This could not be done easily, they realized, because Israel's stated policy was to not make alliances with the enemy. With ingenious subtlety they sent ambassadors to Gilgal, Israel's first permanent settlement in Canaan; the envoys, wearing worn-out clothing and shoes and bearing moldy bread, feigned to be from a distant land and, therefore, not subject to the law against alliance. Gullibly Joshua and the elders accepted the story and swore to maintain peace with the strangers. When the plot was divulged three days later Joshua was helpless to punish the Gibeonites, for the pact was inviolable, but he immediately placed them in bondage. Regrettably, even though in ignorance, Israel had made a union with some of the people of the land, a union which would plague them in days to come (II Sam. 21:1-9).

When the Amorites learned of the new alliance between Israel and Gibeon, five of their kings led their city-states— Jerusalem, Hebron, Jarmuth, Lachish, and Eglon—against Gibeon as a retaliatory move (10:1-5). Under the terms of the mutual assistance treaty Israel was obligated to come to Gibeon's aid which they did after a forced march overnight from Gilgal to the Valley of Aijalon, just west of Gibeon. The Amorites were no match for the hosts of the Lord and they fled to the west down the valley. By way of direct supernatural assistance, the Lord cast down huge hailstones from heaven upon the fleeing hordes. Moreover, in answer to the prayer of Joshua, He permitted the day to lengthen in order that the grisly task might be completed by the light of day. The best explanation for the miracle seems to be that God simply arrested the universe *in toto*, thus permitting the heavenly bodies to maintain their proper interrelationships. There are traditions from other parts of the world which speak of a long day or long night (as the case would be on the opposite side of the globe from Palestine), but there are no evidences that the world has ever "gained" or "lost" a day or any part thereof. Yet, to state that all we have here is Joshua's overactive imagination or a peculiar refracting of the sun's rays which produced the illusion of a longer day[14] is incongruous with the clear statement of the text which says plainly that "the sun stood still in the midst of heaven, and hasted not to go down about a whole day" (Josh. 10:13).

The Amorite kings, thoroughly routed, fled to Makkedah in the Judaean Shephelah where they hid themselves in one of the numerous caves in the region. When Joshua learned of their whereabouts, he left Gilgal once more and went to Makkedah and found the cave of refuge. He summarily dragged forth its pitiful inhabitants and just as summarily hanged and buried them in their erstwhile hiding place. Israel then struck deep into the South and in a series of brilliant campaigns, in which they apparently met only token resistance, conquered all the towns of any importance. That this onslaught did not result in the control of the populace, but only its temporary subjugation, is clear from the fact that a very short time later these same towns continued to resist Israelite ambition and settlement (Jud. 1:1-21).

Northern Campaign (Joshua 11). With the northern and southern parts of the land cut asunder by Israelite control of the central hills and valleys and with the further devastation of the south, there is little wonder that the northern Canaanite populations were becoming fearful for their existence. With determined organization they welded themselves into a vast federation consisting of city-states stretching from the Valley of Jezreel in the south to the headwaters of the Jordan in the north and from the Mediterranean on the west to the slopes of Hermon on the east. Their leader, Jabin of Hazor, gathered them at the waters of Merom, just to the east of his great city. There, with all their chariots and other might and advanced weapons of war, they awaited the Israelite invasion. Having been assured of God's promise of victory, Joshua marched north, met the Canaanites on their own ground, and administered to them a crushing defeat. Hazor itself, a city of perhaps 40,000 people, was burned to the ground while the remaining cities of the coalition were left "standing on their mounds," (Josh. 11:13) a fact, incidentally, which has been thoroughly substantiated by archaeology.[15] All of Canaan now had felt the strength of Israelite conquest, and except for pockets here and there, especially in the plains and along the southern coast, everything theoretically was in Israelite hands. Just how theoretical this was is revealed in the subsequent chapters of Joshua and all through Judges where the unmistakable impression is that any land seizure was only temporary at best and had to be repeated many, many times. Not until David, or certainly Saul, did Israel come anywhere near occupying the territory which was theirs by promise. Almost without exception the tribes were unable to retain the areas which had without doubt fallen to Israel at least during this initial conquest recorded in Joshua 1-11.

Subsequent Attempts to Settle (12-22). After a summary of the conquests (chapter 12), we learn of the attempts by the various tribes to occupy the lands to which they had been assigned, either by casting of the sacred lots or some other means. An indisputable evidence of the failure of the original conquests is found in chapter 13 where a complete catalogue of unconquered lands is given. When he had thus outlined to the nation what their task was, Joshua proceeded to instruct the eastern tribes—Reuben, Gad, and Manasseh—about their inheritance in Transjordan. To Reuben he gave the land synonymous with Moab, just to the east of the Dead Sea. North of the Arnon River, the original land of Gilead, Gad was established. Its territory was to be bounded on the west by the Jordan, the east by Ammon and the Jabbok River, and the north by a line stretching from the southeast corner of the Sea of Chinneroth (Galilee). The area to the north of this and east of Chinneroth, formerly known as the land of Bashan, was assigned to one half the tribe of Manasseh. The other half, of course, had elected to settle on the west of Jordan with the remaining tribes.

In Canaan proper the first matter in the disposition of the land concerned Caleb who, because of his lifelong faithfulness to the Lord, had been promised an individual inheritance by Moses (Dt. 1:36). Joshua honored the agreement by assigning the area around and including Kirjath-arba (Hebron) to the old hero who promptly, in spite of the weight of eighty-five years, drove out the Amorites who had resettled the area following the original conquest. He next allotted Judah the region south of a line extending west from the northern tip of the Dead Sea, bounded on the west by the Mediterranean, on the south by a line from the southern end of the Dead Sea to

THE TRIBAL TERRITORIES

the River of Egypt (Wadi el-Arish), and on the east by the Dead Sea (Ch. 15). Included in Judah was the land of Caleb and also that of the Simeonites (19:1-9) who apparently had become so decimated by their slaughter in the Plains of Shittim (Num. 25:14) they were unable to claim an independent allotment.

To the north of Judah was the tribe of Ephraim whose borders were as follows: on the east, the Jordan; on the west, the Mediterranean; on the south, Judah; and on the north, the Kanah Valley and eastward. In other words, the southern part of the central hill country was the major part of Ephraim's holdings (Ch. 16). Just to the north was Manasseh. It bounded Ephraim on the south, the Mediterranean on the west, the Jordan on the east, and, apparently, the Valley of Jezreel on the north. At least it is clear that the inhabitants of this great plain could not be displaced by Manasseh and that Manasseh, therefore, was also restricted to the central hills and even there in a limited way (Ch. 17).

The allotment of Benjamin is next described. It, strangely enough, seemed to be carved out between the territories of Judah and Ephraim (18:11-28). At any rate, it extended from Jericho on the east to the Sorek Valley just west of Kirjath-jearim and north and south into parts of Ephraim and Judah. The principal thing is that the city of Jerusalem now became Benjamite, for the new boundary of Judah looped to the south of the city along the Hinnom and Kidron Valleys. Jerusalem was not inhabited by Benjamites, however, nor indeed by any Israelites until the time of David who made it his capital.

North of the Valley of Jezreel there were four more tribes. Zebulun was north of Mt. Carmel, east of the Mediterranean, and south of the Upper Galilean Hills. It reached to the east almost to the Sea of Chinneroth (19:10-16). To the south of it and north of Manasseh was the tribe of Issachar. It went to the Jordan on the east, to the foothills of Carmel on the west, and to the beginning of the Lower Galilean Hills on the northeast (19:17-23). Asher settled right on the Mediterranean, north of Zebulun and west of Naphtali. Its northern boundary was the Canaanite region known later as Phoenicia (19:24-31). Finally, just to the east of Asher and north of Zebulun and Issachar was the tribe of Naphtali whose eastern border was the Sea of Chinneroth and the Jordan. It reached in the north all the way to Dan (19:32-39).

The tribe of Dan was assigned a parcel of land cut from that of Ephraim. This unfortunate clan settled west of Ephraim and along the Mediterranean coast where the native Philistines proved too much for them and restricted them in a tiny area in the hills (19:39-48). In a desperate search for extra land the Danites moved from their assigned portion and migrated north of Naphtali to Laish, a sequestered territory of peaceloving peoples. They slaughtered the inhabitants, moved into their homes and fields, and renamed the place after their father, Dan. This event is described in more detail in the Book of Judges (17-18).

Joshua, also, received a portion, for he, like Caleb, had been promised a reward for his faithfulness. He requested, and obtained, a parcel of land in Ephraim and there he built his city, Timnath-serah (19:49-51).

The Levites had been told by Moses that they would not inherit a temporal land, but that theirs was a spiritual reward. Nonetheless, they lived in the flesh and needed a fleshly dwelling place, so the assignment of cities of the Levites was made (Ch. 21). These were forty-eight in number and were evenly distributed throughout the land on both sides of the river. It seems that others besides Levites could and did dwell in these cities, but Levites must dwell in no other than these. Evidently certain religious ceremonies and services which did not have to be performed at the tabernacle itself were carried on by the Levites in their various cities. The life of the Levite was not to be secular in any sense; he could not work with his hands in gainful employment. The only exception to this was that he might keep a few animals and raise a minimum of crops in the "suburbs" of the town, but only for his own use. Of these forty-eight Levitical cities, six were cities of refuge, three on the east of the Jordan—Bezer in Reuben, Ramoth-gilead in Gad, and Golan in Manasseh—and three on the west —Kedesh in Naphtali, Shechem in Ephraim, and Hebron in Judah. The purpose of these cities has already been discussed.

Lest the settlement of the tribes seem oversimplified, let us hasten once again to suggest that this was far from true. The boundaries and allocations just described were more often than not extremely idealistic and very seldom realized by any of the tribes. Judah was plagued by pockets of resistance within its borders and never was able to push to the Coastal Plain or into the Negev to the south (Jud. 1). Ephraim, though in the comparative safety and emptiness of the central hills, was nevertheless beset by the Canaanites, especially in the area around Gezer (16:10). Manasseh was so hard pressed by the Canaanites because of its nearness to the Jezreel Plain that though they brought many of them under tribute they were completely unable to drive them from the land. The Canaanite use of iron, particularly in their chariots, gave them a great advantage over the Israelites. The Book of Judges gives ample testimony that the four tribes north of Jezreel were harassed throughout their early history by the Phoenician Canaanites and other peoples (Jud. 4-5). The undesirable location of Dan which prompted its evacuation has already been mentioned. The situation was very discouraging on the whole and as long as Israel maintained its loosely federated amphictyonic society nothing better could be expected. It was not until the time of the monarchy three hundred years after the conquest that a measure of unity and stability was brought to Israel in its Canaanite environment.

This tendency for Israel to become disparate after its settlement in the various parts of the land is understandable in the light of the extremely fractured nature of its geography. There came to be actually four different communities of tribes, each with its own geographical, cultural, and linguistic peculiarities (Jud. 12:5-6), though, to be sure, these differences came about only gradually. First, the tribes east of the Jordan, both because of their isolation by the river and their tendencies to absorb culture of the people surrounding them, became vastly different in their outlook from the majority of the tribes, those to the west. These tribes feared such a result even very early, for before the men of the eastern tribes were allowed to go home after the Canaanite conquest they were solemnly warned to remain true to the Mosaic faith (Josh· 22:1-6). When they built an altar by the Jordan near Jericho, their motives were questioned by the western tribes and it was only with difficulty that they could persuade Joshua's messengers of the fact that the altar served purely a commemorative function.

The four tribes north of the Jezreel Valley, known later as the Galilee region, also became quickly independent of the mainstream of Israel. Though they must have observed the

annual feasts at the tabernacle as far as we know, they nevertheless seemed so preoccupied with internal affairs and with
defense from their ever present Canaanite neighbors that they
had little time for close contact with the south. The Valley of
Jezreel, which lay between them and the tribes to the south,
provided much more of a barrier between them than it did a
means of access.

Though Judah and the tribes of the central hills were
much closer in their relationships with each other than with
either of the other tribal groups, there was still a certain geographical separation between them; and from time to time
they were kept apart by Canaanites and Philistines who moved
into villages along their common border. There was always
some rivalry between Judah and her northern neighbors, a
rivalry which became full blown in the time of Saul and David
and again following the death of Solomon. All of these factors
tended to produce certain differences within Israel, though, to
be sure, their similarities more than outweighed them. Most
basic to their continued sense of unity was the cult itself, for
their recognition of a common God, a common law, and a common center of worship more than compensated for their lack
of physical and geographical cohesion, though even that com-
monalty of the spirit seemed to be endangered more than
once.

In the process of allocating to the tribes their inheritance
Joshua had selected a place where the tabernacle and ark
were to rest permanently. This had to be a place that was
central and, if possible, at or near a spot already sacred to
Israel's memory. Such a place was Shiloh (Josh. 18:1),
which, though apparently never occupied before, was close to
the famous cities of Bethel and Shechem and was also in the
central and relatively secure tribal area of Ephraim. After
having rested at Gilgal and possibly Shechem since the crossing of the Jordan, the ark finally found a home where it was
to dwell for over 300 years. To Shiloh all the tribes, both east
and west of Jordan, resorted for the annual pilgrimages and
other special occasions; Shiloh they recognized as the earthly
dwelling place of their God. More than any other factor this
served to maintain their unity until a king should come and
transform their entire national composition.

After the conquest had been completed, perhaps within
seven or eight years after the crossing of Jordan, Joshua sent

the two and one half eastern tribes—Reuben, Gad, and Manasseh—back to their wives and children in Transjordan. He
reminded them of their covenant with God and of their need
to assemble at the stated times at the central sanctuary at
Shiloh. They swore their allegiance, but had no sooner done
so and started for their homes when they decided to erect a
memorial altar by the brink of the Jordan. This alarmed the
western tribal leaders, for it seemed to be a breach of the law
which stipulated only one place of worship (Dt. 12:5; Josh.
22:19). A delegation was sent from Shiloh to investigate and
only after much protestation were the eastern tribes able to
convince their brethren that they were up to no mischief. They
built their monument and named it *ed* ("witness").

The closing years of Joshua's life witnessed the futile attempts of Israel to occupy its tribal allotments. By about the
year 1380, sensing that the end was near, the indefatigable
man of conquest gathered his nation about him and addressed
them in sacred convocation (Ch. 23). He first encouraged
them to continue in the will of God, but his encouragement
was interspersed throughout with warnings of the judgment
of God should they defect from that course. He next reminded
them, as they stood in the sacred precincts of the ancient altar
of Shechem, of their entire redemptive history from the call of
Abram to the present moment. He went on to declare that
Israel's responsibility as a result of God's past dealings was
to commit itself once again to the covenant relationship and to
choose God afresh over against the alternatives of false gods.
To lead the way Joshua declared his loyalty to God and vowed
that he and his entire household would serve Yahweh regardless of the consequences. With unanimity the people gave
their assent to the covenant terms. The words were written
down and the event was commemorated by the setting up of
a great stone at Shechem, a monument of witness which would
thenceforth speak of their covenant renewal. Upon the death
of Joshua, his body was entombed at Timnath-serah. In
fulfillment of Joseph's desires, his bones which had been
carried up from Egypt were also buried after these many
years at his family home at Shechem. Finally, Eleazar, son of
Aaron, passed away and his remains were placed in Mount
Ephraim. The record of these deaths and burials seems to
speak to us of the passing of an age. The formation and
settlement of the nation has become a *fait accompli*, at least

in general terms, and a new generation must now rise to perpetuate the glorious heritage of Israel.

Problems After Joshua (Judges 1:1-36). Admittedly, there is an historical problem at the beginning of the Book of Judges, for we find there accounts of the conquest which duplicate those given in Joshua and others which definitely follow that period. Yet, if we recognize that the first two chapters of Judges are not in chronological order most of the difficulties disappear. A possible reconstruction is as follows: Judges 1:1-8 discusses the events of Judah's conquest after the death of Joshua. Then, in verse 8 we learn that Jerusalem *had* been smitten, presumably before the death of Joshua. This means that verses 9 through 2:7 followed the destruction of Jerusalem under Judah but preceded the death of Joshua. The death is described in 2:8-9, as it had been in Joshua 24:29-30, and the passing of the elders contemporary with Joshua is also mentioned as it had been before. Then, after all this, we learn of the succeeding generations of Israel's history in a capsule form. 2:11-23 presents in almost a cyclic manner a preview of the period under the Judges, that entire era from Joshua to Saul. The people went after other gods, they were chastened by God through the instrumentality of foreign invaders, they repented, God raised up a deliverer (the judge), they enjoyed prosperity and freedom, they again went after other gods. Thus the period went on in almost monotonous regularity and as a whole can be written off as an era of failure for God's people.

In the lifetime of Joshua Israel had been unable to drive out their enemies and occupy the land. This was in spite of the presence of God and His stern rebuke at the mouth of the Angel of Yahweh, a rebuke which produced only momentary repentance. In clear language the Lord spoke, angrily denouncing Israel for its sin of breaking the covenant. The record tells us that "the Lord left those nations, without driving them out hastily; neither delivered he them into the hand of Joshua" (Jud. 2:23). The list of these nations is found in chapter 3 and is followed by the account of the first of the enemies of Israel who invaded and subjugated them.

CANAANITE RELIGION

The first sin of Israel following Joshua was inter-marriage with the native populace, a relationship strongly condemned in the Law. This was associated with the worship of Baal and Asherim ("sacred trees or poles" or "groves"), a worship which was carried on within a framework of sexual immorality of the basest sort.[16] Fertility cults were a rather common feature in the ancient Near East, but they reached their culmination in Canaan. They were formulated on the idea that the gods themselves were originally created by an act of reproduction on the part of the pristine forces of the universe and that everything living finds its origin in the same way. Its adherents believed that plants, animals, and men came about by the intercourse of the gods, and that to guarantee the continuance of life the gods must be entreated by ritual and sacrifice. Perhaps to encourage the gods to procreate and produce plant and animal life, the priests and priestesses of the cult would practice "imitative magic."[17] That is, they would engage in sacred prostitution in an effort to cause the gods to emulate their example. If the gods could be so induced there was every prospect for a successful agricultural year. Crop failures and other agricultural calamities were attributed to divine disfavor. The Canaanite ritualistic orgies were carried out either in a temple or in the shelter of green trees or groves which spoke of fertility. The goddess associated with reproduction was commonly known, therefore, as Asherah ("grove") or, plural, Asherim.

We should also at this point briefly discuss the Canaanite pantheon in general.[18] Over all there was a rather shadowy, nebulous figure known as El. He seems to have been most prominent in early Canaanite theology, but was gradually displaced by his son, Baal, though he did continue to exist as Father God. His wife was Asherah, the aforementioned goddess of fertility, who was also, strangely enough, thought to be the virgin goddess. Baal was actually the god who was most directly involved with mankind. The name means simply "lord," and it is most likely that it was originally only a title. Later on it came to be a proper name, but even then seemed to represent many deities or many manifestations of the same god. For example, as we have already seen there was a Baal at Peor in Moab (Num. 25:3). There was also a

Baal-berith (Jud. 9:4) and a Baal-perazim (II Sam. 5:20) and a Baal-zebub (II Kings 1:3) in addition to many others. Yet, there was a personal Baal of whom these were local representations or later expressions. According to some scholars this god had died and was resurrected, having achieved victory over the god of death, Mot.[19] The commemoration of this event was celebrated every fall at the new year's beginning, which coincided also with the time of the former rains. It was thought that the resurrection of Baal heralded the end of the dry, hot unproductive summer during which time Mot was in control, and the beginning of the lifegiving season of planting and growth signalled by the first rainfall of the year.[20] If rain did not come it was assumed that Baal could not escape from the underworld and that Mot had the upper hand. Perhaps in the drought of Ahab's time Elijah makes reference to all this when he taunts the prophets of Baal about Baal's absence at Mount Carmel, an absence which they would feel had caused the drought. When rain did come at Elijah's prayer, all the people could see that Yahweh and not Baal was the one who provided rain and all good things (I Kings 18). The sexual union of Baal and his sister-consort, Anath or Astarte, was held responsible for the rain and consequent fertility of the soil. Therefore, the New Year's festival was an especial time of immorality, for the priests and priestesses, and perhaps the laity as well, were involved in their gross rituals of invocation.

This was the situation, then, when Israel went after other gods and "committed whoredom." This was not merely a spiritual adultery, but one that was physical and actual and which brought Israel into the most heinous of sins. It was this religious background which explains the monstrous enormity of Israel's transgression in going after other gods and forsaking Yahweh.

THE JUDGES (JUDGES 3:8-16:31)[21]

The first oppressor which God raised up to bring Israel to its senses was Chushan-rishathaim king of Mesopotamia (Aram). This conquest must be dated about 1380 B.C. and lasted for eight years (3:8). In answer to their cry for deliverance God raised up Othniel, son-in-law of Caleb, to judge them and save them from their enemy. Because the term "judge" is somewhat misleading here, perhaps we should briefly discuss the judge and his responsibilities. There were at least twelve of them in all, some of whom were contemporaries, and they ministered down until the midst of the eleventh century. Their principal task seemed to be that of arbiter and governor, as the name implies, but they also had the responsibility of acting as military leader as the need arose. One essential prerequisite was that the judge, like the prophet, must be charismatic.[22] This means that he was not elected by the people, nor did he succeed his predecessor by family inheritance or appointment. He had to be chosen of God; the proof of the Divine selection was his being empowered by the Spirit to perform deeds otherwise impossible for mere men (3:10; 6:34; 11:29; 13:25). It seems fairly clear that very few if any of the judges wielded control over all of Israel at once. Rather, they must have been responsible for only very limited areas, in some cases over only a tribe or two. There were probably times during this era when there were no judges at all and other times when there were several at once. For example, it seems that both Jephthah and Samson judged at the same time, the former over Transjordan in the oppression of the Ammonites and the latter over Judah and surrounding area in the oppression of the Philistines. When there were no enemies, there were probably no judges or at least none who are mentioned in the Bible.

Ehud and Shamgar (3:12-31). Under Othniel's inspired leadership Israel regained its freedom from harassment and the land "had rest" for forty years. Then the cycle commenced again and about 1335 B.C. Eglon, king of Moab, attacked Israel and set up a provincial capital at Jericho. This presupposes a defeat of the eastern tribes, at least the tribe of Reuben (which, incidentally, had nearly disappeared from history by now), and suggests the strength of Moab. Again Israel cried out and again a judge was chosen, this time Ehud of Benjamin. By means of a clever ruse Ehud was able to personally assassinate Eglon; in the resulting fray Israel, after an eighteen year servitude, overcame her Moabite foe. Then followed a long time of peace lasting some eighty years and extending well down into the thirteenth century (ca. 1240 B.C.). Probably during this period there was some difficulty with the Philistines, but under the leadership of Shamgar ben Anath this was quickly stifled.

Deborah (Chs. 4-5). The next cycle involved the Canaanites who had become active in the north. Under their leader Jabin of Hazor (possibly a descendant of the Jabin of Joshua's time) they had accumulated a great host in and near the Valley of Jezreel, apparently under the command of a certain Sisera. Utilizing their 900 chariots of iron and other awesome instruments of war they kept northern Israel in bondage for twenty years. Finally, God spoke through His prophetess Deborah, a resident of Ephraim, and commanded her to select Barak of Kedesh-naphtali as the deliverer of His repentant people. When Barak refused to go to battle against the Canaanites without Deborah's presence, the courageous woman consented to go, but reminded Barak that the glory for the victory would not be his but would belong to a woman. Lest we be too harsh with Barak, let us remember that Deborah was the one blessed with the charisma and Barak wanted her to go with him only as a guarantor of the presence of God. 10,000 men of Naphtali and Zebulun rallied to the call of battle and led by Deborah and Barak they marched down the slopes of Mt. Tabor to meet Sisera's hosts in the Jezreel Valley. Against incredible odds, God's forces prevailed through their personal heroism and an assist from the Almighty Hand which caused a rain storm to come suddenly and fill the little River Kishon to overflowing. The chariots, the invincible weapon of the Canaanites, were bogged down in the mud and their crews had to flee for their lives on foot (Jud. 5:21). Sisera himself ran to the tent of a certain Kenite whom he thought he could trust, but when he fell asleep in his hiding place from sheer exhaustion, the lady of the house, whose sympathies obviously were with Israel because of common ancestry or other reasons, drove a tent peg through his temples. Thus Jabin and his forces were devastated by the weak hands of women, but divinely empowered women to be sure. The event was celebrated by Deborah and Barak in one of the most beautiful and stirring songs in the history of literature (Ch. 5).

Gideon, Tola, and Jair (6:1-10:5). The next judge of Israel, Gideon, lived near the beginning of the twelfth century at the time of the Midianite peril. For seven years these fierce desert tribesmen, the first to use camels as a common practice in warfare, overran the land, especially in the north.[23] The critical problem with these invaders was not so much military as economic because their animals threatened to devour the entire produce of the land and strip the country bare. In the midst of this crisis the Angel of Yahweh appeared to Gideon, son of Joash, a resident of the village of Ophrah in Manasseh (6:11). He instructed Gideon to assume the leadership of God's people in their hour of need, but Gideon protested that he was ill equipped for the task, being nothing more than a poor peasant from a poor family. Yet, he recognized the presence of Deity and hastened to make an offering upon a nearby altar. When the sacrifice was prepared the Angel touched it with his staff and fire leaped forth from the crude stone altar and consumed the sacrifice. Gideon fell prostrate before the Angel (who is synonymous with Yahweh again in this case) who assured him that he would not die for having seen the face of God. At this, Gideon built an altar at the spot and he named it Yahweh-Shalom ("Yahweh is Peace").

That night God ordered him to tear down the Baal altars of his father and to cut down the groves associated with them (6:25). With trusted accomplices he carried out the command and built in its place an altar to Yahweh. Upon this altar he sacrificed a bullock to God. His stealthy work was soon found out, however, and the devotees of Baal in the community went to Joash and demanded an accounting for his son's actions of desecration. Joash, probably not a very faithful Baalite (though he had named his son Jerub-baal originally), responded by asking the crowd why it was that Baal did not vindicate himself if his honor had been so much violated. This averted further action against Gideon, who proceeded to summon the standing armies of Asher, Zebulun, and Naphtali in addition to his own Manassehites. After proving the faithfulness of God by "putting out the fleece" he took in his hand the standard of battle and rushed to meet the Midianites in the Valley of Jezreel south of Mt. Moreh.

On the way God informed Gideon that his 32,000 man army was much too large, for in the event of victory Israel would claim success through its military strength and not through God's power. So Gideon permitted all who wished to return to their homes, an invitation which some 22,000 accepted readily. And still the army must be pared down. Gideon led his army to a brook nearby and observed as they drank in preparation for the battle. Of the entire host, only 300 were cautious enough in the face of surprise enemy attack to drink from their hands with upraised heads. The rest immersed their faces in the water and demonstrated their unreliability in emergencies. These Gideon also released. Now with a tiny contingent, which was in turn divided into three companies, he proceeded to the fray. He and his servant had previously overheard some of the Midianite soldiers discussing the impending Israelite invasion. From their place of hiding in the night they were encouraged by a dream which one of the Midianites had had and which he was relating to his companion. The dream virtually guaranteed Gideon success by predicting that the Midianite camp would be overturned; so without further ado Gideon made his charge. Never was a stranger assault made! Bearing only torches concealed in pitchers in one hand and trumpets in the other, the gallant 300 sallied forth. Suddenly, in the thick of the darkness the trumpets blared, the pitchers were shattered, and the brilliant light of the torches stabbed the blackness in all directions. Thinking they had been set upon by untold thousands, the Midianites began to strike out in all directions but succeeded only in decimating their own ranks until only a comparative handful were left. The kings of Midian fled to the east over the Jordan, but not until two were caught and executed. The other two eluded immediate capture thanks to the refusal of the citizens of Penuel and Succoth to divulge their whereabouts, but finally they were apprehended and the reluctant informers were severely chastened by Gideon (8:13-17).

The victory was so glorious in the eyes of Israel that certain leaders appealed to Gideon to proclaim himself king. This is the first reference we have to a clear desire for a monarch, though there may have been such wishes in the past. Gideon refused the offer, acknowledging that God was their King, but he did make a richly decorated ephod which, because of its association with Gideon, became an object of religious devotion and, hence, a "snare" to Israel. Apparently Israel was preserved from enemies all the rest of the life of Gideon, but on the whole the spiritual situation was less than desirable.

Gideon himself married many wives who bore many children, a fact that was to prove grievous in Israel's national life.

After Gideon died (ca. 1150 B.C.) his illegitimate son, Abimelech, who hailed from Shechem, went to his native city, stirred the people up to make him king, and slew the seventy sons of Gideon, his half brothers. One of the sons, Jotham, escaped, prophesying to Abimelech in a clever parable that he would not last long and that Shechem itself would turn on him and reject him (9:7-21). After three years the people of Shechem did indeed become disaffected with Abimelech, and while he was out of town a band of Shechemites led by a certain Gaal declared their independence of him. Zebul, the mayor of the city, notified Abimelech of the plot. He returned, a battle ensued outside the city, and Gaal and his revolutionaries were dispersed. Because he suspected that Shechem as a whole was involved in this affair, Abimelech ordered the city destroyed and its ruins sowed with salt. Some of the refugees fled from the Tower of Shechem to the sanctuary of Baal-berith, but were unsuccessful in eluding Abimelech, for he burned the temple to the ground (9:49). He then turned to the nearby village of Thebez where he also no doubt suspected a pocket of resistance to his rule, but a millstone cast by a woman from the top of the tower abruptly ended his career. Thus the first attempt at Israelite monarchy was aborted, ending in dismal failure.

Jephthah, Ibzan, Elon, and Abdon (10:6-12:15). There next followed a period of stability under the judgeships of two otherwise unknown figures, Tola of Issachar and Jair of Gilead, the territory across the Jordan. In the meantime, the Philistines had entered Canaan in great numbers from an unsuccessful Egyptian incursion (ca. 1200 B.C.) and had added to the smaller Philistine population already settled on the lower Palestinian coast.[24] In their desire for expansion they pushed west by 1100 B.C. and naturally came in conflict with the Israelite tribes, especially Judah. To the east the Ammonites, long dormant, also came to life and pressed hard upon Gilead. It appears that the two judges called by God to deliver from these enemies, Samson in the west and Jephthah in the east, were contemporary or nearly so and that the Philistine and Ammonite oppressions were also at the same time (10:6). Turning to the eastern front first, let us trace the developments there. After the usual apostasy and punishment, this time by Ammon, Israel cried out to the Lord and he raised up Jephthah. This unfortunate man who hailed from Gilead was born of a harlot and therefore was rejected by his brethren and forced to dwell in exile near the eastern Galilean wilderness. His valor was nonetheless recognized; when Israel found itself in danger, he was invited to come back and assume leadership over them. He agreed, but only on the condition that he would not be removed from his position once the victory was achieved. With little option available the Gileadites assented and Jephthah returned to take the initiative against the Ammonite invaders. In an effort to avert bloodshed if possible he wrote a letter to the king of Ammon and reminded him of the peaceful relationships they had had for the past three hundred years since the Exodus (11:15-27). He entreated him to remember that God in the past had always cared for and preserved His people and that He would do so in this conflict, a conflict which was not of Israel's making. The king of Ammon turned a deaf ear to the communication, and the preparations were made for war.

Before Jephthah entered into conflict he made a vow that if God granted him success he would offer up to God the first thing which met him upon his return home. This is often called Jephthah's "rash vow," and rightly so, but in the opinion of the writer the passage has often been misunderstood. We are generally told that when Jephthah came home his young daughter, an only child, rushed out to meet him and that he, fulfilling the terms of the vow, offered her up as a burnt offering to God.[25] This seems highly improbably for the following reasons: (1) We are told that Jephthah was filled with the Spirit of God. It is not likely that a Spirit-filled man would even leave open the possibility of human sacrifice, a practice strongly prohibited in the Law. (2) Jephthah must have been very much aware that the possibility of his daughter's meeting him at his return was great. (3) In verse 31, the conjunction *Vau*, which is translated "and," can be just as well translated "or," with the result that Jephthah promises to present whatever meets him at the door to the Lord or he will offer it up as a burnt offering. In other words, Jephthah has made allowance for his daughter by promising God to give her to Him in a lifetime of service if she should be the first to greet him. (4) When the bereaved father realized that he had given his only child to the Lord, thus losing any possibility of perpetuating his family name, the rashness of his vow dawned upon him. He had no sons and his hope for a descendant rested in this daughter who would now remain unmarried. (5) The fact that the daughter begged permission to go into the wilderness to bewail her virginity seems to bear out the idea of her impending temple service, for if she were about to be sacrificed it hardly seems she would bewail her unmarried state, nor would she spend her last two months away from her father whom she dearly loved. Rather, she would bemoan the brevity of her life. (6) Finally, we read that she "knew no man" which would be a meaningless statement if she had been put to death. But it makes perfect sense if she had now entered a life of celibacy. In addition, we see that the maidens of Israel made it a custom from that time to "lament" the daughter of Jephthah four days out of every year. A possible translation might be that these maidens went annually to "talk to" the daughter of Jephthah.[26] The translation "lament" is based upon the assumption that she had died, an assumption, as we have seen, that is unnecessary.

The tribal jealousy which we had discussed earlier is manifest in the reaction of the tribe of Ephraim to the success of Jephthah and the Gileadites over Ammon (12:1-4). Because Jephthah had not invited them to participate in the campaign, a matter which the judge denied, they decided to burn his house down in retaliation. Their efforts were not successful, however, and the inter-tribal war which developed resulted in the deaths of thousands of Ephraimites. In their haste to return west over the Jordan they were intercepted at the fords of the river by Gileadites who demanded that they identify themselves by pronouncing the word *shibboleth* ("stream"). Because of certain dialectical changes in the Hebrew language, these westerners could not pronounce the "sh" sound, but rather said "s" (12:6). This betrayed the fact that they were Ephraimites and sealed their doom, but at least the land again knew respite from foreign adversity.

The peace gained under Jephthah in the east was unknown in the west where the Philistines became the chastening rod of God to punish delinquent Judah. There was a judge in Judah at the time, a rather obscure figure named Ibzan, but he seemed to have little relationship with the Philistine scourge

(12:8-10). There were also two other minor judges in other parts of Israel, Elon of Zebulun (12:11-12) and Abdon of Ephraim (12:13-15), but they, like Ibzan, seemed to be local judges only who were not involved in the weightier matters of warfare and national security from external forces. So Israel by the first quarter of the eleventh century looked for a saviour once more.

Samson (Chs. 13-16). At the beginning of Philistine oppression the Angel of Yahweh had appeared to a barren woman, the wife of Manoah of the tribe of Dan, and had promised her a son. This son would be unusual in that he would be a Nazarite from his mother's womb and would be used in a special way to bring deliverance to God's people. Manoah was not present at the first visit of the Angel, but when he learned of the exchange he made it a point to be included in the next heavenly visitation. At that time the Angel repeated his promise and when Manoah made an offering the Angel ascended in the flame from off the altar. Awestruck, Manoah fell upon his face with the realization that he had seen God and that God was about to use his yet unborn son for the salvation of Israel.

From the earliest years of Samson's life it became most apparent that God had placed His hand upon the lad, for the Spirit of God began to manifest Himself through him (13:24-25). Yet, it was equally obvious that Samson was not one who would submit willingly to the plan of God. The time came when he saw a lass from Timnath, a nearby Philistine city, and smitten with love for this alien girl he requested his parents to arrange marriage with her. His parents' arguments availed nothing and so the wedding date was set. Earlier, on his way to Timnath, he had seen a lion by the way; with no effort at all he had slain the savage beast. Thus did the Spirit reveal Himself in Samson, who evidently had no unusual physical prowess otherwise. When he returned to his fiancee to celebrate the wedding, he saw the carcass by the way; in violation of his Nazarite vow he touched the dead body to obtain honey made there by a swarm of bees. At Timnath Samson suggested a riddle concerning the lion and honey to the wedding attendants (Jud. 14:14). If they could reveal the meaning by the end of the seven day period which preceded the wedding day he would give them certain items of clothing; if they could not, they each must give him the same. All through the week they tried in vain to solve the puzzle, until finally they prevailed upon the Philistine bride-to-be to exact the answer from Samson. When they told him, he knew they had threatened his fiancee; in a rage he went to the Philistine city of Askelon, slew thirty men, and gave their clothing to the attendants in fulfillment of his vow. Then he stormed off to his own home leaving his intended wife at the altar.

When he began to reflect upon the incident he realized that he might have acted rashly so he went back to Timnath to get his bride; but alas, she had been given to the best man in Samson's absence (14:20). This so enraged him that he caught 300 foxes, tied their tails together, ignited the brands which he had placed between them, and thereby burned the standing crops of the Philistine fields. They in turn burned the home of his erstwhile bride, killing her and her father in the flames. Samson, his wrath yet unsatisfied, fled to the summit of a hill named Etam and there was approached by some of his Judean kinsmen. They demanded that he come down in order that they might bind him and deliver him to the Philistines as a bounty. He agreed, but only under the condition that they themselves would not lay hand upon him. To this they consented, but the moment Samson was among the Philistines he burst his bonds and with a great demonstration of superhuman strength slaughtered 1000 men with the jawbone of an ass (15:15).

Samson's life seemed to be strangely entwined with the lives of ungodly women; perhaps they were his greatest weakness. We learn that he went to Gaza, one of the Philistine's chief cities, and fell to the allurements of a harlot (16:1-3). When it appeared that the Philistines might slay him there he arose in the night, and filled with the Spirit, carried off the huge gates of the city and left them at Hebron, many miles to the west. But the woman who proved to be his ultimate undoing was another Philistine maiden who lived in the valley of Sorek. Delilah, having been heavily bribed by the Philistines, tried on several occasions to learn from Samson the secret of his great strength, but to no avail. Finally, he yielded to the pressure of her demands and revealed that if his hair should be cut he would be as any other man. This certainly does not suggest that the hair in itself possessed any supernatural powers, but only that the uncut hair represented the bond which tied him to God as a Nazarite. Cutting the hair would signify physically the rupture of that bond and the departure of the Spirit from his life. And when the bond was broken, he became as any other man.

In the last scenes of this tragic figure's life we see him blinded and grinding the grain in a Philistine gristmill (16: 21). But at last his day of final triumph came. The Philistines were in convention in the great temple of Dagon at Gaza, and in pursuit of entertainment brought their former nemesis into their midst that they might make sport of him. His hair having grown back and, more important, his faith and power having been restored, he welcomed this moment as an opportunity to vindicate himself and his God among these pagans. At the climax of the frivolity he was led by a lad to the two central pillars of the massive building; exercising the last measure of strength in his possession, he pulled the posts together. The roof, covered with hundreds of the Philistines, collapsed and buried Samson and everyone within. When the dust of the conflagration had settled, it was learned that Samson in death had slain more of the enemy than in the days of his life. And thus, at about 1050 B.C., the threat from the west was at least temporarily held in abeyance and a kind of shaky peace was sustained for a few years.

The preceding sketch of Israelite history in the period of the Judges has been, of necessity, incomplete; for there is little known about the period in Palestine from either Biblical or non-Biblical sources. The account we do have in Judges is centered about the lives and accomplishments of a few individuals who were raised up from time to time to meet specific emergencies. As is so often true in Biblical history only those happenings which directly impinge upon the covenant relationship are prominently featured. The story, after all, is that of God and His people, and even when that people violated the terms of the covenant contract, which was more true than not in this era, the story is nonetheless told faithfully.

One thing becomes absolutely clear in even the fragmented picture of the historical situation that we do have, however, and that is that the imprint of Divine influence and leading are unmistakable. Often, we see, God's glory is reflected in the shadows and valleys of human experience as well as in the moments of man's obedient service.

THE JUDGES OF ISRAEL

Oppressor	Judge	Reference
Mesopotamians (1383-1375)	Othniel (1375-1336)	Judges 3: 8-11
Moabites (1336-1319)	Ehud (1319-1240)	Judges 3:12-30
Philistines (?)	Shamgar (?)	Judges 3:31
Canaanites (1260-1240)	Deborah (1240-1201)	Judges 4-5
Midianites (1201-1194)	Gideon (1194-1155)	Judges 6-8
?	Tola (1152-1131)	Judges 10: 1- 2
?	Jair (1131-1107)	Judges 10: 3- 5
Ammonites (1107-1089)	Jephthah (1089-1083)	Judges 10: 6-12:7
?	Ibzan (1083-1076)	Judges 12: 8-10
?	Elon (1076-1066)	Judges 12:11-12
?	Abdon (1066-1058)	Judges 12:13-15
Philistines (1089-1049)	Samson (1071-1051)	Judges 13-16

THE CONDITION OF THE TIMES (CHS. 17-21)

In chapters 17-21 of Judges we have two accounts of events of special importance during the period of the Judges. They are not so vital because they had political significance, though they did, but because they reveal the spiritual conditions which prevailed during the entire era, conditions which are summed up in the slogan that "every man did that which was right in his own eyes" (17:6; 21:25). Though Israel was theoretically a Theocracy bound to God by a covenant which they had voluntarily accepted, the nation had disintegrated, not only geographically, as we have outlined above, but especially socially and spiritually. Men had lost interest in the heritage from which the nation had sprung and had permitted the outrages of anarchy to supplant a people governed by the Law. We should not get the impression that all men were evil or negligent of the Divine will, however, for we have seen that there were notable exceptions. The Book of Ruth, which finds its setting in the time of the Judges, also exhibits the godly lives of the minority. Still, it is inter-- esting that the two stories which we possess in this last part of the Book of Judges—the appendix as it is sometimes called— describe scenes of almost unbelievable immorality and license.

In chapters 17-18 we learn that there was a man from Ephraim named Micah who had stolen a certain sum of silver from his own mother. When he repented and confessed to her that he had done so, she rewarded his "honesty" by offering him the silver as a gift so that he might make therewith some images. He refused the gift, but his mother made the images anyway and had them placed in a specially constructed shrine. Micah then commissioned one of his own sons to be his priest, completing the requirements for his own independent religious system. In the meantime, a young Levite from Bethlehem, who apparently was looking for employment, ventured to Ephraim where he came in contact with Micah. Micah, after some bargaining, hired the Levite and consecrated him to the priesthood, hoping that by employing a Levite he might lend some semblance of legitimacy to his maverick religion.

At this same time, the tribe of Dan was having its difficulties along the Philistine coastal plain (18:1-2). They were unable to occupy their territory because of the superior Philistine armament and population and they found that the area of the western hills which was left to them was unable to sustain them. So they sent a delegation to search out the land in hopes of finding a better location. In transit they passed through Mount Ephraim and by the home of Micah. They enquired of Micah's priest as to the prospects which awaited them in their search; they were assured by him that all would be well. They went from there to a far northern region inhabited by a people who dwelt in peace and security. And it was there at Laish, just north of the Waters of Merom, that they decided to settle. When they returned to their people and told them of the land of Laish, it was decided to migrate *en masse.* Their route led them once again by Mount Ephraim; when the leaders remembered that it was there that they had met the Levite of Micah, they stopped by. Enticed by the richly decorated shrine and the images of silver, they appropriated them but not before they were discovered by the Levite. They quickly persuaded him, however, that the life of a tribal priest was far more prestigious and lucrative than a mere family chaplaincy and with little reluctance he followed after them. When Micah discovered the loss of his images and priest, he set out after the pilfering Danites, but even when he caught up with them was unable to prevent their thievery. Downcast, he turned back while the Danites went on to Laish where they cold-bloodedly slaughtered the helpless citizenry. But more significant, they set up Micah's silver images and established the Levite, Jonathan ben Gershom, as their priest.[27] Thus idolatry was inaugurated in Israel in a formal way and on a tribal basis. From that day forward, even until the time of Christ, Dan remained a center of idolatry.

The second incident is discussed in chapters 19-21. There we find another Levite from Ephraim, but this one had married a concubine from Bethlehem. She had run away from him to her home, but because he loved her deeply he followed her there and begged her to return. The father insisted that the Levite remain in Bethlehem for several days no matter what, but finally the Levite excused himself and departed with his wife. They had gotten such a late start that day that they had not nearly reached home before it began to get dark. They thought about spending the night in Jerusalem, but because this was not an Israelite city as yet they abandoned the idea. Then they decided to stay in Gibeah of Benjamin even though it was too late to find accommodations. While they prepared to sleep on the street, a citizen who happened to be a native of Ephraim accosted them and invited them to stay with him in the city. To this they willingly assented, but in the midst of the night certain ruffians beset the house demanding that the Levite be sent out to satisfy their depraved natures.[28] The host protested this insult of his guest and offered instead to release his daughter and the Levite's concubine to them.

The next morning the Levite went to the door where he found his ravished wife lying dead upon the doorstep. He picked her corpse up, returned to his home, and then, in an act of unparalleled imagery, dissected her body into twelve pieces and sent them to the leaders of the twelve tribes (19:29-30). Sometimes a person or nation can be awakened to reality only by something so bizarre or shocking that it is impossible to overlook. This was the case in this dark hour. For generations Israel had been lulled into a false

sense of security. They had forgotten the covenant made
with God at Shechem under Joshua. They had gone after
other gods time and time again; though punished every time
by the nations whom God raised up for that purpose, they
were saved by their judges, only to apostatize again. They
had forgotten the very reason for their being. Now, with
the gory, mutilated body of the concubine as a symbol of the
state of their nation, the tribes with one great national response awoke to the critical issues of the day. How could
Israel go so far that such a brutal deed could be countenanced?
Surely the time had come to restore sanity if at all possible.

The tribal leaders with their troops assembled at Mizpeh
and issued a communique to Benjamin that that tribe should
punish the infamous deed which had been perpetrated within
its borders (21:13). Benjamin refused to comply with this
ultimatum and an intertribal war was precipitated, a war
hardly matched for bloodiness. After a series of unsuccessful
maneuvers on the part of the eleven tribes, occasioned by the
unusual resourcefulness of the tiny tribe of Benjamin, the
larger host finally won the day. But they did their work so
well that the tribe was virtually annihilated; with the exception of 600 men who had fled to the hills, men, women, and
children were destroyed. Alarmed at their own devastation
and its results, the Israelites were now confronted with the
problem of an incomplete nation. Theirs had always been a
twelve-tribe confederacy, and it was unthinkable that the
number should ever be diminished. Now, in the heat of
their retributive justice, they had done what they would never
have contemplated in a saner moment. They had wanted to
punish, but it surely was not God's will that they do so this
thoroughly.

The tribal leaders, confronted with this new problem, met
at the central sanctuary and sought a means whereby the
remaining 600 Benjamites could form the nucleus of a new
tribe. This was not as simple as it might seem, for besides
the fact that the Benjamite women had all been slaughtered
the Israelites had made an inviolable vow that they would not
permit any of their women to marry a Benjamite (21:1).
One sage finally suggested a way out of the dilemma. He
asked that a survey be taken to determine if there were any
peoples who had not sent troops to assist Israel's cause. After
careful search it was learned that the city of Jabesh-gilead

had not done so. The elder then suggested that the men of Jabesh-gilead be put to death and their unmarried women be obtained as wives for Benjamin. This was carried out, but unfortunately there were only 400 such maidens, 200 too few. Another man of wisdom proposed that the 200 betake themselves to Shiloh where the maidens of that city were wont to celebrate an annual festival by dancing in an area near the vineyards.[29] When the girls came to dance, the 200 were to seize any whom they wished and make them their wives. Though this was in no way justifiable, it was done, and the completeness of Israel was assured.

Ruth. Thus were the fortunes of Israel, a nation whose people did that which was right in their own eyes. But for God's grace there is no doubt that the covenant community would have ceased to function because of its own neglect of the Divine precepts and its interest in the idolatry and immorality of the peoples among whom they had settled. Yet, we must not believe that there were no righteous souls at all; occasionally, in the midst of the perversion described above, there were found those whose whole intent was to worship the Lord in truth. The outstanding example of this is described in the Book of Ruth, which has its setting in the early part of the time of the Judges. Almost like an oasis of purity and wholesomeness in a desert of corruption and anarchy we read of Ruth and her family.

There had come a famine to the land of Judah so severe that many of the inhabitants, including Elimelech, Naomi, and their two sons, had fled for relief to Moab, east of the Dead Sea. While there, the boys matured and married Moabite women, Orpah and Ruth, but in due course Elimelech as well as his sons died. The three widows were uncertain as to their future, but when Naomi learned that the famine was ended in Judah, she determined to return home. The bond of love between this godly woman and her daughters-in-law had become so strongly knit that they begged her to take them with her. Orpah finally was convinced to remain among her own people, but Ruth was adamant. In as beautiful a passage as we could ever hope to find she averred that "whither thou goest I will go; and where thou lodgest I will lodge; thy people shall be my people; and thy God my God: Where thou diest will I die, and there will I be buried; the Lord do so to me, and more also, if ought but death part thee and me" (Ruth 1:16-17).

Upon her return to Bethlehem, Naomi was greeted by her old friends; saddened at the loss of her family, she requested that they no longer call her Naomi ("pleasant") but Marah ("bitter"). God had sent her away full and brought her back empty; little did she realize, nor could she, that the daughter-in-law who came with her, though a Moabite maiden, was to become the great grandmother of King David! She had not come back empty, but instead brought the source of life's greatest blessing to herself. But it is true she came back with little material wealth. In fact, it is clear that she had had to sell her late husband's property in Bethlehem in order to make ends meet. With no means whereby she might redeem it (buy it back) she and Ruth were destined to poverty, at least until the Year of Jubilee when, of course, the property would come back to them automatically.

In the meantime Ruth would not presume upon the good graces of her mother-in-law, but decided to alleviate the financial burden by doing whatever work she could find. According to Mosaic Law, the poor of the land had the privilege of gleaning the fields of the more fortunate. This meant that they could follow the reapers of the harvest and pick up any scraps which had been left behind. In addition, they could reap the corners of the fields, for these were not to be cut by the owners of the fields for the very purpose of sustaining the poor. It just so happened that Ruth went to the field of Boaz, one of the wealthier and more prominent men of the city, and a near relative of Elimelech, though Ruth did not know this. When Boaz spied the beautiful foreign girl, he inquired as to her identity and background and was told that she was the daughter-in-law of his deceased kinsman. We ought not to read into the story any romantic motifs, at least not at this point, for it seems that Boaz was interested in her because of the family tie. Besides, he no doubt was many years her senior for he addressed her as "my daughter." He told her to remain in his fields if she wished; and to guarantee her success in her efforts commanded his reapers to deliberately leave scatterings where she might pick them up (2:16). He warned them to refrain from bothering her and even (and this was unthinkable in a country where the women drew the water) allowed her to drink of their water. The real reason

for all this kindness was the kinship which bound them together, but Boaz told Ruth that he was doing what he did
because he had heard how kind she had been to her unfortunate mother-in-law.

When Ruth returned with a huge basket of barley at the
end of that first day, Naomi asked where she had done her
gleaning. Upon learning that it had been in the field of Boaz,
she began to meditate upon a plan whereby she might find a
husband for the young widow and at the same time redeem
her property from her creditor. Several weeks later she instructed Ruth to go to Boaz' threshing floor on a certain night
and to lie at his feet. In that time and place such an act
carried no overtones of impropriety whatsoever, for it was
quite legal and customary for a woman to make known her
matrimonial aspirations in such a fashion, especially under
these circumstances regarding property redemption. When
Boaz inquired who she was and what her intentions were, she
was to let it be known that she desired marriage. Naomi, in
accordance with the Law, wished to redeem her property.
Because she was unable, the responsibility to do it rested upon
her next of kin whom she thought to be Boaz. But if Boaz
redeemed the property he must at the same time take Ruth
as wife and rear up children in the name of her deceased husband (Dt. 25:5-10). The plan to make Boaz redeemer, then,
involved his becoming the husband of Ruth at the same time.

When Boaz discovered the intent of Ruth he was overjoyed, for no doubt by now he had been smitten with an overwhelming love for her. Yet, he said, he was not indeed the
next of kin! There was another in Bethlehem who had this
honor; the option to redeem or not redeem must be first
decided by him. The next day Boaz met this man near the
gate of the city and asked him what he wished to do in the
matter (4:1). The kinsman agreed to redeem the property for
Naomi, but when Boaz mentioned to him that he would have
to marry Ruth also, he began to change his mind. The reason for this reversal was that he was married already and
had sons of his own. If he should marry Ruth also and they
had sons, those sons would take possession of their deceased
father's goods and would likely gain other rights as well. In
any event, the man was afraid that such a marriage would not
work to the advantage of himself and his family, so he elected
to turn down the offer. This, of course, left Boaz in the clear,

but there must be a formal ceremony in which the next of kin relinquished all claim of redemption rights and bequeathed them to Boaz. Before the elders at the gate, the usual place for such a transaction, the two men enacted the usual procedure in such matters. The kinsman took off his shoe and handed it to Boaz, which signified that the property rights, including the marriage to Ruth, were now in the hands of Boaz. And Boaz testified to the assembled witnesses that he intended to redeem the property of his kinsman, Naomi, and to marry Ruth and beget sons in the name of her late husband.

Boaz, who, incidentally, was the son of Rahab the harlot (Matt. 1:5), married Ruth and in due time a son, Obed, was born. He was the father of Jesse, the father of David, so we see once again how the hand of God guided the lives of individuals as well as the nation in achieving His desired ends. The simple Moabite maiden who left such a beautiful impression in such dark days was destined to become another ancestress in the family of her greater Son, the Lord Jesus Christ. Not all was bleak in the days of the Judges. There were a few who did not do that which was right in their own eyes, but who determined to follow their God no matter what the cost.

Samuel (I Sam. 1-7). Near the end of the period of the Judges lived one of the most important figures of the Old Testament. He was the bridge between the era of the judges and that of monarchy which he was instrumental in forming. Samuel was considered a judge himself, though certainly not in the sense of a man like Samson, but more importantly he was a priest[30] and prophet. Concomitant with the rise of the monarchy was that of the school of the prophets of which Samuel was apparently the head. Though there had been individual prophets in Israel's history there had not been any established order of prophets up until this time.

The birth of Samuel is another example of the barren mother theme with which we have become so familiar in our study. It seems that his father, Elkanah, lived at Ramathaim-zophim (Ramah) in Ephraim with his two wives, Hannah and Peninah. The latter had borne him several children, but Hannah was unfruitful despite her devotion to God. Peninah would harass the unfortunate Hannah because she was barren, and also because Elkanah, in compensation, showed greater affection toward her. It was their custom to make annual pilgrimages to Shiloh to worship the Lord there at the tabernacle, and every year Elkanah gave Hannah a double portion of offerings to make to the Lord.

One year Hannah knelt before the tabernacle and in great burden of heart began to pray that the Lord would grant her a son. She promised that if the prayer were answered she would dedicate the son to the Lord as a lifelong Nazarite. In the intensity of her supplication she moved her lips and when the high priest, Eli, noted this, he thought she must be drunken (1:10-13). She denied this, of course, and made known to him the burden of her heart. When the priest knew of her faith, he assured her that God would answer her prayer. Within the year the child was born and named Samuel ("asked of God") because he had come as an answer to special prayer. A few years later, when the child was weaned, he was returned to the tabernacle and entrusted to the keeping of Eli who trained him to minister there unto the Lord.

In chapter 2 we find a wonderful poem in which Hannah expressed her thankfulness to God in making her fruitful and in giving her victory over her adversaries. Hundreds of years later, Mary, the mother of our Lord, based her Magnificat on this ancient song of exultation.

Another glimpse of the wickedness of the times is seen in the behavior of Eli's sons, the priests at Shiloh. Whenever the people would bring offerings to the Lord, these wicked men would appropriate them to their own use and in effect steal from God. They had even turned the tabernacle of God into a brothel where they engaged in sexual immorality with various loose women who consorted there for that purpose.[31] But, and perhaps even more astounding, all this was carried on under the very gaze of Eli who did nothing more than register a mild protest. Naturally, such desecration in the priesthood was bound to incur the wrath of God, so it was not long before a prophet was sent to Eli to inform him that the priestly office would be taken from his family and given to another which would more faithfully discharge it. This was later fulfilled in the accession of the priest Zadok and his family to the office in the time of Solomon (I Kings 2:35). But it was more fully realized in the perfect priesthood of Christ (Heb. 2:17).

While all this was going on, Samuel was growing up and gaining favor in the sight of God and men. His faithful mother, who had been blessed for her unselfishness by bearing five more children, came annually to worship and to visit her son. The day came finally when God manifested Himself to Samuel, a remarkable event when we consider that there had been no Divine revelation as a general rule since the time of Moses (I Sam. 3:1). The call of the Lord was so clear that Samuel mistook it for the voice of Eli until Eli convinced him that it was not his. The message of this first revelation was ominous, indeed, for in it God spoke of the overthrow of the Eli priesthood once again; so convinced were Eli and the people of Israel of the validity of the message that they recognized that Samuel was established to be a prophet of God (3:20). In further fulfillment of this and other predictions, Samuel's authority was substantiated, for none of his prophecies failed in any respect.

The Philistines had been but temporarily subdued by Samson. Now, toward the middle of the eleventh century, they arose with greater unity and determination than ever, making a sweeping incursion into the western highlands of Judah and Ephraim. The Israelite army was quickly mobilized to meet the Philistine invaders near Aphek at the western edge of Ephraimite territory in the Plain of Sharon (4:1). The Philistines apparently had little difficulty in this first encounter; when the Israelites had assessed the reason for their defeat, they decided that it was because of the absence of the Ark of God at Shiloh. Another effort was made to repel the invaders, but again Israel was routed, this time at the cost of the lives of Eli's two wicked sons, Hophni and Phinehas, who no doubt had carried the Ark into battle. Furthermore, the Ark itself, which by now was no more to Israel than a superstitious relic of a by-gone age, was carried off by the enemy to their city of Ashdod (5:1).

When news of the defeat of Israel, the death of his sons, and the capture of the Ark was carried back to Eli at Shiloh, the aged priest was so overcome that he fell from the seat upon which he had been resting and broke his neck. At the same time, as though prophetically, the wife of Eli's son, Phinehas, gave birth to a son whom she named Ichabod. The meaning of the name—"where is the glory?"—spoke eloquently of Israel's plight without God. (4:21-22).

The Ark was set up in the temple of the god Dagon at
Ashdod. The very first morning after its arrival there, however, the "corn deity"[32] was found lying on its face before the
Ark. It was set up again, but the following day not only lay
prostrate before the Ark but also broken in pieces. This convinced the Philistines that their god was inferior to the God
of Israel, whom they imagined was confined within the chest,
or at least represented by it; when they broke out with horrible diseases they felt that surely Yahweh was wroth with
them (5:6-7). With dispatch they sent the Ark to Gath,
hoping perhaps that the change would ameliorate Yahweh
somewhat, but the results were just as disastrous there. After
moving it once more, this time to Ekron, and experiencing
similar calamities, they decided that the only wise course was
to return it to Israel. But the problem was how to go about
this. They could not personally escort it there, for this would
expose whoever carried it to Israelite vengeance. On the other
hand, it was unlikely that the Israelites would venture into
Philistine territory to retrieve their sacred relic. Finally a
solution was devised whereby the Ark could be returned and
the Philistines could learn at the same time whether or not
the Ark had been responsible for their misfortunes. They
made a new cart, attached unbroken cattle to it, and placed
the Ark thereon together with objects of gold which would
serve as a trespass offering to the Israelites' God. If the cattle
returned directly to Israel, they could know that Yahweh indeed had occasioned their grief. If, however, the undriven
cattle meandered aimlessly, they would see that their troubles
had been only coincidental (6:3-9).

As soon as the cattle were released, they set out directly
for the Israelite border, a convincing demonstration of God's
power over Israel's enemies. First they reached the Judaean
town of Beth-shemesh, about twenty-five miles southwest of
Jerusalem. The men of the city were so overjoyed to see the
Ark, the tangible expression of God's presence, that they offered the Philistine cattle as burnt offerings which they
kindled with the wood of the cart. With unrestrained enthusiasm some of them peered into the Ark, an act forbidden
in the Law, a breach which cost the lives of many of them
(6:19). Frantically they called to the people of Kirjath-
jearim, a village in the Valley of Sorek some miles to the east,

who sent a delegation to get the Ark and place it in the home of Abinadab, its custodian for at least the next twenty years.

Following the capture of the Ark, and, we suppose, the destruction of Shiloh (ca. 1050 B.C.),[33] Samuel gathered the fighting force of Israel together at Mizpeh. The Philistines learned of this concentration of strength and set out for further conquest. The Israelites knew, of course, that one more decisive defeat could eliminate them as a nation and deliver them into the Philistine orbit. In desperation they cried out to Samuel to pray for them, and the prophet responded in faith. Taking a young lamb as a burnt offering, he prayed to Yahweh who answered in a mighty thunderstorm. This unnerved the Philistine troops who broke formation and were soon beleagured by Israel. The victory so impressed Samuel that he erected a monument at the site, a stone pillar which he named *eben-ezer* ("stone of help") as a tribute to the God of Israel (7:12). And well might Samuel be impressed, for from that day until the time of David, at least, Philistine aggressiveness was curbed. The rest of Samuel's days could be lived in comparatively peaceful labor at Bethel, Gilgal, Mizpeh, and his home town of Ramah, which cities he traveled in circuit as the last of Israel's judges (7:15-17).

And so we reach the end of the period of conquest and judges, an era of frustration, defeat, and failure. Yet, there shines forth from this time an occasional gleam of courage, faith, and dedication. A land had been entered, conquered in some measure, and at least partially settled in answer to the prophetic word of God. Israel had reached peaks of strength and unity interspersed with corruption and defeat, but it had become more and more clear that the loose tribal confederation of the past would not suffice for the present, especially in the light of the fact that all the surrounding powers had well organized and efficient central governments headed by a king. Israel had a King too, but He had been forgotten except by the few. The demand now was for an earthly hero who could give the nation a place in the world and cohesion within the body politic itself. God's answer was to give a king, but to safeguard His interests by providing a corrective and shepherding influence, He also founded the office of the prophet.

---

[1] For a recent and authoritative treatment of the Canaanites, see John Gray, *The Canaanites*, New York, Frederick A. Praeger, 1964.

[2] W. F. Albright, *From the Stone Age to Christianity*, Garden City, Doubleday and Company, Inc., 1957, p. 206.

[3] See a letter from Abdi-heba, king of Jerusalem, to Ikhnaton (Amenhotep IV) in D. Winton Thomas, *Documents From Old Testament Times*, London, Thomas Nelson and Sons, Ltd., 1958, pp. 39-40.

[4] O. R. Gurney, *The Hittites*, Baltimore, Penguin Books, 1964, p. 29.

[5] *Ibid.*, pp. 38-39.

[6] Sabatino Moscati, *Ancient Semitic Civilizations*, New York, G. P. Putnam's Sons, 1960, pp. 110-111.

[7] Samuel Schultz, *The Old Testament Speaks*, New York, Harper and Brothers, 1960, p. 94.

[8] Bernhard W. Anderson, *Understanding the Old Testament*, Englewood Cliffs, Prentice-Hall, 1957, pp. 128-129.

[9] John Garstang, *The Story of Jericho*, London, Hodder and Stoughton, Ltd., 1940, pp. 137-138.

[10] *Ibid.*, p. 136.

[11] Merrill F. Unger, *Archaeology and the Old Testament*, Grand Rapids, Zondervan Publishing House, 1954, p. 163. For the latest information, see Joseph A. Callaway, "The 1964 Ai (et Tell) Excavations," *Bulletin of the American Schools of Oriental Research*, No. 178, pp. 27-28, April, 1965.

[12] For the Biblical importance of Shechem, see Bernhard W. Anderson, "The Place of Shechem in the Bible," *The Biblical Archaeologist Reader*, Vol. 2, Ed. by David Noel Freedman and Edward F. Campbell, Jr., Garden City, Doubleday and Company, Inc., 1964, pp. 265-275.

[13] G. Ernest Wright, *Biblical Archaeology*, Philadelphia, Westminster Press, 1957, p. 46.

[14] Bernard Ramm, *The Christian View of Science and Scripture*, Grand Rapids, Wm. B. Eerdmans Publishing Company, 1954, pp. 156 ff.

[15] Yigael Yadin, "Excavations at Hazor," *Biblical Archaeologist*, 19:12, February, 1956.

[16] For a discussion of the underlying ideas, see Mircea Eliade, *The Sacred and the Profane*, New York, Harper and Row, 1961, pp. 125-128. On the Asherah see Raphael Patai, "The Goddess Asherah," *Journal of Near Eastern Studies*, 24:37-52, January-April, 1965.

[17] John Gray, *Archaeology and the Old Testament World*, New York, Harper and Row, 1962, p. 111.

[18] Gray, *The Canaanites*, pp. 119-138.

[19] For the text see G. R. Driver, *Canaanite Myths and Legends*, Edinburgh, T. and T. Clark, 1956, Baal IV, pp. 116-117.

[20] Moscati, *op. cit.*, pp. 116-120.

[21] The dates for this complex period are those of John Whitcomb, "Chart of Old Testament Patriarchs and Judges," Winona Lake, Indiana, Grace Theological Seminary, 1963.

[22] Max Weber, *Ancient Judaism*, Trans. and ed. by Hans H. Gerth and Don Martindale, Chicago, Free Press, 1952, p. 40.

[23] W. F. Albright, *The Biblical Period From Abraham to Ezra*, New York, Harper and Row, 1963, p. 41.

[24] See p. 154.

[25] George F. Moore, *A Critical and Exegetical Commentary on Judges*, New York, Charles Scribner's Sons, 1895, p. 301.

[26] Schultz, *op. cit.*, p. 111.

[27] This may have been Moses' grandson (18:3); if so, this places the event in the beginning of the period of the judges. See on the problem of "Manasseh" (Jud. 18:30) or "Moses," John W. Haley, *Alleged Discrepancies of the Bible*, Grand Rapids, Baker Book House, 1958, p. 338.

[28] See p. 77.

[29] Evidently Shiloh had become a center of Baal worship by now, or at least the worship of Yahweh had deteriorated immensely (cf. I Sam. 2:12-22).

[30] Samuel was not of the family of Aaron, so could not have been a high priest. He probably was a prophet who was permitted the priestly prerogatives. See Clive A. Thomson, "Samuel, the Ark, and the Priesthood," *Bibliotheca Sacra*, 118:259-263, July-September, 1961.

[31] Of course, this may very likely refer to religious prostitution accompanying fertility rites. If so, the worship of Yahweh at Shiloh must have been little different from that of Baal elsewhere. See A. F. Kirkpatrick, *The First and Second Books of Samuel*, Cambridge, University Press, 1930, pp. 19-20.

[32] Donald Harden, *The Phoenicians*, New York, Frederick A. Praeger, 1962, pp. 86-87.

[33] For archaeological evidence of this, see Millar Burrows, *What Mean These Stones?*, New York, Meridian Books, 1957, p. 80.

Chapter Seven

AN AGE OF GREATNESS

Historical Background

The rise of the Philistine threat which culminated in the destruction of Shiloh in 1050 B.C. signalled the end of any hope of Israel's maintaining itself as a loose federation of tribes with no central authority. Though the Egyptian Empire had for all practical purposes ceased to exercise any kind of direct influence on Israel, the dangers and undesirability of remaining unfederated nevertheless became obvious because other lesser powers all around were strongly organized and becoming increasingly more militant. It is true that Israel's major problem was that she had forgotten God in any national sense, but this was overlooked in favor of the view that her continued existence must depend upon a king like that of the nations round about.

The Philistines, or "Sea Peoples," had succeeded in finishing the task of removing the Hittite menace which the Assyrians had begun shortly before 1200 B.C.[1] They then swooped down into Palestine from Asia Minor, bringing with them Hittite arts and crafts, especially the use of iron, and established themselves on the south Palestinian littoral. Content with this limited area at first, they eventually began to push to the east and north by the turn of the eleventh century and were contained only by the exploits of men like Samson. However, as we have pointed out, they did manage to penetrate into Ephraim far enough to destroy Shiloh and without question they occupied many other sites within Israelite territory by the time of Samuel and Saul. It was this single danger that most prompted Israel to demand a king who would follow in the line of the judges but whose office would be more permanent and stable. Without such a leader, it was thought, the entire nation would be swallowed up by the Philistines.

Toward the north, in Syria, a people known as the Aramaeans were settling. They organized in various states independent of each other but with certain cultural and linguistic affinities.[2] Also during this time of Philistine expansion people such as the Midianites, Ammonites, and Moabites began to make their presence known, especially in the east of Jordan. These we have considered in relation to some of the judges of Israel. One other group, the Phoenicians, lived north of Carmel in strong, independent cities whose main interest was not in territorial expansion, at least in the Near East, but in maritime trade and colonizing. They achieved no prominence before the time of the Hebrew monarchy, but about that time began to enlarge their horizons in many ways. Besides their skill in sailing and building, both of which are mentioned frequently in the Old Testament, they no doubt invented the first practical alphabet, the origins of which may come from as early as 1500 B.C. On the whole Israel maintained peace with these northern neighbors, the kings of Tyre and Sidon especially being very friendly with David, Solomon, and Omri.[3]

The Assyrians, having overthrown the Hittites with Philistine help by 1200 B.C., went on to subjugate all the area around the northern Tigris and marched into Babylonia with great success. Until ca. 1100 under Tiglath-pileser I, Assyrian expansion was limited, but then it renewed with even greater intensity. But the Aramaean States in Syria were successful in preventing any Assyrian movement into Palestine for another 200 years, thus permitting the United Monarchy of Israel to enjoy security from that quarter. The Babylonians continued to be powerless in the wake of Assyrian conquest and were to continue so throughout all this period and on into the seventh century. This era from 1050-930 proved to be one in which the great nations exchanged power, the Egyptians, Mitanni, and Hittites having given way to the Sea Peoples, Aramaeans, and Assyrians. Taking full advantage of all this jousting for power, Israel under its kings reached unparalleled heights of strength, wealth, and security. The lesser nations such as the Edomites, Ammonites, and Moabites were brought within the Israelite circle of domination, friendly neighbors such as the Phoenicians supplied badly needed skills and commodities, and even such enemies as the Philistines and Aramaeans were contained for the most part and even eventually conquered.

SAUL *(I Samuel 8-31)*

His Ascendancy (8-14). When Samuel finally reached an advanced age and it appeared that his death was imminent, the elders of Israel approached him regarding a successor to take his place. His sons they ruled out, for unlike their father they were dishonest and greedy, but the people at least wished Samuel to appoint one who could assert the authority which had been his. This leader must be more than a judge, however; he must be a king like the kings of all the surrounding peoples. In distress Samuel turned to the Lord who assured him that the nation had not rejected Samuel but had rejected Him from ruling over them. He then instructed the prophet to permit a king but to carefully outline what results would accrue from such a decision. The new king would be autocratic and would reduce the young men and maidens of Israel to servitude to satisfy his own interests. In spite of the warnings the people insisted that they have their way, so action was taken to find a likely candidate.

We must not believe that the idea of a king was wrong, for provision for monarchy had been made in Deuteronomy (Dt. 17:14-20), but the present action of the people at this time was premature. God had a king in mind, and had the nation but awaited His will all would have turned out differently. But because they insisted upon this hasty action, God allowed them to have a king and selected the best possible choice under the circumstances.

This choice was Saul, a native of Gibeah in Benjamin, a young man described as a physical giant who was choice and goodly (I Sam. 9:2). While searching for some strayed asses which belonged to his father, he came to the city of Ramah where the prophet Samuel made his home. The Lord had indicated to Samuel that His candidate for king would appear in the city that day, and when Saul came to him to seek advice as to the lost animals, Samuel immediately knew that this huge man was that choice. He entertained him at a religious festival which was being celebrated that day, and on the following day announced to him that God had selected him to rule Israel.

Despite the fact that the prophet followed this declaration by anointing Saul, the Benjamite argued that he was from the smallest of the tribes and was, therefore, an unlikely candidate to be king. Samuel assured him that he would see certain signs by which God would manifest His favor and requested him to meet him later at Gilgal where the man of God would offer sacrifices.

As Saul departed from Ramah he met two men who informed him as to the whereabouts of his asses. Next, he was confronted by three others headed for Bethel and carrying bread and wine. Finally he met a band of prophets coming down a hill singing their prophetic messages. All these happenings transpired exactly as Samuel had said, and by this Saul knew that the prophet spoke truth. Furthermore, Saul proceeded to prophesy with the prophets; having become filled with the Spirit of God, he was changed to another man. This need not refer to any experience of conversion, for his later life would seem to belie this, but meant simply that the rude, unlettered country youth was now given the heart of a king and the wisdom requisite for the kingly office.[4]

It might be well to pause here briefly to discuss the prophetic institution.[5] We have seen that prophetism itself was very ancient, even Abraham being designated a prophet, but as an office we must look for its beginnings no earlier than Samuel and probably under his guidance. In one sense, every godly man of most ancient times was a prophet because God spoke through them to their generations in the absence of any objective standard of truth. When the prophet Moses received the Law at Sinai, however, there was no longer the need that every man receive revelation, for final instruction had been given to all the nation in written form. As special needs arose in the future, though, God spoke to individuals from time to time, as we saw in the time of the judges, but there was no organized prophetism of any kind. When Samuel was made a prophet in an age characterized by little revelation from God, he apparently went on to train others in the prophetic ministry. This is not to say that a prophet could be trained to prophesy, for most assuredly the prophetic calling was charismatic, but once men were called of God they could be trained in certain prophetic functions and arts. The prophets whom Saul met coming down the hill were singing, for example, and Saul, filled with the Spirit, was enabled to

join in with them (I Sam. 10:9-12). The result of this unexpected behavior on his part, unexpected because he had
given no prior evidence of charismatic blessing, caused the
people of the land to ask whether Saul indeed was now one of
the prophets.

We know very little of the ministry of these unnamed and
relatively unimportant prophets, but we may surmise that
they acted as correctives to abuses within both the priesthood
and the monarchy. It is interesting to note that when the
priesthood had reached its spiritual nadir under Eli and his
sons, this was precisely the time when we see the rise of a
strong prophetic movement. And it is also coincident with
the establishment of a monarchy, an office which could very
easily become secularized and which would need continuous
disciplining by prophetic spokesmen. Though the prophets
are usually associated with prediction in the popular mind, it
is clear that this was only one aspect of their ministry. Their
principal task seemed to be to speak to their own day and to
keep the Theocracy in line as much as possible.[6]

After Samuel's death, we hear little of the bands of the
prophets until the time of Elijah and Elisha (ca. 875-800
B.C.), when they again appeared, but with the new designation, "sons of the prophets." We may safely assume that the
prophetic groups continued to exist after Samuel and until
Elijah, but that without the dynamic leadership of such men,
they occupied a much less prominent place in national life at
other times.

Besides the common term prophet (*nabhi*), we find also
the names seer (*roeh* and *chozeh*), watchman, sentinel, and
many others. The first of the terms is by far the most common, however, and basically means "spokesman," both by
etymology and by usage.[7] The classic Biblical definition is
found in Exodus 7:1 and 4:15-16 where Aaron is called the
nabhi of Moses on the one hand, and the mouthpiece or spokesman on the other. In other words, the proper function of the
nabhi was to speak on behalf of or for another person. This
should be the task of the prophet of God, to speak for Him to
the people. The seer, moreover, was a prophet whose receptive
ministry was stressed. That is, he saw revelation from God,
whether with the eye in visions and dreams, by the ear in an
audible voice, or by impressions of other kinds. It is obvious
that a prophet could be both a *nabhi* and a seer; indeed, he

had to be both, for he could hardly proclaim that which he had not seen. Proof that both designations were applied to the same man may be seen in the case of Samuel (I Sam. 3:20; 9:11).

Sometimes critics allege that the earlier prophets of Israel were nothing short of frenzied dervishes who, in an ecstatic frame of mind, pronounced merely babblings which were incomprehensible even to themselves.[8] Such a view is based on the opinion that the Hebrew prophets were analogous to Canaanite and other Near Eastern prophets who did indeed act in a "crazy" way. But there is no way to support this contention, for there is nothing within the Old Testament or apart from it that would bear it out. Even when Saul in an hysterical state of mind "prophesied" (I Sam. 18:10), all that is meant is that he acted like a prophet in the sense that he spoke things typical of a prophet, though in his case with no control over his message.

Similarly, when Saul pursued David to Ramah later on, he was overwhelmed by the Spirit and began to "prophesy" (I Sam. 19:23-24). This resulted in his lying prostrate on the ground day and night making it possible for David to escape. But we must not assume that prophesying and lying prostrate were one and the same or necessary to each other. The prophesying in this case as in the other we have cited probably means nothing more than that Saul broke out into singing or speaking, perhaps in praise to God, but in this unusual circumstance such expostulations were beyond his control. To take the case of Saul, who obviously was demented and irresponsible, and make this typical of the prophetic office is unfounded and unfair. Other examples commonly pointed out will be considered as they appear in the historical narrative.

The time came when Samuel gathered the people together at Mizpeh for the purpose of publicly announcing the identity of the new king. But when Saul was introduced he was nowhere to be found, for in his embarrassment and humility he had hidden himself among the goods of the people (10:22). They shortly located him, and as he stood before them the people were most highly impressed with their new leader from every standpoint. He was physically imposing and had already demonstrated that he was Spirit filled, and yet he was most modest. Surely, from the human standpoint he was a logical choice for a hero who could deliver his people from the Philistine menace. Yet, not everyone thought so, for there were certain renegades who despised this great hulking fellow, perhaps because of his unassuming attitude, and they refused to acknowledge him as their king. But the graciousness of the man is seen in his refusal to be moved by their opposition; even when he later returned in glorious triumph from his first campaign he granted them immunity from reprisal.

The new king was first tested against the Ammonites who, following their king Nahash, surrounded the Gileadite city of Jabesh-gilead with the view of forcing it to capitulate. In desperation the men of Jabesh-gilead begged the Ammonites to make a covenant with them, which they agreed to do, but only on the condition that they thrust out their right eyes. In other words, they would make a league, but the terms of the arrangements would be so costly that the men of Jabesh-gilead would hardly be likely to comply. To this proposition the men of Jabesh-gilead answered that they would make such a league, and at such a price, but only if the Ammonites in turn would give them seven days respite during which time they would try to get help from the Israelites. This strange request was granted because the Ammonites knew that such help would be unlikely; furthermore, they would be much better off waiting for the city to surrender in seven days than they would to undertake a costly siege to starve it out.

When the appeal reached the ears of Saul, who was plowing in the fields near his rude palace at Gibeah,[9] he rose up in fierce anger, seized the oxen with which he was tilling the ground, and slew them on the spot. He cut their bodies into twelve pieces, which reminds us of the Levite and his concubine, and sent the pieces throughout the land with the warning that thus would be done to any Israelite who refused to come to the aid of Jabesh-gilead. With ready response they came from every part of the nation, the first real cooperative effort since the massacre of Benjamin, and they completely overwhelmed the Ammonites. This successful effort by Saul was culminated by his official acceptance by the assembly at Gilgal.

While at Gilgal, and presumably in connection with the inauguration of the king, Samuel delivered his challenging discourse regarding the rejection of Yahweh in favor of an earthly king. He reminded them of all of God's gracious dealings in the past and that without a human king they had done quite well. Nonetheless, he said, God would still be with them and their king if they both would abide by the Law. To strengthen his admonition, Samuel called for Divine sanction, a sanction which appeared in the form of a tremendous thunder and rain (12:17-18). This occurrence, in the midst of the summer when it almost never rains, convinced the assembly that Samuel spoke the truth of God and they could disobey only at the peril of their own lives.

After two years on the throne, Saul had his first engagement with the Philistines. He divided his small army, which was probably nothing more than his personal palace guard and militia, into two groups. One of these he himself commanded and the other entrusted to his son Jonathan. At a given signal the Israelites attacked a Philistine garrison at Geba, but the immensely superior numbers and armament of the Philistines succeeded in repelling the attack and Saul and his men had to flee for their lives to caves and other places of security across the Jordan. Saul himself remained in Gilgal where he waited for Samuel according to the agreement which had been made two years earlier. With the realization that the Philistines were about to destroy him, Saul knew that the only hope was in God. He therefore disregarded the command of the prophet to wait seven days until he could arrive and offer proper sacrifices, and proceeded to do so himself.[10] At precisely that moment Samuel appeared, and when he noted Saul's presumption declared that Saul's reign would not be hereditary because of his disobedience. Dejectedly, and yet with the buoyancy of spirit afforded by the presence of Samuel, Saul turned back to the west toward Michmash where he drew up his lines of battle in preparation for the inevitable confrontation with the Philistines who were stationed there.

One of the most important advantages of the Philistines was their corner on the iron market of their day (13:19-22). Recent evidence indicates that they learned how to smelt iron and employ it for peacetime and military purposes from their close association with the Hittites who apparently were the first to discover its secrets.[11] They recognized the value in maintaining the secret and only by the payment of exorbitant rates could the Israelites purchase iron implements or have them sharpened by the Philistine smiths. In time of war, the Philistines would retain all iron for their own use, leaving other peoples with their weapons of bronze.

After a series of deft maneuvers, and against the superior weapons of the Philistines, Saul and Jonathan gained a very significant victory at Michmash, one which seemed to avert the present threat of complete Philistine domination. But in the course of the battle Jonathan, ignorant of the decree his father had made that the army would fast until victory was won, took a bit of honey on the end of his staff to sustain himself. When the first phase of the encounter was over, the people seized the Philistine spoil of sheep, oxen, and calves, slaughtered them, and ate them with the blood. This infraction of the Mosaic Law Saul tried to compensate for by building an altar at the scene of the battle and offering upon it a legal sacrifice. But when he shortly thereafter tried to ascertain the will of the Lord as to the continuance of the engagement, the Lord did not answer him. This convinced Saul that someone in Israel had broken the fasting vow which had been decreed and he determined to kill the transgressor (14:39). Even when he knew that it was his son he was adamant, and but for the intercession of the people would have carried out his threat.

Saul's conquests are summarized at the end of chapter 14. He fought against the kings of all the surrounding nations, including Moab, Edom, Zobah (an Aramaean state), Philistia, and the Amalekites, and evidently with some measure of success. Yet there was war throughout his reign and into that of his successor, David. Only when Solomon ascended the throne was there a long period of real security and peace.

Saul's Rejection (Ch. 15). The account of Saul's activities against the Amalekites is of special importance because of its relationship to his status as king. Since the time the Amalekites had attacked Israel in the Sinai Peninsula 400 years earlier, God had resolved to destroy them (Ex. 17:14). Now, under Saul, the time had come. Samuel instructed the king to lead a force against Amalek down in the southern desert and to destroy them completely just as Jericho as an "accursed" city had been destroyed by Joshua. Saul complied, but when he returned he brought the king of Amalek back alive and some of the better animals as spoil. Samuel asked him why he had neglected to fully obey the will of God; after he unsuccessfully tried to blame his folly on the pressures of the people who, he said, kept the animals against his better judgment, Saul finally admitted his guilt.   In a remarkable statement Samuel reproached Saul with the words that obedience is better than sacrifice, the alleged purpose for the animals (15:22).   And he stated that because Saul had rejected the word of the Lord, God had rejected him from being king. This, coupled with the earlier declaration to the same intent, made final the impossibility of the house of Saul to occupy the royal throne.   Saul made at least a superficial protest of repentance, but apparently Samuel saw no genuine contrition, for after slaying the king of Amalek himself, he departed from Saul once and for all.

The critics usually feel that there was a personal animosity between Samuel and Saul and that they never did get along together.   It is true that there always seemed to be a conflict between them over something, but to ascribe petty feelings of vindictiveness to Samuel just because Saul had been made king over his objections is to belittle the great prophet.   And when the entire "struggle-motif" is extended to include an antagonism between the sympathizers with royalty and those with the pre-monarchial amphictyonic federation, we feel that criticism has gone too far.[12]   There is absolutely no proof that Samuel or anyone else was opposed to the principle of monarchy when the right man was on the throne. All the conflicts which we see between Saul and Samuel came about because Saul as an individual refused to adhere to the clear precepts of the Law.   The only way we can possibly understand a rivalry between the early prophets and the monarchy is to either believe the prophets were not familiar with the Deuteronomic law which made provision for a king, or that the book of Deuteronomy was written much later by an author of the seventh century.   Both of these conjectures are equally impossible to substantiate.   Samuel was not opposed to a king, as his subsequent anointing and support of David show beyond question, but he was, as a true prophet, opposed to any violation of the will of God whether that violation be by king or peasant.

Saul and David (Chs. 16-26).   With the utter rejection of Saul, the Lord spoke to Samuel about the appointment of a successor.   The prophet was directed to the Judaean town of

Bethlehem where he was to offer a sacrifice at the home of
Jesse. Following this, he asked for the sons of Jesse to pass
before him, for one of them was to inherit the crown. When
all had appeared and the Divine will was still not revealed,
Samuel asked if there were any other sons. Jesse responded
that he had a young lad tending the family flocks. Samuel
summoned him and when he appeared the seer knew at once
that the handsome young man was the future king. He took
the anointing oil, poured it upon David's head, and from that
day the shepherd youth was filled with the Spirit of God.

Almost coincidentally with God's rejection of Saul and
subsequent anointing of David, the Spirit left the king and an
evil spirit began to trouble him incessantly. This evil spirit
"from the Lord" was perhaps a demonic spirit of madness permitted by the Lord to have his way in Saul's life.[13] The only
remedy for his fits of madness was the playing of soothing
music, and for that purpose, David, who was skilled with the
harp, was brought into the royal court at Gibeah. He had not
only established a reputation for unusual musical skill, but
because he had slain wild animals singlehandedly was known
even from his youth as a courageous hero. This so impressed
the king, as did his pleasing demeanor, that Saul eventually
made him his armor-bearer (16:19-23).

After some time David returned to Bethlehem for an in-
definite period; in his absence Saul experienced the most
challenging threat of his career. The evenly matched Philistine and Israelite armies were lined up for battle on either side
of the Elah Valley, southwest of Jerusalem. Rather than
attack it was decided by the Philistines at least to settle the
matter through the hand-to-hand combat of two representative
heroes. Their challenger, a nine foot giant named Goliath,
stood in the valley cursing God and defying Israel to respond
to his challenge. David came to the scene of battle in time to
witness the Philistine's blasphemy against Yahweh; in anger
he decided that if no other Israelite, including the king,
thought enough of the national honor to meet the giant, he
would do so. When he had finally convinced Saul to allow
him to fight, he went forth with only a sling and a few stones
which he picked up from the bed of the stream. With faith in
his heart and a prayer on his lips to the God of Israel, he
slung a stone and brought the giant hulk of a man crashing to
the ground. Summarily, he decapitated the fallen hero and

carried his head and sword back to the Israelite lines in triumph.   In astonishment Saul inquired who the father of this
lad might be, for though he had known David in the past as
his personal musician and armor-bearer, this feat of courage
drew forth admiration for the father who could produce such
a son.

David once again began to dwell in the palace at Gibeah
and in due time the son of Saul, Jonathan, became his closest
friend (18:1-4).   David's estimation in the eyes of the people
was so great that it was not long before the maidens would
recite upon the return of Israel from battle, "Saul has slain
his thousands, and David his ten thousands" (I Sam. 18:7).
At first this seemed to bother the king very little, but as it
became more and more apparent that David was stealing the
affection of the nation, Saul began to regard him with sus-
picion and eventual hatred.   More than once in his demented
state he tried to kill the young hero, but each time David
eluded him.   Finally Saul removed him from his position, but
to no avail, for David's popularity increased despite what
Saul could do.

Saul at last hit upon a way of putting David out of the
way.   He urged David to marry his daughter Merab, but when
the wedding day came she was given to another.   But a second
daughter, Michal, loved David and Saul decided he could use
this situation to his advantage.   He promised David her hand
if he would go first and kill 100 Philistines and bring him the
proof that he had done so.   In his zeal to please the king and
to show his gratitude for the opportunity to marry into the
royal family, David exceeded the demand and slew 200 Philistines.   Saul, who had hoped, of course, that David would
perish in this unreasonable demand, admitted defeat again
and permitted the marriage.   But he was not one to let the
grass grow under his feet.   Having failed in all else, the king
told his son and servants to take the necessary steps to assassinate David, but Jonathan not only was able to convince
his father that this was a horrible wrong, but he also persuaded him to forgive David and reinstate him to his old position in the court (19:1-7).

Once again, however, Saul's wrath overcame him, and he
struck out at David with his lance, narrowly missing him.
David fled to his home in the city, bid farewell to Michal, who
helped him escape, and set out for Samuel's home at Ramah

where he hoped for sanctuary. When Saul's henchmen reached
David's residence, they found him gone, for thanks to the
clever ruse on the part of Michal, he had gotten a long head-
start on them. Saul immediately dispatched his servants to
Ramah, suspecting that David might have gone to join his
old enemy Samuel, but by the time they arrived there, the
prophet and David had gone to Naioth, a place near or at Ramah associated with the schools of the prophets (19:18).
Then the servants met a company of the prophets over whom
Samuel was head; beyond their own control they began to
"prophesy" with the prophets. This perhaps means that they
were overcome by God's Spirit so that whereas they had come
to apprehend David they now became his friends and aids.
When Saul followed the matter up and came to Naioth, he too
began to prophesy, much as he had at his first encounter with
the prophets when he had become "another man." He became so overwhelmed by the Divine presence and power that
he fell upon the ground and with his outer garments cast aside
prophesied all day and night. This was so unusual an experience for Saul that witnesses asked the proverbial question
once more, "Is Saul also among the prophets?" The purpose
for the experience is clear. God had rendered Saul immobile
in this fashion so that David could escape his evil designs and
make his way to security in the wilderness far away.[14]

On his way David passed by Gibeah to confer with Jonathan, hoping desperately that he might find some way of
bringing peace between himself and Saul. Jonathan said he
would make another effort to convince his father that David
meant him no harm and that he would meet him in a field
outside the city the next day to inform him of the results of
his efforts. For fear of his father's knowledge of the tryst,
Jonathan arranged to contact David through certain signals.
He would take his bow and arrows and pretend to be prac-
ticing archery. If he shot an arrow and told the boy with him
to go out beyond to bring it back, David, in hiding, would know
that it was not safe to return to Gibeah. If Jonathan directed
the lad to come in closer, David could know that all was well.

When Saul returned, he waited a day or two before in-
quiring about David; when he learned from his son that David
had gone to Bethlehem without taking leave of him, the king
became infuriated and vowed once more to kill David. Even
Jonathan barely escaped with his life from his father's temper

tantrum; heavy heartedly he returned to the field to signal David that his efforts had failed. With one last farewell, they left each other, not to be reunited until their final encounter at Ziph (23:16-18). David first went down to Nob, where the tabernacle was then located, and after begging the priest there for some bread and the sword of Goliath which had been placed there for some reason, he went on to the Philistine city of Gath. We assume he went disguised, but nevertheless this was a dangerous move, for this was the home of Goliath whom he had recently slain. He was soon identified and reported to Achish, the Philistine king. Only by pretending that he was mad was he able to escape and return into Israelite territory.

He next centered his activities in the Shephelah region of Judah, living in caves and wherever he could find shelter and hiding places. Before long he attracted a renegade band about him, men who were wanted by the law or who were just tired of the decadent society (22:1-2). His family evidently stayed with him for a time, but fearing Saul's retribution upon them for his sake he sent them all to the land of Moab, the homeland of his great-grandmother Ruth. At the direction of the prophet Gad he left the caves at Adullam and went further into the Judaean wilderness to the forest of Hareth. Saul by now had learned of his whereabouts and recent activities from Doeg, an Edomite who had been at Nob when David had visited there earlier. Doeg informed Saul that the priest at Nob had assisted his enemy to escape, so Saul hastened to Nob and ruthlessly slaughtered all the priests there except Abiathar who fled to David and became his personal chaplain. The extremes to which Saul's mental and spiritual condition had driven him become all too apparent in this bloody purge of the anointed priests of God.

David in the meantime had gone to Keilah to deliver the inhabitants of that unfortunate place from a Philistine attack. Acts of deliverance such as this naturally endeared David to the hearts of the Judaeans, so it is with little wonder that we see that they later made him their king so willingly. Saul also went to Keilah, but to seize David; only he was too late. David had gone to the wilderness of Ziph where he was met by Jonathan and encouraged by his continued friendship. Then he moved on to Maon; passing on one side of a mountain while Saul passed on the other, he managed to elude his pursuer once more. At that time an urgent notice came to Saul that the Philistines were attacking again, so he had to leave temporarily, a departure which afforded David some much needed rest.

David and his men found a new hiding place on the western shore of the Dead Sea at Engedi (22:29). Saul, having returned from the latest Philistine campaign, soon learned of his whereabouts and followed him there. The area provided excellent protection for a fugitive because of the hundreds of caves in the steep hillsides, and it was in one of those caves that David next encountered his tormentor. Saul had gone into a cave to rest, and by chance David was already inside. While Saul was deep within the grotto, David took the royal cloak which Saul left in the outer part of the cave and cut off its skirt. Then, pressing close against the wall, David watched Saul pass by. As he did, David came close behind him and called out his name. Stunned, the king turned back and before he could utter a word David related what he had done and hinted that he could as easily have taken the king's head as he did his skirt. Chagrined, Saul could do nothing more than confess his wickedness against his former friend and promise to discontinue his malice. Though Saul immediately returned home, David was not convinced of his sincerity and remained in his place of hiding.

Because David was a Judaean and believed he was suffering for a righteous cause, he felt that his fellow citizens should afford him some relief in his desperate plight. He therefore requested a certain farmer named Nabal to send him forthwith a plentiful supply of food and other provisions in order that he might sustain his band of men (25:8). Nabal refused outright, whereupon David set out to take what he wanted by force and punish Nabal at the same time for his selfishness. His wife, Abigail, became aware of David's intentions against her husband and prepared the materials David had demanded. She met the outlaw on the road, offered him her goods, and begged him not to kill her husband, though, as she said, he was nothing but a fool as his name suggested (*nabal*—"fool"). She had no sooner returned home when her husband died in a drunken stupor. David, whose heart had been won already by the beautiful Abigail, heard of Nabal's death and took the widow to be his own wife. In addition, he married Ahinoam of Jezreel and, of course, already had wed Michal, daughter of Saul.

By now David had moved back to the wilderness of Ziph. Saul, who had so quickly forgotten his pledge to leave David alone, went there after him. Exhausted from his swift pursuit, Saul went to sleep on the slopes of a steep valley while his chief captain, Abner, stood watch. After a time, even Abner could not remain awake, and the whole camp slumbered. With great daring David and his right-hand man, Abishai, stole into Saul's camp, took the king's spear and water canteen, and silently made their way back across the gorge. Again David had had an opportunity to be rid of his adversary—indeed it was all he could do to prevent Abishai from murdering Saul on the spot—but he could not help but realize that Saul, despite his wretchedness, was still the anointed king of Israel. Safely out of reach, David shouted across the ravine to Saul and Abner. He taunted the latter by asking him where he was when his master was robbed of his spear and canteen, and were not Saul so startled by the turn of events, we may well wonder about Abner's outcome. Saul again begged David's forgivenss and seemed deeply repentant. But when David offered to return the king's spear, he indicated how much he trusted Saul's repentance by suggesting that someone from Saul's camp come to where he was to get it. Nevertheless, Saul returned to Gibeah once more and never again attempted to wreak his vengeance on the unhappy David.

Saul's Last Days (Chs. 27-31). David himself felt that this latest withdrawal of Saul was only temporary and that eventually he would be caught. Throwing caution to the winds, he elected to go again to the Philistine king Achish and volunteer his services to him. By now the Philistines had heard of the complete breach between David and Saul, so it is not especially surprising that Achish welcomed David with open arms. Any man who could slay such a warrior as Goliath would make a valuable ally. Achish, as the *seren* ("prince") of the region around Gath, held other towns within his jurisdiction and one of these he selected as a dwelling place for his new friend. In keeping with what we now know about Philistine political organization, it seems likely that David was given the city of Ziklag as a feudal fief to be administered by him in cooperation with Achish.[15] He would be responsible to support Achish both in peace and war and in turn could no doubt count on the assistance of the Philistines. From this base of operations David sallied forth from time to time to do battle with his enemies in the desert while Achish, oblivious to David's real objectives, esteemed his new Israelite ally most highly.

Back in the Valley of Jezreel, the forces of Saul were drawn up in preparation for battle with the Philistines. David himself was numbered among the enemy because of his Philistine associations and so found himself in a most compromising position. He could hardly refuse to fight for the Philistines because he had pledged his support to Achish. On the other hand, he knew he could never bring himself to draw sword against Saul and the Israelites because his true sympathies were still with his people. Fortunately, he did not have to solve the dilemma, for the Philistine princes, suspecting that David would prove disloyal to them in the heat of battle, discharged him and sent him back to Ziklag.

But Saul's predicament could not be solved so easily. He had attempted to ascertain the Lord's will and secure Divine blessing in this important enterprise, but God would not reveal Himself to the unhappy king. Nor could Saul refer to the priests, for he had had them slaughtered at Nob some time before. Even Samuel, the prophet upon whom the king had leaned so heavily, was dead. The only recourse, then, was to enquire of an illegitimate prophet or seer, though Saul himself had decreed previously that such should be destroyed from the land. Finally he located a prophetess in a nearby village, the witch of Endor. Disguising himself as best he could, Saul visited the woman and requested her to bring up Samuel the prophet from the dead. The woman, fearful for the consequence of disobeying the edict concerning such matters, at first refused to comply; but when Saul assured her that she need fear no harm, she proceeded to conjure up the deceased Samuel. To her utter amazement the prophet appeared and predicted that Saul and his son would be with him the next day for the Philistines would win the battle and slay the king and Jonathan (28:19).

There have been a variety of opinions voiced regarding the transaction just discussed. Some say that the entire matter was a vision;[16] others argue that Samuel appeared in the flesh;[17] and still others that the old woman merely deceived the king.[18] The most likely view is that Samuel did actually appear, albeit in a vision, for if the appearance was only a trick of the woman why was she so afraid when it occurred? There is every evidence that necromancers could and did speak to the dead, for there would be no prohibitions against such things otherwise, but whether this woman under her own power, or even with demonic power, could raise up a godly prophet against his wishes is debatable. We must conclude that God commanded Samuel to appear, even using the witch as a medium in this unusual circumstance, for the purpose of giving Saul a final revelation of his destiny and that of the nation. We do not learn much here about the Old Testament view of the condition of the dead except that the dead were thought of as being down in the earth (28:11). Apparently there was no distinction between the resting place of the righteous and that of the evil, for Samuel said that Saul and Jonathan would be with him; with him, that is, in death.

Saul, overcome by the import of the revelation, barely made it back to the battle lines. In the meantime David had made his way to Ziklag where he found the city pillaged and the people, including his wives, carried off by Amalekites (30:1-2). After enquiring of the Lord, he set out for the Negev in hopes of rescuing his loved ones and goods. Having marched rapidly from Jezreel to Ziklag, however, his little army was hardly able to continue to the Amalekite encampments. Some of them dropped from sheer exhaustion while the rest wearily followed their leader onward. They managed to surprise the enemy with the help of a guide whom they had met along the way, and after a fierce encounter dealt the Amalekites a stunning defeat, at the same time saving all the captives alive. Upon their return they came to the famished troops whom they had left behind; after a hassle concerning the division of the Amalekite spoil, David made a decree, from that day a custom of war, that those behind the lines or in reserve should share and share alike with those who actually participated in the fighting (30:24).

Back at Jezreel, the conflict had begun in earnest. Soundly defeated, the Israelites retreated, leaving their dead and wounded, including Saul and Jonathan, behind. Mortally stricken, Saul ordered his armor bearer to finish him off, but from dread of striking the Lord's anointed the faithful servant refused. At this, Saul took his own sword and falling upon it quickly joined his dead son, Jonathan, and Samuel. The Philistines came upon his body and with glee decapitated it and fastened it upon the wall of Beth-shean. In a final gesture of homage and gratitude, however, the people of Jabesh-gilead, whom Saul had rescued from Ammon in his first act as king, came under cover of night and retrieved his body and buried it in their own city which was just across the Jordan in Gilead. A grateful people had remembered their king though the king himself had fallen long since from the eminence which was his under the initial blessing of God.

THE REIGN OF DAVID (II SAMUEL 1-I KINGS 2; I CHRONICLES 11-29)

Rule at Hebron (II Samuel 1-4; I Chronicles 11:1-3). David is by any standard one of the most striking figures of all history. Reared in the simple life of a Judaean village, he very early in life gave evidence of unusual gifts. He was at once a man of courage and valor, a talented musician, and a man of letters who wrote the finest poetry of the Old Testament. Added to all this was the hand of God upon his life, a Divine infilling which made of David the first of the great kings of Israel at the same time that he was the last truly charismatic figure after the order of the judges and Samuel. But perhaps his most outstanding characteristics were his patience and longsuffering in the face of undeserved persecution. Through no doing of his own he had been anointed by Samuel to be king long before Saul officially abdicated the throne, and through a series of reverses occasioned by Saul's bitter envy and hatred had spent many years of his life in hiding and loneliness. Yet, through all this he had constantly been serenely aware that he was in God's will and would be vindicated in God's own time.

We may be sure that David, whether consciously or not, had been slowly building up favor with his fellow citizens throughout the realm, especially in Judah. His early feats of prowess against the Philistines had made him an almost legendary figure; even his disputes with the popular king Saul must have been to many people a source of sympathy for David. Probably with the passing of time and through the advantage of his position as king Saul was able to wean the people of the northern tribes, at least, away from his adversary, but the exploits which David accomplished on behalf of Judah even while he was in flight from Saul succeeded in gaining the almost universal approval of the southern tribe. When the time came he could rule, it was only a matter of formality for Judah to select him as their leader, even though the other tribes, because of their pro-Saul feeling, were a little slower in acknowledging him as sovereign.

Immediately after Saul's death at Gilboa, a runner came to David at Ziklag and gave him the sad news that both the king and his son were slain. The messenger, hoping to get a reward from David, told him that he had personally finished Saul off. But David, who had had many opportunities to do the same in the past but had desisted from lifting his hand against the Lord's anointed, ordered the lying messenger put to death, though for something which he had only pretended to do. Then David burst out into one of the most heart-rending lamentations in the Bible, expressive at once of his great love for Saul and Jonathan and his poetic genius (II Sam. 1:19-27).

With no king at all in the land, the men of Judah at once took David to Hebron, the chief Judaean city, and made him king of their tribe. This is one of the first clear expressions of division in the kingdom since the time of the judges, and it spoke of greater division in the future. It was only with difficulty that either David or Solomon could keep the kingdom intact, and, of course, upon the latter's death it became divided between south and north for the remainder of its history. In the north, while David was being anointed in Judah, Ishbosheth[19] the son of Saul was proclaimed king in the place of his father. The capital was moved from Gibeah to Mahanaim of Gilead perhaps because a great part of the northern tribes was in Philistine hands (II Sam. 2:8-9).

From the very beginning the real power was in the possession of Abner, Saul's chief military officer, and he made every effort both to reunite the nation and procure more power for himself. He attempted to invade Judah, but David's troops, under Joab, met him at Gibeon; after a short skirmish involving the elite from either side, Abner was forced to retreat with the Judaeans in pursuit. Asahel, Joab's younger brother, singled out Abner as his victim, whereupon Abner, the seasoned veteran, turned upon him and slew him. Joab never forgot this and from that day forward looked for an opportunity for revenge.

After this first clash, David grew stronger while the northern tribes became weaker. During the seven years of his residence in Hebron, David's family also began to grow. He had several wives by now, each of whom bore him many sons and daughters; when he later moved to Jerusalem others, including Solomon, were born. But his first wife, Michal, was still not with him. One day, after a falling out between Ish-bosheth and Abner, the latter went to David to try to arrange peace between the two parts of the kingdom (II Sam. 3:12). He promised to deliver Israel to David if David would make an alliance with him, but David insisted that no such league would be possible until Michal were brought to him at Hebron. Abner returned to get her and the bargain was immediately consummated. When Joab, who had been off to war, learned that his arch enemy Abner had been in Hebron and that David had entertained him there and bargained with him, he sent word to Abner that David wished to see him again. Abner returned to Hebron where Joab met him, and feigning friendship Joab assassinated him. David reacted to this with great mourning for Abner, an act incomprehensible to Joab and one calculated to bring about a rift between David and himself.

Back in Mahanaim the situation was ripe for revolution. Abner, the strength of the kingdom, was dead and only the ineffective Ish-bosheth was in control. Hoping to take advantage of the situation for personal gain, two assassins murdered Ish-bosheth in his bed and immediately notified David that the throne in the north was now empty. Again David, unwilling to be advanced in such a bloody way, punished his would-be accomplices by cutting off their hands and feet and hanging them over the pool at Hebron. But the elders of Israel now knew that with Saul's house gone there was only one thing to be done—David must be king over the united nation. They came to Hebron and anointed him ruler over them as the tribe of Judah had already done seven years earlier (II Sam. 5:3).

David's Prosperity (II Sam. 5-10; I Chron. 11:4-19:19). The first official matter was a delicate one, indeed. David had to locate the capital in a place that would be suitable to all the citizens, especially when tribal feelings still ran so high. Hebron was not possible, because it was manifestly Judaean, a fact that the northern tribes would bitterly resent. Yet, he could not turn his back on his loyal countrymen in Judah, for they had stood by him when all else failed. The ideal location, naturally, would be in the center between the two; such a place existed, Jerusalem, but Jerusalem still was occupied by Jebusites as it had been from ancient times. The only solution was a forcible takeover of the city, but this was no easy matter. The old Jebusite city was perched atop a steep, commanding hill surrounded on all but the north by almost perpendicular valleys, the Kidron to the east and southeast and the Hinnom to the west and southwest. In addition the city was well fortified with massive walls, especially in the north where it most lacked natural defenses. Moreover, there was an adequate water supply because of a tunnel leading from the city cistern to an underground spring in the Kidron Valley.[20] But it was this tunnel that was to lead to the city's undoing. David, camped on a hill just to the west of the city, a hill later known as Mt. Zion, promised any-one who could get into the city through the water tunnel a position of honor in the court. Joab managed to do so, opened the gates from the inside, and Jerusalem fell with little struggle (II Sam. 5:6-8; I Chron. 11:4-6).

Now that he occupied the imposing city of Jerusalem, David's reputation began to cross international boundaries. Here was no ordinary tribal chieftain, but a full-fledged king who could match any in the surrounding nations. Hiram of Phoenicia, for example, sent him materials and men to build him a palace consonant with his new position of prestige (II Sam. 5:11-12). But the Philistines recognized him in another sense. They saw the possibility of a crippling, if not fatal, blow to their ambitions to occupy all of Palestine. Most of the country was in their hands thanks to their victory over Saul and Israel at Gilboa, but they had not reckoned on the meteoric rise of this former vassal of theirs from Judah. Now, before it was too late, they moved against David, even to the outskirts of Jerusalem in the Valley of Rephaim. More than equal to the challenge, and with the special promise of God, David moved forth against this foreign threat and thoroughly routed them (II Sam. 5:25).

Once the solidarity of the kingdom was established within and without in a political sense, David realized that such solidarity could be maintained only by a strong moral and spiritual emphasis. The religious life of the nation had more or less fallen into desuetude since the destruction of Shiloh and the removal of the Ark from there to Philistia. Of course, the real core of Israel's faith had begun to deteriorate much earlier, even as early as the next generation or so after Joshua. Now, however, even the external religious trappings had disappeared from the national life. There had been efforts made to restore worship at various sites such as Gibeah and Nob, to be sure, but these were illegitimate as far as the Law was concerned, for the Ark was not there. And even these places suffered under the hand of Saul who not only purged the priesthood of Nob, as we have seen, but also tended toward religious syncretism as is evidenced by the names of some of his sons such as Esh-baal (I Chron. 8:33).

To rectify an obviously improper situation David took steps to bring the Ark back into use from its resting place at Kirjath-jearim. He made no effort to relocate it at Shiloh, Shechem, or some other place made sacred by past associations, but he determined to carry it to his political center, Jerusalem. This was not unlawful in any sense, as some have tried to indicate, for the Law stated only that there should be a central place where the Ark of the Covenant could remain and where the principal festivals of the year could be celebrated. The selection of such a place was supposed to be in the will of God, and we have no evidence that David did not consult the Lord's will when he decided upon Jerusalem. In addition Jerusalem seemed to have some importance in the spiritual history of Israel as we saw in Abram's associations with it.

Perhaps through carelessness, or even ignorance, David set about getting the Ark in the wrong way (II Sam. 6:3-7; I Chron. 13:7-10)). He had it placed upon a cart for the journey from the house of Abinadab to his new tabernacle which he had pitched in Jerusalem. Moses' Law states quite clearly that the Levites were to carry the Ark on staves upon their shoulders and not upon a cart or other vehicle (Ex. 25:14-15; Num. 4:5-8). When, therefore, David's servants were in the process of transporting it unlawfully it began to slide off the cart in a rough place along the way. Uzzah, one of Abinadab's sons, reached out to steady the Ark, an act of impiety which resulted in his death. This so terrified David that he let the Ark remain at the house of one Obededom for three more months, and only then undertook to remove it, this time properly. With appropriate sacrifices and ceremony the sacred chest made its way up the mountains to the royal city. And when, with great pageantry and feeling, the Levites finally brought it within the walls, David was so overjoyed that he danced before the Lord with all his might. Michal, who had been watching from a palace window, ridiculed the happy king for shamelessly exposing himself before the peasantry. To David, this was the last barrier of many which had come between them throughout their tragic marriage, and he rebuked his wife by discontinuing any effort at normal relations with her the rest of her life (II Sam. 6:23; I Chron. 15:29).

When absolute security from outside interference had become a reality, David next decided to house the Ark in a far more impressive and durable setting than the tabernacle which he had pitched on Mount Zion.[21] But Nathan the prophet, who seemed to be God's prophetic instrument in David's life, revealed to the king that God had not lived in a more substantial dwelling in the past and was quite satisfied to continue to live among His people in a humble tabernacle. At least, Nathan pointed out, David was not the one to build such a place as a temple, for his function was that of war. Until the kingdom should be established even more firmly, no thought should be given to the erection of a more permanent place of worship though David could and did go ahead with the plans and collection of materials for a temple (I Chron. 28). Nathan did go on to outline what we know as the Davidic Covenant, however, a covenant which outlines both the prospects of a temple to be built by David's son and successor and, even more importantly, the promise of an eternal kingdom over which would reign the descendants of David (II Sam. 7:12-16; I Chron. 17:11-14). It would culminate in the reign of the chief Son, the Lord Jesus Christ, who would reign forever (Isa. 9:1-7). We should not look upon this covenant as in any sense a replacement of the earlier covenants, as though David dreamed it up for his own personal political advancement, but as a continuation of the great design of God to progressively disclose Himself in salvation through Israel. At the same time we must recognize that this promise to David did eventuate in the founding of a royal family, a concept which originated only at this time in Israel's history. There had been abortive efforts in the past, such as Abimelech's attempt to succeed Gideon, his father, or Ish-bosheth's shortlived occupation of the throne of Saul, but only with David do we have the beginning of true dynasticism.

The list of David's military accomplishments is most impressive. Before many years had passed, and following his initial humbling of the Philistines at Rephaim, he had overcome the Moabites, certain Aramaean states such as Zobah and Damascus,[22] and the Edomites east of the Dead Sea. This extended the borders of Israel from deep in the Negev north to the Euphrates River with the exception of Phoenicia with which he was allied. On the west he pushed as far as the Philistine pentapolis in the southern coast and all the way to the Mediterranean farther north, while to the east he occupied virtually everything as far as the Great Desert. And those lands which he did not actually possess were forced to pay heavy tribute, thus greatly enriching Israel's coffers and providing a standard of life she had never known before.

Encouraged by his great increase in material prosperity, David took steps to be as beneficent as possible to his friends, especially the survivors of Saul's family. One of the sons of Jonathan, a cripple named Mephi-bosheth, he took into the protection of the palace and sustained the remainder of his life as a token of his friendship for his dearest friend. In other ways David showed his great heart of compassion, though his treatment of enemies sometimes seems a little harsh even for holy war (II Sam. 8:2).

The Ammonite wars seemed to give David the greatest difficulty of all as far as his international relations were concerned.[23] These people had been bitter enemies of Israel in the time of Jephthah as we will recall, but peace had been achieved between David and Nahash, king of Ammon. When Nahash died David sent an envoy to bring solace and encouragement to Hanun, the crown prince and son of Nahash. Hanun misinterpreted David's intentions, however, and humiliated the Israelite ambassage, thinking they had come to spy (II Sam. 10:4; I Chron. 19:4). This provoked hostility between the two kingdoms and when the Syrians joined the Ammonites against Israel matters only worsened. Joab managed to defeat the coalition, however, with the result that the Syrians never again attempted to aid Ammon.

Most important in the long run were David's activities while Israel was in battle. According to custom, the king, if physically able, was personally involved in military excursions. David, however, remained in Jerusalem for some reason while Joab and the army sallied forth to Ammon to besiege the capital city, Rabbah (Rabbath-ammon). While at home he became infatuated with Bath-sheba, the wife of Uriah, one of his Hittite mercenary commanders, and committed adultery with her.[24] When she knew she was pregnant, David sent for Uriah and suggested that he go home to his wife for a few days on furlough. Too honorable a man to enjoy the pleasures of home while his men were in the front line, Uriah refrained from going home, but remained on the steps of David's palace for several nights. Thus, there was not any possibility that David could blame the conception of the child on Uriah. This being the case, the only alternative was to remove Uriah so that Bath-sheba could be free to marry him. David therefore arranged for Uriah to carry a note back to Joab in which the king ordered his commander to place the unwitting Hittite in the front lines and then order a retreat without Uriah's knowledge. The dastardly command was carried out, and with a man's blood on his hands, David took the widow to be his wife (II Sam. 11:26-27).

Naturally the whole sordid affair greatly displeased the Lord, and He sent Nathan to David with a parable about a rich man who had stolen the lamb of his poor neighbor though he had many to spare (II Sam. 12:1-6). This story so incensed the king that he ordered the greedy man to pay the penalty, even with his life. When the prophet pointed out that he was the culprit, the whole ugly truth reached David's heart for the first time. In most abject contrition he begged the forgiveness of God for his heinous acts of murder and adultery, and though God did forgive, the illegitimate child died despite David's fervent prayer that it might be otherwise. Another child was born to the marriage later, however, and was named Solomon ("peace"), perhaps to indicate that peace had come again to the repentant king's heart and soul (II Sam. 12:24).

This event just described seemed to be the turning point in David's life and, consequently, in the life of the nation.

Up until now everything seemed to go so well, but after this his personal and family life became a sequence of tragedies. The first recorded instance was the rape of David's daughter Tamar by her half brother Amnon (II Sam. 13:14). This brought on the revenge of her full brother, Absalom, who determined to punish Amnon with death. He arranged a festival after two years to which Amnon was especially invited. When the unwary man arrived he was assassinated by Absalom's servants, and Absalom himself fled the country to Geshur, the homeland of his mother. This internecine strife filled David with such a heavy heart that he resolutely refused to allow Absalom to return home, even though he missed him sorely and may have seen some justification in what was done. Finally after three years, Joab, with great diplomacy, arranged for the reunion, but when Absalom returned to Jerusalem, David would not greet him. Two more years passed, unfortunate years for the stubborn king who because of pride would not make peace with his son. Then the day came when Joab once again interceded, this time with success, and father and son were at one again (II Sam. 14:33).

But the joy of reconciliation was only superficial on Absalom's part. For five long years he had brooded over his father's rejection, a rejection which he felt had been completely unwarranted under the circumstances. And he had had a long time to think of revenge for his father's callous treatment of him. Now that formal friendship had been reached, he could put into effect the plot that had been formulating in his mind. Absalom began to frequent the main gate of the city where he could contact hundreds of persons every day. They came there oftentimes to vent their grievances to the king, but the busy monarch could have but little time for these comparatively petty matters. But Absalom, with sympathetic ear, would listen to their complaints, and would subtly suggest that if only he were king they could get satisfaction. Gradually, he won the multitudes over (II Sam. 15:6); only when it became too late did David sense what was under foot. Gathering his faithful entourage, the king fled from his own palace and city, abandoning it to his traitorous son. Some of his friends he left behind to serve as spies and saboteurs, including his priest Abiathar, another priest Zadok, their two sons, and an old wise man, Hushai. David instructed Hushai to give misleading counsel to the young Absalom so that David's escape and future return could be more assured.

The king and his loyal subjects crossed the Mount of Olives to the Jericho road and went on to the other side of the Jordan where they mustered what troops they had. Back in Jerusalem, Absalom was in firm control and proceeded to demonstrate that he was in the shoes of his father by taking his father's concubines for himself (II Sam. 16:22). Hushai had in the meantime gained the prince's confidence and made every effort to use his office as counselor to David's advantage. Ahithophel, the official court sage, advised Absalom to go immediately in pursuit of David lest David should attempt to come back and retake the throne. But Hushai gave counter advice to the effect that if Absalom attempted to fight David before he had secured his position as king a little more firmly David, the more seasoned warrior, would surely prevail. Of course, all this worked out to David's favor because he had now the extra time he needed to consolidate his own forces and to obtain the help of friendly Ammonites and others. When Ahithophel saw that his counsel was rejected, he hanged himself. Absalom bided his time and when he thought all was ready, headed for Transjordan with his army under the command of Amasa.

A fierce battle ensued in the Forest of Ephraim, near the Jordan, and David's more experienced band of heroes held the day. Absalom himself caught his head in the boughs of a huge oak, and while suspended in the air was thrust through the heart with darts hurled by Joab (II Sam. 18:14). Runners were dispatched to inform David of the victory, but the glad news was more than offset by his knowledge of Absalom's cruel death. With bitter tears he bemoaned the terrible end of his son, though that son had occasioned so much grief in his own life. Joab, completely disgusted by this show of emotion, reproached David, reminding him that time after time he had mourned for his enemies when he should have rejoiced at their defeat and death. First it was Saul, then Abner, then Ishbosheth, and now his own iniquitous son. If David possessed one overriding fault, in Joab's sight that fault was an irresponsible love for all men including his enemies (II Sam. 19:6). And that fault engendered an ill feeling between the two men that was to result in a complete breach.

David resented Joab's presumption and upon his return to Jerusalem appointed Amasa, Absalom's general, commander in Joab's place. Everyone else he graciously forgave, even those who had been most instrumental in the coup which had sent him in ignominy from Jerusalem in the first place, but this forgiving spirit did not ingratiate the king with his people. There had always been a certain animosity against David because of Saul's great popularity, especially among the northern tribes, and Absalom had managed to capture the people's fancy as not even David had been able. It is no wonder, then, that when David returned to his capital, led primarily by men of his own tribe of Judah, seeds of fresh rebellion began to sprout. This time the usurper was Sheba, a Benjamite, who announced that the northern tribes, indeed, had no real share in the king because of his obvious favoritism for the Judaeans (II Sam. 20:1). David thereupon ordered Amasa to take whatever troops necessary to squelch this newest revolution and to show the nation that he was still in control. On the way to battle Joab called Amasa aside as though to confer with him, and instead stabbed him to death. As commander once more, Joab led the king's army north to Abel, in the northern part of Naphtali, where he located Sheba and his band in the shelter of the city walls. When he threatened to burn the city down with all its inhabitants, a wise old woman demanded the reason for the attack. Joab told her that they were after only Sheba, with the result that the head of Sheba came over the wall in a few moments, the price of the city's security having been paid (II Sam. 20:22).

These political emergencies in the realm were followed by agricultural calamities occasioned by a three year drought. In reply to his query concerning the reason for God's judgment in this way, the Lord informed David that Saul's family had mistreated the Gibeonites by breaking the ancient treaty made with them by Joshua (Josh. 9:15), and that the famine came in punishment of this. So David asked the Gibeonites what they wished to be done, but he was totally unprepared for the answer they gave: Saul's remaining sons must be hanged. The king was faced with a serious dilemma. He must grant the Gibeonites their request, but he must try to preserve the family of Saul as much as possible. A compromise was reached in which seven of the sons were delivered to the Gibeonites, but Mephi-bosheth, son of Jonathan, was saved in Jonathan's memory. Then, as a sort of compensation, David sent for the bones of Saul and Jonathan, which still remained in Jabesh-gilead, and had them properly interred at Gibeah, Saul's royal city and real home.

David's Final Years (II Sam. 22-I Kings 2; I Chron. 21-29). One other act of impropriety recorded in II Samuel was David's census of the army. This book says that "he" moved David to number the people (II Sam. 24:1), the antecedent to the pronoun apparently being the Lord, but I Chronicles states that Satan tempted David to sin in this matter (I Chron. 21:1). The reconciliaton, no doubt, lies in the assumption that "he" in Samuel does not refer to the Lord, but to Satan, a fact that becomes clear when we recognize that God does not entice men to commit evil. In any event, the counting of the army seems to suggest a reliance upon the flesh rather than upon the spiritual resources of God and such lack of confidence in God must be punished. In due time David recognized the sin of pride which prompted the enumeration, but already Gad the prophet came with the announcement of Divine judgment. This time David had the choice of seven years of famine, three months flight from his enemies, or three days of plague. Fearing to fall into the hands of men, he rejected the second alternative and cast himself upon the mercy of God to suffer what he must. A great epidemic broke out and took 70,000 lives. In deepest repentance David prayed for the Lord's grace, and by instruction of the prophet Gad built an altar at the threshing floor of Araunah, on the sight of ancient Mount Moriah, where he interceded by sacrifice before the Lord (II Sam. 24:25). God heard, and the pestilence was halted. In time to come Solomon chose this very spot, just north of the old Jebusite city of Jerusalem, as the site for his magnificent Temple and he incorporated it within the city walls.

David's latter years were spent in comparative peace, at least as far as international affairs were concerned. The problems within his family which had been precipitated by his adulterous affair with Bath-sheba continued to rise, however, and his dying days witnessed a struggle for the throne among his own sons. Adonijah, whom he had spoiled with fatherly attention, waited until his father was too senile to interfere and then persuaded Abiathar, David's longtime priest and friend, and Joab, the hero of many a military cam-

paign, to side with him in an effort to take the throne upon
David's decease. Properly, though, the kingdom should have
gone to Solomon by virtue of the Divine promise (I Chron.
22:9-10), so Nathan the prophet, Zadok the priest, and certain
other notables aligned themselves with Solomon in opposition
to the Adonijah usurpation plot.

Nathan encouraged Bath-sheba, mother of Solomon, to
go to the king and inform him that Adonijah was conniving
against her son, the legitimate successor to the crown. While
she was presenting her case, Nathan came into the royal
chamber and seconded what Bath-sheba had said. Convinced
that dirty work was underfoot indeed, the old monarch ordered
Nathan and Zadok to anoint Solomon king without delay. With
dispatch the ceremony took place, accompanied with such
shouting of "God save the king!" that the whole city rang
with the echo. Adonijah, in another part of the city, heard
the commotion, and when he was informed by the son of
Abiathar that Solomon had taken the throne at his father's
instigation, he fled for his life to the security of the great
altar of the tabernacle. For a time no retributive action was
taken by either David or Solomon, but when the final moment
of the king's life had come he solemnly charged his son to
carry out any necessary punishment of the revolutionaries.
Then the great man, seventy years old now, slept with his
fathers and at last had rest after a lifetime of exacting labor
and strife (ca. 971 B.C.).

Solomon wasted no time in establishing his position with
ruthlessness and utmost efficiency (I Kings 2:12). His half
brother Adonijah foolishly requested that he be given his late
father's concubine, an acquisition calculated to eventually give
him royal status, but Solomon wisely saw the implications.
With unleashed vengeance he ordered his strong man, Benaiah,
to murder Adonijah and thus remove any future possibility of
his reviving political hopes (I Kings 2:25). Next, the new
king commanded Abiathar to leave Jerusalem and to surrender his priestly office, the only reason for his salvation
being his holy position. Joab was then considered, and catching wind of a threat to his life, he fled to the horns of the altar,
but to no avail. Benaiah caught him there and summarily
stabbed him to death after dragging him from the holy precincts. Finally, Shimei, a man who had mocked David when
the unfortunate king had been run out of the capital by Ab-

salom (II Sam. 16:5-7), was warned by Solomon that if he ever attempted to leave the city he too would die. Heedless of the warning, he undertook to do just that, and upon his return fell victim to the purge which had already taken such a toll.

SOLOMON (I Kings 3-11; II Chronicles 1-9)

Solomon's Wisdom (I Kings 3-4; II Chron. 1:1-13). It is almost impossible to describe the dramatic and far reaching changes which had occurred in David's forty year reign over Israel. From a badly divided, or at best loosely federated, group of distantly spread tribes, the nation had become united, powerful, and comparatively very wealthy. Whereas the kingdom had been ruled by a man who was not much more than a powerful tribal chieftain in a crude palace located in an insignificant Benjamite city, now a king in the real sense of the term was on the throne. Not only the tribes, but surrounding kingdoms had been either welded together into the Davidic sphere of influence or had at least been reduced to the status of tributaries. The Kingdom of Israel had become a power to be reckoned with, even, perhaps, rivaling the world's leading states. With its strategic location in the Fertile Crescent the nation stood to wield considerable influence in all directions and to extract revenues from trading peoples who must pass through that way. In addition, under David we seem to see genuine signs of spiritual renewal, if the monarchy itself is any gauge, for the greatest religious poetry of Israel's history was written then and in the succeeding generation (II Sam. 22; 23:1-7; I Chron. 23-29). Moreover, there seems to be almost no mention of idolatrous practices in Israel, and we can conclude that the pious king had pretty well purged such things from the realm.[25] Now that he was dead, and his erstwhile enemies had also perished at the hand of his son, we can well understand the significance of the statement that "the kingdom was established in the hand of Solomon" (I Kings 2:46).

Some idea of the new importance of the nation Israel might be seen in the fact that Solomon appeared almost on equal terms with Pharaoh of Egypt. At least, he married Pharaoh's daughter, an accomplishment almost without parallel, for Egyptian princesses were reserved for Egyptian royal-

THE MONARCHY

ZOBAH

Damascus

SYRIA

SEA OF GALILEE

MEDITERRANEAN SEA

• Endor

Mt. Gilboa +

Beth-shan •

• Jabesh-gilead

Jabbok River

Jordan River

Michmash •

Ramah

Mizpah

Aijalon

• Gibeah

Kiriath-jearim •

• Nob

• Jerusalem

Gilgal

Bethlehem

Adullam

Gath

Keilah

PHILISTIA

DEAD SEA

AMMON

• Hebron

Ziph •

Engedi

Ziklag •

Maon •

• Carmel

AMALEK

MOAB

WILDERNESS

OF PARAN

EDOM

SCALE OF MILES

0   5   10   15   20   25   30

ty.[26] But that importance contained within it the seeds of the nation's own demise, for we learn that a quasi-legal religious practice was being carried on outside of Jerusalem at various "high places" (*bamoth*), probably to accommodate Solomon's heathen wives. Such shrines were located on the summits of hills perhaps to indicate a closer relationship to God. In any event, the king himself frequented these places of worship, especially resorting to the great Bamah at Gibeon (I Kings 3:4; II Chron. 1:3).[27] There the Lord approached him very early in his reign and offered him whatever gift he might choose. With unusual discernment the young ruler acknowledged his immaturity and inabilities and requested that above all else he might have the wisdom necessary to govern his great nation. The Lord graciously bestowed not only this, but because of Solomon's selflessness promised him also great wealth and honor among men. The new wisdom was quickly put to the test in Solomon's incredible judgment regarding the two harlots and their babies, a story celebrated for its simple logic and fairness. Like wild fire the king's wisdom became proverbial, so much so that people came from around the eastern world to catch his words.

His astuteness may be seen also in his organization of the kingdom politically. He appointed certain court officials, perhaps after Egyptian models,[28] and also divided the kingdom into twelve administrative districts over which he placed officers. He did not follow the ancient tribal boundaries, thus preventing too much nationalism among the tribes, but he was conscious that he must retain the twelve-fold division lest he entirely reject tradition. These districts were responsible for supplying a certain amount of provision to the court every month, a not inconsiderable task, and they no doubt also supplied manpower in times of public works as well as in war.[29]

Solomon's Building (I Kings 5-8; II Chron. 2-7). Solomon is not primarily known as a man of war; indeed, we have no record of conflict until the end of his reign. His fame lay in his literary and building accomplishments. The former we will discuss below, but with the latter we should spend some time here. Hiram, the friend of his father and king of Phoenicia, when he learned of David's death, immediately offered his services to Solomon in any way he could use them (I Kings 5:1). For this Solomon was most grateful, for he had long since been commissioned by his father to build the Temple in accordance with the Davidic Covenant. Moreover, he had certain other projects in mind which he could accomplish only with the skills for which the Phoenicians were renowned.

In return for a certain quantity of wheat and oil year by year, Hiram would supply cedar and fir from Lebanon as well as skilled craftsmen. Solomon would also use labor from his own country, as many as 150,000 men under conscription, who would serve as hewers of timber, porters, and stone masons. When all arrangements had been made, the work commenced in Solomon's fourth year which, as we have noted, was the 480th year since the Exodus (ca. 966 B.C.). The Temple, fashioned after the general pattern of the tabernacle of Moses, but much larger, was ninety feet long, thirty feet wide, and forty-five feet high. On the front was a porch and in front of that two free standing pillars named Boaz ("strength") and Jachin ("uprightness"). Along the two sides and the back were chambers three stories high, used probably as vestment chambers and storage rooms. The interior was lined with richly decorated boards and beams of cedar. Within and without were lavish carvings and other decorative motifs which combined to make the Temple one of the finest buildings in history. The seven year period involved in its construction suggests something of the magnificence of the edifice.

Also in the Temple area, located on Mount Moriah just to the north of the old Jebusite city, were several other great buildings including the House of the Forest of Lebanon, the Judgment Hall, a Porch of Pillars, a palace for Pharaoh's daughter, and Solomon's own opulent palace. The fancy work in all these projects was under the execution of another Hiram (I Kings 7:13), a native of Naphtali, whose gifts remind us of Bezaleel and Aholiab. The general construction we assume to be under Phoenician direction, for besides being great shipbuilders they also distinguished themselves for their work in stone as we know from many of their temples which have been recently excavated. To suggest that Solomon's buildings, especially the Temple, were influenced to any great degree by Phoenician Baal temples, seems unwarranted, however.[30] It may be permissible to say, perhaps, that there were certain common features among Near Eastern temples in general, and that Solomon's temple adopted some of these features within the framework of the earlier tabernacle arrangement, but even at this point we must be very careful, for anything which would detract from the originality of Israel's faith, even as expressed in the architecture of its temples, is risky.[31] Though we have no record of direct revelation to Solomon in the building of this place of worship (cf. II Chron. 3:3), we may assume that the gift of wisdom with which he was endowed presupposed a knowledge in such matters.

At the conclusion of the Temple construction a tremendous ceremony of dedication was carried out. The Ark was carried from its resting place at Mount Zion and was placed with greatest reverence into the Oracle (Holy of Holies) of the new structure on Mount Moriah (II Chron. 5:7). At that moment the glory of God filled the Temple, as it had the tabernacle in days past, and the nation knew that God was at last pleased to dwell in this new, more permanent residence among them. Following this demonstration of God's presence, Solomon offered the longest prayer recorded in the Bible, a prayer laden with recognition of God's grace, Israel's responsibility, and general recognition of the ancient covenant relationships between them. Nowhere else do we find such clear statements concerning the transcendance of God, and yet such realization that He dwells among and within His faithful people.[32] He prayed urgently that if the nation should ever sin so grievously that it must be carried forth from the land that it might repent and be graciously allowed to return to the praise of God. After the prayer, the ready dedication of the people was expressed by the offering of the greatest magnitude in man's memory— 22,000 oxen and 120,000 sheep.

Solomon's Covenant (I Kings 9:1-9; II Chron. 7:12-22). Some time later the Lord appeared to Solomon again as He had at Gibeon and reviewed with him the glorious covenant promises which He had spelled out to David (I Kings 9:1-9). He assured the king that as long as he faithfully executed his royal function in uprightness and obedience he would forever reign through his posterity. Should he deviate from this holy calling, however, his family and nation would be cast aside, at least for a season, and all the world would know that unfaithful Israel was the object of God's displeasure.

Solomon's Glory   (I Kings 9:10-10:29; II Chron. 8-9).
The last years of Solomon's life, like those of David, were
filled with a mixture of joy and sorrow, triumph and defeat,
but for different reasons. His extensive building programs
had oppressed the people with heavy taxation and hard physical labor which he obtained by corveé.[33] Some of his friendly
neighbors, notably Hiram of Phoenicia, became dissatisfied
with Solomon's business dealings with them. Hiram objected
that Solomon had not lived up to his agreements in that he
had given him poor villages in Galilee as compensation, rather
than the more munificent payment he expectd. To offset this,
Solomon had had to increase the burden of his already over-
laden people. But he partially relieved their situation by fitting out a navy of ships, under Phoenician direction, and
these he sent from his Red Sea port to lands throughout the
known world. These ships came back bearing all manner of
exotic goods which Solomon presumably sold, in some cases
at a very handsome profit.[34]

His rapidly accumulating prestige and wealth were soon
noticed by even distant rulers; some of them began to travel
to the court of Solomon to feast their eyes on what he had
done and to hear from his own lips the words of wisdom for
which he was even more celebrated. Among these royal
figures was the queen of Sheba, a fabulously wealthy land in
the southern tip of the Arabian peninsula, which to this day
is a primary source of rich spices.[35] She came skeptically to
test the king of Israel with difficult questions, but she left
convinced that the half had never been told her concerning
this amazing man. His buildings, his use of pure gold for
even common vessels, and his throne of ivory were her envy
and the envy of all the world.

Solomon's Sin and Death   (I Kings 11). But his prosperity in this sense was more than offset by his poverty in another, his love for women. He took wives from many foreign
nations, including those with whom intermarriage was specifically forbidden in the Law, and this brought about the
result anticipated in the Law—Solomon's heart was turned
from God to the gods of these nations. This need not imply
that he forsook Yahweh entirely, for the text is clear that he
did not, but he probably instituted a rather syncretistic religion consisting of elements from many different ones (I

Kings 11:4-8). We do know that he built chapels for his wives in which they could worship their native deities, and he may have associated with them there in their worship rituals. The result was as God had warned. The kingdom was to be wrested from Solomon's grasp, yet not entirely, because of his father David's sake, and only the tribe of Judah would be retained by the Davidic line (I Kings 11:13). This declaration was soon followed by the outbreak of revolution in various parts of the empire. Hadad, an Edomite prince exiled to Egypt under David but now returned, broke away in the southeast (I Kings 11:14). Then Rezon took over Damascus and from there revolted from Israel and reigned over all the Aramaean states (11:23). Even his own trusted servant Jeroboam, officer over the central part of the nation, declared his independence of the king. In this he was encouraged by the prophet Ahijah of Shiloh who met him one day in a field, seized and tore his garment into a dozen pieces, explaining that the pieces symbolized the tribes. Ten of these he returned to Jeroboam, indicating that he would be the ruler of ten tribes, but two the prophet retained. One piece represented Judah, of course, and the other, as it turned out, stood for Benjamin, the tribe which eventually sided with its southern neighbor (I Kings 11:26-36). This was only fitting because Jerusalem, the city of David, had by now been incorporated into the area of Benjamin. After Solomon knew of the encounter between Ahijah and Jeroboam, he attempted to arrest the latter, but Jeroboam fled to Egypt where he bided his time until the moment of opportunity should come. And that time came quickly, for within a short period Solomon died, having completed an illustrious reign of forty years, but a reign which ended in dismal prospects for the future.

HEBREW POETRY

The most appropriate time and place to discuss the poetical sections of the Old Testament is in connection with the United Monarchy, especially in the reigns of David and Solomon, for it was then that such literature reached its peak in finesse and prolificacy. Of all the books which we consider poetry in our English arrangement of the canon—Job, Psalms, Proverbs, Ecclesiastes, and Song of Solomon—the greater part was no doubt written by either David and Solomon personally or by scribes in their courts. Now certainly some of this is not poetry in the sense in which we regard poetry, for the term covers a much broader area here than is usual now. But if we realize that we are speaking only of literature which can not properly be called history or law or prophecy, then we may use the designation for lack of a better term. As we saw above, the Hebrews designated one section of the canon "Writings," but that is not entirely satisfactory either for it includes materials such as Chronicles and Ezra-Nehemiah which can hardly be considered poetry at all.

Before discussing the five books mentioned just above, we should examine Hebrew poetry as a whole in an effort to detect its outstanding genres and characteristics.[36]   We do not find any emphasis at all on rhyme and very little on metre compared to that of other languages. The principal feature is that of parallelism, the idea that the second or following lines of a strophe somehow parallel the thought of the first. There are several kinds of parallelism, such as (1) synonymous, in which almost identical thoughts are expressed in both lines of a couplet (Ps. 49:1) ; (2) antithetical, in which the second line contrasts with the first (Prov. 15:1) ; (3) synthetical, in which the second line completes the thought of the first (Prov. 4:23) ;   (4) climactic, in which the lines proceed step by step to a climax in thought (Ps. 103:1) ; (5) comparative, in which the second line forms a simile of the first (Ps. 103:12) ; and (6) progressive, in which a new and related thought is introduced in the second line (Job 3:17).   Almost without exception the poetic portions of the Old Testament, whether those in the books listed above or even those in the historical and prophetic books, are represented by one of the foregoing types of parallelism.

The kinds of poetry are as follows: (1) lyric, a poetry to be sung, found most commonly in the Psalms; (2) didactic, or teaching literature, represented by Proverbs and Ecclesiastes; (3) prophetic, found in lengthy sections of some of the prophetic books, notably Isaiah; (4) elegaic, meant to convey grief and mourning, seen in the Lamentations of Jeremiah; and (5) dramatic, meant to be acted, and expressed by Job and the Song of Solomon. One characteristic of all these kinds is that they express the heartfelt feelings of their composers toward their fellow men, especially toward God; whereas other kinds of Scriptural literature reflect the attitude of God and

His feelings toward men. Now surely we cannot make a hard and fast rule along this line, but in general this criterion can stand. And we must also guard against any feeling that these books or portions, because they are human expressions, are not at the same time the inspired Word of God. In some cases, perhaps most, the inspiration involved has to do only with the faithful, inerrant recording of what the poet said or wrote, but in other cases there is actual revelation from God to men through the poet. For example, the psalms which prophesy the messianic activity cannot be merely the reasoning or reflection of a man about these things, no matter how godly he might be, but must be understood as a revelation somehow expressed by the poet in his voluntary utterances.[37]

The Book of Job. There is no doubt that Job was an historical figure (Ezek. 14:14; James 5:11), but there is no way to ascertain when or even where he lived except to say probably in the desert east of Palestine and in the patriarchal period. Most conservative scholars feel, however, that the book was not written that early, but probably comes from the time of Solomon.[38] Liberals for the most part assign it to a much later time, some even dating it in post-exilic times.[39] The author is unnamed and thus unknown, but whoever wrote it has been considered one of the most gifted dramatists in history of literature. His purpose was not, as some feel, to illustrate the patience of a godly man, though that surely is involved, but to attempt to answer the age-old problem of theodicy—why do righteous men suffer if there is a God of mercy and love? Or it might even be to teach that man is to acknowledge the sovereignty of God, no matter what the circumstance, and that his real problem might be the pride of his own righteousness.

The drama begins with a prologue (chapters 1-2) in which Job is singled out by God as an exemplary man whom not even Satan could defeat. Satan is allowed to do what he will to Job, except take his life, and he proceeds to subject Job to the greatest loss and punishment imaginable, but the patriarch stoutly maintains his faith in God. Then we have a series of speeches by three "comforters" who come to Job and try to account for his miserable condition (3-31). There are three cycles of dialogue in this series (chapters 3-14, 15-21, and 22-31) in which each friend speaks in turn and each time is answered by Job who tries to defend his integrity. The main argument they advance is that Job must have sinned, either consciously or not, or he would not suffer as he did (8:3-6). But Job says that he is innocent of any wrong doing and is at a loss to explain his misfortune. A fifth figure, Elihu, then comes into the story and we have his speeches next (32-37). He takes issue with the three preceding counselors whom he considers ignorant (32:3) and then attempts to convince Job through a slightly different line of argument that he is somehow to blame. He especially emphasizes the instruction afforded by suffering (33:29), God's justice in all things (34:10-19), and the Divine transcendance as compared to Job's ignorance and limitations (35:5-6).

Through all this Job has clung to his hope in God, but he eventually begins to question God in this basic issue: why should he, a righteous man, be afflicted (Ch. 31)? Yet, Job did not turn his back on God. Finally, God broke His silence and explained that the gulf which separates Deity and humanity is so great that Job not only should not question his suffering, but should not even try to understand it (40:2). There are some things limited to God and in these areas man is to be silent and let God work out His own wondrous will. In the Epilogue (42:7-17) God restores Job to his original position with even greater blessings than he had known before and makes of Job the intercessor necessary for the salvation of his recent critics. The story ends with the basic question yet unanswered; yet the message of God that He is absolute and does as He will without regard to man's comprehension of His mysteries must constitute the real theme and provide the fullest measure of hope.[40]

Psalms. The Psalms constitute the hymn book of Israel; many of them were sung and recited at festal occasions and probably even in the homes and on the job. Approximately half of the 150 were written by David, who we know had great artistic abilities (I Chron. 13:8); a few were by Solomon, whose reputation also is well established in these pursuits (I Kings 4:29-34); by Asaph, one of David's court poets; by the sons of Korah, another group of professional writers; and one even was written by Moses (Ps. 90). In addition, many are of anonymous authorship and were written over a period of many years, some certainly as late as post-exilic times. We see, then, that the majority of the Psalms come from the United

Monarchy period (tenth century), and only a few from much later. This is in contrast to a view commonly espoused until very recent years that most of the Psalms, if not all, were composed very late, some shortly before the time of Christ. The main theory was that the literature and theology encompassed therein were too elevated or advanced for the primitive period in which David was presumed to have lived.[41] With the discovery of Canaanite poetry of a similar nature and equally advanced from a literary standpoint at Ras Shamra in Syria, dating from four centuries before David, all arguments that David could not have written the Psalms have been quietly laid to rest.[42] Now it is averred that David *did* not write them, except maybe a few, and not that he *could* not.[43]

There are several themes in the Psalms, and sometimes they are divided into groupings corresponding to these themes. We have, for example, penitential psalms which pertain to repentance and sorrow for sin. The best known of these is David's prayer of forgiveness uttered after his sin with Bathsheba (Ps. 51). Others are Psalms 6, 32, 38, 102, 130, and 143. There are also psalms called imprecatory because they invoke the wrath and judgment of God against ungodly men. Examples in which this element is found are Psalms 5:10 and 139:21-22. It is important to remember on those that the poet is not expressing a desire for God's punishment of the wicked to satisfy his own feelings, but because he recognizes that the wicked have offended the honor of God.[44] And there is usually a strong eschatological sense involved. That is, the poet is not so much invoking and expecting the immediate judgment of God, but he is looking forward to the day of the Lord when all unrepentant sinners must be dealt with according to their impiety toward God. Though many scholars would attempt to demonstrate that the Old Testament is morally inferior to the New by referring to these "barbarous" imprecations, the true explanation of the ethical incongruity lies in the mistaken ideas some men have concerning the Biblical doctrine of sin and punishment. When we properly understand the nature of a holy and sinless God, we, with the psalmists, must cry out against the iniquity which so terribly offends Him. We must not mean that we hate men though they sin, for indeed we must love them, but we must hate their sin and unrepentance. To the Old Testament mind the distinction between the two may not have been as clear as it is to us this side of the Cross.

One of the most important collections of Psalms is what we call the Messianic because they prophetically describe the future Messiah of Israel and His work. Many of these depict Him in His regal splendor in which He will come as King to reign over His church (2, 8, 45, 72, 89, 97, 110, 132) and are therefore sometimes called Royal Psalms. Others speak of Him as the suffering One who must taste death before He can wear the crown. Among these are those referring to His betrayal into the hands of sinners (41, 109), His crucifixion (22, 69), and His bodily resurrection (16, 40, 66). Obviously the writers were not always completely aware of the significance of their writings in these areas, though surely at times they knew they spoke of the Anointed One; we can know, as the New Testament writers testify (Heb. 2:6-10; Mt. 27:46, 43; John 19:24; 20:25; Mt. 27:34, 38), that they speak of none other than our Lord. Because of the higher critics' difficulty in accepting fulfilled prophecy, they must assume that these Messianic Psalms speak only in very general terms of some ideal figure of the future or even of the nation itself in some cases.[45] They avoid the implications of the New Testament writers' use of these portions of the Psalms as prophecies which Messiah fulfilled by maintaining that the writers "read into" the life and death of Christ elements from the Psalms. In other words, they say, many of the Messianic Psalms are used in reference to our Lord where such use is historically unjustified. Jesus did not really rise from the dead, but the Gospel writers said he did and supported their claims by referring to these Messianic passages in the Old Testament. This seems to be an extremely frantic effort to deny any Messianic character to the Psalms except that which was idealistic and hardly likely of literal fulfillment.

Proverbs. The Book of Proverbs claims to have been written by Solomon for the most part, and there is no real reason to argue otherwise.[46] We know that he was highly gifted in wisdom and literary talent (I Kings 4:32) and that he wrote hundreds of proverbs and songs which have never been recovered. The main purpose of the book is to disclose human wisdom or observation in the light of that from God. It discusses the whole range of morals and ethics, providing wise insight into human behavior. Despite its seemingly "earthly" approach, there is clearly a recognition of Divine revelation in the guidance of mankind's affairs (3:21-26). Solomon and the other wisdom writers did not merely express their own opinions here, but they regarded God as the fountainhead of all wisdom, and indeed, considered Wisdom (*Chokhmah*) in almost a personified sense, perhaps as a manifestation of the Spirit of God. Wisdom to them was not, in a Gnostic sense, the means of salvation *per se*, but the gift of God available to all men whereby they might know Him and their world as well.

In addition to the portions written by Solomon (chapters 1:1-22:16), we have also the "words of the wise" (22:17-24:34), perhaps by an unknown author; proverbs of Solomon copied out by Hezekiah's scribes and included in the final edition (25-29); the "words of Agur" (30), an unknown figure; the "words of Lemuel" (31:1-9), also otherwise unknown; and an anonymous acrostic poem written in honor of the virtuous woman (31:10-31). Most of the Proverbs are dated much later by the critics because they seem to them to reflect much later wisdom concepts than would be possible in the time of Solomon. However, more and more evidence is being compiled to suggest that such wisdom was very ancient and that Solomon's proverbs were only a portion of the entire literature of this kind which circulated in the Near Eastern world.[47]

Ecclesiastes. No book of the Old Testament has suffered more at the hands of the higher critics than Ecclesiastes because of its alleged secular and pessimistic tone. Many feel it has no place in the canon at all, a rather presumptuous opinion to say the least, whereas others would date it so late that it could scarcely be called Old Testament. It was popular at one time, especially before the Dead Sea Scrolls and other ancient Jewish documents were found, to believe that Ecclesiastes was Hellenistic because it contained ideas allegedly Greek in nature.[48] This is pretty well discredited now because it is recognized widely that Jewish literature from a very early period contained ideas similar to Greek concepts, but completely unrelated.[49] But this has not discouraged the critics from dating the book very late on other, subjective grounds.

The book is essentially a record of the reasonings of "man

under the sun" or the secular man who lives without a recognition of God. The original name of the book was *koheleth*, or "The Preacher"; it was written by "the son of David, king in Jerusalem." It is tempting to identify this preacher and son of David with Solomon, and some scholars do just this,[50] but other evidence seems to rule this out. For example, the writer says that he "was king," indicating that he is not at the time of writing, so this hardly fits in with Solomon who died in office (1:12). Furthermore, he states that his wealth and power exceeded that of any of the kings before him (2:7-9). This does not seem to refer to Solomon because he would not be apt to speak of only Saul and his own father David as "all that were before me in Jerusalem." Yet, as Archer suggests, the above arguments can be explained in various ways reconcilable with Solomonic authorship.[51] Perhaps it is best to take the obvious meaning, that Solomon was the Preacher, but to recognize that there are difficulties in any view.

The authorship of the book is of little consequence, however, compared to the theme, which is "vanity." The writer observes that the human condition is very pessimistic indeed, for time comes and goes, men are born and die, and yet nothing basically changes (1:3-11). As he sees this unending pattern he remarks that there is nothing new under the sun and that everything man can do or become is merely emptiness. The central idea is beautifully expressed in the last chapter where man is described as a house whose pillars and posts become weakened with age, whose windows (eyes) become darkened, whose grinders (teeth) become low and worn out, and whose daughters of music (the voice) are brought low. But this description of man who is old and about to expire is prefaced by the admonition to "remember now thy Creator in the days of thy youth" (12:1-7). This, then, is the key to the book. The Preacher exhorts that man should know God while he is young so that life will have a proper orientation and meaning. If he fails to do this, life will be nothing but emptiness, an experience devoid of purpose and direction and satisfaction. Far from being a pessimistic book, it is a stirring, almost evangelistic sermon which shows the way out of the morass of a godless life into the brilliant radiance of His presence.

Song of Solomon. This short love story, ascribed to Solomon both by internal (1:1) and external evidence, has long been the focal point of vigorous discussion. There are many who would reject it as unworthy of the Old Testament because of its allegedly sensuous and even erotic nature. They say that it speaks only of human love and in such terms that there can hardly be any spiritual edification to the reader.[52] Obviously, if the book was written by Solomon it must have some claim to canonicity because of that fact alone, but the further fact that Jewish tradition as well as the consensus of the Church have accepted its authenticity constitutes a powerful argument.

The real theme of the book, apart from the interpretation forced upon it by critics who seem to delight in pointing out its bold descriptions, is the glorification of true love. One can hardly read it with an open mind without sensing the beautiful concepts related there. It seems that Solomon (for he surely is the king in mind in the story) had fallen in love with a beautiful maiden who, unfortunately, was beneath his class in life, being but a shepherd girl. The narrative relates the struggle of the king, who had everything else he desired but the maiden, to woo her affections, apparently successfully. Primarily we have dialogues in which he describes her and his love for her, and in which she also describes him. The final result is that Solomon wins the maiden and she enables him, by her beauty and character, to see that God's intention is for a man to have one wife and not the many who had come into his life to lead him from God.[53]

It has always seemed most unlikely that the whole episode, as personal as it is, was recorded for only the purpose of giving us instruction in a love affair of the tenth century. Hence, other interpretations have been suggested. The two most widely accepted among conservatives are (1) that the relationship described is that between God (Solomon) and Israel (the maiden), and that God is attempting in this type to show His love for His special people;[54] or (2) that it is an allegory of the love of Christ for the Church.[55] Both of these could be possible interpretations at the same time, so that actually we have an historical allegory showing God's love for Israel, which is made typical by reference to the New Testament Church. In both the Old and New Testaments the figure of Israel and the Church is frequently expressed in the motif of a wife or lover of God. We maintain that the main reason for rejection of the book lies in the failure of the critics to see the ideal love of God which lies beneath the surface of this actual love affair of Solomon.

[1] O. R. Gurney, *The Hittites*, Baltimore, Penguin Books, 1964, p. 39.

[2] John Bright, *A History of Israel*, Philadelphia, Westminster Press, 1959, p. 153.

[3] Donald Harden, *The Phoenicians*, New York, Frederick A. Praeger, 1962, pp. 50-51.

[4] C. F. Keil and Franz Delitzsch, *Biblical Commentary on the Old Testament: Samuel*, Grand Rapids, Wm. B. Eerdmans Publishing Co., 1948, p. 100.

[5] See my unpublished dissertation, "An Investigation of the Person and Work of the Old Testament Prophet of God," Ph. D. Dissertation, Greenville, South Carolina, Bob Jones University, 1963, for a discussion of the prophetic office in general. My remarks in this section are based largely on conclusions made in that study.

[6] George E. Mendenhall, "Biblical History in Transition," *The Bible and the Ancient Near East*, Ed. by G. Ernest Wright, Garden City, Doubleday and Company, Inc., 1965, pp. 47-48.

[7] Theophile J. Meek, *Hebrew Origins*, New York, Harper and Row, 1960, p. 150.

[8] Theodore H. Robinson, *Prophecy and the Prophets*, London, Duckworth and Co., 1923, p. 50.

[9] This site has been excavated by Albright who found it to be most rustic and primitive, just as the Biblical evidence would suggest (I Sam. 11:4-5). See a description in G. Ernest Wright, *Biblical Archaeology*, Philadelphia, Westminster Press, 1957, pp. 67-69. See also Paul W. Lapp, "Tell el-Ful," *Biblical Archaeologist*, 28:2-10, February, 1965.

[10] For the difficult chronological problem here in relation to I Sam. 10:8 and 11:14, see John P. Lange, *Commentary on the Holy Scriptures: Samuel*, Ed. by Philip Schaff, Grand Rapids, Zondervan Publishing House, n.d., pp. 11-13.

[11] W. F. Albright, *The Archaeology of Palestine*, London, Penguin Books, 1956, p. 110.

[12] Johannes Pedersen, *Israel, Its Life and Culture*, Vol. 2, London, Oxford University Press, 1954, pp. 49 ff.

[13] Lange, *op. cit.*, p. 222.

[14] M. S. Terry, *Commentary on the Old Testament: Joshua to II Samuel*, Ed. by D. D. Whedon, New York, Hunt and Eaton, 1873, pp. 415-416.

[15] Martin Noth, *The History of Israel*, New York, Harper and Brothers, 1958, p. 180. For some interesting alternatives, see Hanna E. Kassis, "Gath and the Structure of the Philistine Society," *Journal of Biblical Literature*, 84:259-271, September, 1965.

[16] John Calvin as cited in Lange, *op. cit.*, p. 335.

[17] Keil and Delitzsch, *op. cit.*, p. 262. This means, of course, that it was really Samuel, though in a "spiritual body."

[18] G. Henton Davies, Alan Richardson, and Charles L. Wallis, eds., *The Twentieth Century Bible Commentary*, New York, Harper and Brothers, Publishers, 1955, p. 187.

[19] The Book of Chronicles (I Chron. 8:33) calls him Esh-baal ("Fire of Baal"), which indicates the pagan influences in Saul's own family.

[20] This tunnel, discovered by Charles Warren in 1865, is now known as Warren's Shaft. See J. Garrow Duncan, *The Accuracy of the Old Testament*, London, Society for Promoting Christian Knowledge, 1930, pp. 120-121.

[21] The Tabernacle of Moses had evidently been taken to Nob and later to Gibeon (II Chron. 1:3). This of David was only a temporary expediency.

[22] For David's relationships with the Aramaeans, see Abraham Malamat, "The Kingdom of David and Solomon in Its Contact with Egypt and Aram Naharaim," *Biblical Archaeologist*, 21:96-102, December, 1958.

[23] See on the Ammonite nation, George Landes, "The Material Civilization of the Ammonites," *Biblical Archaeologist*, 24:68-86, September, 1961.

[24] This great sin of David is not mentioned by the Chronicler whose general tendency, under inspiration, of course, was to minimize the sorrier aspects of David's life. For a discussion see Edward J. Young, *An Introduction to the Old Testament*, Grand Rapids, Wm. B. Eerdmans Publishing Company, 1958, pp. 421-422.

[25] David had established the priestly and Levitical orders in Jerusalem and had made special allowance for the encouragement of sacred literature and music (I Chron. 25).

[26] Malamat, *op. cit.*, pp. 91-92.

[27] It seems that Moses' Tabernacle was at Gibeon (II Chron. 1:3) while the Ark was in Jerusalem in the tent which David had built there on Mount Zion (II Chron. 1:4; cf. II Sam. 6:17).

[28] Wright, *Biblical Archaeology*, pp. 70-72.

[29] Martin Noth, *The Old Testament World*, Philadelphia, Fortress Press, 1964, pp. 96-97; I. Mendelsohn, "On Corveé Labor in Ancient Canaan and Israel," *Bulletin of the American Schools of Oriental Research*, No. 167, pp. 31-35, October, 1962.

[30] Harden, *op. cit.*, p. 91.

[31] Merrill F. Unger, *Archaeology and the Old Testament*, Grand Rapids, Zondervan Publishing House, 1954, p. 232.

[32] G. Ernest Wright, "The Temple in Palestine-Syria," *The Biblical Archaeologist Reader*, Vol. 1, Ed. by G. Ernest Wright and David Noel Freedman, Garden City, Doubleday and Company, Inc., 1961, p. 182.

[33] For his extensive fortifications (II Kings 9:15) and other building activity outside Jerusalem, see Yigael Yardin, "New Light on Solomon's Megiddo," *Biblical Archaeologist*, 23:62-68, May, 1960; Excavations at Hazor, *Biblical Archaeologist*, 19:1-12, February, 1956; Nelson Glueck, "Ezion-geber," *Biblical Archaeologist*, 28:70-87, September, 1965.

[34] Cyrus Gordon, *The Ancient Near East*, New York, W. W. Norton and Company, Inc., 1965, pp. 186-187; for the explanation of Solomon's trade in horses (I Kings 10:28-29), see Noth, *The Old Testament World*, p. 260.

[35] Gus W. Van Beek, "Frankincense and Myrrh," *Biblical Archaeologist*, 23:69-95, September, 1960.

[36] Gleason Archer, *A Survey of Old Testament Introduction*, Chicago, Moody Press, 1964, pp. 418-423; G. B. Gray, *Forms of Hebrew Poetry*, London, Hodder and Stoughton, 1915.

[37] Franz Delitzsch, *Biblical Commentary on the Old Testament: Psalms*, Vol. 1, Grand Rapids, Wm. B. Eerdmans Publishing Company, 1948, pp. 64-71.

[38] Young, *op. cit.*, p. 340.

[39] W. Baumgartner, "The Wisdom Literature," *The Old Testament and Modern Study*, Ed. by H. H. Rowley, Oxford, Clarendon Press, 1951 p. 219.

[40] Samuel Schultz, *The Old Testament Speaks*, New York, Harper and Brothers, Publishers, 1960, p. 285.

[41] Robert Henry Pfeiffer, *Introduction to the Old Testament*, New York, Harper and Brothers, 1941, p. 627.

[42] Robert Dick Wilson, *A Scientific Investigation of the Old Testament*, Chicago, Moody Press, 1965, p. 174.

[43] For a discussion of the uncertainties with regard to authorship in critical circles, see Aubrey R. Johnson, "The Psalms," *The Old Testament and Modern Study*, Ed. by H. H. Rowley, Oxford, Clarendon Press, 1951, pp. 181-189.

[44] Archer, *op. cit.*, p. 437.

[45] Sigmund Mowinckel, *The Psalms in Israel's Worship*, Vol. 1, London, Blackwell, 1962, pp. 75-76.

[46] Young, *op. cit.*, p. 328.

[47] Charles T. Fritsch, "The Book of Proverbs," *The Interpreter's Bible*, Vol. 4, Ed. by George Buttrick, *et al.*, New York, Abingdon-Cokesbury Press, 1951, p. 775.

[48] So thought Pfleiderer, for example. See George Barton, *A Critical and Exegetical Commentary on the Book of Ecclesiastes*, Edinburgh, T. and T. Clark, 1908, p. 34.

[49] W. F. Albright, "Canaanite-Phoenician Sources of Hebrew Wisdom," *Wisdom in Israel and in the Ancient Near East*, Ed. by Martin Noth and D. Winton Thomas, Leiden, E. J. Brill, 1960, pp. 3 ff.

[50] Robert Jamieson, A. R. Fausset, and David Brown, *Commentary on the Whole Bible*, Grand Rapids, Zondervan Publishing House, n.d., p. 403.

[51] Archer, *op. cit.*, pp. 462-472.

[52] For views which suggest that the Song is a reflection of pagan cult-material, see Robert Gordis, *The Song of Songs*, New York, Jewish Theological Seminary of America, 1954, pp. 4-8.

[53] Franz Delitzsch, *Biblical Commentary on the Old Testament: The Song of Songs*, Grand Rapids, Wm. B. Eerdmans Publishing Company, 1948, p. 5.

[54] Archer, *op. cit.*, pp. 477-478.

[55] Ernst Hengstenberg, *Commentary on Ecclesiastes*, Trans. by D. W. Simon, Edinburgh, T. and T. Clark, 1876, pp. 297-305.

was going down from Jerusalem to Jericho, when robbers attacked him, stripped him, and beat him up, leaving him half dead. It so happened that a priest was going down that road; when he saw the man he walked on by, on the other side. In the same way a Levite also came there, went over and looked at the man, and then walked on by, on the other side. But a certain Samaritan who was traveling that way came upon him, and when he saw the man his heart was filled with pity. He went over to him, poured oil and wine on his wounds and bandaged them; then he put the man on his own animal and took him to an inn, where he took care of him. The next day he took out two silver coins and gave them to the innkeeper. 'Take care of him,' he told the innkeeper, 'and when I come back this way I will pay you back whatever you spend on him.'"

And Jesus concluded, "In your opinion, which one of these three acted like a fellow-man toward the man attacked by the robbers?"

The teacher of the Law answered, "The one who was kind to him."

Jesus replied, "You go, then, and do the same."

This selection of Holy Scripture in Today's English Version consists of Luke 10.25-37.

The American Bible Society is one of 100 national Bible Society offices throughout the world whose goal is to reach every person with a copy of Scripture in a language he can understand and at a price he can readily afford. In pursuit of this goal the American Bible Society has distributed more than one and one half billion Scriptures since its founding in 1816. If you are interested in sharing the word of God with others by supporting this global task with your prayers and your giving, or would like to order additional copies of this selection (06945), please write to: American Bible Society, 1865 Broadway, New York, N. Y. 10023

AMERICAN BIBLE SOCIETY
New York

TEV860P   ABS-1975-2,000,000- 4,250,000-Q-3-06945-C

THE PARABLE OF THE GOOD SAMARITAN

Luke 10.25-37

A certain teacher of the Law came up and tried to trap Jesus. "Teacher," he asked, "what must I do to receive eternal life?"

Jesus answered him, "What do the Scriptures say? How do you interpret them?"

The man answered, " 'You must love the Lord your God with all your heart, with all your soul, with all your strength, and with all your mind'; and, 'You must love your fellow-man as yourself.' "

"Your answer is correct," replied Jesus; "do this and you will live."

But the teacher of the Law wanted to put himself in the right, so he asked Jesus, "Who is my fellow-man?"

Jesus answered, "There was a man who

CHAPTER EIGHT

A HOUSE DIVIDED

ANCIENT NEAR EASTERN HISTORICAL BACKGROUND

The period of history embraced by the Divided Monarchy began ca. 931 B.C. and continued to the fall of Samaria in 722 under the Assyrians. After that time the southern kingdom of Judah existed alone; but further remarks on this matter must be deferred until Chapter Nine. The era now under discussion was dominated by the meteoric rise of Assyria to the position of dominant power in the Near East, though there were other nations and peoples also important to the overall story. Israel, of course, must occupy chief importance to us, and as we discuss the books of Kings and related matters in Chronicles we shall see how the people of God interacted with these other greater nations. But before we do we must examine at least briefly the affairs of the more important of these surrounding kingdoms.[1]

Assyria. Until the beginning of the Early Iron Age (1200 B.C.) Assyria had remained pretty well obscure since the days of its greatness under Shamshi-adad I (1748-1716). There had been occasional bright lights such as Asshur-rabi I (1441-1425?) and Asshur-uballit (1356-1321), both of whom seemed to give rise to hope of Assyrian renascence, but the real genius of the nation's recovery was Shalmaneser I (1265-1236). Among other things this brilliant monarch completed the conquest of the Mitanni which had begun the preceding century. He was followed by Tukulti-ninurta I (1233-1199) who managed to conquer Babylon and lay claim to a large area around Assyria. For about another century, however, Assyria was able to retain only what she had and little expansion is noted. Then one of the greatest imperialists in world history appeared—Tiglath-pileser I (1116-1078). He is properly considered the founder of the New Assyrian Empire which extended in all directions except south. There he was held in check by the rising Aramaean states which we mentioned earlier.

Not until about 875 B.C., under Asshur-nasirpal II (884-860), were the Assyrians able to move beyond this stalemate and make serious incursions into Palestine. His successor Shalmaneser III (859-825) made many contacts with Biblical kings, some of which have been recorded on various important monuments and other inscriptions. But the real assault of Palestine, including Israel, was under the leadership of Tiglath-pileser III (745-728), otherwise known as Pulu or Pul. He was able to break up the Aramaean alliance completely and carry off many Palestinians as prisoners. In fact, some of the Israelites from the Galilee are numbered among his captives according to his records and the Old Testament as well. The actual attack on Samaria, capital of Israel, was made by Shalmaneser V (727-723), but he died before the conquest could be completed and the task was finished by a usurper, Sargon II (722-706).

Throughout this whole period there were few who attempted to challenge Assyria's supremacy, but by the end of the eighth century there were indications that that domination might soon end. Other nations, especially Media and Babylonia, were beginning to exert pressures upon Assyria and before another century passed The Kingdom of the Tigris had succumbed and passed from history. But Assyria's greatest importance lay in the fact that God had raised her up as a rod in His hand to chasten Israel (Isa. 10:5) ; it is for this reason that Assyria figures so prominently in the Biblical narrative for this period.

Egypt. As we have suggested, Egypt became an almost forgotten nation after its glorious Eighteenth and Nineteenth Dynasties. The Twentieth and Twenty-first especially were times of declension during which Egypt had little or no contact with Palestine or, indeed, any place outside its own immediate borders except the Sinai Peninsula. It was not until the Twenty-second Dynasty, founded by Shishak I (935?-914), that the Land of the Nile began to exercise influence on the Near East. This famous king penetrated into Palestine as far

north as Galilee, leaving behind steles and other markers in
place after place and a full account of his activities on the walls
of the Temple of Karnak in Thebes. The following king,
Osorkon I (914-874), was not quite so successful, however, for
we learn in the Book of Chronicles that Asa king of Judah
defeated his general Zerah as he attempted to invade that
kingdom (II Chron. 14:7-12). This defeat seemed to herald
to Egypt the unmistakable impression that she was not yet
ready for imperialistic ambitions. Indeed, she never was again
in her history except in the seventh century when once more
she pushed up into Palestine. But even this movement was
with Assyrian permission, and was only temporary and most
ineffectual.

Aramaea. It is impossible to consider the history of this
period without a discussion of the Aramaean States to the
north of Palestine.[2] These little kingdoms had come into existence largely through a migration of northern peoples into
the region known as Aram or Mesopotamia (not to be confused with the larger term describing everything between the
Tigris and Euphrates rivers). These immigrants blended
with the peoples already there and by the year 1200 B.C. had
become a rather formidable force. They remained, generally,
independent of each other until the need came for concerted
defensive action. This was in the time of Tiglath-pileser I,
who was unable to annex the stubborn Aramaeans. In fact,
during the age just after Tiglath-pileser, when Assyria receded somewhat, the Aramaeans took the initiative and
founded several settlements in the Tigris-Euphrates region to
the east and as far as Cilicia in Asia Minor on the west. They
also pressed to the south so that by the time of Saul and David
there were several important states just north and east of
Galilee, the chief being Hamath, Damascus, and Zobah.

With the revival of Assyrian power and the height of
Israelite expansion under Solomon these states were largely
limited in scope, in many cases being brought under the control of their neighbors. But once again, after the division of
Israel, the Aramaeans became independent and in the tenth
and ninth centuries waged almost incessant war especially
with the Northern Kingdom. These conflicts figure prominently in the Book of I Kings and will be considered in detail
when we come to them there. Suffice to say that the great

Assyrian rampage of Tiglath-pileser III near the end of the eighth century removed Aramaea permanently from the world scene. It was not until the emergence of Syria hundreds of years later that the people there gained autonomy once again. The important contribution of Aramaea which cannot be overlooked even in this brief sketch is not political, but cultural. The Aramaic language and manner of life pervaded throughout the Near Eastern World, largely because of Aramaea's ideal location in the heart of the Fertile Crescent, so that by the time of Christ the *lingua franca* of that whole part of the world was Aramaic.

Babylonia. A final word should be said about Babylonia, for though this nation remained in the shrouds of her Dark Ages even through this period, there were faint glimmers of hope that the slumber might at last be broken. This hope was concentrated in a people known as the Sealands Dynasty, a rising threat located in the area of the extreme south along the Persian Gulf. They gradually extended their influence, though they lost almost everything along the way to the Assyrians, until there was an ultimate alliance with the Median Kingdom to the north and east which resulted, in the end of the seventh century, in the formation of the Neo-Babylonian Empire.

KINGS OF ISRAEL AND JUDAH

Israel	Judah
Jeroboam I (931-910)	Rehoboam (931-913)
Nadab (910-909)	Abijam (913-911)
Baasha (909-886)	Asa (911-870)
Elah (886-885)	
Zimri (885)	
Omri (885-874)	
Ahab (874-853)	Jehoshaphat (873-848)
Ahaziah (853-852)	
Joram (852-841)	Jehoram (853-841)
Jehu (841-814)	Ahaziah (841)
	Athaliah (841-835)

KINGS OF ISRAEL AND JUDAH (Continued)

Jehoahaz (814-798)
Jehoash (798-782)
Jeroboam II (793-753)
Zachariah (753-752)
Shallum (752)
Menahem (752-742)
Pekahiah (742-740)
Pekah (752-732)
Hoshea (732-722)

Joash (835-796)
Amaziah (796-767)
Uzziah (790-739)

Jotham (750-731)
Ahaz (735-715)

Hezekiah (715-686)
Manasseh (696-642)
Amon 642-640)
Josiah (640-609)
Jehoahaz (609)
Jehoiakim (609-597)
Jehoiakin (597)
Zedekiah (597-586)

ISRAEL AND JUDAH TO THE TIME OF JEHU (I Kings 12:1-
II Kings 9:6; II Chronicles 10:1-22:7)

Dynasty of Jeroboam I (I Kings 12:1-15:26; II Chron. 10:15). After Solomon's death, the throne fell to his son Rehoboam (931-913) who continued to reign in Jerusalem, though he was anointed at Shechem. The selection of this holy place in the north may have been for the purpose of uniting the nation which had given evidence of being already seriously divided in opinion and loyalty. Proof of this may be seen in the appeal made to the king by the northern tribes, led by Jeroboam who had returned to Israel from Egypt (I Kings 12:4). They demanded that the heavy tribute laid on them by his father be alleviated, but the demand went unheeded, for Rehoboam, counseled by his young friends, determined to tax them even more. At this, the representatives of the northern tribes declared their independence of Judah and set about to declare Jeroboam their new king. Rehoboam was not about to permit this revolution without a fight, but when the prophet

Shemaiah reminded him that the Lord had already decreed that this should happen, he desisted from an attack of the north (I Kings 12:23-24).

Jeroboam (931-910), in the meantime, had established the capital of the new kingdom of Israel at Shechem, hoping because of its sacred associations that this site would add legitimacy to the revolution. He also built the city of Penuel, east of the Jordan, as a sort of provincial capital. The most significant act of his early administration, however, was his selection of the cities of Dan and Bethel as centers of a new cult (I Kings 12:29). He fully realized that if his people should return to Jerusalem annually for the stated feasts they might soon become disenchanted with the division of the kingdom and might even desire to rejoin Judah. To prevent this he must arrange for places of worship within his own realm, and yet this worship could not differ a great deal from that with which they were familiar. He therefore made calves of gold which he placed in the new shrines at Dan and Bethel, the extreme north and south respectively, instituting a new priesthood which could officiate at the cultus.

These calves certainly were not images of Yahweh, but only representations of the throne upon which Yahweh stood. We see in this, however, strong Canaanite influences, for some of the Canaanites too imagined their god, Baal, as seated or standing upon a bull, the animal which signified strength and fertility.[3] Thus, Jeroboam had already exposed his people to the dangers of idolatry and nature worship, dangers which became more apparent as time passed. His selection of renegade and unqualified priests also constituted the gravest offense against the law. In this he was reproved by a man of God from Judah who was sent to him by the Lord to Bethel. The king himself was celebrating a feast at the altar there, but the altar was destroyed by the Lord at the prophet's word and the king became paralyzed (I Kings 13:1-6). This blasphemous act of sacrifice at an improper altar and by an illegal priest was long remembered as the sin of Jeroboam whereby he made Israel to sin. Tragically enough, Jeroboam was not dissuaded from a continuation of this evil practice, but enlarged the idolatrous worship which he had instituted and filled the priestly office by bribery.

Soon after this encounter with the prophet from Judah, Jeroboam's son became deathly ill and the king desperately

THE
DIVIDED
KINGDOM

SCALE OF MILES

0   5   10   15   20   25   30

Zarephath

Dan

PHOENICIA

ASHER

ZEBULUN

NAPHTALI

SEA OF
GALILEE

Mt.
Carmel

Kishon River

ISSACHAR

MANASSEH

Shunem

Jezreel

Ramoth
Gilead

MANASSEH

ISRAEL

Samaria

Shechem

Jabbok River

Tirzah (?)

Gilgal

Jordan River

EPHRAIM

Bethel

GAD

DAN

BENJAMIN

Jericho

Ekron

MEDITERRANEAN SEA

Jerusalem

JUDAH

Tekoa

REUBEN

Lachish

DEAD SEA

PHILISTIA

JUDAH

MOAB

Beer-sheba

200 Miles
to Horeb

SIMEON

sought out Ahijah, the prophet who had torn his garment and predicted his rise to power long before it had happened. This man of God had no good words to say, however, and told the king's wife, who had come to him in an ineffective disguise, that their son would die because of the king's evil. Furthermore, the king's family would not continue to occupy the throne, but would be soon cut off completely. Shortly thereafter Jeroboam died, leaving his crown to his son Nadab (910-909) who was no less evil in following his father's pernicious ways (I Kings 14:20).

The situation was hardly any better in Judah, for there Rehoboam permitted all kinds of idolatrous practices to come into the land, though we may be sure they did so without regal sanction. We see such nefarious objects and persons as high places, *masseboth* (religious pillars), *asherim* (groves), and sacred male prostitutes, all of which were so obscene and illegal that we wonder if Judah indeed was any better than her northern neighbor or not (I Kings 14:22-24; II Chron. 12:1). Perhaps under the instigation of Jeroboam, whom he had afforded protection, Shishak of Egypt invaded Judah at this time, carrying away many of the sacred temple objects from Jerusalem (I Kings 14:26). His onslaught did not stop there, for Shishak turned on his old friend from Israel and advanced as far north as the Valley of Jezreel and beyond.[4] Throughout this period we see that there was constant hostility between Israel and Judah, conflict which did not end with the deaths of the first two kings (II Chron. 13).

Rehoboam was followed by his son Abijam who reigned for only three years (913-911) and was, like his father, contemporary with Jeroboam (I Kings 14:31). He too was evil, but because of Yahweh's love for David the throne remained with the Davidic family. Whereas we find several dynasties in the relatively brief period of Israelite history, there is only the family of David in the south, though there were several kings of that line who were anything but godly. During Abijam's reign the Canaanitish religious influence which we saw under Rehoboam continued and even increased. His mother was Maachah, a daughter of Absalom, an evil woman who seemed to only aggravate the apostate situation through her young grandson, Asa, who followed Abijam as king when apparently still a lad. When Asa became king (911-870), one of the first things he accomplished was to remove his grandmother from her throne and with her the objects of worship which she had set up (I Kings 15:12-14; II Chron. 14:2-5). He failed to remove the Israelite high places, though evidently those of the Canaanites were destroyed, but on the whole he did that which was right in the sight of the Lord.

The wars between Judah and Israel continued in the reign of Asa, but there were intermittent periods of peace in which he was able to build strong fortifications against the Northern Kingdom and Egypt (II Chron. 14:6-7). When Zerah, the Ethiopian general under Osorkon I of Egypt, invaded in the beginning of Asa's reign, the latter defeated him in a great battle at Mareshah (II Chron. 14:9-10).[5] Meanwhile, thousands of Israelites, recognizing that God was with Judah and her godly king, came to the south from their homes and made common cause with Judah (II Chron. 15:9). Baasha (909-886) took the initiative against Judah by building a strong fortification at Ramah, mainly to prevent any crossing between the two nations either way (I Kings 15:17; II Chron. 16:1). Asa therefore sent a handsome gift to Benhadad I (890?-841)[6] of Damascus and begged him to break his alliance with Israel and come to his assistance instead. This Benhadad did with the result that several cities in north Israel fell to the Aramaeans (I Kings 15:20). Furthermore Baasha was forced to leave his building program at Ramah to divert his attention to this Syrian threat with the result that Asa took the building stones from the unfinished Ramah and made fortresses of his own on the boundary at Geba and Mizpah. But because he had relied on the Syrians and not God in his dispute with Baasha, the prophet Hanani predicted that he would thenceforth have war (II Chron. 16:7-8). We presume that this occurred, though further war is not mentioned in the Old Testament, but we do know that Asa, because of a certain foot disease, was unable to complete his reign alone. At about 873 he was joined by his son Jehoshaphat (873-848) who became his co-regent.

Dynasty of Baasha (I Kings 15:27-16:22). Baasha, an unknown citizen of Issachar, successfully engineered a plot against Nadab, king of Israel, and founded the second dynasty of that kingdom. He evidently located the capital at Tirzah, though there is some evidence that Jeroboam had done that himself, and he followed closely the pattern of evil which

Jeroboam had established. The result was that Baasha was embroiled in war continually. Furthermore, he was condemned by the prophet Jehu, son of Hanani, and told that his dynasty, like that which he had ended, would be very transitory. After a reign of twenty-four years he died and the throne went to his son Elah (886-885), who, in turn, was assassinated by the captain of his charioteers, Zimri. Zimri managed to retain control for only one week, for the people, who were anything but sympathetic with what had happened, quickly appointed Omri to reign over them. As general of the Israelite army, Omri had the necessary resources to storm Tirzah and burn the royal palace with Zimri inside. Another man, Tibni, now appeared also hoping to take the crown which Omri had won. But Omri was more than a match for this new challenge and without further trouble slew Tibni and proclaimed himself king of Israel (885-874). Thus, in two years Israel had had four kings, a fact which helps us to see the unstable condition of the kingdom at this particular point.

Dynasty of Omri (I Kings 16:23-II Kings 9:24; II Chron. 17:1-22:9). Only six verses are devoted to the reign of Omri, which makes his position seem rather unimportant, but we now know from contemporary historical records, especially from Assyria, that Omri was regarded as a king of great eminence both within Israel and in neighboring nations. In fact, the Assyrians generally referred to Israel by the name *Bit Humria* ("House of Omri") from his time and onward.[7] He was able to bring order out of the chaos into which he had come and to extend Israelite influence farther than it had been since the reign of Solomon. One of the more significant accomplishments, though certainly not a good one, was his alliance and friendly relations with the Phoenicians at Sidon. In fact, the daughter of Eth-baal, king of Sidon, became the wife of Ahab, son of Omri and heir apparent to the throne. This, as we shall see, contributed to the even more hasty demise of the Northern Kingdom and precipitated the captivity that much more. Omri also moved the capital once again, this time to Samaria (880 B.C.), where it remained until the Assyrian destruction in 722. The wisdom of such a choice for a capital may be seen by anyone who visits the mound there and sees its tremendously advantageous location. Evidence of Phoenician collaboration in the building of the palace of

Omri, and that of Ahab as well, has been uncovered by archaeological research at Samaria in recent years.[8]

In 874 Ahab became king of Israel and inaugurated an age of transgression unparalleled thus far. His long reign (874-853) was contemporaneous with that of Jehoshaphat in Judah and of Benhadad I in Damascus. It was also in his time that the Assyrians under Asur-nasirpal II (883-859) began to oppress the Aramaeans and made an effort to include even Palestine in their maraudings. Because of his marriage to Jezebel, the Sidonian princess, he forsook God as not even Jeroboam had done and began to worship Baal. This was the occasion for the ministry of the most important man in the entire period, Elijah the Tishbite. This strange figure came on the scene sometime in Ahab's reign with the declaration that Israel would have no rain until he should give the word. Then he disappeared to the wilderness where he was sustained by God's miraculous use of a raven which carried him meat from time to time. From there he went to the kingdom of Sidon where he found a widow and her son who were starving because of the famine. He performed a miracle by creating an inexhaustible supply of meal and oil and was rewarded by being given shelter for a time under the roof of the grateful woman. His most incredible act, perhaps, came when the child of the Sidonian woman became ill and died. As the Son of God was to do on several occasions in the future, Elijah, by God's power, raised the deceased to life (I Kings 17:21-23).

After three years the prophet went to Samaria for the purpose of informing Ahab that the famine would end. The king had sent his servants throughout the land in search of water and grazing land and had all but given up hope that the nation should survive. Elijah met one of these servants, Obadiah (not to be confused with the prophet by the same name), and told him to fetch the king. Reluctantly, Obadiah did so and when Ahab and Elijah met face to face the king rebuked the prophet for having brought such misery upon the nation. Elijah denied the responsibility and said that it was the wicked king himself who had elicited God's judgment because of his shameful worship of Baal. Thereupon Elijah challenged Ahab to meet him at Mount Carmel, a leading Baal shrine, and see for himself whether the true God was Baal or Yahweh.

Ahab appeared with 450 of his Baal prophets, though Jezebel's own 400 Sidonian prophets of Asherah, who had been invited, evidently failed to put in an appearance. A huge throng of Israelites were there to witness this showdown between the gods, and Elijah advised them to make up their minds whom they would follow. When they failed to respond, he invited the Baal prophets to slay a sacrifice, place it upon their altar, and pray Baal to consume it in fire.[9] He would do the same to Yahweh after they had had their opportunity. But in vain they called their god from morning until noon until at last Elijah mocked them in their unrewarding efforts and asked if their god might not be asleep or away from home. Even when they cut themselves, a popular measure to procure the sympathy of the gods, no response was forthcoming.[10] At last in utter frustration, they abandoned their frenzied efforts and permitted Elijah his turn. Finding some stones of the old abandoned altar of Yahweh the prophet made a new one. Upon it he placed a sacrifice, but then did a very strang thing. He poured barrels of water over the altar and wood and sacrifice, and even filled the surrounding trench with it. Over and over again he soaked the altar until there was no question that only a miracle could ignite it. Then he spoke a short but fervent prayer in response to which fire descended from God and consumed sacrifice, wood, altar, and even the water in the trench. This empirical evidence compelled the assembled throng to acknowledge enthusiastically that only Yahweh was God. Taking advantage of their exuberance, Elijah ordered them to apprehend the prophets of Baal and slay them on the spot. In this dramatic manner Baalism was seriously crippled in Israel, though it continued in one form or another for twenty years or more.

At the conclusion of this overwhelming experience, the rains came and a drought of three years was ended.[11] Ahab, chagrined, rushed back to his country home at Jezreel and related to Jezebel all that had happened. This wicked queen, enraged that her gods had been so treated, warned that if she could get her hands on Elijah the hapless prophet would meet the same fate as had the prophets of Baal. Terrified, Elijah ran from Jezreel, where he had gone ahead of Ahab, and he headed for the land of Judah. Down in the Negev near Beersheba he fell exhausted and wished to die rather than live in the face of such discouragements and dangers

(I Kings 19:4). The Lord sustained him there, however, and led him to Horeb in the plains of Sinai where He appeared to him as He had to Moses nearly 600 years earlier. God told him that He would redeem His people and that Elijah would be His instrument. The Divine help would not come in a mighty overt way, but quietly as in a still small voice. With renewed confidence Elijah left these hallowed precincts and set out to discharge the specific tasks which the Lord had assigned him. He must anoint Elisha ben Shaphat to succeed him as prophet (I Kings 19:19), Jehu ben Nimshi to be king of Israel (II Kings 9:6), and Hazael to be king of Damascus in the place of Benhadad (II Kings 8:13). Only the first of these did Elijah accomplish personally, but through Elisha who followed in his steps the other two were also fulfilled.

On the international scene Benhadad I had begun preparations for war with Israel. He had taken certain northern regions of Israel earlier, though these areas may have been retaken in the time of Omri and Ahab.[12] Now he felt confident enough to actually talk of subduing Samaria itself; so he sent an ultimatum to Ahab to that effect stipulating that Ahab must render a huge payment of gold if he wished to avoid the consequences. Ahab agreed to make such a payment, but Benhadad came the second time and threatened to take the city even if such a ransom were paid. A prophet then came to Ahab and assured him of victory against his Syrian foe. When the drunken Benhadad and his men entered the field of battle they were ill equipped to tackle the courageous Israelite host. But their setback was only temporary, for Benhadad made a second attack. Again Israel won out, this time cornering the Syrian king in the city of Aphek. Failing to follow up this opportunity to finish off his dreaded enemy, Ahab let Benhadad go free. A man of God made it known to him that because of this his kingdom would soon be taken from him and bequeathed to the hands of another (I Kings 20:42).

The setting for Ahab's final rejection involved the neighbor of the king, Naboth, who had a beautiful piece of land which the king wanted for himself. When she noticed how the king moped about, Jezebel asked him for the reason for his dejection. When she found out, she ruthlessly hired witnesses who perjured themselves, swearing to the court that Naboth had blasphemed the king and God. Naboth was therefore stoned to death, and Ahab took his property. Upon this

turn of events, Elijah came to the king and told him that what
he had done would issue in the violent deaths of both Ahab
and Jezebel, and that the dogs would lick their blood where
they had licked that of the murdered Naboth.

About this time a most significant event was shaping
up in the north. Shalmaneser III of Assyria, who had already
enjoyed considerable success in his efforts to annex northern
Palestine, swooped down across the Euphrates with a great
army in an effort to finish this conquest. At Qarqar he met
a massive alliance made up of a large number of kings including Ahab and Benhadad I.[13] According to his own records,
Shalmaneser attributed over 2000 chariots to Ahab alone, a
very significant fact in support of the strength of the House
of Omri at this period. It is difficult to know what happened
for sure at the Battle of Qarqar (853), but it is certain that
Assyria was unable to advance farther south for the time
being and probably not for a number of years.

As soon as this united effort was over, Benhadad and
Ahab renewed their own hostilities (ca. 853 B.C.). It seems
that the Israelite city of Ramoth-gilead was still in Syrian
hands and Ahab would not be satisfied until he had taken it
back. He urged Jehoshaphat of Judah to join with him in
his efforts, and in a rather amazing display of friendship the
king of Judah complied (I Kings 22:4; II Chron. 18:1).
This was an unwise move on his part because the prophet
Micaiah had denounced the whole plan as foolhardy, declaring
that God would dispossess Israel of its king as a result. But,
more influenced by the false prophets of Ahab than by this
stalwart man of God, Jehoshaphat joined in. In the thick of
the fray Ahab was mortally wonded, but bravely fought on
until he expired at the close of the day. Jehoshaphat himself
was nearly slain, and only when he convinced the Syrians that
he was not Ahab was he spared. Ahab's body was carried
to Jezreel where the chariot which bare it, covered with his
blood, was licked by dogs in answer to the prophetic word.
Immediately Ahaziah, son of the king, took the reigns of
authority and did his best to keep the tottering kingdom together (I Kings 22:40).

Jehoshaphat from the very beginning had attempted to
fortify Judah against its enemy Israel (II Chron. 17:1-2).
Furthermore, like his father, he tried to rid the land of
the idolatry which had become such a curse to Israel. Even

beyond this, he took extensive measures to instruct the people in the things of the Lord by sending teachers throughout Judah for this very purpose (II Chron. 17:3-4). In addition, he accomplished great things as far as public works and commerce are concerned (II Chron. 17:12-13). He outfitted a convoy of ships at Ezion-geber, as Solomon had done, but because Ahaziah of Israel was partner with him in the project, the ships were broken up before they ever got to sea (I Kings 22:48; II Chron. 20:37). Perhaps a second effort was made, though this is not clear, but Jehoshaphat had learned the lesson of association with the ungodly and refused to make a similar arrangement with Ahaziah.

Jehoshaphat also had his hands full with the Ammonites, Moabites, and certain other tribal peoples who combined to invade Judah from across the Dead Sea. The prophet Jahaziel assured him, however, that there was no need for alarm (II Chron. 20:15); when Jehoshaphat went to the scene of battle with his large host, he was amazed to see the Ammonites and Moabites engaged in battle with the Edomites. Why or how this came about we are not told, but when it was all over the people had almost totally decimated themselves. Of course, this was not the end of these peoples entirely, for very shortly after this (ca. 850 B.C.) they rebelled against Israel, who had theoretically controlled them since the time of Solomon, and declared their independence under Mesha king of Moab (II Kings 3:4ff).[14] This took place after the death of Ahab, so Joram, son of Ahab, attempted to recover the lost area. He requested and received aid from Jehoshaphat and through a miraculous intervention of God the united forces of Israel and Judah achieved a great military victory; however, they did not succeed in bringing the land of Moab back into Israelite control. At length Jehoshaphat died and was followed by his son Jehoram (853-841).

In the north, Ahaziah (853-852) occupied the throne of Ahab who had recently been killed by the Syrians. This evil son followed his father in all his wickedness and paid dearly for it in many ways. It was in his brief reign that Mesha rebelled from Israel. Ahaziah was unable to do anything about it, perhaps because of an accident which he suffered. Somehow he had fallen through a second story lattice in the palace and tumbled to the floor below (II Kings 1:2). He sent servants to the city of Ekron to enquire of their god

Baal-zebub ("Lord of the Flies") as to the prospects for his recovery. Along the way they met Elijah who told them to save their time by returning to the king at once and informing him that he would not recover. Enraged, Ahaziah demanded Elijah's arrest, but Elijah was delivered on two occasions from those who sought his life. Finally he went willingly to Samaria and told the king that there was no hope because, he, like his father, had repudiated God. Shortly the king died, as the prophet said he would, and yielded the throne to his brother Joram (or Jehoram). This king reigned for twelve years (852-841), contemporary largely with Jehoram (or Joram) of Judah. For purposes of ready identification, we shall refer to the northern king as Joram and the southern as Jehoram, though the spellings are used interchangeably in the Old Testament.

At this point, we resume the narratives of the prophets once again. The time had come for Elijah to pass from the scene. God disclosed to him that he would not die but be assumed bodily. Elisha, recently anointed to succeed his master, followed him about very closely in those days, hoping to be able to witness his departure. The "sons of the prophets" were likewise curious and one day assembled near their headquarters at Jericho to view Elijah and Elisha who had come recently and were preparing to cross over the Jordan. Elijah took his prophetic mantle, swept it over the river, and together the men of God crossed over on dry ground. Sensing that the time of separation was near, Elisha requested that his mentor give him a double portion of his spirit before he left. Elijah replied that this would be possible if Elisha witnessed his disappearance. At that moment a chariot of fire appeared and Elijah was taken up in a whirlwind, but not before he had a chance to leave his mantle behind in Elisha's keeping (II Kings 2:11-12). Amazed by the phenomenon he had just seen, Elisha was no less amazed, perhaps, that he could recross the Jordan as easily as Elijah and he had done at the first.

It is striking that Elisha performed about twice as many miracles as did Elijah, a fitting correspondence to his having received a double portion of Elijah's spirit. In fact, the miraculous makes up such a part of the prophet's ministry that we can do little more than enumerate the instances. We have, for example, the healing of the water at the prophets'

home at Jericho (II Kings 2:21), the smiting of the young
men on the road to Bethel (2:24), the multiplication of the
widow's oil (4:6), the resurrection of the son of a Shunam-
mite woman (4:34-35), the healing of the pot of deadly soup
(4:41), the cleansing of Naaman's leprosy (5:14), the at-
tachment of leprosy to his wicked servant Gehazi (5:27),
the floating of the iron axehead (6:6), the blinding of the
Syrians' eyes (6:18), and even the restoration of a man's
life through contact with Elisha's dead bones (13:21)! As
we said earlier, there were definite periods in Biblical history
in which the miraculous became more or less common; this
time of great spiritual need in Israel and Judah provided the
setting for the miracle-working prophets Elijah and Elisha.
In addition, there were very many more prophets in existence,
though the others are not characterized by their miracles. We
have noted in this period Ahijah of Shiloh, Hanani, Jehu ben
Hanani, Micaiah, and many others. Moreover, as we have
just seen, there were sons of prophets living in various communities throughout the land. These were no doubt the spiritual heirs of the schools of the prophets of Samuel's time who
had remained more or less inactive until they had such leadership as Elijah and Elisha could afford. What their functions
were we cannot even guess, but they presumably were trained
in preaching and singing and certainly in the law.[15]

There were schools which corresponded to these found
among the Canaanites and Phoenicians. Indeed, it was these
who were involved in the conflict with Elijah on Mount Carmel. From all the evidence available it seems far safer to
say that these Baal prophets were modelled after the true
prophets of God than to say that Hebrew prophetism derived
from Canaanite religious practice.[16] Apart from two or there
obscure references to ecstatic dervishes mentioned in such
ancient documents as the Egyptian story of Wen Amon, it is
highly unlikely that the Near East knew anything at all of
prophetism of the Hebrew type except among the Israelites.
As we have noted above, Hebrew prophetism is scarcely ecstatic in nature, and connot be considered as parallel to other
kinds in any respect.

One other matter should be mentioned in regard to the
prophets of Ahab. The first group he had were definitely
Canaanitish and actually called upon Baal in their worship.
When these were extirpated by Elijah, they were replaced by

prophets who claimed to be spokesmen for Yahweh, but who
had never received a Divine call. In other words, there appear to have been two kinds of false prophets: those who
were prophets of false gods and those who were false prophets
of the true God. In either case, they were spurious and were
to be shunned equally.[17]

Relations between Syria and Israel had improved somewhat after the reign of Ahab, so much so that Benhadad was
able to send his chief captain Naaman, a victim of leprosy,
down to Israel to see if he could obtain relief through the
famous prophet Elisha (II Kings 5:5). Joram, however,
interpreted the request as an occasion for Benhadad to make
war with him again. Nevertheless, Elisha learned of
Naaman's coming and arranged to meet with him. After
much hesitation, the Syrian soldier agreed to bathe himself in
the river Jordan as the prophet suggested, a very silly thing
in his sight seeing that the rivers of Damascus, the Abana and
Pharpar, were much cleaner and apparently more conducive
to healing. When his flesh was cleansed he was so overjoyed
that he wished to reward the prophet, an offer which Elijah
refused. Still, out of respect to the God of Israel, who had
made the healing possible, Naaman carried a load of soil from
Israel back to Damascus, intending to make with it an altar at
the temple of Rimmon (5:17-18).[18]

Shortly thereafter, war broke out again between Syria
and Israel. Whenever Benhadad made plans to deploy his
troops at strategic points, the Israelites always seemed to
know in advance (II Kings 6:10-11). Finally, he learned
that Elisha the prophet, through the revelation of God, could
know his every thought. His objective then was to seize
Elisha and put him out of commission. The Syrians went to
Dothan, where Elisha and his servant were staying, and surrounded the city. When the prophet awakened the next morning he saw the huge Syrian contingent, but with his spiritual
vision saw also an army of God on all the surrounding hills.
He then prayed for the Syrians to be blinded, and when they
were, he led them into the city of Samaria. There their eyes
opened, but contrary to the wishes of Joram they were freed
and sent back to Damascus. The result was that Benhadad
sent no more small foraging parties into Israel, but decided to
mass his troops for one grand siege of the capital city (6:24).
The siege was so effective that the people of Samaria were

reduced to cannibalism and were on the point of surrender or extinction.[19]

Elisha, who also was in the city, was the special object of Joram's wrath, for the king accused him of bringing this grief upon the kingdom. Elisha then predicted that within twenty-four hours there would be food in plenty, a suggestion that brought him only ridicule from one of the king's officers who overheard. Elisha replied that the unbelieving lord would not live to share in the promised bounty. The next day the Syrians, who were camped in the valley near the city, heard what they thought were the hoof beats of a great army. Thinking that Joram had hired Hittite or Egyptian mercenaries (II Kings 7:6), they fled their camps and dashed back toward Damascus. In their haste, they left their food and gear behind to be found and appropriated by the starving population of Samaria thanks to some beggars who had come upon the deserted tents. The nobleman who would not believe the prophet was trampled by the rampaging mob as it streamed forth through the gates of the city.

At length Benhadad of Syria became ill and Elisha, under Divine orders, went to Damascus to see him and especially to anoint a successor as Elijah had been commissioned to do at Horeb (II Kings 8:7). Hazael, one of the king's aides, met him and asked how the king would fare. Elisha said that the king would not die of this present sickness but would nevertheless die of something else, and that Hazael would rule in his place. This information Hazael must have taken as a hint, for he went into the royal palace, put a thick wet cloth over the sleeping king's face, and smothered him to death. Hazael then took the throne and reigned for over forty years (841-801).

In the south, Jehoram, son of Jehoshaphat, had been reigning (II Chron. 21:1; II Kings 8:16). He was extremely evil, much unlike his father, but this is understandable in that his wife was Athaliah, daughter of Ahab and Jezebel. In his time of rule the Edomites revolted from Judah, though, as we have seen, they had evidently sided with Judah at the time the Moabites rebelled from Israel. Jehoram was never able to recover Edom, perhaps largely because of a terrible internal disease which he suffered the last two years of his life. Moreover, he was invaded by the Philistines, Arabians, and Ethiopians who continually harassed him along his southern

borders. Finally the tragic reign was ended by death, and the
suffering Jehoram was followed by his son, Ahaziah (841),
who was named for his uncle Ahaziah, the former king of
Israel.

Ahaziah's other uncle, Joram, was the present king of
Israel, and was then at war with Hazael of Damascus over
the disputed city of Ramoth-gilead, the place where his father
Ahab had lost his life some twelve years earlier (II Kings
8:28; II Chron. 22:5). Ahaziah decided to help him in the
campaign, but in the thick of the fray Joram was wounded
and had to be carried to Jezreel. Ahaziah decided to visit
his uncle at the country palace and was there with him when
a very crucial series of events took place.

Elisha, led by God, had sent a young prophet to the battle
field at Ramoth-gilead to anoint a dashing military commander, Jehu ben Nimshi, to be king of Israel (II Kings 9:6).
The prophet instructed him that he was to cut off the house of
Ahab, including the old queen Jezebel, and avenge the blood
of all the prophets who had suffered at their hands. Jehu
left the field to others and returned to Jezreel as quickly as
possible, for he knew, of course, that his king was there re-
cuperating. Without delay, Jehu encountered Joram, took
his bow and arrows, and slew the wicked king (II Kings 9:24).
Ahaziah, king of Judah, was there as we have seen, and Jehu,
knowing that he too was related to the Ahab dynasty, liquidat-
ed him at the same time (9:27). Thus, at once both kingdoms
were shorn of their kings (ca. 841). Jezebel had heard all the
commotion and looked out the window of her chamber. Jehu
spotted her and ordered her chamberlains to cast her bodily
through the opening, which they did. The dogs came and
ate her flesh, as Elijah had predicted, so that there were
barely any remains of the vile woman to be buried.

Dynasty of Jehu (II Kings 9:6-15:12). Jehu did not stop
here. He proceeded to slaughter the seventy sons of Ahab and
even went so far as to annihilate the family of Ahaziah of
Judah whom he found along the way. Then he took measures
to rid the land of Baalism. He invited all the priests and
prophets of Baal to assemble at the great temple of Baal at
Samaria under the pretense of holding an important religious
observance. When they had all come and were securely locked
inside the building, Jehu turned his soldiers loose on the de-

fenseless crowd and soon had finished them off. "Thus Jehu destroyed Baal out of Israel" (II Kings 10:28). It is true that from that time Baalism was a matter of little concern. Yet, we cannot escape the feeling that Jehu more than did the will of God in some ways in his haughty pride and utter ruthlessness. In addition, he failed to remove the golden images from the shrines at Dan and Bethel and apparently resorted there for worship as the kings of Israel had done before him. All this was to cost him a shortened dynasty, for after four generations another family took the throne. Furthermore, the kingdom began to suffer the encroachments of foreign powers early in his reign. We know from the Black Obelisk that Shalmaneser III forced Jehu to pay tribute to Assyria, apparently in Jehu's first year, and it is clear that Hazael of Damascus also threatened from time to time (II King 10:32-33).[20]

In Jerusalem, Athaliah, mother of the late Ahaziah, sat upon the Davidic throne. Her brief reign (841-835) was marked by an effort to destroy all the rest of the royal family, including, naturally, her own grandchildren and children, so that she might hold undisputed sway in the kingdom (II Kings 11:1; II Chron. 22:10). One grandchild, Joash, escaped thanks to a God-fearing aunt and a faithful priest, Jehoiada. When the lad became about seven years old, Jehoiada secretly took him to the Temple into the presence of the nobility assembled there. At a prearranged signal, the royal crown was placed on the boy's head and the shout "God save the king!" rang forth. The queen, in her nearby palace, heard the excitement and rushed into the Temple to learn of its meaning. The priest then ordered her to be dragged into the outer court and slain, removing once and for all any vestige of the Ahab family in Judah. Joash then began to reign (835-796), at first under the governorship of Jehoiada, and then alone. He inaugurated many sweeping changes including the removal of any remnants of Baal worship. Among his other projects in this direction was the restoration of the Temple, a project so successful that he had to restrain the people from their giving. Unfortunately, he also had his failings, notably his lack of effort in removing the high places, though we may assume that only Yahweh was tolerated there at first. Yet, he permitted the worship of Asherah, newly revived, and even sanctioned the stoning of the prophet Zechariah, son of Jehoiada, who

had spoken out against this new apostasy (II Chron. 24:21).
He had to take some of the Temple treasure to buy off Hazael
who had threatened to take Jerusalem, having pressed as far
south as Gath in the Shephelah (II Kings 12:18). His death
was the climax to a trend toward evil, for some of his trusted
servants rose up against him and assassinated him in his bed.

Jehu had died by the year 814 and was succeeded by his
son Jehoahaz (814-798). This unrighteous king was plagued
throughout his life by Hazael and his son Benhadad II (801-?)
of Syria, but in spite of Divine deliverance on many occasions
continued to live in sinful ways. The prophets of Asherah
continued to pervert the people unmolested by the king or
his son Jehoash (798-782) who followed him. The same conditions prevailed into the reign of Jeroboam II (793-753),
though this outstanding figure did manage to regain all the
territory lost to the Syrians and bring to Israel a measure of
the glory she had enjoyed in more happy days in the past.

The prophet Elisha lived on into the reign of Jehoash of
Israel, but at last the time of his death drew near. The stubborn king came to the aged seer and asked him if he had a
message from the Lord. Elisha told the king to take an
arrow and shoot it out the window of the chamber. This done,
he predicted that Jehoash would be able to repel the Syrians
at Aphek. He then told the king to strike the ground with
his bundle of arrows, but suspecting that the old man must be
demented the king only half-heartedly complied. The prophet, in response, told him that he would gain only partial victory over his foes and would eventually be unsuccessful against
them. And Jehoash did barely manage to seize his lost lands
from Benhadad II and pass them on to his son Jeroboam II
(II Kings 13:24-25).

Amaziah had followed his murdered father, Joash, in the
Southern Kingdom (796-767) and continued his basically
good policies. He also avenged the death of his father by
executing his assassins. He then set his sights on Edom in
an effort to bring the former Judaean province back under
his sway. But he made the mistake of hiring Israel to co-
operate with him, and an unknown prophet told him as much.
Heeding the advice, he sent the Israelite troops home, a matter
which did not set well at all with Jehoash. Amaziah went on
into Edom, destroyed the capital city, and carried the nation's
gods home with him as booty. Unfortunately, he set them up

in Jerusalem and worshiped them along with Yahweh, for which the prophet predicted the downfall of the king (II Chron. 25:15).

In the meantime, the Israelite soldiers who had been sent back home vengefully pillaged many villages of Judah on their way while Amaziah was away in Edom. When the king of Judah returned in victory he challenged Israel to make war over the matter, a war which turned out very badly for Amaziah. Jehoash had warned him not to attempt such a contest, but Amaziah, fresh from victory over Edom, paid no heed, much to his sorrow, for Jehoash came into Jerusalem itself and plundered the treasuries of the Temple and the royal palace. Eventually Amaziah, like his father, was assassinated by his own people and died in ignominy at Lachish. His young son Uzziah (Azariah) ascended to the throne in his place (790-739).

The reign of Uzziah is described in Kings, Chronicles, and Isaiah, though the last book merely mentions the fact that the prophet began his ministry in the year that Uzziah died (Isa. 6:1). This king of Judah was righteous for the most part, but he failed to remove the high places and allowed the people to worship there (II Kings 15:4). He undertook successful campaigns against the Arabians and Philistines and extended the kingdom as far to the southwest as the border of Egypt. In line with this he built strong fortifications in Jerusalem and other strategic places including several towers and wells in the desert, the remains of which have been uncovered (II Chron. 26:6-10).[21] In time he gained a widespread reputation for his skill in inventing engines of war and for his military successes. "But when he was strong his heart was lifted up to his destruction" (II Chron. 26:16), and he forgot the source of all his strength. The result was that he became a leper and was forced to dwell in a separate dwelling the rest of his life. His son Jotham (750-731) coreigned with him, apparently, until his death in 739.[22]

In Israel Jeroboam II had been able to retrieve much of the territory lost to the Syrians especially during the reigns of Jehu and Jehoahaz. He probably pushed the borders all the way back to the place they had occupied under Ahab, if not more. The Lord allowed this out of compassion for wicked Israel, though Jeroboam II, like his early namesake, continued the policy of idol worship and toleration of the Baal cults

which still persisted in scattered locales. By 753 he was dead
and his son Zachariah (753-752) took his place in Samaria.

The Collapse of Israel (II Kings 15:13-17:4). This ushered in a period of anarchy and regicide matched only by the
overthrow of the Baasha dynasty 130 years earlier. Zachariah reigned only six months when he was assassinated by a
commoner, Shallum, who held power for just a month. He
then was deposed by Menahem (752-742) who initiated a
barbarous purge of all those in Israel who had refused to
support him in his grab for power. But he was not to be
successful in the long run for the Assyrians, under the mighty
Tiglath-pileser III (745-727), had begun to swoop down un-
impeded upon Syria and even to the gates of Samaria. The
only way that Menahem was spared was by the payment of
a huge sum as a bribe and a heavy tribute thereafter. This
transaction we know from both the Biblical record and the
extensive annals which Tiglath-pileser (Pul) himself left for
posterity (II Kings 15:19-20).[23] The result of this tribute
was an onerous taxation, a burden which no doubt hastened
the end of the kingdom.

Menahem was succeeded by his son Pekahiah (742-740)
who after a short time was removed by his captain, Pekah
(752-732). The chronology at this point is quite confusing,
for it appears that Pekah reigned throughout the period of
both Menahem and Pekahiah. Thiele's solution, that Pekah
actually exercised a measure of authority all through this
time, enough even to be considered a coregency, seems quite
plausible.[24] In other words, he gained full control only after
Pekahiah's death, though he had worked behind the scenes
for many years leading up to this. Sometime in his reign,
possibly about 734 B.C., Tiglath-pileser came down against
Israel once more and carried away certain captives from the
Galilee region and took them to Assyria (II Kings 15:29).
This first phase of the overthrow of the Northern Kingdom
prompted Hoshea ben Elah to put Pekah to death and to
reign in his stead. According to the Assyrian records, Hoshea
was placed on the throne by Tiglath-pileser, and it is very
likely that this is so.[25] We may assume that after Hoshea
assassinated Pekah, he was rewarded by the Assyrian king
with the throne of Israel. In any event, Hoshea did not remain loyal to the Assyrians, and in the reign of Shalmaneser

V (727-722) they came down upon Samaria once more and put Hoshea in prison for a time (ca. 725 B.C.). Upon his release he foolishly rebelled against the Assyrians again and attempted to hold the Assyrian armies off.[26] For three years the siege failed, but in the year 722 the walls were broken down, Sargon II (722-705), who had followed the recently deceased Shalmaneser, entered the city, and carried away all but the peasantry of the land.[27] In line with Assyrian policy the Israelites were settled in various parts of the Assyrian empire and other peoples were moved into Israel to take their places in the care of the soil. The intermarriage of these immigrants with the low class Israelites left behind produced a people known to this day as the Samaritans.

The seventeenth chapter of II Kings reveals in unmistakable terms the reason for the captivity of the Northern Kingdom, reasons which we have seen continually unfolding before us in our study of the history of this faithless people. From the time they had left Egypt until the present they had refused to obey Moses and the prophets and had made a practice of breaking the gracious covenants of God. The Lord had pleaded with them over and over to repent and had sent His servants the prophets to admonish them for their evil, but to no avail. The only remedy was this final and harsh expediency: the nation must learn the meaning of obedience through captivity and punishment.

In Judah Jotham and Ahaz occupied the throne of David throughout these tragic days of their northern neighbors (II Kings 15:32; II Chron. 27). The former king, son of Uzziah, followed closely in his father's steps, both good and bad. He neglected to remove the high places and even failed to observe the Temple ceremonies, but nonetheless made a name for himself in domestic and foreign affairs. He built new fortifications in Judah and succeeded in bringing the Ammonites under tribute. However, he was troubled by Rezin (750-732), king of Syria, though both he and Rezin stood in the shadow of still greater threats from Tiglath-pileser. In the reign of his son, Ahaz (735-715), Pekah, king of Israel, combined with Rezin to invade Judah (II Kings 16:5), a very foolish move when we realize how important it was for these little kings to stand united against Assyria rather than divided against one another. Ahaz, in desperation, sent for aid from Tiglath-pileser, a move that had been very much discouraged by Isaiah the prophet (Isa. 7). The king of Assyria lent his assistance, even going so far as to slay Rezin and carry off the inhabitants of the Galilee, but at a very dear price to Ahaz.

This king of Judah was the most evil in that nation's history up until then. He not only had followed the example of his fathers, but had gone beyond to an unbelievable degree. For example, he offered his own children as burnt offerings and worshiped in the high places and groves (II Kings 16:3-4; II Chron. 28:2-4). And he found it necessary, moreover, to rob the Temple of its treasures to pay Tiglath-pileser for his services. And as though this were not enough, he went to Damascus where the Assyrian king was quartered and seeing the great altar of the Assyrian gods there, ordered one like it to be placed in the Temple at Jerusalem. These gods were powerless to help him, and Ahaz died, having been saved from Assyrian captivity because he had sold his soul to them and for the sake of David whom God remembered.

With Israel in captivity we direct our attention now almost exclusively to Judah. Under Ahaz this kingdom had almost perished because of the hostility of the Syrians, Israelites, Edomites, and Philistines, but Ahaz did survive seven years after Samaria's collapse (II Chron. 28:18-19). He was followed by his son, the good king Hezekiah (715-686), who reversed as much as possible the iniquitous policies of his father. Besides the accounts in Kings and Chronicles, we have the full discussion of Isaiah for this period.

The reasons for the continuance of the Southern Kingdom in these days of Assyrian imperialism must be found in the generally more godly nature of the kings and people of Judah as well as the underlying Davidic covenant promise. But neither of these would prove to be adequate to ensure the perpetual maintenance of the state as a whole. The problem of reconciling the immutable promises of God with the certainty of national annihilation provides one of the principal motifs of the prophetic books. And the reconciliation took the form of the "remnant," a relatively tiny minority of the people who had without interruption been loyal to the covenant terms and who, moreover, were to become special objects of divine grace. As with many of the major Old Testament themes, that of the remnant is only gradually revealed, reaching its fulness in the late pre-exilic and exilic prophets.

THE WRITING PROPHETS

Name	Dates	Object
Obadiah	ca. 840-830	Edom
Joel	ca. 830-820	Judah
Jonah	785-775	Nineveh
Amos	765-755	Israel
Hosea	755-715	Israel
Isaiah	739-690	Israel & Judah
Micah	735-700	Israel & Judah
Nahum	ca. 650-620	Assyria
Zephaniah	635-625	Judah
Jeremiah	627-575	Judah
Habakkuk	620-610	Judah
Daniel	605-536	the Nations
Ezekiel	593-560	Judah
Haggai	520-505	Jews
Zechariah	520-490	Jews
Malachi	435-415	Jews

THE PROPHETS OF THE PERIOD

In addition to the prophets Elijah, Elisha, Micaiah, and others whom we have mentioned in this chapter, there were others whose names, except for one or two (Jonah and Isaiah), are not mentioned in the historical books. They lived in this time, however, and their own books of prophecy provide invaluable information regarding the historical background. Naturally, we will not have time to discuss each prophet fully in a work devoted to an historical survey of the Old Testament, but we should at least list them and give very brief resumes of their historical importance and sketchy outlines of their books.

Obadiah. It is impossible to assign a certain date to this prophet and his book because of the lack of any clear historical references either internally or externally. With Archer and others we date the book from about the latter part of the ninth century, which makes Obadiah contemporary with Elisha.[28] The reason for this is that Obadiah (and this is the theme of the book) predicts that Edom would be destroyed by the Lord for having failed to assist Judah, her brother, in a time of need. We need to look for a time before the destruction of Edom and after such a period of danger for Judah. We have seen that Amaziah demolished Edom ca. 790 B.C., so this makes a possible *ad quem*. Earlier than that, in the reign of Rehoboam (931-913), Shishak of Egypt had invaded Judah and taken the Temple treasures. But we are not informed as to Edom's attitude, though it is not unreasonable to assume that the Edomites failed to assist Judah and even sided with Egypt. The time of Jehoram of Judah may be best, however, for it is very likely that the Edomites assisted the Philistines and Arabians in their sacking of Jerusalem in Jehoram's reign (II Chron. 21:16-17).

Regardless of the time involved, the message is clear. The haughty and proud nation of Edom, secure in its mountains and valleys, would become an object of God's judgment. And the people of God would inherit Edom's territories and dwell in safety.

Outline of Obadiah

   I.   Certainty of judgment (1-9).
  II.   Cause of judgment (10-15).
 III.   Conclusion of judgment (16-21).

— — — — — —

Joel. It is possible that the next prophet in historical order was Joel, but again there is little evidence one way or another. The message of this prophet, who may have lived at the turn of the eighth century (ca. 800 B.C.),[29] is directed to Judah and has as its theme "The Day of the Lord." This expression, which appears frequently in the prophetic books, speaks of the time of Divine judgment and has many connotations. For example, it may speak of an historical day of judgment, or a period of judgment, or even of an eschatological day or period of reckoning. At times, all of these may be in mind because the prophet, looking down through the years, may not distinguish in his mind exactly what fulfillment he sees. This "perspective" nature of prophecy allows many prophecies to have many fulfillments, though these fulfillments generally are somehow related.

So Joel sees the unfolding of Judah's sin and the punishment which must follow. He speaks of the Day of Yahweh when a great nation (Babylon) will come upon the land to lay it waste (1:1-7). But he goes on to extend the promise of forgiveness if the nation will only turn to God (2:12-14). Then, in another aspect of the Day of the Lord, he indicates that the time will come when God will pour out His Spirit upon all flesh with most amazing results (2:28-32; cf. Acts 2:16-21). Finally, he says there will be a great day of wrath in which God will gather the nations of the world to battle (3:1-2), following which He will redeem His own forever (3:18-21). The outline indicates the order in which these events are recorded in his book.

Outline of Joel

I.   Plague of the locusts (1).
II. Prophecy of the Day of the Lord (2:1-27).
III. Promise of the Holy Spirit (2:28-32).
IV. Pronouncement of judgment (3).

— — — — — —

Jonah. It is not difficult to locate Jonah in history, for he is mentioned in the Book of II Kings in relation to Jeroboam II of Israel (14:25). This places him somewhere in the first quarter of the eighth century, in a time when Assyria was relatively quiet. His commission was to preach against Nineveh, the capital of Assyria, and to warn the great metropolis of God's impending doom upon it. He sought to evade the call (Ch. 1), was swallowed up by a great fish (Ch. 2), specially prepared for the occasion we may suggest, and arrived at Nineveh anyway. When there he preached so convicting a message that mass repentance resulted and God withheld what He had thought to do to the city (3:10). Jonah, however, had expected God to visit the city with His wrath, and was bitterly disappointed when the fireworks failed to materialize (4:1). But God (and this is the real theme) asked the prophet if true repentance did not deserve Divine mercy. To this the man of God could give only silent assent.

In addition to the other themes which are stated or implied in the book, there is the important idea here of internationalism. Contrary to the notion popularly propounded that Yahweh was, to the prophets of early times, a local Deity of Israel alone, we see in Jonah that Yahweh was God of Assyria as well, though Assyria might not recognize that fact. She was not only God's "rod" of chastisement, but the object of His tender love.

Outline of Jonah

I.   Jonah's perversity (1).
II. Jonah's prayer (2).
III. Jonah's preaching (3).
IV. Jonah's pouting (4).

— — — — — —

Amos. With the prophet Amos we come to the luxuriant
age of Jeroboam II. As we have seen, this king had regained
the lands lost to Israel just prior to his time and had restored
Israel to a position of great wealth and prosperity. This
produced an atmosphere of materialism and carelessness in
the carrying out of the worship. To counteract this situation
God sent Amos (ca. 765-755), an untrained farmer and shepherd from Tekoa in Judah, to inveigh against the Israelite
court. The message of this "prophet of doom" was anything
but pleasant to Jeroboam and his nobility, and they made
every effort to send the man of God home. But Amos fear-
lessly delivered the burden which God had given him.

We can see from Amos, almost better than in any other
book, the social and spiritual conditions of the eighth century.
The rich were severely oppressing the poor and living in great
opulence in their ivory houses (3:15; 4:1; 5:12). The
people were worshiping unashamedly at the shrines of the
golden calf at Bethel and Dan (3:14; 4:4; 8:14). The
political leaders subsisted largely on bribes and put their confidence in their own military and geographical strength
(2:14-15; 6:1; 9:2-3). As a result, Amos said, the kingdom of Israel would meet a violent destruction at the hands
of a great oppressor (6:14). This was understood to refer
to Assyria, whose troops had already begun to mass for attack under Ashurdan III. In the end the Lord would save
His people and "raise up the tabernacle of David that is fallen"
(9:11). Then nobody would be able to pull them up out of
the land which the Lord would give them forever.

Amos is particularly instructive in showing us that a man
need not be a member of the "sons of the prophets" (the
meaning of 7:14) in order to be called to do the prophet's task.
It seems that he had been engaged in agricultural pursuits
when God issued the Divine call to service, and without further
preparation except for the revelation from the Lord, he set
forth to thunder out the message to the nation of the north.
His was a "charismatic" ministry, one made possible by a

special call and filling by God's Spirit. Sometimes Amos is called the first true prophet, as though Samuel, Elijah, and Elisha were something less, but this is usually so thought because he was one of the first prophets to commit his message to writing.[30] We fail to see, however, how this makes Amos more of a prophet than others who preceded him, for they, like he, all responded to a call from God and exercised a faithful ministry, though they did not record their messages for our day. Some also make a point of proving that Amos, unlike his predecessors, was not an ecstatic phrophet, and that he introduced a long line of prophets who were not after the order of the Canaanitish dervish-type prophets.[31] We have already discussed the fallacy of classifying the early Hebrew prophets as ecstatics, and we would affirm once again that there is not the slightest Biblical evidence to support such a charge. Just because Elijah lived among Canaanite prophets who became overpowered with uncontrollable fits of religious enthusiasm, there is no reason to say that he was of their ilk. This is an argument from silence which is unsupportable.

Yet we may say that with Amos a new direction seemed to be undertaken. Now we have men whose main function is not that of working miracles, but of serving as correctives to the unstable monarchy and priesthood which characterized this period. But we must hasten to say that we cannot charge the prophets with political or cultic ambitions as some scholars would have us do. Amos or any other true prophet was not interested in the monarchy because he had political interests of his own; he wanted only to deliver to the kings the "thus saith the Lord." Likewise, he did not desire to involve himself in the responsibilities of the priesthood as though he himself desired to be a priest or wished to introduce a new way of worship.[32] He wanted only to rid the priesthood of the undesirables, of whom there were many, and bring the people back to the faith of their fathers as expressed in the ancient law codes. The prophets were reformers, then; not reformers in the sense that they had developed higher and more refined theological concepts than already existed under such "crude" prophets as Samuel and Elijah, or even Moses, but in the sense that that early revealed covenant faith had been forsaken in the present generation and needed to be regained. They did not develop a new "ethical monotheism"[33] as the critics say, but only urged a return to the pure monotheism presupposed by the law.

Amos, as the first of these "new prophets," created by his inspired ministry a certain tension between prophet and priest and king that could be resolved only by repentance by priest and king alike and a national return to God. This was the burden of his message, together with the alternatives for obedience and disobedience. If the nation would come back to God, there would be salvation and healing; if not, there would be certain judgment, though the immutable covenant with Abraham, Moses, and David required an ultimate day of glory and triumph for the saints.

Outline of Amos

I.   Punishment of the nations (1-2:5).
II. Punishment of Israel (2:6-9:15).
    A.   Nature of the sin (2:6-16).
    B.   Promise of judgment (3-4).
    C.   Plea for repentance (5).
    D.   Prediction of captivity (6)
    E.   Prophecy of Amos (7).
    F.   Promise of restoration (8-9).

— — — — —

Hosea. The last of the prophets whose ministry ended in the eighth century was Hosea. It is likely that his prophetic activity stretched over a period of at least forty years (ca. 755-715), embracing the reigns of several kings of Israel and Judah. He was sent especially to Israel with his message of Divine love in an effort to turn the nation once again to the God who had given it *raison d'etre,* but the nation would not respond. Like Amos, Hosea could see only captivity by Assyria if Israel persisted in sin, and he, indeed, lived to see that tragic day.

The life of the prophet reflected the relationship between God and His people in a most lucid way. The Lord told the man of God to go and marry a woman who would become a harlot (1:2). Without argument, the faithful prophet did as he was told. After three children were born, all of whose names suggested the evil about to come to Israel, the faithless wife, Gomer, departed. Some time passed and one day the hapless Hosea saw Gomer in the employ of her masters (3:1). Rather than revolting at the sight of his wife turned prostitute, the heart of the good man reached out to her and he bargained with her owners to buy her back to himself.

Though some would dismiss this as only a legend or parable, it seems that the only realistic interpretation is to take it as a true account in the life of the prophet.[34] Hosea, having suffered such an experience, could now understand well the broken heart of God who had loved His own bride, Israel, so much that He had brought her out of the bondage of Egypt (11:1). Even now, God stood with outstretched arms ready to forgive and cleanse His adulterous wife, but the nation would not hear (6:1-3; 11:8; 14:1). Like a silly dove Israel had hired herself out to other lovers such as Egypt and Assyria, and God's great love had gone unrequited (7:11). At last God had had to turn His people over to those who would chastise them (9:1-6), until finally they would see the error of their way and return to Him (13:9-14). Someday they would acknowledge His love and He would restore them freely (14:4).

Outline of Hosea

I.   Illustration of Divine Love (1-3).
    A. Marriage of the prophet (1).
    B. Message of the prophet (2).
    C. Mercy of the prophet (3).

II.   Indication of Divine Love (4-14).
    A. Defection of the people 4-7).
        1. Their sinfulness (4-5).
        2. Their stubbornness (6).
        3. Their silliness (7).

    B. Destruction of the people (8-12).
        1. Weakness of their gods (8).
        2. Wasting of their goods (9).
        3. Wresting of their glory (10-12).

    C. Deliverance of the people (13-14).
        1. Sin of Israel (13:1-8)
        2. Salvation of Israel (13:9-14:9).

------

[1] For this period, except for the dates, we are following basically the outline of John Bright, *A History of Israel*, Philadelphia, Westminster Press, 1959, pp. 209 ff. The dates earlier than the death of Solomon are based on the chronology of W. F. Albright as found in Edward F. Campbell, Jr., "The Ancient Near East: Chronological Bibliography and

Charts," *The Bible and the Ancient Near East*, Ed. by G. Ernest Wright, Garden City, Doubleday and Company, Inc., 1965, pp. 291-292. The dates for the Divided Kingdom era are based on the chronology of Edwin R. Thiele, *The Mysterious Numbers of the Hebrew Kings*, Chicago, University of Chicago Press, 1951.

[2] See especially Benjamin Mazar, "The Aramaean Empire and Its Relations with Israel," *Biblical Archaeologist*, 25:97-120, December, 1962; also Merrill F. Unger, *Israel and the Aramaeans of Damascus*, Grand Rapids, Zondervan Publishing House, 1957.

[3] Merrill F. Unger, *Archaeology and the Old Testament*, Grand Rapids, Zondervan Publishing House, 1954, pp. 236-237; Martin Buber, *Moses*, New York, Harper and Row, 1958, pp. 147-149.

[4] John Gray, *Archaeology and the Old Testament World*, New York, Harper and Row, 1962, p. 146.

[5] Bright, *op. cit.*, p. 215.

[6] This king is mentioned on the Milqart Stele found near Aleppo, Syria. For the text see D. Winton Thomas, *Documents From Old Testament Times*, London, Thomas Nelson and Sons, Ltd., 1958, p. 239.

[7] *Ibid.*, p. 49.

[8] Donald Harden, *The Phoenicians*, New York, Frederick A. Praeger, 1962, p. 52.

[9] As the god of rain and lightning, Baal, if he really existed, should have had no difficulty in igniting the sacrifice. In fact, he should have been able to prevent the three year drought. See Sabatino Moscati, *Ancient Semitic Civilizations*, New York, G. P. Putnam's Sons, 1960, p. 117.

[10] For an example of this in the Ras Shamra literature, see G. R. Driver, *Canaanite Myths and Legends*, Edinburgh, T. and T. Clark, 1956, p. 109.

[11] This, of course, showed that Yahweh, not Baal, was God of rain, fire, and every other force of nature. Cf. Josh. 10:11; I Sam. 7:10; 12:18. See Frank E. Eakin, "Yahwism and Baalism Before the Exile," *Journal of Biblical Literature*, 84:413, December, 1965.

[12] Bright, *op. cit.*, pp. 221-223.

[13] For the text of the Kurkh Stele, which records this campaign, see Thomas, *op. cit.*, p. 47.

[14] This is recorded on the Moabite Stone. For the text see Thomas, *op. cit.*, pp. 196-197.

[15] See my unpublished dissertation, "An Investigation of the Person and Work of the Old Testament Prophet of God," Ph.D. Dissertation, Greenville, South Carolina, Bob Jones University, 1963, pp. 284-287.

[16] Edward J. Young, *My Servants the Prophets*, Grand Rapids, Wm. B. Eerdmans Publishing Company, 1952, pp. 25 ff.

[17] Merrill, *op. cit.*, pp. 258-279.

[18] J. Garrow Duncan, *The Accuracy of the Old Testament*, London, Society for Promoting Christian Knowledge, 1930, p. 167.

[19] For the chronology, see John Gray, *I and II Kings, A Commentary*, Philadelphia, Westminster Press, 1963, p. 466.

[20] For the text of the Black Obelisk, see Thomas, *op. cit.*, p. 48.

[21] Nelson Glueck, "The Seventh Season of Archaeological Exploration in the Negeb," *Bulletin of the American Schools of Oriental Research*, No. 152, pp. 18-38, December, 1958.

[22] A seal of Jotham was found at Elath, on the Red Sea, supporting the statement of II Kings 14:22 that Uzziah "restored Elath." See Thomas, *op. cit.*, pp. 48-49.

[23] *Ibid.*, pp. 54-56. Several kings of Israel and Judah are mentioned by name in these texts.

[24] Thiele, *op. cit.*, pp. 114-115.

[25] See the Nimrud Tablet in Thomas, *op. cit.*, p. 55.

[26] For the view that Hoshea was carried off before 722 and was not returned to Samaria, see Bright, *op. cit.*, p. 258.

[27] Sargon has recorded this in his Annals found at Khorsabad. For the text see Thomas, *op. cit.*, p. 59.

[28] Gleason Archer, *A Survey of Old Testament Introduction*, Chicago, Moody Press, 1964, p. 288.

[29] A. F. Kirkpatrick, *The Doctrine of the Prophets*, London, Macmillan and Co., Ltd., 1901, pp. 58-60.

[30] John Bayne Ascham, *The Religion of Israel*, New York, The Abingdon Press, 1918, p. 115.

[31] Alfred Guillaume, *Prophecy and Divination Among the Hebrews and Other Semites*, New York, Harper and Brothers, 1938, p. 110.

[32] Aubrey Johnson, *The Cultic Prophet in Ancient Israel*, Cardiff, University of Wales, 1944, p. 52.

[33] Edward W. Hopkins, *The History of Religions*, New York, The Macmillan Company, 1918, p. 431.

[34] Keil thinks that the marriage was symbolical only. Cf. C. F. Keil, *Biblical Commentary on the Old Testament: Minor Prophets*, Vol. 1, Grand Rapids, Wm. B. Eerdmans Publishing Company, 1948, p. 38. On the other hand, see Edward B. Pusey, *The Minor Prophets*, Vol. 1, Grand Rapids, Baker Book House, 1950, p. 21.

CHAPTER NINE

CATHARSIS BEFORE CALAMITY

HISTORICAL BACKGROUND

The history of this period (722-586) and shortly after is the history of three great empires which succeeded each other.[1] Assyria had reached its zenith in the eighth century and continued to maintain it well into the seventh. But by 625 there was no question that her former glory was irrecoverable and within a decade she passed from the world scene entirely. Babylonia, under the inspiration of the Sealands Dynasty, had already shown signs of awakening as early as the end of the eighth century, but only at the founding of the Neo-Babylonian Empire under Nabopolassar (626), an event coincident with and contributory to the collapse of Assyria, did the lower Mesopotamian land resume the importance it had lost a thousand years earlier. What it had regained, it lost very rapidly, for by 539 Cyrus of Persia had reduced the great head of gold to dust and the Persian Empire took its place. This massive empire, spread from Greece in the west to India in the east, continued throughout the rest of the Biblical period and not until Alexander the Great destroyed its last stronghold at Arbela in 330 B.C. did it pass into oblivion to be supplanted by the Macedonians.

Other nations such as Egypt, Aramaea, Elam, Media, and Urartu must be considered in their relationships to these three great powers, as, of course, must Judah, but it might be best to establish such relationships not independently but as they occur in the detailed exposition of the historical narrative. To this we shall now direct our attention.

Sargon II, the conquerer of Samaria, found himself in difficulty from the very beginning of his reign. The Sealands

Dynasty, at the head of the Persian Gulf, fell into the hands of a Babylonian nobleman, Merodach-baladan (722-711), who, with assistance from the Elamites, a neighboring people, declared Babylonia independent. Because Sargon was busy in the west and south at the time, he had no recourse but to permit Merodach-baladan to remain in power for a few years. When he did manage to expel him, the persistent Babylonian came back again very shortly and was not successfully removed until Sennacherib of Assyria (705-681) did so in 703 B.C. Sargon also had to contend with invaders from Asia Minor and, in the north, with Urartu (Ararat), a people whom he destroyed with the help of savage tribesmen from south Russia.

In Egypt the Twenty-second and Twenty-third Dynasties were competing in a divided land. They both soon collapsed and were followed by the Twenty-fourth (725-709), the dynasty in power at the time of Israel's captivity. This feeble government also ended in a short time because of the rise of the Ethiopian invaders who now swept into Lower Egypt and established the Twenty-fifth Dynasty (715-656). Their first king, Piankhi, brought Egypt back to a place of comparative influence, enough so that Hezekiah would try to get her to assist Judah in its efforts against Assyria.

REIGN OF HEZEKIAH (II Kings 18-20; II Chronicles 29-32)

Hezekiah ascended the throne of his father Ahaz in 715 B.C.,[2] just six years after Sargon had destroyed Samaria. This good king set out immediately to rid the kingdom of everything which had contributed to Israel's downfall, including the bronze serpent of Moses which had still been kept but had been turned into an object of idolatry (II Kings 18:4). The result was a religious reformation the like of which Judah had not seen in all her history and which she would never see again. Even the pious of Samaria were invited to come to Jerusalem to participate in the worship of Yahweh (II Chron. 30:1), something they had not been able to do legitimately since the kingdom was divided 200 years before. This action may also suggest some sort of effort at reunification of the nation politically as well, and if so this constituted a brazen act of rebellion against Assyria, for Samaria now was an Assyrian province.[3]

Ahaz had remained subservient to Assyria, but Hezekiah, in line with his desire to reverse his father's policies, decided to rid Judah of Assyrian domination. He apparently was too preoccupied throughout the reign of Sargon with his programs of domestic reforms to think much about revolution, but when Sennacherib became king he no doubt thought that the change in administration was propitious for his moves in that direction. Besides, Egypt once more was powerful under the leadership of Piankhi and could be relied upon to help remove the Assyrian menace. Isaiah insisted, however, that Hezekiah have nothing to do with the Egyptians, for they could not be trusted (Isa. 31:1-3); instead the people should be putting their trust in God.

The first act of resistance to Assyria consisted of the withholding of tribute which had been paid since the time of Ahaz (II Kings 18:7).[4] This act was evidently timed to coincide with Sennacherib's difficulties in Babylonia with Merodach-baladan and with increased Egyptian boldness under Shabako (710-696). In fact, Merodach-baladan even came to Judah to gain Hezekiah's support in his campaign against Assyria. Other lesser states such as Tyre and some of the Philistine cities also became involved and together with Judah formed a coalition to withstand what they knew to be certain Assyrian retribution. At this time Hezekiah rebuilt the fortifications in Jerusalem and environs (II Chron. 32:1-9), constructing a water tunnel from the spring Gihon outside the city into the Pool of Siloam within (II Kings 20:20). With courage and faith he awaited the impending assault of Sennacherib, feeling that his God would surely prevail no matter what the odds.

In the year 701 Sennacherib moved west and south sweeping all resistance from his path until he reached Judah and Philistia. He even defeated the Egyptian army at Eltekah, but did not venture into Egypt. He then turned on the Philistine cities, which he easily destroyed, and finally set out for Judah. After taking some forty-six Judaean cities he approached the city of Jerusalem itself. It was then that Hezekiah offered to come to terms by paying an immense sum to protect the city from destruction (II Kings 18:13-16).

At about that time Hezekiah became so ill that he thought he was going to die (II Kings 20:1; II Chron. 32:24; Isa. 38:1). In desperation he turned to the Lord, and the Lord sent Isaiah to him with a message that he would live after all because God had heard his prayer. As a sign that the healing was a certainty, the Lord caused the sundial to go backward ten degrees thus lengthening the day by some forty minutes. After the miracle, Merodach-baladan of Babylonia came to visit Hezekiah, ostensibly to wish him speedy recovery, but actually to enlist his support against the Assyrians (II Kings 20:12-13). This Hezekiah cheerfully volunteered, and in a most amicable spirit took the Babylonian on a guided tour of the city and Temple, showing him everything sacred and profane. This Isaiah condemned bitterly, predicting to the king that the time would come that these same Babylonian people would come into Jerusalem on an errand of destruction and would carry off the same holy treasures they had seen now (Isa. 39:6-7).

There was evidently a second campaign by Sennacherib against Hezekiah several years later, for the story of the destruction of Assyria's army by the Angel of Yahweh, an event which could not have occurred in the siege of 701, must have happened later.[5] This second account is no doubt the one described by Isaiah 36:2-37:36, II Kings 18:17-19:36, and II Chronicles 32:9-21. This must be dated about 689 B.C., for Tirhaka of Egypt, mentioned in connection with the siege, began to reign at that time.[6] Sennacherib sent some of his ambassadors to Jerusalem to persuade Hezekiah to submit voluntarily, but he refused to come to terms. Yet, the king knew that he was in the gravest peril and so he sent for Isaiah the prophet. Contrary to his earlier advice to yield to the Assyrians in the siege of 701, the prophet now urged the king to stand firm, for God would trouble Sennacherib by a rumor that assistance was coming to Judah from another source (Isa. 37:7). But even when the Assyrian king heard that Tirhakah, the Ethiopian king of Egypt, was on his way, he refused to be deterred from his objective in destroying Jerusalem.[7] Again he issued an ultimatum to Hezekiah to surrender while he could. This time Isaiah responded that because Sennacherib had blasphemed the God of Judah in comparing Him to the impotent gods of the nations which Assyria had conquered, Assyria would not enter Jerusalem, but would be forced to retreat to her homeland in shame. That night the Angel of Yahweh swept over the Assyrian camp and slew 185,000 troops, a calamity which gave Sennacherib no choice but to return home.[8]

A few years after his return to Nineveh Sennacherib was murdered in the temple of Nisroch by two of his sons and was succeeded by a third son, Esarhaddon (681-669).[9] This able ruler stabilized the unsettled condition of government in Babylon by recognizing the validity of Marduk, the chief Babylonian deity, thus obtaining popular support for Assyria. He later pressed on into Egypt, hoping to eliminate the harassment which had come from that source ever since the founding of the Ethiopian Twenty-fifth Dynasty. By 671 he had defeated Tirhakah and went all the way to Memphis which he occupied and made the center of his Egyptian domains. When his army left, however, Tirhakah rebelled; when Esarhaddon returned to put down the insurrection he took sick and died along the way. His son Ashurbanipal (669-633) carried on, successfully routing Tirhakah and eventually (ca. 663) going as far south as Thebes (No).

Hezekiah coreigned with his son Manasseh for the last ten years of his life; when he died the young prince was ready to take the authority immediately. He continued to rule for fifty-five years (695-642), which includes the years of co-regency. He immediately made known the fact that he would set a new record in Judah for wholesale apostasy by building altars to the Baalim and planting groves to Asherah. Moreover, he served the hosts of heaven, the planets and stars, and even built altars in their honor within the Temple (II Kings 21:3-7; II Chron. 33:2-7). Like Ahaz, he offered his children as sacrifices in the Valley of Hinnom and consulted witches and other workers of evil. In fact, we learn that no king of either Israel or Judah exceeded him in the abundance and nature of his iniquity.

Kings does not tell us that Manesseh ever repented of his sins, but Chronicles makes a point of informing us that the Assyrians came and carried him off to Assyria in bonds (II Chron. 33:11).[10] When this happened we cannot tell, but apparently the experience humbled the king so that when he returned to Jerusalem he turned to Yahweh, destroyed all the pagan altars and images, and repaired the neglected altar of God. But all this reformation was not sufficient to erase the prophets' declaration that Jerusalem would be dealt with in the same manner as was Samaria (II Kings 21:10-16). The revival under the leadership of Hezekiah had only stopped the gap between Ahaz and Manasseh temporarily; Manasseh's long reign had completely reversed any trend toward righteousness, sounding the death knell for Judah.

THE PROPHETS OF THE PERIOD (725-675)

Isaiah. Even before the collapse and captivity of Samaria there had arisen in Judah a man whose prophetic ministry was to make of him one of the most illustrious figures in history. Isaiah ben Amoz became conscious of the call of God in the same year that king Uzziah of Judah died, ca. 739 B.C. (Isa. 6:1). All through the incredibly difficult days of Tiglath-pileser's conquests of Samaria and on into those of Ahaz and Hezekiah of Judah the courageous seer spoke the counsel of God. Apart from Jeremiah there is no prophet whose life and ministry are better known and none can excel him in the strength and beauty of his prophetic declarations.

Isaiah apparently came from a high social stratum in the city of Jerusalem. All through his life he rubbed elbows with royalty and occupied a place of unrivaled opportunity as far as policy shaping was concerned. Jotham, Ahaz, and Hezekiah, especially, knew him intimately and depended upon him to an immeasurable degree, though his counsel was as often flaunted as not. But though he had come from good material circumstances his eyes were not closed to the needs of the poor and afflicted. With boldness and zeal he attacked the social ills of the day, not because he was a social reformer, but because he recognized that these abuses merely represented the terribly sick spiritual life of the nation (1:3-9). In ancient Israel there was no distinction between the secular and sacred; a weakness in any part of the Theocratic body was a blight upon the whole corpus.

The prophet first became involved politically, at least on any significant scale, at the time of the Pekah-Rezin coalition against Judah (735-732). As we said before, Ahaz decided that the only alternative he had was to appeal to Tiglath-pileser III for assistance. Isaiah realized, however, that if Ahaz would quietly trust the Lord, the Syrian-Israelite alliance would come to naught (7:4). But Ahaz would not believe even when a special sign was given, so Isaiah had to tell him that his request of Tiglath-pileser would result in Assyria's domination of Judah. The sign, of course, was that a virgin would conceive, bear a son, and call his name Immanuel ("God with us"). This prophecy naturally had some reference to a young woman of Ahaz' day, but found its ultimate fulfillment in Jesus Christ, God in the flesh (7:14; cf. Matt. 1:23).[11]

Another child was born, this time to the prophet and his wife, and the Lord told Isaiah that the Northern Kingdom would fall before the child became of age (8:3). In the midst of these dire predictions, Isaiah confidently believed that God would ultimately restore His people through a holy Child who would become the "Prince of Peace" (9:6). At the same time, Assyria, the threat to Judah and the whole world, would be broken by the Lord who had used the nation only as a rod to chasten His own nation (10:5). Babylon, Moab, Syria, Ethiopia, Egypt, Arabia, and Tyre also were embraced in the prophet's denunciation; all were doomed to destruction because of their pride and arrogance.

Israel and Judah must recognize that they were not exempt from God's wrath. Even reliance upon Egypt would not help (30:1-17), for the Egyptians were men and not God, their horses were flesh and not spirit (31:1-3). Only when the two nations repented and returned to God could they be assured of continued existence and of a future made bright with the promises of a new heaven and earth (Ch. 35).

The time came when Samaria fell, and Isaiah turned his full attention to Judah, warning that kingdom of the folly of repeating the sins of her northern neighbor. When Hezekiah became king, the prophet found a willing heart to which he could outline the Divine will. The good king, whose activities we have already described, was assured by Isaiah in his very first year on the throne that the Assyrians would not be able to injure Jerusalem (14:4-23). When the invasion of Sargon II in 714 took place, Isaiah warned Hezekiah against trusting the Egyptians or Philistines, maintaining that the latter themselves would become slaves of Assyria (20:4). Though Judah must not seek help in resisting Assyria, they must themselves resist the oppressor through their faith in God (31:5).

In the invasion of Sennacherib in 689, Isaiah recommended that Hezekiah stand fast and watch the miraculous deliverance which the Lord would effect (37:33). The death of the 185,000 troops attested the fact that God answered prayer and had a further purpose for His people. Through all his trying relations with the Assyrians Hezekiah found a comforting and capable support in the prophet. After the death of Hezekiah we no longer hear anything of Isaiah, though Jewish tradition says that he was martyred by the ungodly Manasseh.[12]

The last twenty-seven chapters of Isaiah (40-66) express an entirely different approach to the prophet's ministry. Whereas the first part was largely historical, though interspersed heavily with various oracles, this latter section is wholly predictive, with special heed being paid to the eschatological aspects of Israel's future. This part of the book has been denied to Isaiah by recent higher criticism, but on the flimsiest of evidence. There is no question that the early Jewish and Christian writers believed in the unity of the book, and, of course, Jesus and the Apostles invariably ascribed the last section to Isaiah (John 12:38; Luke 4:17; Mt. 3:3; John 1:23; Rom. 10:16, 20). The internal evidences, too involved and lengthy to be considered here,[13] also point to the unavoidable conclusion that the prophet wrote the entire composition. The chief reason for the rejection of Isaianic authorship for this part is that there are so many detailed and specific predictions that supernaturalism must be presupposed in order to believe that Isaiah wrote it. The only alternative to the critic is that this section is history and not prophecy.[14] But if we accept the Biblical doctrine of verbal inspiration, the difficulties along this line cease altogether.

We can see that Isaiah's purpose in writing is to comfort the captives and those who still live under the shadow of impending captivity (40:1). The time will come when the glory of the Lord will be revealed and "the word of our God shall stand forever" (40:8). This will be accomplished through the Servant of Yahweh (42) who will be filled with God's Spirit and will bring judgment upon the Gentiles (42:1; cf. Mt. 12:18). The folly of idols will be seen (44:9), and indeed they will be destroyed. Among the instruments of the Lord in performing His will in the future will be Cyrus, a king who will contribute to the building of the House of the Lord in Jerusalem. He will also figure in the destruction of Babylon, from whence the chosen of the Lord will be delivered (44:28; 45:1).

The highlight of these glorious chapters is certainly the elaboration of the Servant concept as seen in 52:13-53:12.

The Servant will be humiliated, beaten, and put to death, all for the sins of His people. He will be the means of bringing forgiveness to mankind and will eventually triumph even over sin and death. That this refers primarily to the Messiah is agreed by most interpreters, though many say that the Servant is either idealistic or speaks only of the future nation Israel which shall be God's means of redeeming the world.[15] The inescapable individualism of the passage, coupled with the fulfillment in Christ, suggests without question that Isaiah is painting in starkly realistic lines and colors the real and vital function of the Son of God in the prophetic future.

The remaining chapters of the book outline the benefits to be derived from the Servant's vicarious work. Included are satisfaction for the thirsty (55:1), forgiveness to the penitent (57:13), salvation to the Gentiles (60:3), and the reconstitution of Jerusalem, Israel, and the whole earth as the dwelling place of God and His saints for evermore (65:17-66:24). Words of greater comfort to people uprooted from their homes and land can scarcely be imagined. The imagery and poetic genius in which the thoughts are couched but add to the grandeur of the glorious promises.

Outline of Isaiah

I. Rebellion (1:2-6:13).

II. Retribution (7:1-12:6).

III. Retaliation against foreign powers (13-27).

IV. Repentance (28-39).

    A. Ephraim threatened (28).
    B. Zion strengthened and enlarged (29).
    C. Israel rebuked for alliances (30-31).
    D. Israel promised goodness and judgment (32).
    E. God's enemies threatened with retribution (33).
    F. Threatenings made to enemies and promises to Israel (34-35).
    G. Current history described (36-39).

V. Restoration (40-66).

    A. Relation of Israel to the Lord (40-48).
    B. Relation of Israel to the world (49-66).

Micah. The contemporary of Isaiah in Jerusalem was Micah, a lesser figure whose life nearly paralleled that of his colleague. Like Isaiah this prophet inveighed against the social and moral aberrations of the time, paying special heed to the corrupt rulers and priests and the false prophets who cried "Peace!" when there was none (3:5). The people were trusting in the ceremony of their religion but had completely forgotten the spirit behind it all; thus, the prophet struck out against their empty formality, in scathing terms telling them that the Lord had no use for their hypocritical sacrifices. What He did demand was that they "do justly, love mercy, and walk humbly with God" (6:8).

But despite the headlong plunge of Judah into disaster, in the footsteps of Israel, God would some day remember His people for good (4:1-7). The Temple mountain would be exalted above all the earth; the nations, forgetting their war and conflict, would all flow unto Jerusalem; and the Lord would reign forever and ever (4). His ruler who would come and accomplish this, in addition to the overthrow of Assyria and the wicked nations, would originate in Bethlehem Ephratah (in Judah). He would permit the ravaging of His people for a time in order to teach them His displeasure at their sin (5:2-3). Then, in a demonstration of His wondrous grace, He would have compassion on them and remember His eternal covenant with Abraham and Jacob (7:19-20).

Outline of Micah

I.   Condemnation of idolatry (1).

II. Corruption of the people (2).

III. Craftiness of the leaders (3).

IV. Consummation of the Kingdom (4).

V.   Conquest of the Messiah (5).

VI. Controversy with the nation (6).

VII. Consolation of the nation (7).

THE LAST YEARS OF JUDAH

Ashurbanipal had extended Assyria's might farther than any of his predecessors, but the end of his empire was soon to come because of certain national and international complications which began to set in.[16] In Egypt the Twenty-sixth Dynasty under Psammeticus I (663-609) had commenced; this able ruler carried on the independent policies which had harassed Assyria under Tirhakah. Because Ashurbanipal was preoccupied with the Babylonians (though his brother was king there), Elamites, and barbarian borders from the north, he was unable to look to his interests in the south. Chief among these newcomers from the north were the Medes, a people who figured very prominently in the eventual collapse of Assyria.

Ashurbanipal was able, however, to meet the emergencies and in a series of lightning moves regained at least a good measure of the old Assyrian solidarity. He took Babylon from his own brother, crushed the Elamites, and brought Manasseh of Judah back under his firm control in spite of some resistant efforts on the part of Psammeticus (II Chron. 33: 11). He then devoted the remainder of his life to the collection of antiquities and construction of libraries and archives. Thanks to his efforts in this line we have the famous Babylonian Creation and Flood Epics[17] in a well-preserved form as well as thousands of other tablets representing countless ancient historical and legendary sources.

Ashurbanipal's son, Ashur-etil-ilani (633-629), had a very obscure and apparently unsuccessful reign, and was followed by his brother Sin-shar-ishkun (629-612) who lived to see the kingdom totter, fall, and almost pass into oblivion. The Median king Cyaxares (625-585) began to trouble Assyria as soon as he took his throne, and his ally Nabo-polassar of Babylonia (626-605) actually declared his independence of Assyria and defeated Sin-shar-ishkun at Babylon. Egypt, in the meantime, became friendly to Assyria, probably realizing that a weak but alive Assyria was better than an insuperable Medo-Babylonian front in the north and east. At any rate Psammeticus attacked the Babylonian armies in Mesopotamia in 616, thus preserving Assyria a little longer. Two years later, however, Cyaxares took the city of Asshur, and then after two years more (612) the Babylonians and Medes together took the capital, Nineveh. Sin-shar-ishkun, who died in the battle for Nineveh, was replaced by Ashur-uballit II (612-609). This unfortunate heir of Assyria's death struggle soon lost Haran and by 609 every vestige of Assyria's glory had passed from the world scene.[18]

After Manasseh died (642), the throne of Judah was temporarily occupied by his young son Amon (642-640). This chip off the block, after filling the land with idolatry again, was murdered by his servants in his palace (II Chron. 33:24). His son and successor was Josiah (640-609), a boy of eight years who became as renowned for his piety and zeal for the Lord as his father and grandfather were for everything opposite. When he came of age, he set about to repair the Temple, which had fallen into disgraceful disrepair, and in the process was introduced to a certain scroll which had been found concealed in the walls of the building (II Kings 22:8). Upon examination, he found it to be a copy of the Law of Moses, something which had not been in circulation since the time of Hezekiah at least. Whether this was the entire Law or only a part such as Deuteronomy we cannot say for certain, though it seems unlikely that only part of the Law would have been suppressed by Manasseh or otherwise lost.[19]

When the king had finished perusing the book for himself, he recognized the awful indictment it contained with regard to himself as an individual and to the nation as a whole. He therefore sent it to Hilkiah the priest for his reactions, and the priest took it to the prophetess Huldah. This godly woman, having seen the message of the scroll, predicted that the curses written within it would pass upon Judah because Judah had wantonly broken the covenant which had bound the nation to God. Josiah himself, however, because he had repented and humbled himself before the Lord, would not have to witness Judah's tragic end with his own eyes. For his sake, the nation would last until he had finished his days (II Chron. 34:24-28).

The king then took the Law, and standing before the assembled nation began to read it in their hearing. With one accord they responded by reaffirming their faith in God, and at least superficially experienced a revival as sweeping and thorough as that in the reign of king Hezekiah. Superficial it was, for it bore no lasting fruit, no sign that God could understand it as sufficient reason for His holding back the wrath promised by Isaiah and Micah. Yet the instruments of heathen worship were demolished, the hireling priests were cut off, and the groves and shrines both in the valleys and the high places were cut down and burned. Josiah even destroyed the worship center at Bethel as the man of God from Judah had predicted long centuries before (II King 23:15; cf. I Kings 13:3). The climax to it all was a magnificent Passover feast, the greatest seen in the kingdom since the days of Samuel. No king did so much for God and so zealously in such a short period of time; yet, the nation could not be saved. Its iniquities more than outweighed any possible benefits to be derived from the piety of its remarkable king.

When Ashur-uballit of Assyria had gone to Haran to retake his city from the Babylonians, he had been assisted by Necho II of Egypt (609-594) who had rushed up through Palestine for that purpose. Josiah, both hoping to rid himself of Assyrian aggression once and for all and also deeply committed to Babylonia, elected to meet Necho at Megiddo and thwart his attempts to come to Haran in time to be of any help to the Assyrians. The valiant king was mortally wounded in the battle there and was carried back to Jerusalem dead (II Kings 23:29). It does seem, however, that this tactic delayed Necho enough so that when the Egyptians arrived at Carchemish, the site of the battle, the Babylonians and their allies had already overcome the Assyrians and removed them forever from the world scene.[20]

The Egyptians took advantage of the situation to install themselves in Palestine and Syria while Babylonia was stabilizing itself to the east of the Euphrates. Having slain Josiah, they took upon themselves the responsibility of appointing a king in his place, his own son Jehoahaz (II Kings 23:30). Very shortly, though, this appointee was removed for some sort of insubordination and carried off to the Egyptian provincial capital at Riblah in Syria and from there to Egypt where he died (II Kings 23:33; II Chron. 36:4). Necho then placed another son of Josiah, Eliakim (609-597), on the throne, and changed his name to Jehoiakim. In exchange for his advancement, Jehoiakim was required to send an exorbitant tax to Egypt, a tax which the people bitterly resented.

Under Jehoiakim, the recent reform of Josiah was all but forgotten, for the king was anything but a spiritual leader. We see especially in the book of Jeremiah the religious conditions of the time, also the weakness of the king in every respect. He was interested only in satisfying the wishes of his Egyptian overlords in order that he might retain his petty power. But his power was to be threatened, this time by the Babylonians, who now had time and resources to press south of the Euphrates and down into the territory which Egypt had held now for only four or five years.

Nebuchadnezzar, the young commander of the Babylonian armies, decided to turn his attention to Palestine in 605 and with little effort overran the Egyptians at Carchemish and pursued them deep into Palestine.[21] Back in Babylon Nabo-polassar had died and the news of that death sent Nebuchadnezzar back to the capital so that he might safeguard his interests there. When he had become crowned king (605-562), he returned to his campaign in Palestine and for three years remained there. It seems likely that Jehoiakim had submitted to him in his first onslaught (605), rebelled for three years when Nebuchadnezzar had had to retire (II Kings 24:1), and then fell back in line when the Babylonian finished his second campaign. This submission in 605 must have included the deportation of many people from Judah to Babylon, including Daniel and his friends (Dan. 1:3). It would also mark the beginning of the seventy year captivity of Judah predicted by Jeremiah (Jer. 25:11).

In 601 Nebuchadnezzar faced Necho again near the Egyptian border; evidently Necho was so successful this time that the Babylonians had to retreat and leave Palestine unprotected for several years. Finally, they marched west again in 597, but before they could get to Jerusalem to punish the rebelious Jehoiakim, he died, perhaps the victim of assassination (Jer. 22:18). His son Jehoiakin could hold out only three months and finally he, with members of his family and other important persons, was deported to Babylon (II Kings 24:10). One of these deportees seems to have been the prophet Ezekiel (Ezek. 1:2). As for Jehoiakin, he was kept under house arrest in Babylon all through the reign of Nebuchadnezzar, but when that king was followed by Evil-merodach (562-560), the latter removed Jehoiakin from his imprisonment, exalted him above other captive kings, and even gave him a lifelong allowance (II Kings 25:27-30).[22]

Jehoiakin's uncle, Mattaniah (597-586), was placed upon the powerless throne of Judah, and received the new name Zedekiah (II Kings 24:17). This worthless fellow, who seemed to lack conviction and strove only to be popular with his lords (Jer. 38:5), also had the problem of not being regarded as the true king of Judah since Jehoiakin was still alive, though a captive in Babylon. But he was able to rebel successfully against Nebuchadnezzar largely because of problems Nebuchadnezzar was having with Jewish captives in Babylonia and also because of certain false prophets in Jerusalem who encouraged the people there by predicting that the Babylonian yoke would be broken within a very short time. Jeremiah rejected such ideas, for he had clearly taught that the captivity would last seventy years. He suggested that there was no alternative but to peacefully submit to the Babylonian suzerainty, a position which he upheld even when Jerusalem fell under siege in 588-86.

This final conquest of Judah by Nebuchadnezzar involved the destruction of Lachish, Azekah, and other surrounding posts first, as we know from the Lachish Letters;[23] when nothing was left but Jerusalem, it became the object of the major thrust (Jer. 34:7). In the meantime the Egyptians marched north to engage the Babylonians, but they were completely unsuccessful in stopping the Babylonian takeover. Together with their new king Hophra or Apries (588-568) they were forced to withdraw leaving Judah at the mercy of Nebuchadnezzer.[24] The king of Babylonia was not disposed to be merciful and in short order he took the city, arrested Zedekiah, carried him to Riblah, and then blinded him after forcing him to witness the execution of his sons (II Kings 25:6-7). The unfortunate king eventually died in Babylon.

A month later Nebuzaradan, captain of the Babylonian guard, returned to Jerusalem and burned its buildings to the ground. Only the poor of the land were left to care for the land but the rest, together with the objects of special value from the Temple, were taken to Babylon. Others of the rulers were dragged off to Riblah where they were executed, probably because they had been ringleaders in the stubborn resistance to Nebuchadnezzar. Some, such as the prophet Jeremiah, were allowed to remain in the city because it was thought, mistakenly of course in his case, that they had been pro-Babylonian all along. With the absence of the king, the state formally ended, but Nebuchadnezzar decided to preserve the new province to a limited degree at least by appointing Gedaliah as ruler (II Kings 25:22). His tenure was all too brief, because for his efforts to placate the survivors he was branded a traitor to the Jewish cause and assassinated by Ishmael, a member of the royal family who had fled to Ammon. The villains involved in the plot then fled to Ammon while Gedaliah's friends carried the prophet Jeremiah with them to Egypt, fearing, of course, that Nebuchadnezzar would somehow hold them accountable for what had happened. What happened to Judah after this we cannot tell, though it is likely that the provincial status did not last long and that both Samaria and Judah were incorporated together as a province.

THE PROPHETS OF JUDAH (650-585)

Though the dominant figure by far for this entire time was Jeremiah the prophet, there were several others whose ministries must have made a tremendous impact on the nation in these critical days of its history. The situation roughly paralleled that of the Northern Kingdom in the days of Amos, Hosea, Isaiah, and Micah, and so we expect to find many of the elements of social and spiritual decay which we saw then. These latter prophets were no less vociferous and courageous in their denunciations than their earlier brethren. At the same time, they contain no fewer messages of hope and restoration. God must punish Judah, they said, but His everlasting covenant demanded that He remember them in their ruinous state and regather them to Himself and to their land. Most important of all, He would save them, and through them save the world by that Anointed One of Israel known by all the prophets.

Nahum. It is impossible to date the book of Nahum, except in general terms, because of a lack of internal or external evidence. We do know, though, that his message consisted of a prediction that Nineveh, the great Assyrian capital, would be laid low (3:1-5). The book must be earlier than 612, then, for that was the date of Nineveh's conflagration under Nabo-polassar and the Medes. And it must be after the fall of Thebes (No) because Nahum compares the devastation of Nineveh with that of Thebes (3:8) which had already perished under the blows of Ashurbanipal (663 B.C.). We may assume then that Nahum lived in the latter part of the seventh century, though we know practically nothing else about the man.

He first outlines the majesty of God as seen in His mercy to His own people and His judgment upon the nations (1:2-7). Then he goes into a dramatic description of the subjugation of Nineveh by a tremendous host of chariots and infantry which would completely overrun the city (2:4-13). Finally he states that there would be no possibility of recovery for Assyria, for the kingdom, though an instrument in the hands of the Lord, had become bloody, and like Jehu had overreached itself in doing God's will.

Outline of Nahum

I. Psalm of praise (1).

II. Prediction of defeat (2).

III. Panorama of ruin (3).

— — — — — —

Zephaniah. The prophet plainly informs us that he lived in the reign of Josiah of Judah (1:1), presumably before the great revival of that king in 622, for there is no mention of such an event. His message, like that of Joel, revolves about the theme of the Day of Yahweh, though in his case this Day refers to the judgment of Judah exclusively. It will be a day of wrath, a day of trouble and distress, a day of wasteness and desolation, a day of darkness and gloominess, a day of clouds and thick darkness, a day of the trumpet and alarm against the fenced cities, and against the high towers (1:15-16). It will also include the Philistines, Moabites, Ammonites, Ethiopians, and Assyrians, for all these nations have vaunted themselves in sinful pride against the Lord of all the earth.

The leadership of Jerusalem has been corrupt and venal and there is no recourse but punishment (3:1-7), but God will one day remember His dispersed people and will be in their midst to save them (3:17) making them a people noteworthy in all the world because of His blessing upon them (3:20).

Outline of Zephaniah

I. Retribution exhibited (1).

II. Repentance encouraged (2).

III. Restoration explained (3).

Habakkuk. This prophet gives us no certain hint as to the date of composition of his little book, but his frequent reference to the Babylonian (Chaldean) uprising, an event which he undoubtedly sees as imminent, suggests a date of about 630 B.C., just before the Neo-Babylonian Empire was established by Nabo-polassar (1:6).

His message is that God will raise up the Babylonians to execute His will against the Assyrians and Judah, much as He had raised up the Assyrians to afflict Israel. But they, too, would go beyond the Divine will and would have to be punished for their presumptuousness. Their bloodiness, their drunkenness, their idolatry—all would serve to undermine them and reduce them to eventual oblivion (2:12). The whole process would result in the praise of God and salvation of all who would trust Him. The interesting note at the end of the book to the effect that the composition had been dedicated to his chief singer might indicate that Habakkuk was a musician as well as a prophet (3:19).

Outline of Habakkuk

I.   The prophet's protestation (1).

II. The prophet's prediction (2).

III. The prophet's prayer (3).

— — — — — —

Jeremiah. Just as Isaiah had towered over his contemporaries at the time of Israel's last days of history, so Jeremiah one hundred years later looms largest on the scene of Judah's final hours. While more is known about him than any other prophet because of his extensive autobiographical notations, there is no book of Scripture more difficult to follow because of the lack of any consistent chronological scheme. It might be best in the long run, therefore, for us to try to follow his life according to the periods in which it was divided, largely as it related to the reigns of Josiah, Jehoiakim, and Zedekiah, and to consider the prophecies relevant to each time.

Jeremiah was born in Anathoth, just north of Jerusalem, and may have come from a priestly lineage (1:1). At an early age he was called to the prophetic ministry; in fact, God told him He had selected him even before he had been born. His task was clear: he must "root out, pull down, destroy, throw down, build, and plant" (1:10). From the beginning (627 B.C.; cf. 1:2) he saw that Jerusalem would be stricken by a power from the north, resulting from the unbridled evil of the nation. When this came about, Egypt would be unable to give them help (2:18) nor would their idols rise up to support them (2:28). Only repentance would suffice (4:1), but this must come quickly, for the noises of war were already resounding in the distance (4:19).

Like his contemporaries, Jeremiah read clearly the symptoms of a sick nation. The rich had oppressed the poor, the prophets taught lies, and the priests served only for material gain. What was worse, the people loved it that way (5:31)! Their sacrifices, therefore, were hollow and meaningless (7:21-24) and they believed that in spite of their iniquitous ways there would be peace (8:11). All of this brought no joy to Jeremiah's heart; indeed, the "weeping prophet" wished that he might have unending tears to express the full measure of his grief over Judah's plight (9:1-2).

No prophet ever used object lessons more than Jeremiah to teach visually what he found it difficult to convey by words alone. For example, he illustrated the torn and battered condition of Judah by a linen sash which he had buried in a hole (13:1-11). Later, he broke a clay pot into tiny fragments to show the completeness of Judah's destruction (19:1-12). He eventually went so far as to make a yoke of wood which he wore on his neck as a symbol of the bondage under which the nation must serve because of its stubborn resistance to God (27:1-2).

The prophet's ministry seemed to intensify after the death of Josiah when the captivity was not only nearer in point of time, but more certain and essential because of the reversal of Josiah's reformation principles under Jehoiakim. This evil king would meet a violent death, according to Jeremiah, and would not be mourned by his own people (22: 18-19). His son Jehoiakin (Coniah) would go to Babylon in chains and die without an heir on the throne of David (22: 30). In his place, however, a righteous Branch would shoot up and be the means of saving God's people and keeping the covenant promise alive (23:5-8). This Branch, of course, was to be the Messiah, the same one predicted by Isaiah as the root out of a dry ground (Isa. 53:2).

Specifically, Jeremiah said, Judah would be led off by Nebuchadnezzar and serve Babylonia for seventy years

(25:11), though Jeremiah had done his utmost for twenty-three years to warn the people of this very thing and to encourage them to repent. Other nations also would fall under the heel of the Chaldeans, so it would be fruitless to trust in them, even in Egypt. Naturally, such a message was unwelcome to the proud king Jehoiakim and his visionless counselors, so the outspoken prophet was placed under arrest (26: 8-24), narrowly escaping death. While in prison, Jeremiah wrote a scroll (presumably much of his present book) and sent his servant and scribe Baruch to read it at the Temple. Baruch was apprehended by the authorities, however, and the scroll was confiscated and taken to king Jehoiakim. As it was read to him the king took the scroll and cut it in pieces and threw it into a blazing fireplace. Thereupon the Lord commanded Jeremiah to write an identical scroll, which he did, and to which he added many other words. Besides showing the tenacity of the prophet in the face of the greatest adversity, this event is very instructive in showing us how scripture came to be written.[25] Especially significant are the statements which emphasize the verbal aspects of the revealed message (36:17-18; 28, 32).

The third phase of his ministry concerned Jeremiah's relationship with Zedekiah. When Zedekiah had taken the throne of Judah through the permission or even orders of Nebuchadnezzar, he had immediately rebelled. When the Babylonians came south to chastise him, he, and others with him, thought that the Egyptians, who were advancing north, would be able to save Judah from the wrath of Nebuchadnezzar. But Jeremiah stoutly affirmed that the only sane policy was to submit to Babylonia and put no trust in Egypt (37: 6-10). When the Babylonians left Jerusalem to meet the Egyptians, Jeremiah was placed under arrest as a Babylonian sympathizer (37:14-15). When Egyptian help failed eventually, the prophet was released for the inadequate Zedekiah knew he was more valuable to him in freedom than in bondage, though he dared not release him completely for fear of the Jews' reaction (38:19). Until the fall of the city, then, Jeremiah remained in the outer court of the prison.

During all this time of incarceration, Jeremiah continued to sound forth the unwelcome message that captivity by Babylonia was unavoidable (21:3-10) and that even the king would die (21:7). Yet, he proclaimed that there would be a remnant that would be saved, a few like good figs who would be carried off but who would return and form the nucleus of a new kingdom (Ch. 24). Other prophets disagreed, notably Hananiah, and argued that the Babylonian scourge would end soon, perhaps as early as two years (28:1-4, and Jehoiakin would return to his throne. Jeremiah contested this, of course, and predicted instead the death of the false prophet, an event which did come to pass and which but strengthened Jeremiah's position (28:15-17). In a more positive vein, Jeremiah also wrote letters to the captives in Babylonia in which he urged them to settle down where they were, for seventy years must pass before there was any hope of return (29:1-23). Any prophets and priests among them who prophesied otherwise and who were living iniquitous lives would suffer the judgment of the Lord (29:32).

But they must not get the equally erroneous impression that there would be no return at all, for this was decidedly not true. Israel would be restored and would participate in a new covenant, one which would be engraved not on stone but within their hearts (31:31-34) and which would be accompanied by joy and prosperity (33:1-18). As a token of his own personal confidence in the return, Jeremiah redeemed a piece of land and hid the deed in an earthen jar, fully expecting his heirs to return to claim it. The price he paid was high, an evidence that to him the land was not worthless, even though it would soon fall to Babylonia, but rich in the use to which the returnees would put it (32:6-15).

Finally, the city was broken up and Zedekiah led off to Riblah to be blinded. Jeremiah, thought by even the Babylonians to be their compatriot, was allowed to live and even to remain in Judah. As we noted before, he remained in the land for but a short time, for after the assassination of Gedaliah he was spirited off to Egypt along with Gedaliah's other friends. There he remained for the remainder of his life, perhaps living long enough to have written all of the books of Kings (ca. 560 B.C.), though this may be doubtful. In Egypt the prophet continued his ministry, predicting such matters as the conquest of Egypt by Nebuchadnezzar (43:8-13), the fall of the Philistines (Ch. 47), Moabites (Ch. 48), and many other nations (Ch. 49). Babylon especially would be destroyed by the Lord because of her obstinate refusal to recognize Him as God (Chs. 50-51). Marduk and Bel would be completely unable to stave off the ruin which would come at the hands of the Medes and Persians.

Thus the courageous man of God lived out the remainder of his days in a strange and distant land, never to return to the city he loved. Misunderstood by both friend and enemy, Jeremiah had suffered as have few others in the proclamation of truth. But his stout heart was unbowed and his faith in God remained constant. The prophet of tears knew of a day when God in triumph would wipe them all away.

Outline of Jeremiah

I.   Judah before the fall of Jerusalem (1-38).

    A.   Jeremiah's task (1).
    B.   Judah's sin (2:1-3:5).
    C.   Warnings of judgment (3:6-6:30).
    D.   A call for repentance (7-10).
    E.   The linen girdle (11-13).
    F.   Promise of captivity (14-17).
    G.   Visit to the potter (18-19).
    H.   Jeremiah's arrest by Pashur (20).
    I.   Prophecy of Babylonian conquest (21-29).
    J.   Promise of return (30-33).
    K.   Captivity of Zedekiah (34-35).
    L.   Writing of the scroll (36).
    M.   Jeremiah's arrest under Zedekiah (37-38).

II.   Judah during the fall of Jerusalem (39-45).

    A.   Jeremiah's protection (39).
    B.   Death of Gedaliah (40-41).
    C.   Jeremiah's advice (42).
    D.   Jeremiah in Egypt (43-45).

III.   Oracles about the nations (46-51).

    A.   Egypt (46).
    B.   Philistia (47).
    C.   Moab (48).
    D.   Ammon (49:1-6).
    E.   Edom, Damascus, Kedar, Hazor, and Elam (49:7-39).
    F.   Babylon (50-51).

IV.   Appendix (52).

The Book of Lamentations. While in **Egypt**, or shortly before his having gone there, Jeremiah wrote a poetic description of his beloved city as it lay in the flames of Nebuzaradan's torches. No elegy ever written is more profoundly moving than that of the prophet, for no other is filled with the intensity of meaning and importance as is this. This is not just the description of a beautiful, proud, ancient city—though it is all that—but the picture of the Day of Yahweh as it related to the heart of the covenant people. Symbolically, Jerusalem spoke to Judah of their crushed hopes, desires, and aspirations. Relatedly, it spoke of her dismal failure to serve the Lord. The smoke and ashes suggested disintegration of the national goal. All that the people can do now is mourn their condition and reach out to God in loving penitence and faith, hoping that in His mercy He might give them a ray of assurance that this is not all. Of course, there is no suggestion that the picture might be changed, at least not in this book, for that was not its intention; but to the reader familiar with the glowing promises of restoration in the writings of the prophets, even this bleak and desolate scene would one day be changed, and all men would turn for salvation to the City of David, made new by the glorious presence of the Lord.

---

[1] For fuller historical detail see John Bright, *A History of Israel,.* Philadelphia, Westminster Press, 1959, pp. 288-319.

[2] The dates for the kings of Judah are those of Edwin R. Thiele, *The Mysterious Numbers of the Hebrew Kings,* Chicago, University of Chicago Press, 1951.

[3] W. F. Albright, *The Biblical Period From Abraham to Ezra,* New York, Harper and Row, 1963, p. 77.

[4] This is the interpretation of Bright, *op. cit.,* p. 267.

[5] See Bright's extensive excursus on the historical and chronological problems of this period in *op. cit.,* pp. 282-287.

[6] Martin Noth, *The Old Testament World,* Philadelphia, Fortress Press, 1964, p. 249.

[7] Sennacherib states that he had shut Hezekiah up in Jerusalem "like a caged bird." See the text of the Taylor Prism in D. Winton Thomas, *Documents From Old Testament Times,* London, Thomas Nelson and Sons, Ltd., 1958, pp. 66-67.

[8] Herodotus described the defeat of an Assyrian army by a plague, but there is no evidence of a plague in the Biblical account. We have no alternative but to accept a miracle. Cf. Merrill F. Unger, *Archaeology and the Old Testament,* Grand Rapids, Zondervan Publishing House, 1954, p. 269.

[9] The Prism of Esarhaddon found at Nineveh confirms this. See Thomas, *op. cit.*, p. 72.

[10] In line with this see Thomas, *op. cit.*, p. 74. The Chronicles passage may refer to the conquest of Ashurbanipal, however.

[11] Because the word *almah* can mean "young woman" or "virgin," it seems that the passage must have a twofold application; otherwise, the virgin birth aspect would have been meaningless to Ahaz. Yet, the primary reference was to the Virgin Birth, for Matthew plainly tells us so. For the view that only the birth of Christ is in mind here, see Edward J. Young, *The Book of Isaiah*, Vol. 1, Grand Rapids, Wm. B. Eerdmans Publishing Company, 1965, pp. 289-291. For the view that both a woman in Ahaz' time and a future Virgin (Mary) are intended, see Robert Jamieson, A. R. Fausset, and David Brown, *Commentary on the Whole Bible*, Grand Rapids, Zondervan Publishing House, n.d., p. 437.

[12] George L. Robinson, "Isaiah," *The International Standard Bible Encyclopedia*, Vol. 3, Ed. by James Orr, Grand Rapids, Wm. B. Eerdmans Publishing Company, 1960, p. 1496.

[13] O. T. Allis, *The Unity of Isaiah*, Philadelphia, The Presbyterian and Reformed Publishing Company, 1950.

[14] Bernhard W. Anderson, *Understanding the Old Testament*. Englewood Cliffs, Prentice-Hall, 1957, pp. 399 ff.

[15] Otto Eissfeldt, "The Prophetic Literature," *The Old Testament and Modern Study*, Ed. by H. H. Rowley, Oxford, Clarendon Press, 1951, pp. 147-151.

[16] Bright, *op. cit.*, pp. 291 ff.

[17] For these texts see James Pritchard, ed., *Ancient Near Eastern Texts Relating to the Old Testament*, Princeton, Princeton University Press, 1950, pp. 60-99.

[18] For the last years of Assyria, see William W. Hallo, "From Qarqar to Carchemish: Assyria and Israel in the Light of New Discoveries," *Biblical Archaeologist*, 23:34ff, May, 1960.

[19] Martin Kegel, *Die Kultusreformation des Josias*, cited in Gleason Archer, *A Survey of Old Testament Introduction*, Chicago, Moody Press, 1964, p. 92.

[20] Hallo, *op. cit.*, p. 61.

[21] David Noel Freedman, "The Babylonian Chronicle," *Biblical Archaeologist*, 19:50-60, September, 1956.

[22] For the "Jehoiakin Tablets" see Thomas, *op. cit.*, p. 86.

[23] *Ibid.*, pp. 213-216.

[24] Martin Noth, *The History of Israel*, New York, Harper and Brothers, 1958, p. 285.

[25] For an interesting discussion of this, see J. Philip Hyatt, "The Writing of an Old Testament Book," *The Biblical Archaeologist Reader*, Vol. 1, Ed. by G. Ernest Wright and David Noel Freedman, Garden City, Doubleday and Company, Inc., 1961, pp. 22-31.

CHAPTER TEN

RETURN AND RENEWAL

THE BABYLONIA-PERSIA CONTEST

While Nebuchadnezzar had been employed in the conquest of Judah, Cyaxares of the Medes had been making territorial acquisitions of his own.[1] He went as far west as Asia Minor and occupied everything in the east and north of Babylonia. His death occurred at about the time of the fall of Jerusalem (ca. 585) and he was followed by Astyages (585-550) who was able to stay on peaceful terms with Babylonia throughout the reign of Nebuchadnezzar. In the south, Egypt, under Hophra, continued to endanger Babylonia's holdings in Palestine. As long as that king remained in power Egypt was not punished, but when Amasis (568-525) took the throne in a coup, Nebuchadnezzar swept down into Egypt and registered a decisive blow against the new king. This seems to have succeeded in humbling Egyptian ambitions, for until Egypt fell to the Persians in 525 B.C. she remained relatively quiet.

After the reign of Nebuchadnezzar the Babylonian Empire began to disintegrate rapidly. His son Evil-Merodach, who released Jehoiakin from imprisonment, reigned for only two years (562-560). He was followed by Neri-glissar (560-556), Labashi-Marduk (a few weeks), and, finally, by a usurper of the royal family, Nabonidus (556-539). This man was from Haran and worshiped the moon god Sin. He brought images of this god to Babylon, an act which irritated the Babylonians immensely; moreover, he neglected the religious rites of the Babylonians while engaged in conquest and in an insatiable search for antiquities which he collected into museums. Eventually he took up residence in Teima, a small land in the Arabian desert, installing his son Belshazzar as

regent in Babylon in his place.   Most galling of all to the
Babylonian priests was Nabonidus' failure to observe the national religious festivals, especially that of New Year's Day.
On that day the gods were led down the great processional way
and the people reaffirmed their allegiance to them.   When the
king neglected these ceremonies, the people felt their nation
to be in jeopardy because of the natural wrath of the gods.
In fact, when Cyrus of Persia took Babylon by storm in 539
he credited Marduk, the chief Babylonian god, with having
given him victory because Nabonidus had forsaken the cultus![2]

The Median threat was increasing in the meantime, until
the southern Median province of Anshan revolted from the
Empire under the leadership of Cyrus the Persian (550-530).
In short order Cyrus had taken all the old Median empire and
began to push westward into Asia Minor.   By 546 B.C. he
had gone as far as the Aegean Sea and even threatened Greece
for a time.   After further expansion in the east, Cyrus began
to concentrate on the divided and tottering empire of the
Babylonians.   He appointed Gobryas, a former Babylonian
general, to take command and to march on his old capital.
By 539 Gobryas surrounded it, having met little resistance
along the way, and without a struggle the city capitulated.
Nabonidus fled in panic, but was later recaptured, and Belshazzar lost his life.   Thus, a new era of history commenced,
an era bound to have influence in changing the fortunes of
God's people.

THE AGE OF THE CAPTIVITY

The Prophet Ezekiel.   Not much is known of the lives of
the Jewish captives following the first deportation from Jerusalem in 605 B.C.   We do know that there were very few
Jews left in Judah at all, perhaps no more than 20,000 according to W. F. Albright, and that most of these were from the
lower classes and had been left to care for the soil and crops.[3]
Evidently other people were not sent to Judah from other
parts of the Empire, so that from the time the city was destroyed in 586 until the first wave of migration back occurred
ca. 535 there was very little change in the land in any way.

But this was not true in Babylonia, Egypt, and elsewhere,
for in these areas the Jews had been taken in great numbers
and began to settle down in large colonies.   We should not

imagine the captivity to be one in which the dispossessed
Jews were placed in large concentration camps or anything of
the kind. Instead they were allowed to have their own homes,
engage in businesses of one kind or another, and practice their
religion as best they could without a Temple (Jer. 29:5-7;
Ezek. 8:1). Indeed, the synagogue arose during this period
to compensate for the loss of the Temple and to provide a place
where the pious could gather to study and hear the Word of
God. There is even evidence that a Temple was built at
Elephantine in Upper Egypt where the Jews had a large community on an island in the Nile.[4]

Some of the captives became prominent in government,
business, and in other phases of national life, so much so that
when the time came seventy years later that they could return to Jerusalem, very few had any desire to do so. Far
from being oppressive the captivity was to many of them an
opportunity to prosper materially as they never had at home.[5]
One of the great dangers was not that the people would be
eliminated as a race while in captivity, but that not enough
of them would want to leave it and return home to continue
the occupation of the Promised Land. Only the persistent
and continuous encouragement of men such as Ezekiel, Daniel,
Ezra, and Nehemiah assured a restoration at all; and even
with their leadership Judaism as a Palestinian movement
seemed at times to be in danger of failing.

According to Ezekiel's own testimony, he was among
the captives taken in the siege of 597 (1:2), along with king
Jehoiakin. He and his wife evidently lived in a colony of
Jews who had settled along the banks of the Chebar Canal,
a few miles from Babylon. As far as we can tell he spent
his entire life there, preaching and writing from 592 B.C.
until about 560. And a strange life he lived! No prophet
writes in such symbolic imagery as does Ezekiel; to him must
go the credit for the first extensive use of apocalyptic.[6] By
this is meant the presentation of future events, both political
and spiritual, in a "hidden" way; that is, a way that is not
immediately clear in its interpretation. It has the added
feature, moreover, of viewing time in a cyclical way, as a
series of events which are more or less repetitious from one
age to the next, but which will culminate in the breaking
through of God into history and the establishment of another,
spiritual order. It differs from ordinary prophecy in its

very use of imagery and symbolism and in its emphasis on God's dramatic self-initiated visitation in the Last Day. Much apocalyptic literature defies rational interpretation in itself, but when attached to clearer passages and wellfounded eschatological principles, it becomes rich in its meaning.

After an initial vision of cherubim and wheels, the priest-prophet received his prophetic commission: he must speak a message demanding repentance to the captive people among whom he lived (2:3). In spite of God's judgment in sending them there, they obstinately refused to open their hearts to Him and acknowledge their many sins. As a watchman, Ezekiel must speak forth the message of warning in order to deliver his own soul from guilt of the nation's blood. If they responded, all would be well, but if not at least the prophet could not be blamed for not trying to alert the people about God's judgment (3:17-21; 33:7-16). Then, in two symbolical actions—the model of a siege against Jerusalem and the cutting and dividing of his hair—Ezekiel demonstrated visually how that the city would be attacked by Nebuchadnezzar and how some of the people would be burned, some would be slain with the sword, others would be scattered to the four winds, and a tiny remnant would be saved to form the nucleus of a new nation (5:3-4).[7]

Ezekiel spoke directly to the needs and conditions of Judah by pointing out the idolatry which had occasioned their removal from the land and which had produced the violence and devastation which their holy city was to suffer. He referred to the abominable practices of the Jews in their Temple worship (8:10), the wicked counsel of the rulers (11:2), and the deceitfulness of the false prophets (13:2). The situation was so hopeless that even if Noah, Daniel, and Job were to intercede on their behalf (14:14), the people of Judah could not be spared. Judah was worse than her sister Samaria and than any of her ancestors (16:47), and it was for her own sin, and not that of her fathers, that she must be punished (18:4). And despite the fact that the Lord had been gracious to Judah, she had not acknowledged Him, but had turned her back. Still, the Lord would not forget but would cleanse the wicked nation and eventually bring it back to Himself (20:33-44).

Judah was not the only nation to be struck with the rod of God's anger. The Ammonites, Moabites, Edomites, Philis-

tines (Ch. 25), Tyre (Chs. 26-28), and Egypt (Chs. 29-32)
all would feel His reproach and come to realize that He is
God of all the earth. The reason for this would be their
antagonism toward God's people, for though God had permitted it, He had not sanctioned its unlicensed use. Besides,
all these nations had failed to observe that the God of Israel
was the true God; they had consciously rejected the light
that He had given them.

One of Ezekiel's major themes is that of the future
covenant. He, like Jeremiah especially, had to reconcile the
present state of affairs with the glorious promises of Israel's
past. God had told Abraham that He would make of him a
great nation, He had confirmed this covenant pact with Isaac
and Jacob, and had revealed through Moses the Theocratic
principles which had given the covenant relationship a greater
tangibleness and framework in the form of a nation miracu-
lously delivered in the Exodus and organized at Sinai. He
had, moreover, spoken to David regarding the royal line
which would forever reign in the Kingdom of God, and had
specifically stated that that Kingdom would, of course, abide
eternally. The Assyrian rampage of 722 had dealt a severe
blow to Israel's hopes, for after that the nation had become
only a small part of what it was in the promise, though it
was true that the Davidic tribe of Judah still existed, albeit
very tenuously. Now, however, even Judah had gone and the
nation as a political entity had ceased to exist. The people
for the most part felt that God had broken His covenant with
them, and that there was now no possibility of its renewal.
The prophets, though, did not view these events in this light,
but they, too, suffered the shock of an uprooted kingdom.
Theirs was the dilemma of reconciling the exile nation with
the immutable covenant of God. And through the revelation
of God, the solution became apparent. The nation Israel had
disappeared for all practical purposes, but the covenant had
not been forgotten. It would now continue, but would be expressed in a different way. The dispersed Jews would return
to their homeland, but not to resume their old relationship;
rather, a new covenant would be made with them, one which
further expanded and interpreted the previous ones (34:20-
31). In the future God would "sprinkle water upon them"
and they would be given a "new heart" in which would abide
the Spirit of God (36:25-38). This renewal of the nation

and its inspiration by the Spirit are depicted by the prophet as a resurrection of a valley full of dry bones (Ch. 37). Israel, as dry bones which cannot live, would be reassembled and rejuvenated with God's Spirit and David would reign over the nation, now united into one people.

But this final restoration of Israel would be preceded by great international movements directed against the Lord and His covenant people. Gog and Magog (symbolical of the world powers) would swoop down upon Palestine in the last days and seek to destroy the saints (Ch. 38). God, however, would cause them to fall upon the mountains north of Israel and would consume them so completely and universally that seven months would be necessary for the burial of the dead (39:12). This eschatological picture of God's vengeance upon the nations and His protection and revival of His own small kingdom must have seemed very remote to the tiny remnant to whom the prophets preached, for the great nations had seemed to make a mockery of Yahweh and the promises. Yet, the prophets maintained in the face of all the odds that the eternal covenant was a reality and that Israel, both physically and spiritually, would rise to take her place of world dominance.

Ezekiel, as a priest, naturally had a strong interest in the more cultic aspects of the covenant of the future, so we find a large section of his book (Chs. 40-48) devoted to a delineation of the future glorious Temple, its altars and instruments, the new priesthood, the division of the land, the order of worship and liturgy, and other such matters. Some of this was fulfilled in the return of the exiles who rebuilt the Temple under Zerubbabel, but by far the most spoke of an eschatological day in the end of time. Whether or not Ezekiel speaks in literal or figurative terms is much disputed, but there is no doubt that the theme here as elsewhere is that of a fulfillment of the wonderful promises of the Lord to His people of all ages. The present world order, though it apparently triumphs now over the righteousness and truth, will be discarded by God's direct intervention into the affairs of nations, and a new order will be instituted to take its place, an order characterized by the eternal fellowship of God with His covenant people.

Outline of Ezekiel

I. Prophet's call and commission (1-3).

II. Prophecies against Judah (4-24).

    A. Destruction predicted by sign and symbol (4-7).

    B. Vision of Jerusalem's sin and punishment (8-11).

    C. Necessity of punishment (12-19).

    D. Last warning before Jerusalem's fall (20-24).

III. Prophecies against surrounding nations (25-32).

    A. Ammon (25:1-7).

    B. Moab (25:8-11).

    C. Edom (25:12-14).

    D. Philistia (25:15-17).

    E. Tyre (26:1-28:19).

    F. Sidon (28:20-26).

    G. Egypt (29-32).

IV. Final restoration.

    A. Events preceding establishment of kingdom (33-39).

    B. Worship in the Kingdom (40-48).

        1. Temple (40-43).

        2. Worship (44-46).

        3. Land (47-48).

— — — — — —

Daniel. In Nebuchadnezzar's first campaign in the reign of Jehoiakim (605), certain choice young men were spirited off to Babylon, including Daniel, Hananiah (Shadrach), Mishael (Meshech), and Azariah (Abed-nego). They were trained to serve in the court of the pagan king, but these four at least refused to forsake the laws and customs of their fathers in order to conform to Babylonian conditions. For this God blessed them with the result that they became especially adept in knowledge, learning, and wisdom. Daniel, moreover, became an authority in matters of dreams and visions, even surpassing those wise men of the kingdom whose special forte was in these areas (1:17-20).

Daniel was evidently only a lad when he went to Babylon in 605, for he continued to prophesy until at least 539 B.C. His ministry was, therefore, contemporary with the reigns of all the kings of Babylonia from Nebuchadnezzar to the end of the empire under Nabonidus and Belshazzar. And he lived even under the rule of the Persian king Cyrus and his provincial ruler Darius the Mede. His book, written partly in Hebrew and partly in Aramaic, is divided into two sections: the first six chapters which have to do with his own experiences and the last six which describe his visions concerning the future. He is not counted among the prophets because he did not occupy the prophetic office, but his book is placed among the Major Prophets because Daniel did possess the gift of prophecy. As a statesman he made his greatest impact upon his times through the message which he delivered and interpreted.

Daniel seemed to be both respected and feared by Nebuchadnezzar. Very shortly after the king had succeeded his father on the Babylonian throne he had dreamed a dream which he not only could not interpret but which he had even forgotten by the time he awoke. The imperious king summoned his wisest counselors, but they protested that without a knowledge of the contents of the dream they could hardly interpret it (2:8-9). Dissatisfied with this perfectly legitimate excuse, the king ordered the wise men to be executed. Daniel, however, managed to gain an audience with Nebuchadnezzar in time to prevent the massacre, and after he had given full recognition to God as the source of his wisdom, revealed both the dream and its meaning to the monarch. This persuaded the king to advance the young counselor and Daniel became the overseer of the wise men.

Some years after that, Nebuchadnezzar erected a ninety foot tall golden image in a conspicuous place and decreed that all men should bow down to it at a given signal. The Babylonian concept of the king as a representative of Marduk is seen here clearly, and Daniel was not about to show any such deference to a foreign god.[8] How Daniel escaped the consequences we are not told, but his three friends were apprehended when they refused to show obeisance to the king's image. With incredible hardness the king ordered these three to death in a huge furnace heated to utmost capacity. But in the midst of the flames appeared one "like the Son of God" who so protected the faithful young men that they came forth unscathed. This could not but help raise the prestige of Yahweh in Nebuchadnezzar's eyes so he decreed that from then on the God of the Hebrews must be given full recognition as an acceptable deity in the realm (3:29).

Sometime in his reign Nebuchadnezzar had another dream in which he saw a great tree stripped of its branches and leaves and reduced to a mere stump. This stump then became like a beast of the field for seven years, eating grass and being driven from place to place. Daniel predicted that the king himself, represented by the tree which he had seen in his dream, would become demented, and as a wild beast would roam about unable to control even himself to say nothing of the kingdom. After seven years his sanity would return and he would acknowledge the supremacy of Almighty God. This did happen according to Daniel, though there have as yet been found no secular documents from this period to support a seven year period of incapacity for Nebuchadnezzar.[9] And we must question that the king from this time became a convert to Yahweh. Rather, as was the custom in the times, he merely recognized now more clearly than ever that Yahweh was a great god and that, indeed, Yahweh of the Hebrews might actually be synonymous with Marduk or some chief Babylonian god.

In Daniel's latter years, he became involved especially with Belshazzar, son of Nabonidus and last regent of Babylon.[10] This impious prince who ruled in the absence of his father held a great banquet during which he desecrated the sacred vessels of Solomon's Temple by drinking wine in them (5:2-3). This blasphemous act, apparently in the last night of Belshazzar's reign (539 B.C.), so angered the Lord God of Israel that He caused a strange writing to appear on the banquet room wall, a writing which predicted the overthrow of the mighty Babylonian Empire that very night. Daniel was called to interpret the unknown characters; and after berating the prince for having followed in the proud and sacrilegious steps of his predecessor, Nebuchadnezzar, he pronounced the doom of the prince and his city. That very night the Persians and Medes, under Gobryas (possibly the same as Darius the Mede),[11] invaded the city and without resistance occupied it and slew the prince. Daniel, who had been promoted to third place in the kingdom (next to Nabonidus and Belshazzar), went uninjured because Darius saw in him a man who could be useful in the solidification of his new empire.

Daniel's experiences with the Persians, though brief, were fraught with dangers and marvelous deliverances by the Lord. He had been appointed as a chief official in the city, but other dignitaries, jealous of his position, had cajoled the king into making a decree that no one should worship his own god for a certain period under penalty of death. Daniel, of course, continued to pray daily to the Lord, and so was brought before the king and sentenced to death. Though the king certainly did all he could to find a means of excepting Daniel, the irreversible Persian law, which even the king must observe, could not be circumvented. The aged seer was therefore cast into a den of lions, but he was protected from the ravenous beasts by the presence of the Lord. His salvation from such dire circumstances convinced the king that Daniel's God must surely be a first rate deity, ranking on a level with those others whom he recognized (6:26-27).

The dreams and visions which Daniel had personally or which he interpreted for the king are based upon one main theme: the nations of the world and their relationship to the covenant people of God. Nebuchadnezzar had seen a great image whose head was gold, whose breasts and arms were silver, whose belly and thighs were bronze, whose legs were iron, and whose feet were part iron and part clay. Daniel revealed that Nebuchadnezzar himself was the head of gold, and that the other parts were kingdoms which would rise successively after him. There would be a stone cut without hands which would demolish the image; this stone represented the kingdom of God which would overthrow the governments of men and take their place forever (2:44-45). This is amplified in chapter seven where we have the vision of Daniel concerning the four great beasts. The first, like a lion, corresponded to the first kingdom, that of Nebuchadnezzar of Babylonia (or the head of gold). The second, like a bear, was Medo-Persia, and its being raised up on one side suggested the superiority of Persia over Media. This paralleled the breasts and arms of silver. The third beast, like a leopard, had four heads and four wings, and, we shall see, represented Greece (or the belly and thighs of bronze). The fourth beast was indescribable, but its iron teeth show us the correspondence with the part of Nebuchadnezzar's image made of iron. Its ten horns were reduced to seven and then increased by one to a total of eight (7:24). This last horn, a usurper, spoke against the "most

High" until he was destroyed by the Kingdom of God (the stone cut from a mountain without hands).

In chapter eight Daniel records a vision in which he sees two animals, a goat and a ram. The latter (Medo-Persia) pushed out in all directions until it was finally overcome by the goat (Greece). The goat had a great horn (ruler) between its eyes, but its horn was broken off in its prime and replaced by four others. From one of these four another ruler would rise up who would stand against the people of God, but who would also be broken off. This very likely refers to the Macedonian Empire whose chief king, Alexander the Great (d. 322 B.C.), died in his prime and was followed by his four generals who divided his empire. And from Seleucia, one of these parts, came Antiochus Epiphanes (Antiochus IV) who reigned from 175-163 B.C. This wicked king despoiled the Temple in Jerusalem, offered sacrifices of swine upon its altars, and even erected a statue of Zeus within its confines. Jews under Judas Maccabaeus revolted and restored the Temple to its proper usage.[12] This whole remarkable prophecy (found both here and in greater detail in chapter eleven) is the reason why critical scholarship has had to reject the historicity of Daniel or at least the possibility that the book was written as early as the sixth century. Because it so clearly outlines Greek and Seleucid history as it actually occurred, the popular solution is to say that an anonymous writer composed the book after 165 B.C.[13] Without going into the arguments here, may we simply say that the only valid reason for rejecting Danielic authorship is the impossibility of verbal inspiration. But those who do accept this high view of Scripture have no difficulty in believing that God revealed these amazing events hundreds of years before they happened.

In chapter nine Daniel predicted that seventy weeks must pass before the climactic eschatological day would be completed. It is generally agreed that the term "week" (*heptad* in Greek) does not refer to seven days but to seven years, and that seventy weeks are therefore 490 years. This period would begin with the decree for the rebuilding of the Temple and would be broken up into three eras. After seven weeks (forty-nine years) the city would be rebuilt; sixty-two more weeks (434 years) the Anointed One (Messiah) would be cut off; and after one more week (seven years) everything else would be completed including the anointing of the most

Holy. Besides the critical school, which refers to this passage as imaginative apocalyptic and makes no effort to give it prophetic significance, we have two main views. The a-millennial is that these periods are figurative but that there is here a picture of the final restoration as represented by the death and resurrection of the Lord and establishment of God's eternal kingdom through the Church.[14] The pre-millennial interpretation is that the time spans are literal, dating from the decree of Artaxerxes in 458 B.C., and that Christ died 483 years after that. Then there is disagreement as to whether the seventieth week was fulfilled immediately after the death of Christ or whether there has been a lapse of time since the death of the Lord; and the seventieth week, therefore, remains yet to be fulfilled in the time of great tribulation which the Scriptures imply will endure for seven years.[15] In any event, the detail is amazing and the purpose is clear: God will permit the kingdoms of men to go on for just so far, and then He will step in and through His Son introduce everlasting peace and righteousness.

Outline of Daniel

I. The deportation (1).

   A. Captivity of Judah (1-2).
   B. Choice of children (3-7).
   C. Conviction of Daniel (8-16).
   D. Capabilities of the four (17-21).

II. The great image (2).

   A. Dream of Nebuchadnezzar (1-13).
   B. Desire of Daniel (14-23).
   C. Description of the dream (24-35).
   D. Declaration of the dream (36-45).
   E. Distinction of Daniel (46-49).

III. Nebuchadnezzar's decree (3).

   A. Command of Nebuchadnezzar (1-7).
   B. Conduct of the three children (8-12).
   C. Conclusion of their disobedience (13-25).
   D. Confession of Nebuchadnezzar (26-30).

IV. Nebuchadnezzar's humiliation (4).

    A. Nebuchadnezzar's pronouncement (1-3).
    B. Nebuchadnezzar's problem (4-18).
    C. Nebuchadnezzar's prospects (19-27).
    D. Nebuchadnezzar's punishment (28-37).

V. Babylon's destruction (5).

    A. Defilement of the kingdom (1-4).
    B. Declaration to the kingdom (5-29).
    C. Destruction of the kingdom (30-31.

VI. Daniel's faithfulness (6).

    A. Daniel's favor (1-3).
    B. Daniel's foes (4-9).
    C. Daniel's faithfulness (10-23).
    D. Daniel's freedom (24-28).

VII. The four earthly kingdoms (7).

    A. Daniel's dream received (1-14).
    B. Daniel's dream revealed (15-28).

VIII. The type of Antichrist (8).

    A. Impartation of Daniel's vision (1-12).
    B. Inquiry concerning Daniel's vision (13-14).
    C. Interpretation of Daniel's vision (15-27).

IX. The seventy weeks (9).

    A. Daniel's research (1-2).
    B. Daniel's repentance (3-15).
    C. Daniel's request (16-19).
    D. Daniel's revelation (20-27).

X. The defeat of Persia (10).

    A. Daniel's vision (1-9).
    B. Daniel's visitations (10-21).

XI. Antichrist (11).

    A. The prefiguring of Antichrist (1-20).
    B. The presenting of Antichrist (21-29).
    C. The profanities of Antichrist (30-45).

XII.   The triumph of God's people (12).

    A.   The tribulation of the end (1-4).
    B.   The time of the end (5-12).
    C.   The triumph of the end (12-13).

THE PERSIAN EMPIRE

The Persian conquest of Babylon by Cyrus the Great inaugurated still another phase of Jewish national life. This energetic emperor, who exercised power over the greatest realm hitherto known, had the eastern world at his feet by 539 B.C.[16] In 538 Cyrus issued his famous decree that all captive peoples might return to their native lands, thus reversing the oppressive policies of the Assyrians and to a lesser extent that of the Babylonians. The contents of this decree are found in the so-called Cylinder of Cyrus, a large clay monument unearthed in the last century, and, of course, in the Biblical books of II Chronicles (36:22-23) and Ezra (1:1-4). This wise leader felt it would serve his interests better for people to return to their homelands and resume their religious and cultural practices without outside interference. When a people could be internally independent and happy, they would be far less apt to promote unrest in the Empire. Thus, the setting was laid for Judah's return to Jerusalem.

Cyrus reigned until 530 B.C. when he was killed in battle. His son and successor, Cambyses (530-522), maintained his father's holdings and even added to them by subduing Egypt (525). Amasis, king of Egypt, died in the process of Persian conquest and his son Psammeticus held out for only a few months. With his defeat Egypt became a Persian province, which it remained for over a century. Cambyses had slain his own brother Bardiya when he first became king, but in 522 an imposter named Smerdis (or Gautama) seized the Persian throne in Cambyses' absence and pretended to be the deceased Bardiya. Completely broken by the news, Cambyses committed suicide and his officer, Darius Hystaspes, took command. Darius, in spite of almost overwhelming odds and beset by unrest throughout the Empire, managed to liquidate Smerdis and proclaim himself king (521-486).

After a year or two Darius was able to consolidate the Empire which had for several years seemed on the verge of collapse. He engaged himself not only in military operations, but accomplished notable building enterprises including the new capital at Persepolis, a canal from the Nile to the Red Sea in Egypt, and extensive highways throughout his vast realm.   Toward the close of his life he tried to annex Greece to his territory, but suffered a crushing defeat at the Battle of Marathon in Greece (490).   His son Xerxes (486-465), known as Ahasuerus in the Book of Esther, attempted to follow up the Greek campaigns of his father but was defeated at the naval battle of Salamis, though he had been successful in annihilating the Spartans at Thermopylae and actually reached the city of Athens.   He also had his hands full with troubles at Egypt and Babylon and eventually met violent death at the hands of an assassin.

One of Xerxes' sons, Artaxerxes (464-423), followed him but his reign was for the most part quite unsuccessful.   He had constant difficulty holding his Egyptian province and was completely unable to push westward against the Greeks.   As a matter of fact, by this time Persia had begun to lose its grip on the world and to slide backward, a slide that would culminate in its destruction under Alexander a century later. The only interruption to this pattern was the reign of Darius II (423-404), a gifted king who was able to establish Persian authority in Asia Minor once more and even to subjugate Athens for a time.   He was followed by Artaxerxes II (404-358) who gradually lost his empire through rebellions all over the world.   The details of this period or of those which followed are not relevant to our study in this book, however, so we will bring our discussion of historical backgrounds to a close here.   Suffice to say that the Macedonians under Alexander the Great finished the Persian Empire at the Battle of Arbela in 331.   This new Empire in turn was broken up by 322 B.C. into at least four parts; though a Hellenistic influence held on for over a hundred years more there was no more empire until Rome appeared late in the third century, incorporating nearly all of the Near East into its hegemony by 63 B.C.   This was to lay the political foundation of the New Testament.

THE FIRST RETURN FROM BABYLONIA

After Cyrus had made his decree authorizing the Jews to return to Jerusalem, he provided them with such assistance as they would need to make the journey and to begin to rebuild their countries. He placed Sheshbazzar, who may have been a son of Jehoiakin (I Chron. 3:18), over the exiles and later made him governor over the Judaean section of the satrap. In all there were over 50,000 people who returned, including over 7,000 servants. Two of the chief figures, besides Sheshbazzar, were Joshua the priest and Zerubbabel who came shortly after. These two godly men took the initiative in setting up the broken altars of Yahweh in the blackened ruins of the Temple and actually inspired the people to lay the foundation for a new temple in its place (Ezra 3:9-10). The joy which accompanied the beginning of this work can well be imagined, since for fifty years there had been no sacrifice. This was the beginning of a new era for them, an era in which God would truly begin to fulfill the promises of the prophets concerning a glorious future occasioned by the return and restoration.

The chronology of the books of Ezra-Nehemiah is a little complicated, especially at this point (ch. 4), but it seems likely that the next events of history we see come from the period of Darius of Persia shortly after he had become king.[17] The only sources of information we have concerning the beginning of this time are the prophets Haggai and Zechariah, so it will be well to refer to them now very briefly.

Haggai. From the time the Temple was begun (ca. 536) until the commencement of the ministry of Haggai (520) there was a span of sixteen years. During that time the initial enthusiasm of the people had worn off and the unfinished foundations remained as an ugly reminder of an uncompleted task. The people themselves had begun to provide their own residences and under the sanction of Cyrus and Camyses and the blessing of God had made a good start to recovery, though the undertaking staggers the imagination. This is, however, the motivation that prompted Haggai to speak. The people had no right to care for their own selfish needs while the Temple of the Lord lay in an unfinished state (1:4-6). His message was so well received that the people immediately undertook the resumption of the work and within five years had completed it (by 516). Thus, as Jeremiah had said, the captivity would last for seventy years, a captivity in which

God could not be honored in sacrifice because of the lack of a Temple.

It is true that there were those present who had remembered the magnificent temple of Solomon and who now wept at the comparison with this meagre structure (2:3). But Haggai strengthened them with the affirmation that this house would be filled with the glory of the Lord in an even greater measure than was the Temple of old. The people had come home and God would remember His covenant with them (2:9).

Outline of Haggai

I. Rebuilding encouraged (1).

    A. Excuses of the people (1-2).
    B. Exhortation of the prophet (3-11).
    C. Effect of the plea (12-15).

II. Restoration explained (2).

    A. Comparison of temples (1-3).
    B. Covenant of the Lord (4-9).
    C. Condemnation of the people (10-19).
    D. Choosing of Judah (20-23).

— — — — —

Zechariah. The prophet Zechariah, a contemporary of Haggai, had also the burden to rebuild the Temple, but his vision, expressed largely in apocalyptic terms, was much broader than just that. He saw a measurement and rebuilding of not only a physical Jerusalem, but that of a spiritual city wherein salvation could be found for all mankind (2:11-12). This salvation would become possible through the Branch, the anointed one of God, who would build the Temple of God (3:8). The city itself would be filled with joyous people who would be indeed the people of God (8:8). The time would come that ten men would seize the skirt of one Jew and beg him to reveal to them the way of salvation (8:23).

The king of the city would come to it in humility and justice, bringing salvation, and yet would accomplish the destruction of God's enemies (9:9). Jerusalem would be free from idolatry and from false prophets who made it their business to deceive (13:2). But, as Ezekiel taught, this future glory must be ushered in by tribulation. Jerusalem must experience the wrath of the nations in the last days and await the deliverance of the Lord (14:1-3). But that deliverance would surely come when the feet of the Lord stood upon the Mount of Olives and divided it in two, proclaiming thereby the message of doom upon the nations assembled against Jerusalem for battle (14:4-11). The wicked would be crushed, the feasts of the Lord would be resumed, and everything would be holy unto the Lord (14:20-21).

Outline of Zechariah

I. Series of visions (1-6:8).

    A. Call to repentenance (1:1-6).
    B. The horses (7-17).
    C. The horns and carpenters (18-21).
    D. The measurer (2).
    E. Cleansing of the priest (3).
    F. Candlesticks (4)
    G. The flying roll (5:1-4).
    H. The flying ephah (5:5-11).
    I. The flying chariots (6:1-8).

II. Symbolical crowning of the priest (6:9-15).

III. Problem concerning fasting (7).

IV. Promise of restoration (8).

V. Future of the Kingdom (9-11).

    A. Rejoicing of Jerusalem (9).
    B. Restoration of Jerusalem (10).
    C. Revelation to Jerusalem (11).

VI. Future of the king (12-14).

    A. Punishment by Jerusalem (12).
    B. Purification of Jerusalem (13).
    C. Plague of Jerusalem's enemies (14).

For the completion of the Temple we must turn back to Ezra where we find it discussed more fully. The citizens of the land, the Samaritans, had requested that they might assist in the rebuilding, but their offer was declined on the grounds that this was a Jewish project (4:1-6). This suggestion that the Samaritans were less than Jewish and were therefore unqualified to participate in the formation of the new state produced a friction between the two peoples which increased with the passing of time and was most apparent in the time of Jesus (John 4). The Samaritans and their Arabian and Ammonite allies then attempted to frustrate the work, which may

be one of the reasons for its delay until the resumption under
Haggai and Zechariah.   When it was resumed, Tatnai, govern-
or of the Persian lands west of the Euphrates, sent a letter to
Darius informing him of the Jews' activity and asking him to
search in the official archives to see if there were any legal
basis to what they were doing (5:6-17).   This Darius did,
and to the chagrin of the opposition the original decree of
Cyrus was found which not only authorized the Jews to do
this rebuilding, but offered them help.   Darius therefore ordered the opposition to cease and told Tatnai to supply to the
Jews such things as they might lack (6:8).   Within six years
the Temple stood complete, though the city was still a pile of
rubble for the most part and the walls still lay shattered.

Esther.   Events are very obscure throughout the rest of
the reign of Darius and into that of Xerxes.   We may assume
that the work of rebuilding the state of Judah continued,
though with great harassment from many sides.   The Jews in
exile prospered for the most part, but there were certain anti-
Jewish currents which began to make themselves felt.   This
is the main gist of the book of Esther, a rather strange composition which does not even mention the name of God, but
whose every page reflects the intense awareness of God's
presence and power on behalf of His exiled people.

The setting of the book is in the reign of Ahasuerus
(Xerxes), and the first events are in his third year (483).
It seems that the king was celebrating a magnificent feast
which had gone on for seven days.   All the lords and ladies
of the empire were there and spirits were high indeed. Near
the end of the week the king, who was in a drunken stupor,
was urged by his counselors to invite his queen Vashti to the
feast in order that her great beauty might be admired.   The
king unthinkingly complied, but the noble Vashti refused to
come (2:12).   The counselors then advised the king that he
would have to rid himself of Vashti because of her disobedience, for if word of this should get out into the realm, all wives
would take the cue to disobey their husbands.   Reluctantly
Xerxes followed the advice and followed it up with a decree
that any disobedient wife should be treated in the same
fashion.

The king then set out to look for another queen.   All the
beautiful and intelligent maidens of the realm were brought

before him, and one in particular caught his eye—Esther, the young cousin of Mordecai the Jew. Shortly after the marriage, Mordecai overheard a plot against the life of the king. He conveyed the information to his cousin and she relayed it to her husband in Mordecai's name. In the meantime, a greedy man named Haman had been promoted to a place of prominence in the empire. Everyone acknowledged his eminence by bowing before him when he made an appearance—everyone but Mordecai. This so infuriated Haman that he set out to devise a way of removing the irksome Jew. When all other plans failed, he decided that a nationwide purge of the Jewish people would be best so he convinced the king to decree such a purge by telling him that the Jews were seditious (3:8-9). Now, Xerxes, who seemed to act rashly in any event, did not know that his beloved Esther was a Jewess or he would never have made this irreversible decree. When Mordecai learned that a date had been set for the purge of his race, he quickly reached Esther with the news and advised her that she might be the means of salvation for her people (4:14).

After much soul-searching, Esther agreed to do what she could. She would go to her husband unannounced, though this could result in her death according to Persian custom, and would invite him and Haman to a series of banquets. Amazingly, the king was well disposed to the idea and agreed to attend when Esther should name the date. Haman, overjoyed at his great success in removing the Jews and also being invited to such an important function, went away to his home, only to meet the hated Mordecai along the way. When the Jew would not prostrate himself, Haman went home in a rage and while there accepted his wife's suggestion that he build a huge gallows on which to hang his enemy.

That night the king could not sleep and called for the state records to be brought and read to him. It was brought to his attention afresh that his life had been saved by a certain Mordecai; when he asked if Mordecai had ever been rewarded for this, the answer was no. Haman, who had come to the palace early in the morning, was asked by the king what he could do to honor a man in a special way. The selfish Haman thought that the king must have him in mind, so he advised the king to give the man a place of great authority and to bestow lavish gifts upon him. At that, Xerxes told Haman to go to Mordecai and so honor him (6:10).

When the banquet day came Haman was there with the king and queen when the queen requested that her people might be spared. It now dawned upon Xerxes that he had sentenced his own wife to death with her people. When he learned further that Haman had been instrumental in the matter he had the wretched man hanged on his own gallows. Another decree was issued stating that though the first could not be changed, the Jews now would be able to defend themselves. This so encouraged the Jews and unnerved their enemies that when the appointed day of purge arrived the tables were turned and the Jews succeeded in thwarting the designs of their foes. In commemoration of the Divine deliverance, they celebrated the Feast of Purim ("lots"). The lots which had been cast by their oppressors to determine the order in which they would die now fell favorably in their direction (9:26). Mordecai, the faithful servant of God, enjoyed the honor of the man who thought to do him harm.

We see, then, how that God's people, even in exile, were remarkably protected in this circumstance and many others which we presume must have been similar. Though the book of Esther is not regarded favorably by higher criticism,[18] usually because of its allegedly secular tone and incredible turn of events, there is no reason historical or otherwise to deny the authenticity of the events and persons which it describes.

Back in Judah the original settlers under Shesh-bazzar and Zerubbabel had laid a good foundation in many respects, at least as far as the material progress of the state was concerned. The Temple had been rebuilt and some effort made to fortify the city of Jerusalem. The people were getting along comfortably enough as we have seen in the books of Haggai and Zechariah and apparently enjoyed some measure of independence under the Persians even though their neighbors in all directions persisted in their harassment. The government was that of a high priestly rule, though there were officials designated as governors who were appointees of the Persian king. Judaea itself was not an individual political entity, to be sure, but was part of the larger satrap which consisted of the Persian lands west of the Euphrates.

Sheshbazzar, Zerubbabel, and Joshua the priest had all passed from the scene by the close of the sixth century and the leadership which followed them did not seem to measure up to their stature at all. We have no record of a governor after

Zerubbabel until the time of Nehemiah (444), but the high priestly line continued under Joiakim (ca. 510-475) and Eliashib (475-425?). These men were unable to establish a spiritual leadership which was so necessary, with the result that the cult had fallen into bad times indeed. Moreover, and relatedly, the people had begun to intermingle with the natives of the land, even going so far as to intermarry with them. This, we presume, was the state of affairs for over fifty years until Ezra came to Jerusalem in the company of a great crowd of exiles (Ezra 7:6-10).

This godly man was a direct descendant of Aaron and was therefore qualified to occupy the priestly office. Furthermore, he was a scribe or scholar in the matters of the Law and had authority to render interpretations of it and make legal copies of it. At a time when the returned people had begun to forget their past as well as the covenant promises of the future, Ezra came to them and made of them a nation with renewed direction and purpose. It is certainly overstating the matter to say that Ezra was the founder of Judaism,[19] for Judaism is simply the post-exilic expression of the ancient Old Testament faith. But that it was a different expression and was greatly influenced by Ezra cannot be challenged. The reemphasis on the Law and ceremony, the rise of the synagogue movement with its careful attention to the study of Torah, and the final shaping of the Old Testament canon— all these were largely affected by Ezra and his spiritual heirs.

We first meet Ezra in the seventh year of Artaxerxes I (458) when he came, under the authority and assistance of that king, from Babylon to Jerusalem. He came for the purpose not only of leading a caravan of the pious back to the fatherland, but to seek the Law of the Lord, to do it, and to teach it to the community (Ezra 7:10). The ecclesiastical character of Ezra's movement is seen in the extensive lists of priests (10:15-44) and other people who had either accompanied him to Jerusalem or who came under his direction when he located there. He especially was concerned about the lack of separation among the priests and Levites in the community, for though they had not forsaken the faith and adopted other gods, they had intermarried with foreign women (9:1-2). This so aroused him that he broke out into prayer immediately upon his arrival and interceded for his wayward people. The result was a great assembly of the population from throughout the little country followed by national repentance. This in turn was followed by a proclamation that the whole nation must convene at Jerusalem, failing which the disobedient would lose their earthly goods. The purpose for the gathering was to take action to remove the foreign wives of those who had married outside the covenant. The response was so universal and overwhelming that there is every reason to believe that a genuine revival was experienced under Ezra's leadership (10:12).

This more favorable condition was maintained for ten years or more, but then difficulties crept in again. It seems that sometime near 446-445 B.C. work on the walls and buildings, which had slowly been making progress, was stopped by the interference of the hostile neighbors, and even that which had been rebuilt was in some way destroyed (Ezra 4:24; Neh. 1:3). The antagonists had written a letter to Artaxerxes informing him that under Ezra's leadership the Jews had not only reestablished the cult, a matter which the king had permitted, but had gone beyond the king's express command by fortifying Jerusalem. They charged that the Jews were a notoriously seditious people and that Artaxerxes would do well to look out for his interests lest they conspire against him and hide behind their new walls. The king did indeed discover that the Jews had such a reputation in the past, so he sent immediate word that the work must cease until further word should be given.

This discouraging setback was related to Nehemiah, the Jewish cupbearer of Artaxerxes, when certain travelers from Judah came to see him at Susa (ca. 444 B.C.). Nehemiah, though he apparently had never been to Jerusalem, nevertheless had the well-being of his ancestral home deep in his heart and was very upset. His anxiety over the ruined condition of the city showed so plainly in his countenance that the king asked him what ailed him. With a prayer upon his lips, Nehemiah told all that had happened among his countrymen and courageously begged permission of the king to go to the Holy City to see what he could do. Amazingly, Artaxerxes, who had only recently ordered construction of Jerusalem to cease, acquiesced and sent his trusted servant on leave of absence (Neh. 2:6). More than that, he sent letters of conveyance with him which guaranteed him not only a safe journey but access to any materials he might need from the provincial governor to resume the work at Jerusalem. Sanballat, governor of Samaria, and Tobiah, governor of Ammon, were naturally upset by this reversal, but because of the king's sanction of it there was little they could hope to do by way of force to prevent the work under Nehemiah.

Nehemiah's first task was to assess the amount of damage done and the extensiveness of the labor and materials necessary to finish the great task. At once he aroused the people of Judah to action, assuring them of both Divine and royal authorization. The opponents, who hoped that they might join the project now that they could not prevent it, were forbidden any part one way or the other (2:17-20). The workers were divided up into gangs according to their occupations, places of residence, and families, and each became responsible for a different section of the wall of the city. We cannot pause here to trace the lines of the walls and locations of the many gates, but the information presented has been remarkably well verified by archaeological exploration of the ancient city walls.[20]

When Sanballat, Tobiah, and their allies saw that they could not dissuade Nehemiah from his project, they resorted to a course of action which became increasingly more violent. At first they mocked the effort of the Jews, branding it as "feeble." The walls, they said, were so inadequate that even a fox by brushing against them could cause their collapse (4:3). When ridicule failed and the work was nearing completion, it became clear that mere words could not prevent it. Heedless of Artaxerxes' decree that the work be unhindered, the Samaritans, Ammonites, Arabians, and others took up arms and began to physically impede construction. This only served to make Nehemiah more vigilant; in a remarkable display of preseverance and fortitude he ordered his men to work in shifts day and night and to fight with one hand while they built with the other. No wonder the entire wall was erected in only fifty-two days!

Still the enemy persisted. With all possibility of preventing the fortification of Jerusalem gone, they hoped they could induce Nehemiah to negotiate with them in a neutral place. But as far as the Jewish leader was concerned, there was nothing to negotiate, for he clearly had the upper hand. Undaunted, they composed an open letter which they read loudly outside the city so as to attract the attention of the populace.

In the letter they maintained that the purpose for the walls was to allow the Jews to rebel against the Persians so that Nehemiah could be the king (6:6-7). This ridiculous accusation Nehemiah hotly denied and the people were quick to see the subtlety behind it. Finally, they essayed to diminish Nehemiah's good reputation among the citizens by attempting to persuade him to take sanctuary in the Temple, arguing that such a valuable man should not expose himself to danger. But Nehemiah saw through this scheme all too well and revealed to all that the one who had rendered the advice was a crony of the opposition who had tried to weaken his position by making him appear cowardly.

At last, the problems of material reconstruction were pretty well solved and Nehemiah had time to direct his attention to other matters of even greater importance. In the twenty-five years or so since the great revival of Ezra, social and religious relapses had taken place on every hand. This seems to be difficult to understand, and, indeed, has led some such as John Bright to date Ezra after Nehemiah for, it is argued, if Ezra's revival was the success he says it was in his book, why was there a need so soon for another one, especially if Ezra were still living there among the people? There is merit to this argument, but it is not conclusive we feel. For one thing, the problems do not seem to be exactly the same as Ezra had faced earlier, the main difficulty now being the oppressive usury which Jew was exacting from Jew. It is true that some of the same matters which Ezra had handled had to be dealt with again, but we must realize that the Jews had historically been prone to quickly defect from a position or attitude of revival, even in as little time as twenty-five years. How it could happen beneath Ezra's nose may be explained by assuming that Ezra by this time was no doubt advanced in years and was simply not alert to what was going on. It is true that Nehemiah himself had been back for ten years or so before he instituted his reforms, but such matters as the building of the walls and city and the securing of a solid position in the face of great opposition from without could easily have prevented his taking a more active role in domestic and spiritual matters.

He first struck out against those who were exploiting their fellow citizens by charging unduly high rates of interest contrary to the Law (5:1-5). He argued that since the impoverished Jews had sold themselves to the surrounding heathen and had been redeemed by those who had returned from exile, it was especially serious that Jew should so oppress Jew by inflicting unpayable rates of interest on loans. He said that as long as he had been governor (444-433) he had worked for no wages and had not burdened the people in any other way. The least they could do was emulate his example and ease their common yoke.

Nehemiah also set about allocating to the people their dwelling places on the basis of their genealogical records as they existed since the time of Zerubbabel and Joshua. Following this a great crowd gathered before the Water Gate to listen to the reading of the Law by Ezra the scribe (8:1-8). On a specially erected platform he opened the scrolls and when he began to read the people stood reverently before him. With clarity and expression he expounded the ancient covenant truths while the assembly wept in the presence of their convicting precepts. But Nehemiah exhorted them to rejoice, for this was a day of gladness, a day when they could celebrate the actuality of the return from exile and the reestablishment of their sacred community. The next day the covenant renewal was consummated by the observance of the Feast of Tabernacles, the principal feature of which was the daily reading of the Law by Ezra. This was the first time the Feast had been celebrated since the time of Joshua the son of Nun; and now, after 800 years, it signified the beginning of a new era in Israel. The faith of their fathers had become bound up in the Law (which means here the entire Old Testament) and Judaism became a religion of the Book more than anything else.

As evidence of this new direction we see the repentance of the people, a repentance conditioned upon their failure to faithfully follow the precepts of Moses. And so, at the same time, we see that Judaism, as we may now call their religion, was not unrelated from its earlier composition. It found its roots deep within the historical dealings of God with Israel just as Christianity must find its source in Judaism and the Old Testament. In united recitation the Levites recounted God's past blessings and leading and acknowledged that their disastrous afflictions had come about deservedly. But God had not discontinued His convenant with them. He had only temporarily withheld its blessing. Now they had returned as

God had said they would through the prophets; they had become conscious that though things would never be exactly the
same as they were before the Exile, God had not forsaken the
covenant. He had caused them to pass through the fires of
purgation in order that they might return refined and ready
to resume their obligations to Him. To this end they solemnly
rededicated themselves and all that they possessed on that momentous day (9:38).

It is clear that Nehemiah returned to Susa shortly after
the Feast of Tabernacles and the subsequent ceremony of
covenant renewal (ca. 433). He remained there for an in-
definite period, and then obtained leave again from the king
(presumably Artaxerxes I) to return to Jerusalem. When he
reached the city, he found deplorable conditions abounded in
every area of life though he had been absent for but a few
years at the most. For one thing, Eliashib the priest had not
only permitted Tobiah to make an alliance with him, but the
crafty Ammonite had been given an apartment within the
sacred Temple of the Lord, a clear violation of the Law of
Moses (13:4-5). Angrily, Nehemiah evicted Tobiah and
ordered the polluted chambers cleaned thoroughly. He then
observed that the Levites were not supported by the gifts of
the people and that they had to go to work in the fields to
maintain their families. He assailed the people for their
stinginess and saw to it that they paid the Levites their due.
The Sabbath too was being violated by both Jew and Gentile
who came and bought and sold in the city on the day of rest.
Nehemiah quickly put a stop to this activity, but the caravan
merchants continued to linger outside the city all through the
Sabbath waiting for the first day of the week to come so that
they could resume their business. Even this Nehemiah considered a breach of the spirit of the law, so he warned these
Gentile traders to stay a comfortable distance from Jerusalem
lest they fall into his hands. Finally, he had to deal with the
oft-recurring problem of mixed marriages, though Ezra had
settled this matter with them over thirty years before (13:23).
The problem had become so serious that the children of these
marriages had a strange lingo, half Hebrew and half foreign.
With a burst of temper the energetic reformer forced compliance with the law of marital purity, apparently with success.

With this, Nehemiah's career passes from history; in fact, the course of Old Testament history reaches its completion. The only other allusions to the period are found in the book of the last prophet of the Old Testament, Malachi.

Malachi. In order to see that there were unhealthy trends in normative Judaism immediately after the time of Ezra and contemporary with Nehemiah, we must examine briefly the book of Malachi. This prophet, whose indictments seem to point to the same conditions as prevailed in Nehemiah's age, largely concerned himself with invectives against the terrible travesties of law and righteousness which he saw on every hand. Though it is true that the Jews never were idolatrous after the Exile, it is equally true that they very seldom matched up to the Lord's expectations. Malachi could point out such things as their offering of inferior animals to the Lord (1:8), the sinfulness of the priests, and their mixed marriages, but they would only reply, "Wherein have we offended the Lord?" They had come through the Exile, they had rebuilt their country, they had become covenant-conscious once again. Yet, their very security had produced a callousness of spirit and heart and had bred indifference and coldness into their relationship to God and each other.

But Malachi stated in no uncertain terms that the Day of the Lord was still coming, a day when the Lord would appear among them to purify and judge (3:1-3). Then would they offer the good sacrifices which they were so unwilling to do now. They had robbed Him now by failing to bring proper offerings, but if they would test Him they would find that He could bless them beyond their wildest expectations (3:10). Those who were unprepared for His coming would be consumed by His wrath, but those who obediently awaited and feared Him would be blessed with healing and salvation. The sign of the appearance of the Lord would be the preaching of Elijah which, as Isaiah had said, would be the voice of one crying in the wilderness with a message of judgment, repentance, and hope. The covenant had been reaffirmed over and over, even as late as this time of the prophet, but the fulfillment and perfect realization must await that wilderness voice which would pronounce jubilantly and with authority, "Behold the Lamb of God which taketh away the sin of the world."

Outline of Malachi

I.   Reminder to the nation (1:1-5).

II. Reproof to the profane (6-14).

III. Rebuke to the priests (2).

IV. Restoration of the nation (3).

V.   Reign of the Sun of Righteousness (4).

INTERTESTAMENTAL HISTORY

Apart from the uncertain references of Josephus and documents such as the Elephantine Papyri we know virtually nothing of Jewish affairs to the end of the Persian period and on into the Hellenistic. It seems fairly clear, however, that the pattern as seen in the last chapter of Nehemiah and in the prophet Malachi must have persisted more or less until the breakup of the Macedonian Empire (322 B.C.). After that the successive dominations of the Ptolemies of Egypt and the Seleucids of Syria and Babylonia brought in certain modifications of the Judaistic faith, though minor to be sure, which continued to manifest themselves until and including the time of Jesus Christ and even beyond. The struggle for Jewish independence under the Maccabbees (167-135), followed by the Hasmonaean Dynasty of Jewish kings (135-63 B.C.), also made its contributions to the nation and people, notably in the rise of parties such as the Pharisees, Sadducees, and Essenes.[21] The Judaism of the Roman period (after 63), therefore, had much in common with that of Ezra, but the accretions from the sources mentioned, embodied largely in terms of Hellenistic philosophy, Persian religious concepts to a limited degree, and the oral law (Mishnah), all combined to make that later Judaism also something quite different.[22] The hostility of Judaism to Christ and the Gospel cannot be explained as a clash between Judaism and Christianity; it was rather, a clash between the Judaism perverted through four centuries of history since Ezra and the fulfillment of Judaism of the Old Testament as expressed by Christ and the Apostles. "In the fullness of time God sent forth His Son," the crucial and culminating act of all history and that toward which the Old Testament story we have been studying constantly was pressing.

¹ For the historical background of this period, see John Bright, *A History of Israel*, Philadelphia, Westminster Press, 1959, pp. 332 ff. The dates are primarily those of Edwin R. Thiele, *The Mysterious Numbers of the Hebrew Kings* Chicago, University of Chicago Press, 1951, pp. 153-166.

² This information is on the famous Cylinder of Cyrus. For the text see D. Winton Thomas, *Documents From Old Testament Times*, London, Thomas Nelson and Sons, Ltd., 1958, pp. 92-94.

³ W. F. Albright, *The Biblical Period From Abraham to Ezra*, New York, Harper and Row, 1963 p. 87.

⁴ The Elephantine Papyri, first found a hundred years ago, speak of the affairs of the Jewish Colony in Egypt. Some of these go back as far as the beginning of the fifth century B.C. See Thomas, *op. cit.*, pp. 258-268. See also Emil G. Kraeling, "New Light on the Elephantine Colony," *Biblical Archaeologist*, 15:50-67, September, 1952.

⁵ John Gray, *Archaeology and the Old Testament World*, New York, Harper and Row, 1962, p. 189.

⁶ This was not a later development from the third or second centuries B.C. as Rowley implies; cf. H. H. Rowley, *The Growth of the Old Testament*, New York, Harper and Row, 1963, p. 92.

⁷ C. F. Keil, *Biblical Commentary on the Old Testament: Ezekiel*, Grand Rapids, Wm. B. Eerdmans Publishing Company, 1948, pp. 84-85.

⁸ Sabatino Moscati, *Ancient Semitic Civilizations*, New York, G. P. Putnam's Sons, 1960, p. 88.

⁹ This is not surprising in the light of the fact that very few records from this period were preserved at all. See David Noel Freedman, 'The Babylonian Chronicle," *Biblical Archaeologist*, 19:59, 1959.

¹⁰ For texts which mention Belshazzar, see Thomas, *op. cit.*, p. 90.

¹¹ John Whitcomb, *Darius the Mede*, Grand Rapids, Wm. B. Eerdmans Publishing Company, 1959.

¹² Flavius Josephus, *Antiquities of the Jews*, XII, 5-6, *Josephus' Complete Works*, Trans. by William Whiston, London, Tallis, n.d.

¹³ William O. E. Oesterley, *An Introduction to the Books of the Old Testament*, New York, The Macmillan Company, 1934, pp. 334-337.

¹⁴ Herbert C. Leupold, *Exposition of Daniel*, Columbus, Wartburg Press, 1949.

¹⁵ Robert D. Culver, *Daniel and the Latter Days*, Chicago, Moody Press, 1954.

¹⁶ Bright, *op. cit.*, pp. 356 ff.

¹⁷ For the view that Ezra preceded Nehemiah, see Gleason Archer, *A Survey of Old Testament Introduction*, Chicago, Moody Press, 1964, pp. 396-398.

¹⁸ For example, see the remarks of Bernard W. Anderson, *Understanding the Old Testament*, Englewood Cliffs, Prentice-Hall, 1957, pp. 504-508.

¹⁹ Jacob M. Myers, *The Anchor Bible: Ezra-Nehemiah*, Ed. by W. F. Albright and David Noel Freedman, Garden City, Doubleday and Company, Inc., 1965, p. lxii.

[20] J. Garrow Duncan, *The Accuracy of the Old Testament*, London, Society for Promoting Christian Knowledge, 1930, pp. 105 ff.

[21] For this period, see F. F. Bruce, *Israel and the Nations*, Grand Rapids, Wm. B. Eerdmans Publishing Company, 1963; Werner Foerster, *From the Exile to Christ*, Philadelphia, Fortress Press, 1964.

[22] W. F. Albright, *From the Stone Age to Christianity*, Garden City, Doubleday and Company, Inc., 1957, pp. 345-380.

BIBLIOGRAPHY

A. Books

1. Archaeology and Texts

Albright, W. F. *The Archaeology of Palestine*. London, Penguin Books, 1956.

Barton, George. *Archaeology and the Bible*. Philadelphia, American Sunday School Union, 1937.

Bruce, F. F. *Second Thoughts on the Dead Sea Scrolls*. Grand Rapids, Wm. B. Eerdmans Publishing Company, 1964.

Burrows, Millar. *What Mean These Stones?* New York, Meridian Books, 1957.

Cadbury, Henry J., ed. *Annual of the American Schools of Oriental Research*. Vol. 10. New Haven, Yale University Press, 1930.

Driver, G. R. *Canaanite Myths and Legends*. Edinburgh, T. and T. Clark, 1956.

Garstang, John. *The Story of Jericho*. London, Hodder and Stroughton, Ltd., 1940.

Gray, John. *Archaeology and the Old Testament World*. New York, Harper and Row, 1962.

Hole, Frank and Robert Heizer. *An Introduction to Prehistoric Archaeology*. New York, Holt, Rinehart, and Winston, 1965.

Owens, G. Frederick. *Archaeology and the Bible*. Westwood, New Jersey, Revell, 1961.

Price, Ira. M. *The Monuments and the Old Testament*. Philadelphia, American Baptist Publication Society, 1907.

Pritchard, James, ed. *Ancient Near Eastern Texts Relating to the Old Testament*. Princeton, The Princeton Press, 1950.

Thomas, D. Winton. *Documents From Old Testament Times*. London, Thomas Nelson and Sons, Ltd., 1958.

Thompson, J. A. *The Bible and Archaeology*. Grand Rapids, Wm. B. Eerdmans Publishing Company, 1962.

Unger, Merrill F. *Archaeology and the Old Testament*. Grand Rapids, Zondervan Publishing House, 1954.

Wright, G. Ernest. *Biblical Archaeology*. Philadelphia, Westminster Press, 1957.

2. Commentaries

Barton, George. *A Critical and Exegetical Commentary on the Book of Ecclesiastes*. Edinburgh, T. and T. Clark, 1908.

Culver, Robert D. *Daniel and the Latter Days*. Chicago, Moody Press, 1954.

Davies, G. Henton, Alan Richardson, and Charles L. Wallis, eds., *The Twentieth Century Bible Commentary*. New York, Harper and Brothers, 1955.

Delitzsch, Franz. *Biblical Commentary on the Old Testament: Psalms.* Vol. 1. Grand Rapids, Wm. B. Eerdmans Publishing Company, 1948. *Biblical Commentary on the Old Testament: The Song of Songs.* Grand Rapids, Wm. B. Eerdmans Publishing Company, 1948.

Fritsch, Charles T. "The Book of Proverbs." *The Interpreter's Bible.* Vol. 4. George Buttrick, *et. al.*, eds. New York, Abingdon-Cokesbury Press, 1951.

Gordis, Robert. *The Song of Songs.* New York, Jewish Theological Seminary of America, 1954.

Gray, John. *I and II Kings, A Commentary.* Philadelphia, Westminster Press, 1963.

Hengstenberg, Ernst. *Commentary on Ecclesiastes.* Trans. by D. W. Simon. Edinburgh, T. and T. Clark, 1876.

Jamieson, Robert, A. R. Fausset, and David Brown. *Commentary on the Whole Bible.* Grand Rapids, Zondervan Publishing House, n.d.

Keil, C. F. *Biblical Commentary on the Old Testament: Ezekiel.* Grand Rapids, Wm. B. Eerdmans Publishing Company, 1948. *Biblical Commentary on the Old Testament: Minor Prophets.* Vol. 1. Grand Rapids, Wm. B. Eerdmans Publishing Company, 1948.

Keil, C. F. and Franz Delitzsch. *Biblical Commentary on the Old Testament: The Pentateuch.* Vol. 1. Grand Rapids, Wm. B. Eerdmans Publishing Company, 1948. *Biblical Commentary on the Old Testament: The Pentateuch.* Vol. 3. Grand Rapids, Wm. B. Eerdmans Publishing Company, 1948. *Biblical Commentary on the Old Testament: Samuel.* Grand Rapids, Wm. B. Eerdmans Publishing Company, 1948.

Kirkpatrick, A. F. *The First and Second Books of Samuel.* Cambridge: University Press, 1930.

Lange, John P. *Commentary on the Holy Scriptures: Samuel.* Ed. by Philip Schaff. Grand Rapids, Zondervan Publishing House, n.d.

Leupold, Herbert C. *Exposition of Daniel.* Columbus, Wartburg Press, 1949.

McNeile, A. H. *The Book of Exodus.* London, Methuen, 1908.

Moore, George F. *A Critical and Exegetical Commentary on Judges.* New York, Charles Scribner's Sons, 1895.

Myers, Jacob M. *Ezra-Nehemiah, The Anchor Bible.* Ed. by W. F. Albright and David Noel Freedman. New York, Doubleday and Company, Inc., 1965.

Pusey, Edward B. *The Minor Prophets.* Vol. 1. Grand Rapids, Baker Book House, 1950.

Rylaarsdam, J. Coert. "Exodus," *The Interpreter's Bible.* Vol. 1. Ed. George Buttrick, *et. al.* New York, Abingdon-Cokesbury Press, 1951.

Skinner, John. *A Critical and Exegetical Commentary on Genesis.* New York, Charles Scribner's Sons, 1910.

Terry, M. S. *Commentary on the Old Testament: Joshua to II Samuel.* Ed. by D. D. Whedon. New York, Hunt and Eaton, 1873.

Thomas, William Henry Griffith. *Genesis: A Devotional Commentary.* London, Religious Tract Society, n.d.

Young, Edward J. *The Book of Isaiah.* Vol. 1. Grand Rapids, Wm. B. Eerdmans Publishing Company, 1965.

3. Evidences

Duncan, J. Garrow. *The Accuracy of the Old Testament.* London, Society for Promoting Christian Knowledge, 1930.

Haley, John W. *Alleged Discrepancies of the Bible.* Grand Rapids, Baker Book House, 1958.

Wilson, Robert Dick. *A Scientific Investigation of the Old Testament.* Chicago, Moody Press, 1965.

4. General Studies

Anderson, Bernhard W. *Understanding the Old Testament.* Englewood Cliffs, Prentice-Hall, 1957.

Freedman, David Noel and Edward F. Campbell, Jr., eds. *The Biblical Archaeologist Reader.* Vol. 2. Garden City, Doubleday and Company, Inc., 1964.

Harrelson, Walter. *Interpreting the Old Testament.* New York, Holt, Rinehart and Winston, 1964.

Noth, Martin. *The Old Testament World.* Philadelphia, Fortress Press, 1964.

Rowley, H. H., ed. *The Old Testament and Modern Study.* Oxford, Clarendon Press, 1951.

Schultz, Samuel. *The Old Testament Speaks.* New York, Harper and Brothers, 1960.

Wright, G. Ernest, ed. *The Bible and the Ancient Near East.* Garden City, Doubleday and Company, Inc., 1965.

Wright, G. Ernest and David Noel Freedman, eds. *The Biblical Archaeologist Reader,* Vol. 1. Garden City, Doubleday and Company, Inc., 1961.

Young, Edward J. *Studies in Genesis One.* Philadelphia, Presbyterian and Reformed Publishing Company, 1964.

5. Geography

Baly, Denis. *The Geography of the Bible.* New York, Harper and Brothers, 1957.

Glueck, Nelson. *The Other Side of the Jordan.* New Haven, The American Schools of Oriental Research, 1940.

Pfeiffer, Charles F., ed. *Baker's Bible Atlas.* Grand Rapids, Baker Book House, 1961.

6. History

Albright, W. F. *The Biblical Period From Abraham to Ezra.* New York, Harper and Row, 1963.

From the Stone Age to Christianity. Garden City, Doubleday and Company, Inc., 1957.

Bright, John. *A History of Israel.* Philadelphia, Westminster Press 1959.

Bruce, F. F. *Israel and the Nations.* Grand Rapids, Wm. B. Eerdmans Publishing Company, 1963.

Foerster, Werner. *From the Exile to Christ.* Trans. by Gordon E. Harris. Philadelphia, Fortress Press, 1964.

Garstang, John. *Foundations of Bible History.* London, Constable and Company, 1937.

Gordon, Cyrus. *The Ancient Near East.* New York, W. W. Norton and Company, Inc., 1965.

Gray, John. *The Canaanites.* New York, Frederick A. Praeger, 1964.

Gurney, O. R. *The Hittites.* Baltimore, Penguin Books, 1964.

Harden, Donald. *The Phoenicians.* New York, Frederick A. Praeger, 1962.

Moscati, Sabatino. *Ancient Semitic Civilizations.* New York, G. P. Putnam's Sons, 1960.

Noth, Martin. *The History of Israel.* New York, Harper and Brothers, 1958.

Rowley, H. H. *From Joseph to Joshua.* London, Oxford University Press, 1950.

Thiele, Edwin R. *The Mysterious Numbers of the Hebrew Kings.* Chicago, University of Chicago Press, 1951.

Unger, Merrill F. *Israel and the Aramaeans of Damascus.* Grand Rapids, Zondervan Publishing House, 1957.

Whiston, William, trans. *The Complete Works of Flavius-Josephus.* London, Tallis, n.d.

Whitcomb, John. *Darius the Mede.* (International Library), Philadelphia, Presbyterian and Reformed Publishing Company, 1959.

Wilson, John A. *The Culture of Ancient Egypt.* Chicago, University of Chicago Press, 1963.

7. Introduction

Allis, O. T. *The Five Books of Moses.* Philadelphia, Presbyterian and Reformed Publishing Company, 1943.

The Unity of Isaiah. Philadelphia, Presbyterian and Reformed Publishing Company, 1950.

Archer, Gleason. *A Survey of Old Testament Introduction.* Chicago, Moody Press, 1964.

Enslin, Morton Scott. *The Literature of the Christian Movement.* New York, Harper and Brothers, 1938.

Gray, G. B. *Forms of Hebrew Poetry*. London, Hodder and Stoughton, 1915.

Green, William H. *Old Testament Canon and Philology*. Princeton, Press, 1889.

Harris, Robert Laird. *Inspiration and Canonicity of the Bible*. Grand Rapids, Zondervan Publishing House, 1957.

Kuhl, Curt. *The Old Testament: Its Origins and Composition*. Trans. by C. T. M. Herriott. Richmond, John Knox Press, 1961.

Oesterley, William O. E. *An Introduction to the Books of the Old Testament*. New York, The Macmillan Company, 1934.

Pfeiffer, Robert Henry. *Introduction to the Old Testament*. New York, Harper and Brothers, 1941.

Rowley, H. H. *The Growth of the Old Testament*. New York, Harper and Row, 1963.

Ryle, H. E. *The Canon of the Old Testament*. London, Macmillan and Company, Ltd., 1895.

Warfield, Benjamin Breckinridge. *The Inspiration and Authority of the Bible*. Philadelphia, Presbyterian and Reformed Publishing Company, 1948.

Weiser, Artur. *The Old Testament: Its Formation and Development*. Trans. by Dorothea M. Barton. New York, Association Press, 1961.

Würthwein, Ernst. *The Text of the Old Testament*. Trans. by Peter R. Ackroyd. New York, The Macmillan Company, 1951.

Young, Edward J. *An Introduction to the Old Testament*. Grand Rapids, Wm. B. Eerdmans Publishing Company, 1958.

8. Religion and Theology

Ascham, John Bayne. *The Religion of Israel*. New York, The Abingdon Press, 1918.

Buber, Martin. *Moses*. New York, Harper and Row, 1958.

Eliade, Mircea. *The Sacred and the Profane*. New York. Harper and Row, 1961.

Guillaume, Alfred. *Prophecy and Divination Among the Hebrews and Other Semites*. New York, Harper and Brothers, 1938.

Hopkins, Edward W. *The History of the Religions*. New York, The Macmillan Company, 1918.

Johnson, Aubrey. *The Cultic Prophet in Ancient Israel*. Cardiff, University of Wales, 1944.

Kirkpatrick, A. F. *The Doctrine of the Prophets*. London, Macmillan and Co., Ltd., 1901.

Meek, Theophile J. *Hebrew Origins*. New York, Harper and Row, 1960.

Mendenhall, G. E. *Law and Covenant in Israel and the Ancient Near East*. Pittsburgh, The Biblical Colloquium, 1954.

Mercer, Samuel A. B. *The Religion of Ancient Egypt*. London, Luzac, 1949.

Moorehead, William G. *Studies in the Mosaic Institutions.* Dayton, W. J. Shuey, 1896.

Mowinckel, Sigmund. *The Psalms in Israel's Worship.* Vol. 1. London, Blackwell, 1962.

Noth, Martin and D. Winton Thomas, eds. *Wisdom in Israel and in the Ancient Near East.* Leiden, E. J. Brill, 1960.

Oehler, Gustave. *Theology of the Old Testament.* Grand Rapids, Zondervan Publishing House, 1883.

Pedersen, Johannes. *Israel, Its Life and Culture.* Vol. 2. London, Oxford University Press, 1954.

Rad, Gerhard von. *Old Testament Theology.* Vol. 1. Edinburgh, Oliver and Boyd, 1962.

Robinson, Theodore H. *Prophecy and the Prophets.* London, Duckworth and Co., 1923.

Vos, Geerhardus. *Biblical Theology.* Grand Rapids, Wm. B. Eerdmans Publishing Company, 1954.

Weber, Max. *Ancient Judaism.* Trans. and ed. by Hans H. Gerth and Don Martindale. Chicago, Free Press, 1952.

Young, Edward J. *My Servants the Prophets.* Grand Rapids, Wm. B. Eerdmans Publishing Company, 1952.

9. Science and the Bible

Clark, W. E. LeGros. *The Antecedents of Man.* New York, Harper and Row, 1963.

Messenger, Ernest Charles. *Evolution and Theology: The Problem of Man's Origin.* New York, The Macmillan Company, 1932.

Morris, Henry. *The Twilight of Evolution.* Grand Rapids, Baker Book House, 1963.
Studies in the Bible and Science, Philadelphia, Presbyterian and Reformed Publishing Company, 1966.

Putnam, William Clement. *Geology.* New York, Oxford University Press, 1964.

Ramm, Bernard. *The Christian View of Science and Scripture.* Grand Rapids, Wm. B. Eerdmans Publishing Company, 1954.

Reymond, Robert L. *A Christian View of Modern Science.* Philadelphia, Presbyterian and Reformed Publishing Company, 1964.

Ronan, Colin Austair. *Changing Views of the Universe.* New York, The Macmillan Company, 1961.

Schubert, Charles and Carl O. Dunbar. *Outlines of Historical Geology.* New York, John Wiley and Sons, Inc., 1947.

Whitcomb, John C. and Henry M. Morris. *The Genesis Flood.* Philadelphia, Presbyterian and Reformed Publishing Company, 1963.

B. Periodicals

Albright, W. F. "The Hebrew Expression for 'Making Covenant' in Pre-Israelite Documents," *Bulletin of the American Schools of Oriental Research*, 121:21-22, 1951.

Callaway, Joseph A. "The 1964 'Ai (et Tell) Excavations." *Bulletin of the American Schools of Oriental Research,"* 178:27-28, April, 1965.

Eakin, Frank E.   "Yahwism and Baalism Before the Exile." *Journal of Biblical Literature,* 84:413, December, 1965.

Freedman, David Noel. "The Babylonian Chronicle." *Biblical Archaeologist,* 19:50-60, September, 1956.

Gerstenberger, Erhard. "Covenant and Commandment." *Journal of Biblical Literature,* 84:50, March, 1965.

Glueck, Nelson. "Ezion-geber." *Biblical Archaeologist,* 28:70-87, September, 1965.

"The Seventh Season of Archaeological Exploration in the Negeb." *Bulletin of the American Schools of Oriental Research,* 152:18-38, December, 1958.

Hallo, William W. "From Qarqar to Carchemish: Assyria and Israel in the Light of New Discoveries." *Biblical Archaeologist,* 23:34ff, May, 1960.

Kassis, Hanna E. "Gath and the Structure of the Philistine Society." *Journal of Biblical Literature,* 84:259-271, September, 1965.

Kline, Meredith. "Law Covenant." *Westminster Theological Journal,* 27:19ff, November, 1964.

Kraeling, Emil G. "New Light on the Elephantine Colony." *Biblical Archaeologist,* 15:50-67, September, 1952.

Landes, George. "The Material Civilization of the Ammonites." *Biblical Archaeologist,* 24:65-86, September, 1961.

Lapp, Paul W. "Tell el Ful." *Biblical Archaeologist,* 28:2-10, February, 1965.

Malamat, Abraham. "The Kingdom of David and Solomon in Its Contact With Egypt and Aram Naharaim." *Biblical Archaeologist,* 21:96-102, December, 1958.

Mazar, Benjamin. "The Aramaean Empire and Its Relations With Israel." *Biblical Archaeologist,* 25:97-120, December, 1962.

Mendelsohn, I. "On Corveé Labor in Ancient Canaan and Israel." *Bulletin of the American Schools of Oriental Research,* 167:31-35, October, 1962.

Patai, Raphael. "The Goddess Asherah." *Journal of Near Eastern Studies,* 24:37-52, January-April, 1965.

Thompson, Clive A. "Samuel, The Ark and The Priesthood." *Bibliotheca Sacra,* 118:259-263, July-September 1961.

Van Beek, Gus W. "Frankincense and Myrrh." *Biblical Archaeologist,* 23:69-95, September, 1960.

Yadin, Yigael. "Excavations at Hazor." *Biblical Archaeologist,* 19:1-12, February, 1956.

"New Light on Solomon's Megiddo." *Biblical Archaeologist,* 23:62-68, May, 1960.

C. Dictionaries and Encyclopedias

Brown, Francis, S. R. Driver, and Charles Briggs. *A Hebrew and English Lexicon of the Old Testament.* London, Oxford University Press, 1962.

Robinson, George L. "Isaiah." *The International Standard Bible Encyclopedia.* Vol. 3. Ed. by James Orr. Grand Rapids, Wm. B. Eerdmans Publishing Company, 1960.

Webster's New Collegiate Dictionary. Second Edition. Springfield, Mass., G. & C. Merriam Company, Publishers, 1953.

D. Miscellaneous

Hebrew Union College. Jerusalem, Israel. Lecture by G. Ernest Wright, July 21, 1965.

Holyland Hotel, Jerusalem, Israel. Lecture by Manasseh Harel, July 17, 1965.

Merrill, Eugene H. "An Investigation of the Person and Work of the Old Testament Prophet of God." Unpublished Ph.D. dissertation, Bob Jones University, Greenville, South Carolina, 1963.

Whitcomb, John C. "Chart of Old Testament Patriarchs and Judges." Winona Lake, Indiana, Grace Theological Seminary, 1963.

INDEX

INDEX